GHETTOS, TRAMPS, A

GHETTOS, TRAMPS, AND WELFARE QUEENS

Down and Out on the Silver Screen

Stephen Pimpare

OXFORD
UNIVERSITY PRESS

OXFORD
UNIVERSITY PRESS

Oxford University Press is a department of the University of Oxford. It furthers
the University's objective of excellence in research, scholarship, and education
by publishing worldwide. Oxford is a registered trade mark of Oxford University
Press in the UK and certain other countries.

Published in the United States of America by Oxford University Press
198 Madison Avenue, New York, NY 10016, United States of America.

Library of Congress Cataloging-in-Publication
Data Names: Pimpare, Stephen author.
Title: Ghettos, tramps, and welfare queens : down & out on the silver screen /
Stephen Pimpare.
Description: New York : Oxford University Press, 2017. |
Includes bibliographical references and index.
Identifiers: LCCN 2016045873 (print) | LCCN 2017010956 (ebook) |
ISBN 9780190660727 (alk. paper) | ISBN 9780190660734 (epdf)
Subjects: LCSH: Poor in motion pictures. | Homeless persons in motion pictures. |
Motion pictures—United States—History and criticism.
Classification: LCC PN1995.9.P63 P56 2017 (print) | LCC PN1995.9.P63 (ebook) |
DDC 791.43/6526942—dc23
LC record available at https://lccn.loc.gov/2016045873

9 8 7 6 5 4 3 2 1

Printed by Sheridan Books, Inc., United States of America

Portions of Chapter 5 were first published as "The Welfare Queen and the Great White Hope," *New Political Science*, Vol. 32, No. 3. Reprinted by permission of Taylor & Francis.

Portions of Chapter 8 were first published as "The Poverty of Relentless Disappointment," *Talk Poverty* and the Center for American Progress (August 22, 2014). Reprinted with permission.

CONTENTS

KEY U.S. FILMS DISCUSSED, 1902–2015

187
A Corner in Wheat
A Dog's Life
A Film Johnnie
A Little Princess
A Night Out
A Piece of the Action
A Raisin in the Sun
A Tree Grows in Brooklyn
Acid Rain
Adventures of Robin Hood
American Heart
American Hobo
An Angel on Abbey Street
Angela's Ashes
Angels with Dirty Faces
Ann Vickers
Annie!
Ask the Dust
Ballast
Barfly
Beasts of the Southern Wild
Beggars in Ermine
Beggars of Life
Being Flynn
Between Showers
Billion Dollar Hobo
Bindlestiffs

Blackboard Jungle
Body and Soul
Bound for Glory
Bowery Blitzkrieg
Boxcar Bertha
Boy of the Streets
Boys of the City
Boys Town
Boyz N the Hood
Brick City
Broken Blossoms
Brother Can You Spare a Dime?
Brother to Brother
Bulworth
Bum Man: Hero of the Homeless
C.H.U.D.
Candyman
Carrie
Chains of Gold
Chi-Raq
Chop Shop
Cinderella Man
Citizen Ruth
City Lights
Claudine
Clockers
Coal Miner's Daughter
Complex: Life Inside a Sect 8 Apt

INTRODUCTION

Long ago, when the American cinema was young, Gilbert Seldes insisted that "we do not go to the movies for any of the reasons which the producers of the movies consider fundamental." It was not, he thought, to see the handsomest new stars and gawk at their fancy clothes, to be swept away to exotic locales and hear new and exciting stories, or to escape from our drab lives for a few hours. Not even to learn something new. Instead, Seldes was convinced that people go to the movies "because the moving picture *moves*," and "simply to be at the movies"—to share in a common experience with other people. "The mad King of Bavaria liked to have productions of grand opera at which he was the only spectator," he wrote. "That was part of his madness. Sane people enjoy the presence of their fellow beings" (Seldes, 1937, pp. 8–9).

So, if we consider the videocassette recorder (VCR) and then the profusion of digital video disks (DVDs), on-demand digital downloads, and giant-screen home theater systems, which make possible large numbers of people sitting at home, alone, watching films, we are now all Mad Kings of Bavaria. This does not mean that Seldes is wrong about the satisfaction and comfort we derive from this shared experience (Aristotle had something to say about that, as well, in his *Poetics*), but perhaps it's not quite so simple, since so many seem to find so much pleasure (or at least spend so much time) watching movies alone. Still, Pauline Kael felt similarly (as have many critics), and issued a warning that seeing a film on television is an entirely different, and inferior, experience than seeing it in a theater, on a big screen, with a crowd (Kael, 1994, p. 124).

The principal aim of *Ghettos, Tramps, and Welfare Queens* is to find representations of poor and homeless people and the places they have inhabited throughout the century-long history of American cinema, and to describe them. All told, I'll examine just shy of 300 films released between 1902 and 2015 that fit this category.

Table 0.1 Number of Key Films Discussed, by Decade of First Release

Number of key films discussed, by decade of release (total = 299)

1902–09	04	*1940–49*	25	*1980–89*	36
1910–19	21	*1950–59*	05	*1990–99*	53
1920–29	11	*1960–69*	11	*2000–09*	52
1930–39	42	*1970–79*	19	*2010–15*	20

There are other films, mostly made early in the twentieth century, that would appear from synopses to be relevant, but they can't be discussed because they have been lost, which is the case for seventy percent of all features made in the silent era (Pierce, 2013). A few others seem to still exist, but I have not been able to find and view them prior to publication of this book. I have ignored television series for this project, although I have included a handful of relevant made-for-television movies. My focus is on American movies, and although I will refer to a few foreign pictures, it is only to draw a contrast. I only discuss (or even name, for that matter) films that I have viewed. I've tried to do that in a theater when possible, but, in the overwhelming majority of cases, I have watched them like a Mad King of Bavaria—in their DVD versions (and some videocassettes!) on a modest-sized screen, at home, often alone. I'm not sure what the alternative would be, given the demise of the revival movie house and the constraints of time. Moreover, I'd note that the ability to pause and ponder, to freeze frames to study composition, to rewatch scenes, and to accurately capture dialogue offers its own advantages. Still, if, as Seldes, Kael, and some scholars suggest (see Klinger, 2006; Tryon, 2009), this is an inferior means by which to experience a movie, so be it.

Many books have sought to identify and interpret the images of particular groups in movies made in the United States. *The Celluloid Closet* (Russo, 1987), the book that gave some initial inspiration to this one, offered a critique of the ways in which gay men and lesbians were represented (or ignored) on film, a book itself made into a movie (1995). We have volumes about the political world as it appears on film (Christensen and Haas, 2005; Rogin, 1987; Neve, 1992; Giglio, 2002; Kirshner, 2012), surveys of the cinematic city (Sanders, 2001), and discussions of race (Bogle, 1973/2007; Davis, 2000), crime (Rafter, 2006), and women in the movies (Haskell, 1987). There are books about the working class (Ross, 1998; Bodnar, 2003/2006; Zaniello, 2003; Greene, 2010), silent-era "social problem" films (Brownlow, 1990; Sloan, 1988), and Great Depression–era films and other aspects of 1930s culture (Bergman, 1971; Shindler, 1996; Denning, 1997; Kelley, 1998; May, 2000; Bernstein, 1985; Dickstein, 2009). We can, in addition, point to classic essays on the Western (Warshow in Lopate, 2008; Bazin, 1971), horror flicks (Wood, 1979/2002), film noir (Schrader in Lopate, 2008), the intersection of race and gender (hooks, 2012), the screwball comedy (Cavell in Lopate, 2008), and science fiction (Sontag, 1965/2001).

Yet, for all this, there has been little attention given to poverty and homelessness (James Agee might be his own exception, I suppose). Linda Fuller (in Min, 1999) offered a brief review in her "Images of the Homeless in Motion Pictures," but that essay was scarcely more than a list of films and provided little analysis. Some years earlier, in a volume that Fuller edited, William Brigham (1996) offered a deeper and richer chapter-length review of homelessness on film, but perhaps inevitably, given the constraints of space, focused narrowly and schematically on only three dozen or so movies. Lisen Roberts (2003) discussed six films ostensibly about poverty that could be used in the sociology classroom, but one of them was about child abuse rather than poverty, by her own admission, and the discussion of content was intentionally limited—the focus was pedagogy, not poverty. Kevin Brownlow (1990) includes a chapter on films about poverty in his indispensable book about the silent era, but his analysis doesn't extend beyond the 1920s, and includes films that are not about poverty per se, but class or other topics, like tuberculosis. In *Hollywood Speaks Out*, Robert Hilliard (2009) also included a chapter on poverty (along with chapters on anti-Semitism, race, politics, homophobia, and more), but it leaned heavily on *Grapes of Wrath* and the Depression era, with only a passing glance at later endeavors, and it was, inescapably, brief. This is part of a pattern, by the way: while inquiries into the presence or absence of poverty in the films of the 1930s are well represented in these studies, the rest of American history is largely absent.

Not only has there been no comprehensive history of poverty and homelessness in the movies, analysis has often (although not always) been undertaken by film scholars. I am trained as a political scientist, by contrast, and write and teach about poverty, inequality, and the history of U.S. social welfare policy, not culture. While I do now and again draw on works from film theory, literary criticism, and cultural studies, I don't do so extensively, and I don't do so systematically. That is intentional. The goal here is not to investigate homelessness and poverty in film as a film scholar or cultural critic would, but to see the ways in which poverty policy and policy history appear on screen; document the ways in which individuals, families, and neighborhoods are represented; and ask how well that comports with our historical knowledge and the current reality; and, in turn, to then ask questions about what that might tell us about the state of social policy as it affects populations living in poverty. It is an exercise in evaluating the *authenticity* of those portrayals more than it is unpacking the cultural or social meanings contained in them. It's a corrective, in a small way, since there is a tendency among some scholars to over-interpret, it seems to me. Here's a caution against that, as told by Graham Greene, who had many of his novels and stories adapted for the screen:

> I remember that when my film *The Third Man* had its little hour of success a rather learned reviewer expounded its symbolism.... The surname of Harry Lime he connected with a passage about the lime tree in Sir James Frazer's *The Golden Bough*. The "Christian" name of the principal character—Holly—was obviously, he wrote, closely con-nected with Christ's—paganism and Christianity were thus joined in a symbolic dance. The truth of the matter is, I wanted for my "villain" a name natural and yet disagreeable, and to me "Lime" represented the quick-lime in which murderers were said to be buried. An association of ideas, not, as the reviewer claimed, a symbol. As for Holly, it was because my choice of name, Rollo, had not met with the approval of Joseph Cotton [who, Greene writes elsewhere, thought it too effete]. So much for symbols. (Greene in Parkinson, 1993, p. 468)

The lesson is not that we should avoid rooting around for meaning in movies: Greene confirms that the choice of name was not arbitrary and that it was designed to have effect. What we should do, however, is to separate our "readings" of a film from the intentions of the filmmakers (and note the plu-rals there—*intentions* and *filmmakers*), since a film (or a scene, or a line, or a character's name) might have multiple meanings, and what the screenwriter intended may be something quite different from what the actor intended or the director intended or even the editor intended. I won't hesitate to write about what I think these films mean and what they mean to me, but I will hes-itate to identify those meanings as purposeful unless I can find some evidence to support the claim. That is, I'm interested less in intent than I am in effect.

A related goal moves beyond the descriptive to the comparative to answer two questions: Have cinematic representations of homelessness and pov-erty changed over time, and are there patterns to be discerned? (Spoiler: The answers are, in order, yes and yes.) Finally, I offer a preliminary response to a handful of harder questions about causation and consequence, building on an inquiry begun by sociologist Herbert Gans a half-century ago (Gans, 1964; Gans 1993): Why are these portrayals as they are? Where do they come from? Are they a reflection of American attitudes and policies toward marginalized populations, or do they help create them? What does this all mean for politics and policymaking?

While I am not a film scholar, I do approach the subject as an enthusiast. I watch movies for the same reasons others do, I suppose—to be distracted, to be transported, to be entertained (*pace*, Gilbert Seldes). I tend to appreciate films that show me something of people or worlds, real or imagined, that I don't know about. In this way, movie-going can be an exercise in empathy-generating, allowing us to be pulled in by a compelling narrative or by appealing (or repugnant) characters in a way that can offer us a fleeting sense of what it might be like to live another's life. There's reason to believe that literature can do this and that readers of novels or poetry might be more empathetic than others, says Elaine Scarry (2012), noting "the capacity of literature to exercise and reinforce our recognition that there *are* other points of view in the world, and to make this recognition a powerful mental habit" (see also Kidd and Castano, 2013). Why shouldn't the same hold true for film? This could be especially important if representations of poor and homeless people are consistently guilty of misunderstanding or misrepresenting those populations, and if, in turn, significant numbers of moviegoers walk away convinced that they have gained some true insight, when they have instead only had their own biases reaffirmed. You can tell by the way that I frame this that I think there's something to that particular worry.

Defining Poverty and Homelessness

I've not tried to present a catalogue of every instance of, or reference to, homelessness or poverty in American film. Instead, I've emphasized movies or scenes that are "about" poverty or homelessness in some way, or for which these states are important to the narrative, or that offer an unusual perspective. So, while in *Alien vs. Predator* (2004), first contact is made with homeless people living under a bridge, there's not really anything more to observe, it seems to me, and it does not, therefore, make its way into my bibliography of key films and will not, you may be relieved to learn, be discussed in these pages again. There are films, like Jaume Collet-Serra's *Orphan* (2009), that are not about children abandoned by their parents to face the world poor and alone, even if that is what those children are, but horror films or domestic tragedies. They are not included, nor are films like *Antwone Fisher* (2002), which is about the foster care system, or *Stage Door* (1937) and other movies about supposedly poor girls who come to New York or Hollywood to make it, and then, in short order, do: They are not materially poor, but abstractly or *romantically* poor, and some, like Kathryn Hepburn's character in *Stage*

Door, are actually heiresses escaping their gilded cages, a female counterpart to the Impostor Tramp characters I'll discuss in Chapter 11. King Vidor's *The Crowd* (1928) has a bit of unemployment, but there doesn't seem more to say about it than that (Vidor himself pushed aside notions that there was deeper import here; see Brownlow, 1999, p. xxiii). His *Hallelujah* (1929) could, theoretically, be discussed in terms of rural poverty, but that's not the subject of the picture: While the characters are black tenant farmers, there's little or no attention paid to questions of deprivation or need. It's a romance and revenge drama, one that, while enlightened for the time in its own way, I suppose, still traffics in hoary old stereotypes. *The Struggle* (1931) is a story about an alcoholic who becomes "a begging bum" in the words of some taunting children and, briefly, homeless, squatting in abandoned buildings, but it's a story about alcohol (framed, with the first title card, within the context of Prohibition) and not about poverty. It's not homelessness that D. W. Griffith wants to explore here, but the consequences of drink, which he does in sentimental fashion, as is his wont. Despite a title that might suggest some affinity with this project, *Tramp, Tramp, Tramp* (1926) is about a shoemaker's son who enters a cross-country footrace to save his father's business and win the girl. Much mayhem, you will be pleased to know, ensues, but it's of no use here except, possibly, for the casual use of the word "tramp" in the title and what that might mean. *Ask the Dust* (2006) is set in Depression-era Los Angeles, focusing on a young writer (Colin Farrell) six months behind on his rent and down, literally, to his last nickel. He sells a story, flirts with a waitress, looks handsome, has writer's block, and feels sorry for himself, but it's not a story about the Depression per se: it could be set in any time period, almost anywhere. Andrea Arnold's *Fish Tank* (2009) is another movie that doesn't make the cut, since it's not American-made and not about poverty but merely another example of how effectively some British filmmakers have captured working-class people and their daily lives. And to focus on class is not the same as focusing on poverty: All the works of Edith Wharton might be included in a discussion of class, but only *The House of Mirth* (2001) deals directly with poverty. This is why films based on the novels of Henry James are not included here. Although they are surely about class in the late nineteenth and early twentieth centuries, among other things, they are not about poverty, and they are most surely not about poor people. And even though cowboys are rootless, as Robert Warshow (1954) observes—they are itinerants, perhaps even vagabonds of a sort—it's by choice and, more important, not a measure of need but a measure of freedom and a successful effort to live the kinds of lives they value. Cowboy status does not indicate want, and, therefore, does not qualify them for inclusion here either. You get, I trust, the idea.

Estimated US Poverty, 1904–2014

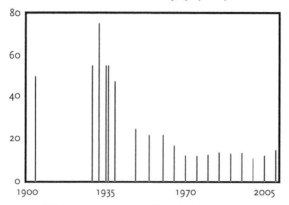

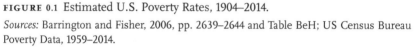

FIGURE 0.1 Estimated U.S. Poverty Rates, 1904–2014.

Sources: Barrington and Fisher, 2006, pp. 2639–2644 and Table BeH; US Census Bureau Poverty Data, 1959–2014.

Poverty is not class, I've asserted, and homelessness is not mere vaga-bondage. So what does mark people or a place as "poor," then? The U.S. Census Bureau identifies poverty with an income threshold. For 2014, this "poverty line" for a family of four was about $25,000, and some 48.4 million Americans had total incomes below it, amounting to 15.3 percent of the total population (Short, 2015). Other measures show that poverty was probably around 50 percent at the beginning of the century (with rates that were much higher among certain groups) and as high as 75 percent at the worst of the Depression in 1932, before it fell back to between 45 and 50 percent by 1939. Thanks to the recovery (slow though it was), the full-employment program that was World War II, and the booming economy and strong social supports of the postwar years, poverty rates may have fallen to as low as 22 percent by 1954. Still other measures show an overall poverty rate of 26 percent in 1967, declining to 16 percent by 2012, and an elderly poverty rate dropping from some 40 percent in 1967 to 15 percent in 2012 (Wimer, Fox, Garfinkel, et al., 2013; Fox, Garfinkel, Kaushal, et al., 2014).

There's a lot that's wrong with these measures, and we should take all of them with a grain of salt. But that doesn't matter much, anyway: we can't use this technique to identify poor people in the movies, since we tend not to have precise income data for movie characters. But if we don't know what people's income is, how can we know if they are poor or not?

If you find an individual or family surviving onscreen with the aid of food stamps, cash welfare programs, and the like, they will be included here, since eligibility for those programs is determined, at least in part, by income, and those thresholds are often at or just above the official poverty line. I am interested in representations of social welfare programs, too, and in the people who administer them—so we'll also attend to welfare offices, to public housing projects, and to social workers.

Poverty, most would agree, is a state of material want: not having enough food or money to buy enough food, lacking shelter (or electricity or heat), or not being able to afford gasoline to get to work or to the grocery store. It's not merely need, however, but the attendant struggle, too—if part of your day is spent worrying about where food or money for food will come from, even if you ultimately get enough, or worrying about how you will stay warm, even if you find yourself warm enough that night, or scrambling to find a place to sleep, although you may succeed, those are all indicators of poverty. Poverty is anxiety-filled, time-consuming, and labor-intensive. It is precisely that relentless day-to-day anxiety, by the way, that rarely appears on film.

My way of thinking about what constitutes poverty owes something to economist Adam Smith's approach as he articulated it in *Wealth of Nations* (1776/1904, Book V.II):

> Every man is rich or poor according to the degree to which he can afford to enjoy the necessaries, conveniences, and amusements of human life. By necessaries I understand, not only the commodities which are indispensably necessary for the support of life, but whatever the custom of the country renders it indecent for creditable people, even of the lowest order to be without. A linen shirt is, strictly speaking, not a necessary of life. The Greeks and Romans lived, I suppose, very comfortably, though they had no linen. But in the present times, through the greater part of Europe, a creditable day-labourer would be ashamed to appear in public without a linen shirt, the want of which would be supposed to denote that disgraceful degree of poverty, which, it is presumed, no body can well fall into without extreme bad conduct.

Poverty is more than mere material want, and Smith's "custom of the country" approach helps us see how it can be as much cultural and social as it is economic. If you forego acquisitions that those around you have—a students' field trip or equipment to play a sport, ordering lunch when your co-workers do, acquiring the latest fashions—then that, too, suggests a kind of poverty; an economic shortfall that reveals itself as social isolation or the inability to act as those around you do. This is one way to see the blindness in claims by activists like the Heritage Foundation's Robert Rector (Rector and Sheffield, 2011), who, in observing that most poor people now have stoves and air conditioners and televisions and DVD players and so on, suggests that such people are therefore not poor, not truly in need of assistance and, in effect, scamming the system (it's also a bit silly because while "luxuries" like televisions have gotten relatively inexpensive, necessities, like housing or education, have gotten radically more expensive).

Another economist, Amartya Sen, offers a better way of thinking about what it means to be poor. Poverty, for Sen, is a *lack of freedom*, an inability for people, as he puts it, "to lead the kind of lives they value—and have reason to value" (Sen, 1999, p. 18). As sociologist Loïc Wacquant (2008, p. 168) writes, "Aside from being deprived of adequate conditions and means of living, to be poor in a rich society also entails, to varying degree, being assigned to the status of a *social anomaly* and being deprived of control over one's collective representation and identity."

Political scientist Murray Edelman (1995, pp. 99–100) captures another useful perspective:

> The conditions in which the poor grow up and live accordingly need to be recognized as art forms themselves, as well as obstacles to the good life. The environment becomes a never-ending drama that teaches people to be afraid, humble, subservient, ashamed, hopeless, or all of these. The components of this spectacle include the neighborhood that is conspicuously shabby and contrasts revealingly with affluent areas; lack of enough money to live "respectably," forcing people to behave in ways they have been taught to see as immoral, petty, or illegal; police patrols and other actions that remind residents they are distrusted, even as they offer some protection; deprivation of quality clothes and appurtenances that mark a desirable way of life, as pictured in advertisements and in public displays by the comfortable; demeaning treatment by teachers, social workers, police, bureaucrats in welfare and other government agencies, employers, prison guards, and the armed forces.

To be poor is to inhabit a separate sphere, to live in a world apart. Thus, in film it is geography that often marks poverty—the crowded immigrant slums, the "ruin-porn" streets of the inner cities, always under the close supervision of the police, or the gray, dilapidated landscapes of the rural outcast.

It is clear from this discussion that I am using a fairly amorphous definition of poverty, and not offering a standard that permits a clear demarcation between films sufficiently about poverty or homelessness to be included and films that may have indications of or reference to poverty or homelessness, but that aren't really about poverty. I'm okay with that, in part because that helps make an important point: there is no such thing as "poverty" per se. Poverty is an economic state, a social state, perhaps even an emotional state. Justice Potter Stewart famously claimed that the Supreme Court couldn't define "pornography," but said, "I know it when I see it." Something similar might be the case for poverty and homelessness, and while you might not always even be able to see it, you surely know it when you experience it.

The Real-World Causes of Poverty and Homelessness

There have been two ways that people have thought about the causes of poverty and, as a consequence, two ways of thinking about what should or should not be done to ameliorate it. For many, the roots are behavioral, lodged inevitably in the failure of individuals to act morally or responsibly—to be sufficiently diligent, chaste, sober, and thrifty (see Schwartz, 2000). If people delayed childbearing until they were married and financially secure, stayed in school and then went on to college, worked hard and consistently at whatever job was available, and were scrupulously careful with their resources, they would be much less likely to be poor (Lowell, 1884; Murray, 1994; Bailey, 2003). As a natural consequence of this diagnosis, the remedies prescribed tend to center upon the reform of the individual, inculcating in them the personal habits and discipline that will speed their advancement toward security and financial stability. Only as a very last resort should assistance be given, and rarely as cash, since aid too easily obtained will only encourage idleness and dependence: it takes away the necessity for self-help. As one late–nineteenth century charity reformer put it, "It is hardly too much to say that people do not beg because they are poor, but that they are poor because they beg. . . . For centuries the stream of charity has been steadily flowing, and the flood of poverty has been growing; and we have not stopped to consider that it might be merely cause and effect" (Almy, 1900). But these are ideas that still sit at the heart of many people's notions about the causes of poverty and the best remedies for it: witness South Carolina Lieutenant Governor Andre Bauer speaking in 2010 about the school lunch program:

> My grandmother was not a highly educated woman, but she told me as a small child to quit feeding stray animals. You know why? Because they breed. You're facilitating the problem if you give an animal or a person ample food supply. They will reproduce, especially ones that don't think too much further than that. And so what you've got to do is you've got to curtail that type of behavior. They don't know any better. (quoted in Cary, 2010)

This, as we'll see, is a way of thinking about the roots of poverty and the best solutions for it that suffuses American film and, indeed, American politics and culture more broadly. This may be properly understood as the conservative or Republican view, but it is also the dominant one, one that resonates with many policymakers who identify as Democrats, liberals, or even, sometimes, radicals. *The Other America* (1962/1997), a book written by American socialist Michael Harrington, which is often credited with helping to inspire Lyndon Johnson's "War on Poverty," is suffused with Culture of Poverty rhetoric. These are the unworthy poor or undeserving poor, poor because of their own *misconduct*.

The second way of thinking about why people are poor is rooted not in individual or personal failure or the dysfunction of poor families and communities, but, rather, in the failure of political, social, or economic *institutions*, an analysis generally associated with the political Left. People are poor because of *misfortune*: there are not enough jobs, or the jobs that are available pay too little or offer only irregular work; many public schools poorly prepare their students to compete against students who have come from better-funded schools in wealthier neighborhoods; they are poor because of active racial discrimination in the labor market and the difficulty of finding safe, affordable childcare; and because they have illness or disability that renders them badly suited for the modern labor market. This different kind of diagnosis suggests different remedies, and instead of seeking to alter individual behavior, it calls for relief and regulation: raising the minimum wage, creating jobs, providing access to day care and greater social welfare program supports, and so on.

The weight of evidence available from anthropology, sociology, social work, history, psychology, economics, and political science tells us that the second kind of explanation is the better one (for summaries, see Austin, 2006; Schiller, 2007; Rynell, 2008; Iceland, 2013), and, therefore, the second set of remedies is likely to be more effective. That may sound like bias, but it's no more bias than it is to report that the weight of scientific evidence tells us that global climate change is real, accelerating, and human-made or that there is no demonstrable link between childhood vaccinations and autism.

This is not to say that there are not people whose poverty might fairly be attributed to their own bad decision-making. But even when that's the case (and it's a small portion of the problem at best), what it reveals is the key difference between poor and low-income households and more financially secure ones: when a better-situated person does something dumb—and most of us do, at one time or another, make decisions that make our financial lives worse—they can survive the event. But for a financially insecure household living on the edge, it's more likely to be a crisis that brings about their poverty, as it has always been, which is why, contrary to widespread assumptions, most poverty spells are relatively short and are a much more common experience that people tend to think (Edwards, 2014).

This is worth underlining, since it gets at a blind spot common to almost all thinking about the scale and scope of poverty from left and right alike. The official overall poverty rate for 2014 was about 15 percent, as we've seen. That is a "snapshot" measure, telling us how many people had total income below the poverty line for the year of the survey used to gather those data. But people move in and out of poverty over time, and might be doing okay for six months of the year, but lose a job and have no income at all for the next six, a dynamic that wouldn't be captured by such measures. So, if we step back a bit and look at an entire four-year period from 2009 to 2012 and ask how many people were poor for at least two consecutive months at some point during that time, the poverty rate was actually 34.5 percent. By contrast, only about 2.7 percent were poor for the entirety of that period (U.S. Census, 2014). Long-term, persistent poverty is real, make no mistake, and it's a problem we should pay attention to, but that's not what most poverty looks like.

In fact, the causes of poverty haven't changed much since the Middle Ages. Most poverty was and is the product of *insecurity + crisis*, emerging in economically fragile households after the illness, injury, or death of a main breadwinner, the birth of a child, or the loss of a job (which is more likely to happen in economic downturns). Most households are simply unprepared for such economic shocks: according to one 2013 survey, fully 76 percent of Americans had savings equal to no more than six months' worth of living expenses, 50 percent had less than three months' cushion should an emergency occur, and 27 percent had no savings at all (Johnson, 2013; see also Hacker, Rehm, and Schlesinger, 2010, p. 16). For many hundreds of years now, we have found that people are most likely to experience poverty in childhood (when they generate expense without providing income), upon becoming parents (as their expenses rise and their availability for work declines), and in old age (as they become, once again, unable to work). Poverty has been concentrated in overcrowded ghettos, where heating has been a crucial expense (coal or wood in the past, electricity or gas today) and poor nutrition has been pervasive (and more common even than starvation). Social networks and mutual aid have always been crucial to survival (from family, neighbors, civic associations, and guilds), while homeless people and "the wandering poor" have been shunned and treated as criminals. Women have always been disproportionately poor, and poor women have always worked: the presence of women in the labor force is not a phenomenon of second-wave feminism, an all-too-common claim that is possible only if the historian ignores the experiences of poor women and, especially, African American women (Jütte, 1994). Moreover, contrary to notions that there is a "culture of poverty," or that relief so degrades the spirit that one comes to shun work and independence, there is, in fact, little difference about opinions of welfare—and those opinions are largely negative—between welfare recipients and non-recipients (Schneider and Jacoby, 2003; Seccombe, 2010; but see Wertheimer, Long, and Vandivere, 2001, for contrary evidence). People would rather work than be on relief, and, in fact, the overwhelming majority of all federal social welfare benefits—Social Security, Medicare, Medicaid, Supplemental Security Income (SSI), Food Stamps, Temporary Assistance to Needy Families (TANF), the Earned Income Tax Credit (EITC), and school lunch—go to populations of people who have traditionally been thought of as "deserving": children, the elderly, working people, and the disabled (Sherman, Greenstein, and Ruffing, 2012).

Culture, Opinion, and Policy

The evidence I have recounted about the causes of poverty and the behavior of poor people is not widely known by the public or most policymakers. Since the 1960s at least, poll respondents have been consistently more likely to cite "lack of effort" rather than "circumstances beyond their control" as the main cause of poverty, often pointing to drug or alcohol use, lack of motivation, or welfare itself as the culprit. The percentage of the public that thinks it is government's obligation to do something about poverty has been declining for decades, while majorities, sometimes large majorities, have asserted that most people on welfare could get along without it and that there were plenty of jobs available, if only people would seek them out (American Enterprise Institute, 2003; see also Feagin, 1975; Lepianka, Oorschot, and Gelissen, 2009; Draut, 2002). These attitudes are unusual: Americans are more likely than their counterparts in other rich democracies to attribute poverty to lack of work effort or other personal failures than to failures of public policy or the economy, much less likely to believe that luck plays an important role in determining income, and less likely to believe that there's a public obligation to help care for those who, for whatever reason, are unable to care for themselves (Alesina and Glaeser, 2004; Stokes, 2013). This is all despite (or because of?) the fact that the United States has higher rates of poverty, child poverty, elderly poverty, infant mortality, inequality, violence, and incarceration, and lower rates of life expectancy, upward mobility, and access to health care than other rich democracies (see, e.g., Economic Policy Institute, 2013; Pimpare, 2008).

That points us toward four questions:

1. Why is there such distance between what social science research tells us to be true about the main causes of poverty and what Americans believe to be true?
2. How has that changed over time?
3. Where do those beliefs come from?
4. Is mass culture—including film—a cause of those beliefs, a reflection of them, or a bit of both?

The first thing to note is that Americans are, for the most part, ignorant about matters of public policy. I do not mean that they are stupid, but simply that they rarely possess substantive knowledge. This is not a new development, either, despite the frequency with which people of a certain age tend to bemoan the current generations' supposed lack of knowledge: Reviewing some fifty years of public opinion survey data, Delli Carpini and Keeter (1996) find that the public's substantive knowledge has changed very little over time (see also Lippmann, 1925; Kohut, 2007; Prior, 2005). This is not to say that citizens do not have *opinions* about policy, but to say that those opinions tend to be ill informed, shallowly held, and tenuously connected to any empirical realty. This should not be especially surprising. Most people are too busy managing their lives to work their way through complicated issues, and don't have the training, education, experience, or expertise (not to say inclination) to know how to evaluate competing Congressional budget plans, say, or contradictory claims about the work-disincentive effects of cash assistance programs. This is often very complicated stuff, and it's useful in this regard to remember that even today fewer than one-third of adults have a college degree, according to Census Bureau data.

That said, media surely play a role in this widespread ignorance. Most of the academic literature in the social sciences on media effects has focused on television and, more specifically, on news or public affairs programming. That may or may not apply to fictional accounts in film, which we'll turn to shortly, but it's worth recounting some of what that research has shown.

We know that regular viewers of television news possess greater knowledge of politics and public policy than do those who view less news and more entertainment (Prior, 2005). *Repetition* turns out to be important for the long-term retention of information (Albertson and Lawrence, 2009; Graber, 1988), and both the *quantity* and the *prominence* of coverage on particular issues are, similarly, important to whether people's policy knowledge improves over time (Barabas and Jerit, 2009): More is better, in short. Or rather, more is more effective, since other studies tell us about propaganda effects and the ways in which incorrect information can be distributed, accepted as true, and retained or incorporated into people's worldview. One survey, for example, found that those who watched no news at all were more likely to correctly answer basic factual questions than viewers of Fox News (Farleigh Dickinson, 2012; see also Kull, Ramsay, and Lewis, 2003/2004; Pew, 2012, Section 4), while another showed that Fox viewers were less likely to trust scientists and, as a consequence, less likely to believe that the global climate has been radically altered by human activity (Hmielowski, Feldman, Myers, et al., 2014). Likewise, how issues are framed—whether it's a poverty story focused on an individual's actions or on a bureaucratic failure, for example—matters to how people respond to it, and to how they think about where to place blame (Iyengar, 1990). In that vein, local television news coverage of crime has long possessed a racialized frame and a racial bias, which, in turn, negatively affects white viewers' opinions of African Americans (Gilliam and Iyengar, 2000; see also Gilens, 1999; Kilty and Swank, 1997; Clawson and Trice, 2000; Dyck and Hussey, 2008; Kort-Butler and Hartshorn, 2011). These effects matter: all else being equal, people with higher levels of accurate political knowledge are more tolerant of differences among people, participate more (by voting, making campaign contributions, and volunteering), and are better able to identify policies that are in their own interests and then act on that knowledge (Delli Carpini and Keeter, 1996). In sum: Knowledgeable people make better citizens.

Turning our attention to film specifically, there's been a long-standing effort to link behavior on film to behavior among children—risqué sexual content was the concern at first, then violence, starting with the Payne Fund studies of the 1920s and 1930s, which purported to identify the negative effects of movies on children's attitudes, behavior, school performance, and even sleep patterns (Sklar, 1975/1994; Doherty, 2007), to more recent research that consistently identifies connections between long-term exposure to film or television violence and aggressive behavior (Anderson, Gentile, and Buckley, 2007). Other research draws links between smoking on film and the likelihood that younger viewers will do so themselves (Sargent, Beach, Dalton, et al., 2001; Centers for Disease Control [CDC], 2012), causing potentially hundreds of thousands of people to start smoking who otherwise wouldn't (Center for Tobacco Control Research, 2013).

Studies of particular films also suggest that they have some power to alter thinking. An experiment using Michael Moore's *Roger and Me* (1989) found that viewers were made more cynical, not only about the film's subject, General Motors, but about American business more generally (Bateman, Sakano and Sakano, 1992), and an earlier analysis of *All the President's Men*

(1976) found that viewing it reduced trust in the political system and increased reported alienation from it, just as still earlier work offered evidence that *Birth of a Nation* (1915) stoked racist attitudes, and that *Gentleman's Agreement* (1947) decreased anti-Semitism (Elliott and Schenck-Hamlin, 1979). Spike Lee's *Malcolm X* (1992), by contrast, raised consciousness about race (Davis and Davenport, 1997), and *The Cider House Rules* (1999) appears to have increased viewers' support for abortion under certain circumstances (Mulligan and Habel, 2011). Without *The China Syndrome* (1979), Gary Weimberg (1981) suggests, the disaster at the Three Mile Island nuclear power plant would have been a media event but perhaps not a political one, with implications for subsequent energy policy-making, while *The Day After Tomorrow* (2004) may have both increased viewers' concerns about global climate change and increased their reported willingness to alter their own energy consumption and even voting behavior (Leiserowtiz, 2004). *Wag the Dog* (1997), a more recent experiment discovered, increased subjects' willingness to believe in government-orchestrated conspiracies (Mulligan and Habel, 2013), as did Oliver Stone's *JFK* (1991), which appeared also to reduce viewers expressed desire to vote (Butler, Koopman, and Zimbardo, 1995). Whether their behavior actually changed, as with *Day After Tomorrow* viewers, is unknown. By contrast, Moore's *Fahrenheit 9/11* (2004), while it may have increased negative sentiment about President George W. Bush, may have also increased viewers' participation in political discussions (Stroud, 2007). Whether any of these effects were enduring also typically remains unexamined, although one experiment (Adkins and Castle, 2013) found that not only did *The Rainmaker* (1997) and, to a lesser extent, *As Good As It Gets* (1997), inspire viewers to express more liberal views on health policy, but those effects were still in evidence two weeks after the screenings.

That's some of the impact upon viewers. What can we say about media influence on policymakers and upon policymaking itself? First, we should note that studies seeking to identify the effects of ideas upon policymaking are limited, and the literature as a whole has a problem charting the specific processes by which ideas or changes in ideas influence policy or policymaking processes (Campbell, 2002; Christensen and Haas, 2005, p. viii). We don't, as yet, really have the tools for this, although the evidence is robust that public opinion—whatever its sources—does affect policymaking, on some issues and in some periods more than others, to be sure (Shapiro, 2011). There's a related question: If one of the places from which we acquire ideas about the political and the social world is through television and film, we need to consider the fact that these cultural products draw upon the ideas held by those who create and produce them. But those ideas (and belief about their worthiness and profitability) come from somewhere as well—from prior cultural artifacts, from the detritus of our personal pasts (family, school, religion), from our ongoing encounters with the culture and with the world. Cause and effect may well be impossible to untangle, and it may not be profitable to even attempt to do so. Nonetheless, while this book reveals the ideas and images of poverty that have been contained in American film, it also seeks to understand something about where they come from and what effect they have.

There remains significant space to argue about which kinds of exposure to which kinds of images over what duration have which kinds of effects, and I'm not willing to go as far as either Carl Sandburg (in Bernstein, 2000, p. xi), who claimed that "Culturally speaking, there are arguments to be made that Hollywood ... is more important than Harvard, Yale or Princeton, singly or collectively"; or J. Hoberman (in Lopate, 2008, p. 533), who suggested that "Hollywood is the main repository of cultural memory—and authority." Morris Dickstein (2009, p. 529) seems to get closer to a defensible claim: "Artists and performers rarely succeed in changing the world, but they can change our feelings about the world, our understanding of it, the way we live in it." Likewise, the claim of *Ghettos, Tramps, and Welfare Queens* is a modest one: Images on film can have effects, and if politics, at least in part, is a struggle over which stories we tell ourselves about our country, then one thing seems likely: Movies matter.

IN THE GHETTO: POOR PLACES AND THE PEOPLE IN THEM

THE EVILS OF THE CITY

Musketeers of Pig Alley, Broken Blossoms, The Blot, The Usurer's Grip, A Corner in Wheat, Orphans of the Storm, Sidewalks of New York, The Ex-Convict, The Kleptomaniac, One Is Business the Other Crime, Boy of the Streets, Dead End, Boys Town, Men of Boys Town, The Hoodlum Priest

At least since the Progressive era, reformers worried about urban poverty have identified the city itself as an important part of the problem. The concentration of diverse populations (each with their own unhealthy habits, odd customs, and foreign values), packed into close quarters (with bad influence spreading easily from family to family), far from the natural world (surrounded by tall man-made buildings, the ground paved over with brick, scarce trees, the sky hidden and sooty), all elevate need from merely an individual or familial tragedy into something like a contagion that breeds criminals and crime. Robert Hunter (1904, p. 192), a student of poverty in the late nineteenth century, thought there being no place to play but in the streets "the most widespread evil of child life in the largest cities," which, Jacob Riis argued (1890/1993), fostered bad habits that would lead inexorably to prison or the relief rolls, to disdain for work, and to a propensity for—anticipating Henry Hill's great fear in *The Music Man*—gambling. For evidence of children's alienation from the natural world, all one has to do is "take into a tenement block a handful of flowers from the fields and watch the brightened faces," as they become, as Riis would have it, transformed entirely by the mere sight of such natural beauty. "I have seen an armful of daisies," insists Riis, "keep the peace of a block better than a policeman and his club" (p. 136).

This is part of the thinking that gave birth to Central Park, the movement to build playgrounds, and the infamous "orphan trains" of Charles Loring Brace's Children's Aid Society, which shipped poor children, many of whom were not, in fact, orphans, to upstate New York or out West to be raised by foster parents—and to work their land. (Should you like an overlong, historically inaccurate, made-for-television treatment of the phenomenon, see 1979's *Orphan Train*.) That faith in the restorative powers of the rural landscape remains with us today in Fresh Air Funds, which raise money to send inner-city children off to summer camp; or, in a different way, the Department of Housing and Urban Development's Moving to Opportunity program, which in the mid-1990s helped some people in very poor areas relocate, with the result that their physical and mental health did indeed seem to improve, even if their economic state did not (Ludwig, Duncan, Gennetian, et al., 2012; Turner, Kissane, and Edin, 2012; Ludwig, Duncan, Gennetian, et al., 2013; but see also Chetty, Hendren, Klein, and Saez, 2013).

The city, especially in its poorest parts, is a corrupting force, the thinking goes, one that turns children into villains and breeds pauperism. Such children may be saved, but only by separating them from the causes of their destruction—their corrupt, idle families and the wicked, dark ghettos. As one physician told the New York State Legislature in the 1860s, "The younger criminals seem to come almost exclusively from the worst tenement house districts." They are a "nursery of crime," he observed (Elisha Harris in Hunter, 1904, pp. 194–195).

Many early state and local film censorship efforts were directed at limiting children's access to the cinema, which was thought to be yet another dangerous influence, and concern for movies' effects on children were used as justification for broader efforts at censorship (Pearson and Uriccio in Stokes and Maltby, 1999). By contrast, settlement house leader and urban reformer Jane Addams saw the educational possibilities of the medium, and she established a nickelodeon right in Hull House to show movies to her poor, immigrant clients (Grieveson in Stokes and Maltby, 1999).

Perhaps unsurprisingly, when American movies have ventured into the "slums," they have been obsessed with gangs of what Riis called "ruffians" or "street Arabs," homing in on the organized, criminal activities of young men. The Los Angeles and New York drugs-and-gangs movies of the 1980s and 1990s might come to mind (*Boyz N the Hood*, for example), but those films are descendants of gang and gangster films of the 1930s, which we'll turn to shortly. Even earlier than that, however, with D. W. Griffith's 1912 *Musketeers of Pig Alley*, the poorer parts of the city meant chaos, danger, and dysfunction.

Musketeers, the title card tells us, is set on "New York's Other Side," where a "poor musician" sets off to earn some money, leaving behind his wife (Lillian Gish) and her mother, who soon dies of an apparent heart attack. His wife, the "little lady," is accosted by the gang leader of the Musketeers, but she rebuffs him; upon the young husband's return (having sold his violin), he is beaten and robbed

FIGURES 1.1, 1.2, AND 1.3 Jacob Riis's 1888 Photograph Of "Bandit's Roost" (*Left*); And *Musketeers Of Pig Alley*, Biograph Company, 1912 (*Top Right* And *Bottom Right*).

by the gang leader and his sidekick. Vowing to get his money back, he sets off to Pig Alley, which has the feel of another alley, the Bandit's Roost made famous by Jacob Riis's photographs and was, in fact, filmed nearby (Schickel, 1975).

Throughout this journey, we are introduced to some of the diversity of the turn-of-the-century slum: a few glimpses of a Jewish street merchant, a Chinese man passing through the Alley, pushcart peddlers, gangs of newsboys, men drinking, women chasing after rambunctious children. What's notable is that we see that violence in the slums can have its most baleful effects on other poor people, a reality reflected all too rarely: often in the movies violence emerges from the poorer places to pose a threat to the middle or upper classes, a bias and misconception that many hold even today—even while crime in the United States has been in steady decline since the 1990s, fear of crime has often been on the rise (Saad, 2011).

Griffith shows us another ghetto in *Broken Blossoms* (1919). In, this case, Lucy (Lillian Gish) lives in a gloomy slum along the Thames and is regularly beaten by her father, a boxer and an alcoholic. The homes are small, dark, dirty, and overcrowded. The women are exhausted, harried, and abused (we witness verbal assaults and must assume they suffer physical harm as well), while the men are lazy and loud and, often, drunkards (the Chinese men are

FIGURE 1.3A "Whatever you do, dearie, don't get married." *Broken Blossoms*, United Artists, 1919.

opium addicts). "Whatever you do, dearie, don't get married," a neighbor admonishes young Lucy. The alternative seems to be prostitution, but they warn Lucy away from that route, too. What hope does she have? This is a particularly gendered perspective on very poor neighborhoods, in which men are all but useless and women can do little but sell themselves once to one man or to many men over and again. This view, too, was prominent among the reformers of the late nineteenth and early twentieth centuries (see Lowell, 1884, e.g.), and, as we'll see, it will endure in film.

The earliest years of the American cinema are littered with such stories of the desolate and the destitute. Many of these first short films are set in the tenements and the slums of New York's Lower East Side, a reminder of the fact that the moving picture was born in the Progressive era and that New York was the film industry's first home, before it migrated to the West Coast for better weather and light, a broader range of easily accessible locations, less regulation, and cheaper labor (Sanders, 2001, pp. 24–25). Many of these pictures seem to be trying to puzzle out the relationship between poverty and crime, and they can be quite sympathetic to the young gang members, at least until the 1980s, when the protagonists became black. Some filmmakers will try to demonstrate how it might seem rational for poor young men to join a gang, since it might offer safety, upward mobility, respect, income, and someplace to belong, and many of their films empathize, some very deeply, with young men born into a world in which their options are so limited and their lives are little valued by anyone other than, if they were lucky, a devoted sister or a caring neighborhood priest. Referring back to the discussion in the introduction, they are prone to offering us a structural explanation for poverty rather than a behavioral one. As we'll see later, the portrayal of the would-be rescuers of poor children and others in the ghetto is problematic in a thousand ways, but here it's worth noting the contrast: on one hand, we find simplistic views that suggest that all a boy in trouble needs is one caring adult (making the adult the protagonist, typically). By contrast, in some films and in most realities, the forces aligned against such young men are too strong and too varied to be overcome by one committed reformer. That's why it can be so refreshing, in an odd way, when the reformer fails, since that's the more likely real-world result.

The first film to attend specifically to the effects of the city on poor, impressionable young men would appear to be *Sidewalks of New York* (1931). Because it seeks to trace the origins of violence and crime, it's a different kind of beast than *Musketeers,* which seems to exist in a bit of a vacuum, as Kevin Brownlow (1990, p. 187) observes. In the earliest films, the criminals are just crooks, without an apparent cause for their behavior, although there are exceptions: *Regeneration* (1915) is one (see Chapter 4), and even earlier, in *The Ex-Convict* (1904), a recently released prisoner tries and fails to get honest work, despite having saved the young child of a wealthy family from being run over by a car. Desperate, he resorts to begging for change, and when that fails, he breaks into the wealthy family's home. He's caught, but they take pity on him and change their mind about involving the police. The wealthy family then befriends the man and his poor family. The moral is clear—if you make it hard for an ex-convict to get along by legitimate means, he will, out of necessity, resort to illegitimate ones. Edwin Porter's *The Kleptomaniac* (1905) had similar sympathies: a wealthy woman caught shoplifting at a high-end department store and a poor woman who steals a small bit of food for her children are both arrested; the wealthy woman is set free, while the other is sent off to jail, her children torn from her. Not subtle, but the point is made (with a critique of the American criminal justice system that resonates even today). Griffith's *One Is Business, the Other Crime* (1912) offers another kind of contrast, juxtaposing wealthy newlyweds with a "poor couple, out of work, in sore straits." About to be evicted, the unemployed man searches for work, to no avail, while his wife sits helplessly at home, sobbing, weak and sick from hunger. An empty cradle in the room suggests either a baby on the way, or one that has died. Meanwhile, the wealthy man takes a $5,000 bribe to award a railway company a contract. Increasingly desperate, the poor man breaks into the rich man's house to steal the bribe, but when he's caught by the wife, "the burglar begs for mercy." While the wife is inclined to grant it, when the wealthy man comes home he wants to calls the police. But, she scolds, "he is no worse than you!" Chastened, he returns the bribe and, what's more, tracks down the poor man to offer him a job.

The Blot (1921), directed by Lois Weber, who had experience as a social worker in New York and Pittsburgh (Brownlow, 1990), offers another unusual but relatively sympathetic take on poverty and poor people. The film introduces us to Professor Griggs, who, we are told, subsists on "less than a bare living wage" and is engaged in an "endless struggle with poverty." We meet his wife, who is distressed to hear that Griggs has invited the minister home, since the best she can offer him is weak tea and bread that is spread with too little "butter substitute." The camera offers us shots of worn furniture and a threadbare carpet; later we'll see paint peeling from the home's exterior and learn that they are behind on their mortgage. Their daughter's gloves have holes, and her shoes have thin, worn soles. The Griggs occupy a clear position within the film's class hierarchy but one that is hard to describe: they live what seems, in many respects, a middle-class life, with a large, reasonably well-furnished home and a well-educated, professionally employed patriarch. But the rail-thin Mrs. Griggs steals food from the neighbors' trash to feed her cats, and she is clearly beaten down by privation: sour, angry, bitter, jealous, and resentful. Similarly, we see the minister, like the professor, barely scraping by on his paltry wages. Their status is meant to be "the Blot," an issue that had been receiving attention from prominent magazines like *Literary Digest* and *The Atlantic Monthly* (Parchesky, 1999; deLong, 2010).

The poverty here is material, while the social divide among classes is not so great, and it is the professor and minister's professional standing that what makes them worthy, at the end, of the intervention of a rich trustee's son. This inchoate class commentary is part of what makes the film odd (Carl Sandburg complained of its "slovenly handling of pertinent issues" [in Bernstein, 2000, p. 83]). Despite Weber's background and her ambitions—"I'll tell you what I'd like to be, and that is, the editorial page of the Universal Company," she once claimed (Stamp, 2004)—*The Blot* ultimately pretends to be about "the poor" without really showing us poor people. Instead, we meet the middling classes struggling to maintain their status.

This is an old problem. In one of the short educational films produced in the early twentieth century by the Russell Sage Foundation, *The Usurer's Grip* (1912), we find a seemingly poor couple, with a sick child, having been ensnared by a loan shark, the moral being that poor people should establish savings accounts, a prominent goal of Progressive era reformers. But this is more a middle class household of non-ethnic whites, and that serves a function: by avoiding depictions of the very worst tenement poverty, the film (and the Sage Foundation) avoid drawing attention to one main argument against urging the very poor to save money—they are too many more urgent needs for that to be responsible behavior.

Most films of the early twentieth century have been lost (see silentera.com; Pierce, 2013), so we can't make pronouncements about the balance of class interests in them. Brownlow (1990, p. 290) feels that "the poor were shown less and less during the twenties," while another analysis shows that films that featured "progressive reform of society" were at their peak in 1918, 1930, and 1938 (May, 2000, p. 275, fig. 4). But if what survives of these earlier pictures is representative (and there's no reason to believe it necessarily is), even in this period, in "social problem" films, it was the middle and upper classes who occupied most of American screen time. Some of that, I would suggest, is merely the product of screenwriters' writing what they know.

There are, nonetheless, more radical critiques: One of the most sympathetic views is also among the earliest, yet again from D. W. Griffith. *A Corner in Wheat* (1909) takes us from the fields to the speculator, to the trading floor, to a wealthy dinner party, and then to the bakery, where a poor woman, accompanied by her child, is unable to afford a loaf of bread. Griffith lets us know that the fault is not hers, but the doing of the money-men. When there is soon no bread at all, thanks to "advances" in the price of flour, leaving a long line of poor, hungry men, it is the supercilious rich his camera cuts to. When the speculator, just having cornered the entire global market, falls into a gain elevator and dies, we do not mourn. And when a desperate mob threatens to riot in the bakery, we sympathize with them, and not with the police officer who beats them back, nor with the owner who protects his business. As the final fade-out lingers on the dejected farmer, replanting his small crop after

FIGURES 1.4 **AND** 1.5 D. W. Griffith juxtaposes an extravagant dinner party (*left*) with a long line of people unable to afford bread (*right*). *A Corner in Wheat*, Biograph Company, 1909.

its recent failure, we must be meant to wonder: What's it all for? It's an oddly affecting film, layered and complex despite its scant fourteen minutes. It's the farmer and the poor city-dweller pinioned by the financiers and the merchants, though the merchants are, to some extent, at the mercy of the speculators, too. Rarely will we see poverty on screen in this kind of political economy context, nor do we often see the effort to link the misery in cities with misery on the farm (although we will see a bit of this in the 1930s).

But as Sklar (1975/1994, p. 57) comments, "For every *Corner in Wheat*. . . . there was another Griffith film that sentimentalized the rich," as Griffith does even here, in the end. Indeed, Griffith's radicalism has softened to a pallid kind of centrism by 1921, and *Orphans of the Storm,* an explicitly anti-Communist (anti-Bolshevik, specifically) piece of propaganda, trying to draw lessons from pre-Revolution France for early twentieth-century America. Two children, one the royal issue of an encounter between a noblewoman and a commoner (Louise), the other simply born into a household of "direst poverty" (Henriette), are raised together in the poor household until the plague leaves them orphans and renders Louise blind. The context is in part the contrast between "limitless luxury" and "unspeakable poverty" (surely there's a bit of *Prince and the Pauper* here). Ragged peasants stare longingly at bread in the window of a bakery, bread soon distributed to the emaciated people by the rebellious chevalier. The women cradle and coo at the loaves as if they were babies. Louise is conscripted into service by a clan of street beggars led by a "disreputable old scoundrel" whose public plea is "Charity? Charity?" while, "inflamed by her virginal beauty," a marquis arranges to abduct Henriette, the same marquis who crushes a boy to death under the wheels of his carriage, then blithely offers a coin to the mother. "Dead? Sorry. . . . Are the horses hurt?" Lest we not believe such casual indifference to human life, Griffith notes in the title card that this is *"an historical incident."* Griffith takes great pains to show the decadence of the aristocracy, calling the marquis's parties "dissolute orgies," which take place while "poverty murmurs ominously outside the gates." But it's the chevalier who will save Henriette, and thus we have aristocratic heroes as well as working-class ones, and villains of the nobility and villains amongst the very poor. It is the dangers of the mob that seem to most concern Griffith, and the lessons to be learned about the consequences of class antagonisms. When the "riff-raff" are exuberant with victory and drunk with their newfound power (and seek to slake their thirst for vengeance), the results are just as barbarous as when the arrogant and frivolous aristocracy rule blithely from afar. The rich man's gilded ball or the pauper's bacchanal can each lead us to ruin, Griffith seems to say. It's a wildly immoderate film about political moderation.

But to return, finally, to *Sidewalks of New York*—that pattern of generally eliding the roots of crime will change most dramatically here. Some kids in the tenement district beat up the rent collector at the behest of their mothers. Soon enough, the landlord himself, Homer Van Dine Harmon (Buster Keaton) joins his terrified collector, and they arrive in the middle of a street brawl over a stickball game. Harmon falls in love with Margie, the sister of one of the "ruffians" who belong to a gang of pickpockets run by Butch, but when Harmon appears in court with the boys after the melée, a police officer warns him away from trying to help:

> Mr. Harmon, I don't think you understand. You see, young man, these poor children are born in poverty and reared in ignorance. The gutter's their cradle, and later their playground. They give them to the streets, and most of them die there from policemen's bullets. The judge knows all this, that's why he let you take the blame today. You can stand it.

Harmon is apparently moved by all of this, and tells Margie he wants to "come down here and see how you people live," to which she replies, indignant: "Well, we ain't no zoo!" He just wants to help "take them out of the gutter and give them a place to play," he protests. But she knows his type: "too polite to be up to any good." He pleads that he's an orphan himself, and buys her flowers. We soon cut to a newspaper headline: *Philanthropist Converts Tenement Into Gymnasium for East-Side Kids*. It's called "Harmony Hall," naturally, reflecting a pattern common in real world, then and now—the self-aggrandizement attached to many philanthropic bequests. While he's doing this to win the girl, not out of concern for the children, note that getting them off the streets is itself understood to be improving—and it succeeds: By the end, the worst of the young men has rebuffed Butch in order to come to the rescue of Harmon and all, presumably, will live happily ever after.

It's a typically Progressive kind of analysis, and establishes what will be a common trope in films ostensibly about the urban poor: The wealthy philanthropist is the actual center of the narrative, and the downtrodden objects of his attentions are merely a means toward another end (although in later films it is often the do-gooder's own redemption that's the outcome).

Boy of the Streets (1937) offers a similar kind of social diagnosis. It opens with two cops walking their beat and wondering if they didn't have it better when they were kids. "We had the woods to tramp in, the fields to play in, and decent homes to live in." But "look at these rat traps they call shelters," one says, pointing to a tenement building. Jackie Coogan (from *The Kid*) is Chuck, the head of a Lower East Side teenage gang, which, in what will be the general

with Helen Hayes, "Susan Lenox,
Her Fall and Rise" with Greta
Steffy, Mrs. Daisy Stanley, Mrs.
Berenice Campbell, Miss Hazel Cain

reau, vice oracle; Mrs. Florence
Mrs. Merle Jones and Mrs. Mayme
Kirchner, marshals and Mrs. Lilah
Segroll, musician.

Philanthropist Converts Tenement Into Gymnasium For East-Side Kids

Homer Van Dine Harmon, up-town millionaire, has con-
verted one of his Eastside tenements into a combination gymnasium and social center for the use of the children of the
Eastside. It is Mr. Harmon's contention that if the children
have this recreation, they will soon
become interested in the various
sports that will be afforded by Mr.
Harmon in his new gymnasium.

(Continued on Page Five)

amusing to lie on the bed and fire
bullets from a .38 calibre gun into
the dresser and wall, the wife and
mother-in-law of Jack Griffin, resident of 7032 Spad place, were of an
entirely different opinion and sought
the aid of the Culver City police
when they failed to subdue Griffin

FIGURES 1.6 AND 1.7 *Sidewalks of New York*, MGM, 1931.

FIGURES 1.8., 1.9, AND 1.10 "Heaven help us," implores Mary Brennan, in *Boy of the Streets*, Monogram Pictures, 1937 (*left*). More haggard women. *Boy of the Streets* (*center*); and *One Third of a Nation*, Dudley Murphy Productions, 1939 (*right*).

pattern, causes some trouble without being truly dangerous. A wealthy young woman inherits the tenement where he and his family live, and is appalled and more than bit repulsed by the place (as Kay will be in *Dead End*), a building that is "breeding disease in every poor devil who has to live here," she's scolded by the local doctor.

Chuck tries to help out a neighbor girl at loose ends when her tubercular mother is sent off to a sanitarium by getting her a job singing in a local café; she's underage, and found out by the police and two social workers from the Children's Aid Society—sour, dour, matronly busybodies, who threaten to take her away ("women reformers," Chuck derisively calls them). It's a problem the socialite (and the film) solves by paying for her to go off to boarding school, which is at least better than her efforts to improve the squalid building: She brings wallpaper, and offers plants, lamps, and rugs, which, as Chuck points out, is pretty "dumb," since no one wants or needs these things and will most likely sell them as soon as they can; this is an old pattern of philanthropic cluelessness (see Pimpare, 2008); but the movie is not only aware of the social distance between the would-be benefactor and the ghetto resident, but aware enough to have a character point it out explicitly. This is unusual in the entire history of American film. Chuck, with few options, winds up working for a local gangster, but is shot during a caper, repents, and joins the Navy. There's no pat moral here, except perhaps the suggestion that poor kids in the slums, even the good ones, have two routes up and out—the Mob or the armed forces.

Released in the same year as *Boy of the Streets, Dead End* (1937) sets in motion an entire stream of films, although none will be better than this original. The opening screen crawl tells us, "Every street in New York ends in a river. For many years the dirty banks of the East River were lined with the

FIGURE 1.11 "What do they want?!" wonders the clueless socialite *cum* landlord of the residents of her run-down tenement. "They don't know," is the response. "They've never *had* anything." *Boy of the Streets*, Monogram Pictures, 1937.

tenements of the poor. Then the rich, discovering that the river traffic was picturesque, moved their houses eastward. And now the terraces of these great apartment houses look down into the windows of the tenement poor." This seems to establish right away that the rich here are the interlopers; moreover, they do it for frivolous reasons—because it's "picturesque."

Here we see what makes a city a city, perhaps for the first time: the close, almost claustrophobic abrasion of class and type. The children of the neighborhood swim in the dirty river and play in the street, and we see doormen shoo them away, as a policeman does to a homeless man sleeping on a bench in front of the high-rise's entrance just as the film opens. The wealthy apartment dwellers navigate through them with trepidation, sometimes being pelted by slingshot-launched rocks. One of the kids has tuberculosis, another tells of being hit by his drunken father, and another assaults a rich boy and pulls a knife on the boy's father, events that will lead to his eventual arrest.

Meanwhile, Kay (Wendy Barrie) is a woman who is trapped much as *Broken Blossoms'* Lucy was, and little pleased with the bargain she has cut

FIGURES 1.12, 1.13, 1.14, **AND** 1.15 Setting the scene for *Dead End*, Samuel Goldwyn Studios, 1937.

to escape poverty by becoming a "kept woman"—but "frightened of being poor again: I've seen what it does to people," she says. She flirts with Dave (Joel McCrae), a former gang member himself struggling to find work as an architect even though he has six years of college under his belt. He dreams of tearing down the tenements (as the protagonist will many years later in *The Architect*). But when Kay decides to drop in on him and discovers the place to be loud, dirty, garbage-strewn, and crawling with large roaches, she flees, disgusted. He witnesses this, and realizes she's probably not for him after all.

Drina (Sylvia Sidney) is a department store worker on strike, a strike she defends as simply a fight for what she's earned through hard work. She stuffs newspaper into her shoes to cushion her step and prolong their usefulness. She's also in love with Dave. At the same time, Baby Face Martin (Humphrey Bogart), having escaped the neighborhood through crime, is back to see his estranged mother, who disowns him as a murderer, "a butcher," and his former girlfriend, now a prostitute with tuberculosis (it was syphilis in the stage play; note Buhle and Wagner, 2002, p. 12).

So, almost everyone (even a few of the wealthy), has reached a dead end here—ending up with grim lives and little hope. As Dave says to Drina, "What chance do they have in a place like this—they have to fight for everything,

FIGURE 1.16 The large roach on an overflowing garbage can that marks the end of the romance for Kay. *Dead End*, Samuel Goldwyn Studios, 1937.

they get used to fighting. 'Enemies of society,' they say in the papers. Well, why not? What've they got to be so friendly about?" It's that old notion of the city: It's the ghetto itself, the closeness, the lack of privacy—and the scarcity— that are corrupting of the human spirit and particularly dangerous to children. The sense here is very much that these boys are lost causes and are more likely than not to end up like Martin did.

Dead End was something of a smash, and both it and the Dead End Kids had "more sympathetic impact than [playwright Sidney] Kingsley, [screen-writer Lillian] Hellman, or director William Wyler expected (or even desired on behalf of those lumpen social by-products)," as Buhle and Wagner put it (2002, p. 129). New York senator Robert Wagner, a chief architect of key New Deal programs, was even Samuel Goldwyn's guest at the premier (Bergman 1971/1992, pp. 152–153).

In subsequent films, the young men become the Dead End Kids, the Little Tough Guys, the East Side Kids, and finally the Bowery Boys, appearing (with various cast changes) in eighty-some films of wildly varying quality up until the late 1950s. *Crime School* (1938) was the first, and already the specificity and sharpness are gone now that the screenplay is no longer by Hellman. Instead of an urban scene in tension and transition, with rich and poor forced to occupy the same space and, and a consequence, contemplate and confront each other (perched literally at the edge of the city, no less), we are greeted here with a generic urban street scene in which the Kids gather and cause small-scale disruption and commit modest crimes: shoplifting and stealing bicycles, watches, car hood ornaments and the like; noise-making, stoop-sitting, and typical teen-aged mocking of authority.

But just when it seems fairly tame, they nearly kill a pawnshop owner with a hammer during an argument over money. During a court hearing, the sister of gang leader Frankie—they're orphans—begs the judge to allow him to come home instead of sending him to reform school. She explains that the young men have to be tough to survive on the streets, and that she's working hard and going to school so that she can move him to a better neighborhood. "If you want to do something for these boys, why don't you clean up the slums! Why don't you give them a decent place to live in! Give them some of the things other boys have. Give them a chance in life." But, says the judge in response, "You can't blame it all on environment. Some of our greatest men have come out of those same tenements."

But in Hollywood, most of those we've seen come out of the slums have been gangsters. And so we have the tepid liberalism of Warner Brothers that too often gets mistaken for social radicalism, in part, perhaps, because compared to the politics of the other Hollywood studios it was radical. As Andrew Sarris (1998, p. 26) put it, "Underneath all that grime there was as much sentimental piety and conformist cant among the Brothers Warner as there was in L. B. Mayer." Harry Alan Potamkin, writing in 1930 of movies with some putative reformist spirit, complains that "the social criticisms in these films, as in the war films, are *merely remarks*, they do not inform the progression of the film. An incisive, informative point of view is lacking" (in Jacobs 1977, pp. 155–156; italics added). The social conditions poor people grow up in make it that much harder for them to survive, much less thrive, and that should be remedied (or at least acknowledged, anyway); but the burden in films is nonetheless typically on them to obey the law, to strive, and to seek a way out, whatever the obstacles and whatever the odds. The remedy's the same for conservatives and liberals alike—work, obey, and strive, if you want to thrive. What distinguishes the liberal is the recognition that this simple formula is not so simple for some groups of people.

And what distinguishes the true radicals, who are as absent from American moving pictures as they are from American politics, is the belief that the world, ultimately, cannot be reformed but must be transformed into something else entirely. Even in the 1930s, with the country on the edge of economic and social collapse, Hollywood couldn't see fit—with an exception or two to be noted—to imagine a new economy, or even a new kind of city in which geography doesn't doom some children to poverty or prison. Moreover, we should remember that Warner Brothers finally gave up on "social problem" films when confronted by fights in their own studio for union recognition and violence on the picket lines in the mid-1940s, reportedly vowing to stop "making pictures for the 'little man'" (Neve 1992, p. 89). Jack Warner would later become a friendly witness to the Communist witch-hunts of the House Un-American Activities Committee, and Warner's studio would be among those most scrupulous about adhering to the blacklist and investigating its employees and applicants. By the early 1950s, they "had lost much of their reputation as a liberal studio with a specialisation in working-class themes" (Neve 1992, pp. 108, 183).

That's not to say there's no effort at social commentary in *Crime School*, and when the boys arrive at the house of reform, it's grim: they are told that they have arrived too late for dinner, so they won't get fed, and when Frankie complains, he's hit, and later whipped for fighting. When a state inspector, played by Humphrey Bogart, fires the most ruthless guards and the alcoholic doctor and then observes that the institution is meant to be a reformatory school and not a prison, he's admonished by the superintendent: "Your experience has been in settlement work, Mr. Braden. You'll find this is just a little bit different." Bogart takes over, employs his softer methods to cajole and encourage the boys, and after some slapstick interludes and some non-trivial resistance (which includes a boiler explosion and fire, and later some gun play), he prevails, naturally enough. The boys are paroled and sent back to the streets.

The movies that descend from *Dead End* become less and less about the city and the slum. *Crime School* is about juvenile delinquency, and 1938's *Angels with Dirty Faces*, although there's a nice opening panorama establishing the close quarters of the Lower East Side tenements, is about what happens when those juveniles grow up: it's a gangster film. In this picture, young Rocky observes to his buddy Jerry, justifying a heist, "What we don't take, we ain't got." But they're discovered, and while Jerry escapes after pulling his buddy from the path of an oncoming train, Rocky is caught and sentenced to The Society for Juvenile Delinquents, transferred to reform school, and, finally, to the state penitentiary. Upon his release, adult Rocky, now played by Jimmy Cagney, is a full-fledged gangster and murderer, while Jerry is a priest. (Is it prison itself that made Rocky go bad, we are meant to wonder? Reform school "made a criminal out of him. But he's not bad," we hear.) The Dead End Kids steal Rocky's wallet, thinking him just another rube, and soon enough he's taken them under his wing. But he also gets the boys to go to the parish Boys Club for a game of basketball (the priest has been trying, to no avail) and speaks with Laury (Ann Sheridan) "a snappy-looking dish ... for a sociable worker." In the end, Rocky is executed, thanks to the Hays Code's requirement that no bad deed go unpunished (see Doherty, 2007, p. 91), and Father Jerry asks the Kids to "say a prayer for a boy who couldn't run as fast as I could," again suggesting that maybe Rocky would have stood a chance at redemption had he not gotten caught up in the system, a concern consistent with *Crime School.*

The Angels Wash Their Faces (1939), despite the title, is not a sequel. It begins in a reformatory, but one that seems, by all accounts, the very model of a benevolent institution devoted to improvement and preparing young men to return to society. Gabe is paroled and moves with his sister back to the tenements, where he is soon accused of causing a string of fires actually set by a local gangster. It's up to the Dead End Kids to save him. They do, and in the process they bring down the gangster and corrupt city officials, clearing the way for some of the slum to be torn down and replaced with parks and playgrounds (just as it is in *One Third of a Nation;* see Chapter 7). We can see some New Deal ethos slip in, along with some of the Progressive notion that the remedy for the ghetto is to send children out to the countryside or, at the very least, to bring some of the countryside into the city. We can also see that, long before the "urban renewal" programs of the 1960s or the destruction of public housing under the Department of Housing and Urban Development's HOPE VI programs more recently, slum clearance has been a favored response to concentrated poverty: if we can't remove the children from the slums, we must destroy the slums themselves.

Little Tough Guy (1938) features most of the Dead End Kids on loan to Universal Studios. Kay is angry with her mother for having sent her father to the factory during a strike and encouraging him to work as a scab: Kay worries about whether he'll be able to look his friends in the eye. Her mother worries about paying the bills. He gets caught in a scuffle and is wrongly accused of killing a police officer. When he is convicted, the family is shunned. Kay loses her job, her brother loses his friends, and what's left of the family is evicted and forced to move to the tenements. This is unusual in itself—to see the process by which people slide into poverty and enter into the ghetto. Here again we find the Dead End Kids, now joined by Kay's brother Johnny. Meanwhile, Kay's working in a burlesque house, and Johnny, after throwing a rock through a car window, is sent to a detention home. He promptly escapes with the help of the Kids, who are engaging in something of a petty crime spree financed by a rich young man who wants to live vicariously through them—he envies the improvisational and chaotic nature of their lives. But he double-crosses them, and soon enough Johnny nearly dies in a gun battle with police, while his accomplice does die. And why? Because his father crossed a picket line, his sister lost her job, and they had to move to the ghetto, where he fell in with the wrong crowd. Note that the social commentary doesn't seem to have much diminished, even removed from Warner Brothers. He *had* to steal, he tells the judge, to help his mother and sister. The Kids, at the end, are sent off to reform school, along with the rich kid accomplice and Johnny.

The year 1939 brings us *Hell's Kitchen* and *They Made Me a Criminal*, and brought the Kids back to Warner. In *They Made Me a Criminal*, Johnnie, a carousing boxer (John Garfield), wrongly accused of murder, is on the run and traveling the country by rail. He finds himself on an Arizona ranch, where the Dead End Kids are picking dates (!) as part of some ill-defined reform effort overseen by an East Side priest. The boxer insists he's no tramp when told he has to work if he wants a handout, but, although he's indignant at the mere suggestion, what is he but a tramp? They nurse him back to health after he passes out from hunger, and he winds up hanging around, teaching the Kids to box, steal, and lie, among other things. And yet, eventually, they teach him more, as he risks his own freedom to help them attain stability and security, and stays to build a new, above-board life. *Hell's Kitchen* gives us Buck Caesar (the product, predictably enough, of reform school), a mobster released on a suspended sentence, who tries to demonstrate his good behavior to the judge by making a donation to Hudson's Shelter for Homeless Boys. Hudson's turns out to be a brutal place in which the boys are beaten, punished by having their rancid and already insufficient rations reduced, and worse: one boy dies after having been locked in a freezer to teach him a lesson ("We call it Hell's Kitchen," says one of the Kids, "and sometimes we don't say 'kitchen'"). Among its residents are the Dead End Kids. Caesar's lawyer and nephew (played by Ronald Reagan) suggests that the racketeer can bolster his image as a civic leader even more effectively by being made a superintendent of the shelter, and Buck soon is. Trying to convince him of what the school could be, a teacher asks him if he's seen *Boy's Town*: "It shows you what can be done," she says, "when a home's run with honesty and kindness and understanding. A school like that's making good citizens out of waifs from the street! And we could do the same thing here." And so they do, including instituting mechanisms for self-governance, paying the boys wages for their work, and a starting a school hockey team. Buck, like Johnnie in *They Made Me a Criminal*, is redeemed by the boys, even if they are not yet fully reformed themselves (as Buck tells them, "It's okay for you to like me, but it's not okay for you to *be* like me"). As with *Boys Town* itself, if more tentatively, the message is that "there are no bad boys," only bad environments.

FIGURES 1.17 AND 1.18 Civilian Conservation Corps Camp, Bayard, Nebraska (*left*); and *Pride of the Bowery*, Monogram Pictures, 1940 (*right*).

After 1939, Warner released all the Kids from their contracts, and Monogram Pictures picked up most of the actors for a series now called "The East Side Kids." *Boys of the City* (1940) finds the Kids trying to stay cool on a hot summer day, getting, inevitably, into trouble. In lieu of reform school, they're sent off to a camp in the Adirondacks—another in the line of films with the assumption that getting troubled and trouble-making children and teens out of the pernicious influence of the city is the key. But they never get as far as the camp, waylaid at an old mansion and trapped in a rickety haunted house plot. *Pride of the Bowery* (1940) goes one better: here the Kids wind up in a camp run by the Civilian Conservation Corps, the New Deal program designed to bring low-income young men (and eventually, women) out of the city to work (for modest wages, most of which were sent to their parents) on planting trees, building parks, clearing brush, building paths and roads, and the like. The camp is portrayed as clean and well-managed, with a firm but benevolent hand; it occupies the young men with a range of productive work and educational activities, and the food is good and in ample supply. It's an effective bit of New Deal propaganda, in its own way, although the historical record largely confirms the film's portrayal (see Hiltzik, 2011).

Once again, a change in environment helps expose the Kids' *true* characters, as one of them allows himself to be accused of a petty crime protect a friend. This is one of the few instances in which the Depression intrudes in any specific kind of way—in most of this line of films, it's merely the cause of a constant search for work, if it appears at all.

Bowery Blitzkrieg (1941) returns to an examination of the merits of reform school (1942's *Mr. Wise Guy* will have all the Kids in reform school yet again, although innocent of the crime of which they're accused, for a change). It opens with two police officers debating, in an echo of *Boy of the Streets*, whether reformatories are the answer for the neighborhood kids, and the impending execution of a local boy gone bad serves as background noise. The lesson here is that even a kid apparently on the straight and narrow is just one corrupting influence away from turning to a life of crime—it's that precarious— while a reform school kid headed for trouble can be saved by a loving but disciplined home.

By the time the Kids are repackaged yet again as the "Bowery Boys" (for another forty-plus films), the dark social realism of many of the early movies is gone, and, as many have observed, the franchise seemed to have been following the path of Abbott and Costello as much as anything, moving almost entirely into location- and gimmick-based comedy, with titles like *Bowery Buckaroos*, *Bowery Boys Meet the Monsters*, and *Let's Go, Navy!*

But those earlier films, especially *Dead End* and some of the first Warner Dead End Kids outings, show an effort to think about the slum and the city, where juvenile delinquency comes from and what might be done about it, and, notably, an almost crusading concern with the evils of the punitive reformatory system, concerns that hark back to the juvenile justice reform movements of the late nineteenth century. It is one of the ways in which we can see how Progressive era social concerns and social diagnosis lingered into the 1930s, showing up in national policy and in film culture, in remarkably similar ways.

Boys Town (1938) is in that tradition. The opening title cards let the viewer know that the film is based on Father Edward Flanagan (here played by Spencer Tracy) and an actual orphanage in Omaha: "This picture is dedicated to him and his splendid work for homeless, abandoned boys, regardless of race, creed or color." It's unclear how many Jews or African Americans were in the actual Boys Town then, but we do know that one of its first benefactors was Jewish, and that a bus was made available to bring boys to a synagogue in Omaha—separate Protestant services were held on campus—and that the Ku Klux Klan threatened Flanagan with harm if he brought his inter-racial troupe of "The World's Greatest Entertainers" to town (Lonnborg 1992). Across both films I noticed only two black or brown faces, which probably understated, if only modestly, the diversity of the place, which was real enough to concern some of the locals (Reilly and Warneke, 2008).

The film begins in the cell of a man on death row, and yet again the intimation is that he is there because of his early encounters with the reformatory. "When I went in, coppin' a loaf of bread was a job; when I come out, I could rob a bank!" he wails. "Where was the state when a lonely, starving kid cried himself to sleep in a flophouse, with a bunch of drunks, tramps, and hoboes.... I had to be tough to get along." He insists that if he had had one friend when a child, he wouldn't be where he was. These words reverberate through the mind of Flanagan, there to offer comfort, as he walks home. On the way, conveniently enough for the narrative, he passes through a street in which a dozen or so young boys are fighting, smashing store windows, and looting. We find that he's running "Flanagan's Refuge," a flophouse for grown men for whom, he has come to realize, he can do little but offer food and a bed: "It's too late," he says ruefully. He intervenes and prevents the kids involved in the small-scale riot from being sent to reform school by pledging to assume responsibility for them. With his bishop's permission, he rents a house and begins to build a home for them. The home grows, even as he meets with resistance—it's a hopeless cause, they say, the boys are "savages" and destined to become "human derelicts," fit only to be manacled and shut away. Young Whitey Marsh (Mickey Rooney) seems determined to prove the cynics right, but the film suggests that if Whitey is to have any chance at all, it's the nurturing approach of Boys Town and not reform school that can do it. And, sure enough, it does. The slums are dangerous, but those harms can be repaired, if caught in time. "There is no bad boy," intones Flanagan. It's a more flaccid version of *Dead End* and *Crime School*.

Men of Boys Town (1941) brings us right back to the same place, with Whitey (still Mickey Rooney) as town "mayor" and the very model of an upstanding resident. Flanagan (Tracey again) is facing money troubles, as usual, thanks to continuing expansion and an apparent refusal to turn away any homeless boy who shows up. Now he is rescuing a boy from the penitentiary because of crimes he committed against his abusers at the reformatory. Same message, in other words, hammered home in a slimmer and slighter film trying even harder to make the young men adorable and impish. When we do see inside the reform school (Whitey is wrongfully committed there, for a time), it's brutal: emotional abuse, solitary confinement, torture, and even murder. Flanagan delivers an impassioned plea against the prison model of reform, setting the wheels in motion for a Boys Town there.

As in any genre, it seems as if the same film is made repeatedly. Witness *The Hoodlum Priest* (1961). Like the later Dead End Kids movies, this isn't really about the ghetto (though set in St. Louis, and based on a real priest there and his halfway house), but about the possibility of redemption for juvenile delinquents. As *Boys Town* does, it argues that guidance, discipline, care, and tough love are, ultimately, more effective remedies than punishment and prison. The priest here is a Jesuit, and he spends his time in the world of his young criminals in order to understand them and more effectively reach them. "You can't change a man by punishing him," says the priest after telling the tale of his own rough childhood as the son of a coal miner, "you just build his hatred." What's missing here is any condemnation of the city per se—it's not a character the way it can be in some of these other juvenile delinquency films, and there's no real effort to explain what causes crime (except for the effects of prison itself). There is one sharp line, even if it risks slipping into triteness: one of the young hoodlums is convicted (rightly) of murder and sentenced to death, and a police officer, not without some sympathy, says to an anti–death penalty protester, "You're not gonna change the world by carrying around that sign, buddy," to which the man replies: "I'm not trying to change the world, I'm just trying to keep the world from changing me." It's a powerful statement about one of the important functions of political action and activism—to act as a moral person, even when it feels futile to speak or act out, or even when it is truly futile.

Otis Ferguson (in Wilson, 1971, p. 234), in a long lead-up to a short review of *Boys' Town*, wrote the following:

> Still the films about slum children come along—forget sordid matters of finance for a minute and you can close your eyes and see Hollywood with one burning reform project and plan for world redemption: getting the young toughies off the streets and giving them a nice glass of milk. There probably hasn't been so much compassion for and understanding of the offspring of the masses since the Sermon on the Mount, but the comment on picture making goes beyond that. Childhood is one of the few remaining fields where you can base a picture on a known fact and not find yourself in the middle between the Legion of Decency howling down from one side and various other political or social or racial trash blowing up from the other.

There may be merit to this idea that social critique is more palatable to studios and the censors if it is disguised, although other critics pointed to other methods. Pauline Kael (1994, p. 344) claimed that "melodrama was always the chief vehicle for political thought in our films," while Graham Greene (in Parkinson 1993, p. 411) observed in passing that one can get away with much more on film if it is presented "in fancy dress." But Ferguson is surely on to something, and it's not just Hollywood that sees the effects on children as the worst effects of the slums: as we've seen, this has been a key strain of urban reform and a central preoccupation of urban reformers since the late nineteenth century. It's not surprising, then, that it would find its way into film, and continue to.

2 MODERN GANGS AND GHETTO GURLS

Boyz N the Hood, Straight Out of Brooklyn, Menace II Society, New Jack City,
Fresh, Clockers, Chi-Raq, Colors, Crooklyn, Red Hook Summer, Waging a Living,
Do the Right Thing, Gangs of New York, The Cool World, A Raisin in the Sun,
Brother from Another Planet, Pawnbroker, Killer of Sheep, Just Another Girl on the
IRT, On the Outs

The early film gangs of the Lower East Side were never particularly ethnic. There was something vaguely Italian, perhaps, in the Brooklyn accents of some of the Dead End Kids, but that was about it. When late–twentieth century filmmakers turned their cameras to gangs in the cities, however, they would focus on young, African American men. There is, arguably, a logic to this: According to FBI Uniform Crime Report data, violent crime rose dramatically from the late 1960s to the early 1990s, and this was especially true in poorer neighborhoods; since African Americans were (and are) disproportionately likely to be poor, they were thus more likely to be both victims and perpetrators of crime. These trends became a staple of television news and of political discussion more broadly, reaching a kind of hysteria that continued long after crime had, in fact, begun to decline (we still don't really know why).

We'll turn later to the dystopic images of the city itself in the post-1970s period, but for now let's keep our attention on how American film has taught us to think about young men in the poorest parts of the city, and how those images changed over the century. The more recent films are much darker than their ancestors. They are darker in tone—less hopeful about the possibility of redemption, more prone to display—and even revel in—wanton violence, and sometimes peopled with characters so cruel they might be considered sociopathic. But they are darker in a literal way, too, in that African Americans and to a lesser extent Latinos come to occupy center stage. While Khalil Muhammad (2011) traces to the late nineteenth century the political conflation of

US Homicide Rate, 1950–2010
per 100,000 people

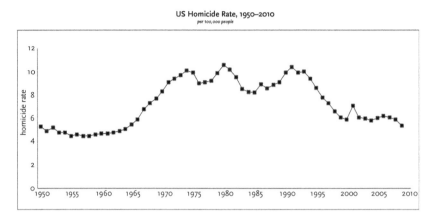

FIGURE 2.1 The rise and fall of murder rates in the U.S. Adapted from van Zanden et al., 2014, Figure 8.1, "Homicide Rates in Selected Western Countries, 1950–2010."

criminality with *blackness*, in the late twentieth century we see it in full flower in the movies.

Boyz N the Hood (1991) begins with the sounds of a confrontation and gunfire, then these words fill the screen: "One out of every twenty-one Black American males will be murdered in their lifetime." The next screen reads: "Most will die at the hands of another Black male." At the center of the story, which begins in 1984, is one young man, Tre (played by Desi Arnez Hines II and then Cuba Gooding, Jr.). His parents, who live apart, are hardworking, educated, responsible, and doing their best, against all odds, to protect him, to teach him values and respect, and to ensure he can make something of himself. But it's them against an entire neighborhood, filled with violent, vicious, misogynist men and lazy, cruel, slatternly women. This

FIGURE 2.2 AND 2.3 The modern ghetto: Black bodies in a desolate landscape, with Ricky as a child, *Boyz N the Hood*, Columbia Pictures, 1991 (*left*); and *Fresh*, Lumiere Pictures, 1994 (*right*).

is a film that simultaneously wallows in and argues against the stereotypes of black urban poverty.

Seven years later, the boys are young men. Tre is in school and has a job at the mall, and his friend Ricky, already a father, has a chance at a football scholarship if he can manage a minimal score on the Scholastic Aptitude Test (SAT). His other friends are in and out of jail, and the neighborhood is little changed, populated by crack-addicted, irresponsible young mothers and men who pull out a sawed-off shotgun if you look at them wrong, all occupying a space that looks nothing like the New York film ghettos we were accustomed to earlier in the century. In the midst of this, from Tre's dad (Laurence Fishburn) comes a radical analysis of the functions of the ghetto itself—arguing that the gun shops and liquor stores and cocaine flooding into the neighborhoods all exist in order to hasten the demise of black men and women themselves. It's an admonition against violence rooted in the claim that it's a sucker's game, since you are ultimately only doing the white man's bidding. It's all the more poignant, if dramatically unsurprising, that Ricky eventually

FIGURE 2.4 The gruesome, un-romanticized death of Ricky, *Boyz N the Hood*, Columbia Pictures, 1991.

gets gunned down. Tre sets out for revenge, but with the voice of his father fresh in his mind, he returns home before the attack is in motion.

It's hard, although not impossible (see *George Washington*), to imagine a film like this made by a white director, and some of its richness and its impassioned plea to end the violence in poor, African American communities must surely be because it is autobiographical, drawn from the experience of young writer and director John Singleton (Barboza, 2009). Only 33 of the 565 people who directed the 500 top-grossing movies released between 2007 and 2012 were black (Women's Media Center, 2014), and thus most makers of films about black neighborhoods have been telling made-up stories, filming their own ideas about what such worlds are like, rather than sharing something they know. These differences matter and help explain why so few modern movies attend to low-income communities of color, while those that do tend to do it poorly: few of those involved in their production bring any of their own knowledge or experience to bear. And that may be why it's harder to get authentic portraits of any "other" on film than to get them, say, in print—the barriers to entry for a movie are so much greater than they are for reporting, for fiction, for music.

Straight Out of Brooklyn (1991), released in the same year, brings us across the country to public housing projects in Red Hook, with another young black man at the center of the story. Dennis (Lawrence Gilliard, Jr., who'll go on to play D'Angelo Barksdale in *The Wire* and appear in the forgettable *Kill the Poor*) is angry and frustrated: his father, disgusted at years of manual labor that have gotten him little, rages against whites, beats his wife, and, in one of his drunken fits, destroys what little property the family has managed to accumulate. Dennis is surrounded by violence, failure, and despair, and wants more. He laments to his friends: "Look at us, man. Look at you. All we do is walk around these projects all day.... We gotta get *paid*, man. We gotta get *paid*. Everybody out there's getting' paid but us." Dennis's plans, alas, revolve around stealing from a drug dealer, and we know it will end badly. Director Matty Rich comes from the projects himself, and there's dimension to the characters, a richness to the place, and like Singleton, he was young when he made the movie—just nineteen. It's a sympathetic portrait of people in bad straits with few options, but it makes no excuses for them, either. Much of the tragedy visited upon Dennis (and more that is surely to come after the film ends) is his own fault, a result of searching for an easy way out, ignoring his girlfriend's increasingly insistent pleas to be patient, keep his head down, and work hard. Those pleas are sometimes made with the Manhattan skyline in the background—that's the promised land here, the place to escape to.

FIGURE 2.5 "There's no wrong way out of here," says Dennis. Dennis and Shirley look out from the ghetto at the promised land in *Straight Out of Brooklyn*, American Playhouse, 1991.

He can't and won't listen, though, partly because he's a teenager and it's his nature, but also because he saw where working hard and playing by the rules got his father—nowhere. This is the lesson of Elliot Liebow's classic text of urban ethnography, *Tally's Corner* (1967/2003), in which extended study reveals that multiple generations of black men were unemployed and hanging out on the street corner not because they passed down laziness from one

FIGURE 2.6 Looking out into the Other City. "The more people there is, the lonelier it gets." *Fresh*, Lumiere Pictures, 1994.

generation to the next, but because each generation struggled for themselves to find a place in the mainstream economy, only to be rejected by it in turn. They didn't give up, but were given up on. *Straight Out of Brooklyn* winds up being at its heart a conservative kind of film, nonetheless, since we have to conclude that Dennis should have taken the slow and steady path, and followed his girlfriend's cautious advice.

Menace II Society (1993), like *Killer of Sheep* before it (discussed later in this chapter), makes the comparison between Watts in Los Angeles of the 1965 rebellions—when more than 30,000 poor, desperate, ill-treated, and forgotten African Americans erupted, finally, in frustration—and its more recent history of gangster violence and deep poverty, violence that is presumed to be less consciously rooted in oppression and abuse. It begins with a young black man, O-Dog (Larenz Tate), casually killing a Korean shop owner for perceived disrespect, and moves quickly to a flashback of news footage of the 1965 events. In voiceover, O-Dog's accomplice, Caine (Tyrin Turner), recounts his parents' post-riot lives: drug use, drug dealing, murder, domestic violence, jail. "I caught on to the criminal life right quick. Instead of keeping me out of trouble, they turned me on to it." By the time Caine finished high school, both of his parents were dead: doomed from the start, we are presumably meant to think. The film charts Caine's exploits after he's been shot in a carjacking that kills a friend, in revenge for which he kills the culprits; he steals cars, robs people at gunpoint, gets arrested, gets beaten by the police, gets a girl pregnant and refuses to acknowledge that the child is his. He is, in some ways, the alter-image of Tre in *Boyz N the Hood*. He's charming, in his own way, but dangerous.

The movie is conflicted about how to think about this place. On one hand, it suggests that there's little chance that Caine (or any of his friends) could have grown up to be anything other than they did. On the other, it hints at how Caine (although perhaps not his friends) could have escaped this fate: he's got loving grandparents who have tried to raise him well, a smart girlfriend (like Tre's in *Boyz*) who's struggling to raise her own son as best as she can, an opportunity to move away with one set of friends to Kansas, or with others to Atlanta (again, escape from the city is the salve), and he himself is sharp and capable. So what's ultimately the point here about the ghetto generally and South Central L.A. specifically? That Caine is killed before he can leave town, although O-Dog is not, might say something about justice, or the lack of opportunities for escape. The film's directors, twin brothers Albert and Allen Hughes, were born in Detroit to an African American father and Armenian mother, and raised by their mother in the Los Angeles suburb of Pomona. They dropped out of high school to make music videos, and did well quickly, making *Menace* when they were twenty years old.

New Jack City, like *Straight Out of Brooklyn* and *Boyz N the Hood*, was released in 1991 (it was a good year for films by and about African Americans, which also brought the release of *Five Heartbeats, Jungle Fever, Mississippi Masala*, and *A Rage in Harlem*, among others) and offers a stark contrast to the humanism of *Boyz* and *Straight Out of Brooklyn*. Better thought of as a gangster movie rather than a ghetto film, it does nonetheless have pretentions of being something more. As the camera pans in for an aerial tour of Manhattan, we hear radio reports about high unemployment, poverty, inequality, drug-related shootings, and crack cocaine–addicted babies (an urban legend of the era), before focusing in on Nino Brown (Wesley Snipes), a crime boss wearing some of the worst 1980s clothing you'll ever see. Later, when Nino proposes taking over the burgeoning crack market, he couches it in a speech about the poor getting poorer and the rich getting richer and the evils of the Reagan era, saying that as a result poor people just want to get high to escape their troubles. But the film doesn't seem to believe this much, and it feels tacked on in an effort to give it weight and meaning, as does some speechmaking at Nino's trial at the end of the film—it's an indictment akin to the one Tre's father gives in *Boyz N the Hood*, but without a coherent political or economic critique. Sanders (2001, p. 375) gives the film too much credit when he suggests we can trace its roots back to *The Roaring Twenties* or to an array of Cagney vehicles.

That the director, Mario Van Peebles, is black, complicates claims about the relationship between Singleton and Rich's race and their more closely observed stories. Black men can make one-dimensional, stereotyped movies about the ghetto just as effectively as white men can, it would seem. Maybe it's personal experience that accounts for some of this difference—Peebles did not grow up poor in South Central, but in Europe and then later in a much different part of Los Angeles as the son of director, writer, producer, and actor Melvin Van Peebles. Mario had acting roles since childhood, and had a career in investment banking before turning to directing (Starpulse.com, n.d.). Perhaps what's most important here is class, then, not race.

That Boaz Yakin, the director of *Fresh* (1994), was born in New York City to Israeli parents of Syrian, Egyptian, and Polish ancestry further hinders our ability to make simple claims about how a filmmaker's race affects their portrayal of poor African Americans. The character Fresh is about twelve years old (Michael is his given name), living in a crowded apartment with his grandmother, aunt, and a dozen cousins; he struggles to get to school on time, and is reprimanded for being disruptive. He flirts awkwardly and tentatively with a pigtailed girl, and gets teased for it by his friends. He travels from his home in Brooklyn to visit his father (who is an alcoholic, perhaps, and living in a dilapidated mobile home) and plays speed chess in Washington Square Park.

And he sells crack cocaine for one local drug dealer and heroin for another. His sister is a junkie, beholden to one of the dealers. The young girl he likes get shot through the neck, caught in the crossfire when a young man kills someone who bested him on the basketball court (and filmed in a way that underscores how little weight most movie shootings have; this is shocking, and awful, among the most powerful deaths on film). *Fresh* may be one of the most accomplished and surest of the pictures in this sub-category, at least initially. Like many of its brethren, it's interested as much in observing as in telling a story or building a conventional narrative, until it becomes something of a caper film as Fresh sets a complex scheme in motion to escape his life and free his sister. Here, too, the Brooklyn ghetto is a place to escape from, although it's less clear to Fresh that the available alternatives are much better. As he looks across the river into Manhattan, just as we see in *Straight Out of Brooklyn*, he frets that "The more people there is, the lonelier it gets."

When Spike Lee's *Clockers* (1995) moves us to the Gowanus Houses in Brooklyn (they are called the Nelson Mandela Houses here), the credits roll over graphic images of bloody gunshot victims, and the kids hanging out and goofing off are of a different sort than those he will show us in *Crooklyn*: they are armed, angry, dealing drugs, periodically degraded through public strip searches at the hands of aggressive (white, bitter, alcoholic, racist) police, and pinioned between those cops and their dealers, who abuse and degrade them in their own ways.

This is the ghetto of the *Straight Out of Brooklyn* universe, but *Clockers* is a gangster story (and a whodunit), not a story about poverty or race per se (although it is concerned with the power of addiction and the corrupting influence of bad role models). It is not, as Lee had hoped (see Massood, 2001), either a radical departure from the others in the genre or the film that will make subsequent drugs-in-the-ghetto movies unnecessary, yet one of its differences is that these men are three-dimensional characters, not cardboard

FIGURES 2.7 AND 2.8 Red Hook, in *Straight Out of Brooklyn* (*left*), American Playhouse, 1991; and the Nelson Mandela Houses, *Clockers*, Universal Pictures, 1995 (*right*).

FIGURE 2.9 In the world of *Clockers*, escape is to be found even farther away from the city. Universal Pictures, 1995.

cutout villains, and they are understood by the other black men and women in the community to be as much a danger, or more, as the police are ("you are selling your own people death" one young mother says). And these men teach the boys around them the same ruthless, bloody ways, something Lee will return to, from the perspective of the women in their lives, in *Chi-Raq* (2015), a modern retelling of *Lysistrata* that puts much of the blame for gang warfare on the poverty, unemployment, and hopelessness endemic to the modern Chicago ghetto. *Clockers* (like *Chi-Raq*) is clumsily didactic on more than a few occasions (viz: "selling your own people death"), but it seems an honest effort to argue that it's not too hard to understand why boys living in this world might emulate those who have money and respect, and to insist that we can understand and empathize with them without waving away what they do. And yet, it winds up with an awkward sense of morality, in which at least two cold-blooded murderers go free, apparently because a cop likes them and sympathizes with them.

Colors (1988) tells this kind of story from the perspective of the police. It's another tale of Los Angeles gangs, and a buddy pic—though one with a shade more dimension to the characters than is often the case, perhaps because the two main cops are played by Sean Penn and Robert Duvall—that offers a long car chase early on, making the point that this is a crime drama, not a ghetto story. It's among the few films to focus mostly on Latino rather than black gangs and gang members. But there's no interest in the neighborhood, except for a brief community meeting early on, where some residents beg the police to do something about the violence, and no interest in causes, nor any real interest in characters. But it's useful as a reminder of why Americans might think that the use of illegal drugs was higher among people of color, even if the evidence tells us that drug use doesn't appreciably vary by race (Department of Health and Human Services, 2012; Burston, Jones, and Saunders, 1995).

There are exceptions to the kinds of films we've discussed, ones that offer a different view of contemporary communities of concentrated poverty and the people in them. Lee's *Crooklyn* (1994) may be the most notable in terms of its portrayal of poorer African Americans as three-dimensional people. It's set in the 1970s, and mostly about smaller-scale matters than *Do the Right Thing*: How a working-class family, with five kids, manages to get through the day, and the ordinary (and occasionally tragic) things that happen as the kids grow up. They struggle some times more than others, having the electricity turned off and taking food stamps from a neighbor, but these are small events and anomalies—the hard times most Americans will face now and again (although they live in a Brooklyn brownstone that would be worth millions today). In *Red Hook Summer* (2012), Lee goes back to public housing, but with interests and tone more aligned again with *Crooklyn* than *Clockers* (containing an odd call back to *Do the Right Thing* as we see Mookie, now a middle-aged man, still delivering pizzas for Sal's Famous). It's not a story about drugs and crime, but about Flik, who comes from Atlanta to spend the summer in Red Hook, Brooklyn, with his preacher grandfather, and about how they negotiate each other and the neighborhood. Despite the fact that late in the film the preacher is revealed to have been sexually abusing boys, we get here a picture of the projects that doesn't pathologize them or make them seem foreign and exotic—in fact, they are filmed mostly in the daytime, in summer, and they seem like any other New York working-class community. As Roger Ebert wrote, "This looks like a good enough neighborhood—like the kind of urban stage the proletarian dramas of the 1930s like to start with" (Ebert, 2008, p. 168). As Lee himself wrote (in Ebert, 1997): "In this script I want to show the black working class. Contrary to popular belief, we work. No welfare rolls here, pal, just hardworking people trying to make a decent living" (pp. 541–542). It's a reminder that the day-to-day struggles of the working poor are largely missing from American film, although there is at least one fine documentary that offers this kind of insight, called *Waging a Living* (2005).

While it may end, famously, in an eruption of violence, *Do the Right Thing* (1989) is also offering us a portrait of real people, not caricatures. It shows how a community that first appears much like the one in *Crooklyn* can end up looking like Watts in the midst of a riot or drug war. The opening credits flash while Public Enemy's "Fight the Power" throbs on the soundtrack, and as the film unspools it provokes questions about who should be fought and where the power lies, and what the most effective means of fighting are. What *is* the right thing? Does anyone here do it? (It is a far less facile exploration than that makes it sound.) Part of what has made this movie such a broad and continuing subject for discussion and debate, beyond its sheer entertainment value, is that is doesn't offer a simple answer to the question, and allows viewers to walk away with their own conclusions. The battles here, on one sweltering summer Saturday, are between poor black residents of Bed-Sty (Bedford-Stuyvesant) and the Italian pizza shop owners and Korean grocery owners; between the black residents themselves (fighting over loud music, drinking, and the perennial debate over who was more important, Malcolm X or Martin Luther King); between blacks and Puerto Ricans; between old and young; among the Italian pizza shop owners; between blacks and a white gentrifier who owns a brownstone on the street; between everyone and the police. It's not a realist account—maybe a hyperrealist one?—but it works harder than most to show, as 1931's *Street Scene* did, the way that marginalized populations in poor neighborhoods find themselves at each other's throats, lashing out when they can at local sources of economic power (the pizzeria, the grocery), rather than directing their energies and analysis outward at the forces that keep them in an insular ghetto with so few avenues of escape. Put differently, they attack Sal's Pizza because the consequences of attacking the police are too great. That it doesn't know whether to side with Martin or Malcolm is shrewd in its own way, given that most readings of the advances of the 1960s suggest that both approaches—the peaceful resistance and its more threatening cousin—came together to create space and pressure for social change, and there was arguably less distance between them ultimately than conventional wisdom suggests. The film is more clearly about race than class, or, perhaps the ways in which class solidarity is frustrated and hindered by racial animosity—animosity that has historically been actively cultivated in order to frustrate solidarity.

One of the most recent films about gangs in poor places is set furthest in the past, Martin Scorsese's *Gangs of New York* (2002). When young Amsterdam (Leonardo DiCaprio) returns after sixteen years in a reformatory-*cum*-orphanage on Blackwell's Island, he sighs: "Every year the reformers came; every year the Points got worse, as if it liked being dirty." It's an unusual kind of claim, as if New York's Five Points slum of the mid–nineteenth century was itself a force, one that fought against efforts at improvement. It's pathological, he seems to say, so beset by a culture of poverty that it cannot be saved. Despite the stereotypes of the Five Points that is the setting for *Gangs*, it was, in truth, a mostly working-class neighborhood, albeit a desperately poor one, to be sure. There was probably little more fatal violence there than in the rest of Manhattan at the time, and the violence, even when it was gang-related, was as much intra-ethnic (Irish gangs fighting Irish gangs) as the Catholic–Protestant divide that tends to be the focus in the film (although the Nativist–Immigrant divide was real, to be sure) (see Anbinder, 2001). It doesn't do much more insult to the truth than do movies about more recent periods, ultimately. Everything's a shade more violent and squalid than it probably was, a bit more one-dimensional, with the ordinary, normal business of the majority—struggling to find work, trying to raise a family, taking pleasure and comfort where and when they could—wiped from the screen, perhaps merely because such "ordinariness" is not dramatic. Almost everyone here is a thug, including the police and members of the fire brigade gangs, and everything is dysfunctional, dark, and dirty. It's all irredeemable, and thus looks a lot like Hollywood ghettos set in other historical periods, including the fact that, widespread praise for Daniel Day Lewis and other performances notwithstanding, the characters are cartoonish, with motivations that can be consistently hard to discern. It is, at its heart, a gangster story, one about the slow pursuit of revenge.

FIGURES 2.10 AND 2.11 Another view of Manhattan from Brooklyn, after the Draft Riots. *Gangs of New York*, Miramax, 2002.

Shirley Clarke's neo-realist *The Cool World* (1964), with a young Frederick Wiseman as producer, laid the groundwork for a lot of the modern films about young men in poor neighborhoods beset with violence and despair. It is at pains to humanize them, to understand the opportunities and constraints of the world in which they live, and it will plant its DNA in *Boyz N the Hood* and *Clockers* (and *Claudine*, for that matter, which we'll discuss in Chapter 5) more than *New Jack City*, drawing some of its own from *A Raisin in the Sun* (1961), which we should talk about briefly. I'm not certain *Raisin* is a movie about poverty, although I'm in the minority, judging by available reviews and commentary. It shows us a black family on the South Side of Chicago, with too many people in too small an apartment, sharing a bathroom with the neighbors, and complaining about how little light they get, but they are solidly working class. The recently retired matriarch, newly widowed, worked all her life as a cook in white homes, as does her daughter-in-law. Her son is a chauffeur, and her daughter is a college student with her sights set on medical school. There's a young grandson, who sleeps on the living room couch for lack of a bed, and a new baby on the way, which may or may not be aborted because of the strain it would put on the already stressed household. They are surely insecure, teetering on the edge of poverty, one crisis away from dire straits, as are so many, but *Raisin* gives us an African American family that is better off than the white Dolans in *A Tree Grows in Brooklyn* (see Chapter 7). We need to be wary of the trap that so many films get caught in: to use black as a proxy for poor. The political right has worked for decades to associate welfare and crime with African American populations as part of their southern strategy, which counts on racist appeals to get working-class whites to vote Republican. So, especially—although not exclusively—for white filmmakers, black can become cinematic shorthand for poor (or crime-laden, or dysfunctional, or dangerous).

Returning to *Cool World*: Duke (Rony Clanton) is a young man who doesn't see many options for himself, but is sure he can make himself known, respected, wealthy, and feared by taking over as leader of a gang. Acquiring a gun becomes his first task. Meanwhile, we see prostitutes and drug dealers, junkies, thieves, and gangsters, but we also see parents doing their best to get by with three children crammed into dirty, run-down, rat- and roach-infested one-room flats, people going to work while complaining bitterly about their low wages, others going off dutifully to church, grandparents knitting and fretting over their grandkids, old men playing checkers on the sidewalk, college students back for the summer, and all the dreary daily business of any neighborhood. That is, it is a poor place, one with crime, drugs, and dangers, but that's not *all* there is; it's not yet the hopeless urban wasteland American film will make of it. And it's that context, that effort to show a complicated world filled with complicated people, that distinguishes *The Cool World*, setting it apart as more authentic and, as a consequence, more attentive to the dignity of its subjects, perhaps all the more notable given that Clarke was not African American but of Eastern European background. For what it's worth, Dwight McDonald (1969, pp. 323–327) would say that I have gotten it exactly wrong, and that it offers such a stereotypical portrait of Harlem and its residents that Southern racists should welcome showings of it.

We get another three-dimensional portrait in *The Brother from Another Planet* (1984), when an alien (Joe Morton) lands near Ellis Island and finds his way to West Harlem. The people he meets are ordinary and decent working folks, with the occasional junkies, criminals, and creeps here and there. Director John Sayles takes what many would think of as a "poor" or "black" neighborhood and instead just shows us a neighborhood, with some faint echoes of 1948's short documentary *In the Street*, which offered us about sixteen minutes of hidden-camera footage of East Harlem residents going about their day. Sayles, too, is just observing, showing us a Harlem that is neither romantic nor exotic, a stance all the more unusual coming from a white director.

It's not merely the location, but there is something about the tone of *Brother* that echoes *The Pawnbroker* (1964), released in the same year as *The Cool World*. Sol Nazerman (Rod Steiger) is a Holocaust survivor running a pawnshop in Harlem, and, although he's in denial about this, laundering money for a local gangster. Marilyn (Geraldine Fitzgerald) is a social worker of sorts seeking supporters for her youth program who tries to befriend him. The customers are in various states of desperation and despair, but the film doesn't tend to judge them too much and is, instead, inclined toward a kind of clear-eyed pity, or empathy, perhaps. It's not their story though, nor that of his young apprentice, Jesús: Flashbacks to his time in a German concentration camp serve as reminders that this is Sol's story, a story of "the walking dead," as he's called—empty, alone, and ultimately in even worse shape than the desperate people who show up in his shop selling the last of what they own for a dollar or two.

There are two ways in which the differences between films like *The Cool World* and their most recent counterparts set in essentially the same neighborhoods reflect different realities, not merely different sensibilities. First, the fight between rival gangs that ends *The Cool World* is a fistfight, not a gunfight. Thinking, by contrast, of *Boyz N the Hood* and then the battle scenes in *Gangs of New York*, it's hard not to wonder what Five Points would have been like if semi-automatic weapons and cocaine had been available. The other difference is that *The Cool World* works hard to show us the full range of opportunities available beyond joining a gang: that's the richness of the movie, the diversity of life and lifestyle presented. In more recent films, there's a hopelessness that often pervades, and there's a reality to that—by the mid-1960s, poverty was in decline, even for African Americans, falling a full 25 percentage points from 1959 to 1973 according to Census estimates. But three decades later, fewer young black men have access to a path from deeply poor neighborhoods to a stable working-class or middle-class life, in large part because in the 1960s there were better jobs available to those with less formal education, and there wasn't yet a mammoth machinery, operating under the guise of safety and crime control, incarcerating massive numbers of young men of color. It is not unreasonable to suggest (even if we could argue this point) that there was more reason to be hopeful about the prospects for a young, African American man in 1964 that there is today.

We see some of that transition period in *Killer of Sheep* (1977), set in a pre–*Boyz N the Hood* post-riots Watts. It's among the earliest neo-realist, semi-improvised glimpses into American poverty after *The Cool World*, and it paves the way for films like *Gummo, George Washington* (see Chapter 8), and Burnett's own *My Brother's Wedding*. Stan (Henry G. Sanders) works in a slaughterhouse and gets by, but little more. All his schemes turn to nothing,

FIGURE 2.12 "You can't give away nothin' to the Salvation Army if you're poor!" *Killer of Sheep*, Milestone Films, 1978.

and the look on his face as they fail is heartbreaking. Try as he might, he's not getting anywhere, even if he is doing better than his relatives and neighbors. His pride and his hopefulness are what make his failures tragic. "I ain't poor!" he insists, defensively, when vaguely accused of thinking himself middle-class.

> I give away things to the Salvation Army. You can't give away nothin' to the Salvation Army if you're poor. Now, we may not have a damn thing sometimes. . . . You wanna see somebody that's poor, you go around and look at Walter. Now he be sittin' over an oven, with nothin' but a coat on, and, and, sittin' around rubbin' their knees all day, eatin' nothin' but wild greens picked out of a vacant lot. Now that ain't me, and damn sure won't be.

But it might as well be him. Much of the rest of the film lingers on children playing and fighting and killing time, as kids do, only here it's among the rubble—deserted train tracks and burnt-out buildings and others that look as if they might topple over at any moment. It allows us to observe at length, to get a feel for the space, and for the grimness of the locale. It's shocking to think of how much worse, in its own way, the neighborhood will be by the time we get to *Boyz N the Hood*, for as grim as it is, there are not yet armed gangs terrorizing the neighborhood, killing people on a whim. But one can also see how generations of living in the world of *Killer of Sheep*, where hope for something better seems futile—even a trip to the racetrack here fails because of a flat tire—might lead, perhaps not inexorably but with a surefooted logic, to a world that looks like *Boyz N the Hood*.

Is it any better for young women of color? *Just Another Girl on the IRT* (1992) takes us to Brooklyn again, in the projects a bit further out into the borough, and this story is told through the eyes (and the voice) of Chantel, a funny, self-assured high school student who has ambitions (including college and maybe medical school), parents who fight and work hard (and part of what they fight about is that hard work doesn't seem to get them anywhere), a part-time job, and caregiving responsibilities for her younger brothers. That it's a female voice is unusual, but especially so in these 1990s life-in-the-black-ghetto films. She gets pregnant, and all of her ambitions are at risk. In denial, she spends the money her boyfriend gave her for an abortion on clothes and manicures, and hides her pregnancy with a girdle and loose clothes. She gives birth, and instructs her boyfriend to put the baby out with the trash. He doesn't, ultimately, and she keeps it, staying at home and going to community college. It seems unlikely she'll make it to medical school, or at least much less likely. And even if she didn't live in the projects, her life would be, at best, complicated.

FIGURE 2.13 *Just Another Girl on the IRT*, Miramax, 1992.

It's another film that observes more than judges, and it cares deeply about Chantel. It's a messy and complicated story, but one that only occasionally feels contrived. Lives are often messy, and some are messier than others, especially if there are fewer resources at hand to mitigate that messiness. This is a film made predominantly with non-professional actors, with a fair bit of improvised dialogue, and that's all to the good, bringing viewers into worlds and introducing them to people they don't regularly encounter in the movies.

On the Outs (2004) follows the lives of three young women in low-income Jersey City, which makes it, too, unusual: not only that it's women at the center of the narrative(s), but that it's New Jersey, not New York City or Los Angeles. Marisol steals to buy crack, leaving her daughter go hungry; while she's in jail, her aunt falls sick, sending her daughter off to foster care. Oz, just released from jail, sells the drug (but doesn't use) while her mother waits for a bed in a residential drug treatment program. She lives with not only her mother and grandmother, but a developmentally disabled brother, another nod to a reality most filmmakers seem unaware of: the higher incidence of disability (developmental, physical, mental) in poor communities and the greater likelihood of forming intergenerational households to pool scarce resources (Taylor, Kochnar, Kohn, et al., 2011). Oz's brother later dies from an asthma attack. Suzette, the youngest, is infatuated with an older man; she gets pregnant, has an abortion, and gets sent to jail when caught holding the man's gun, which he used to kill a small boy who was trying to rob him (who, we should note, was armed himself). They all lose what they care about most, and often it's because of the men in their lives. The settings are real enough, and the characters are well drawn: they are recognizable as people, not a screenwriter's ideas of people. The viewer is not made a voyeur, the violence is not fetishized, and the poverty is not romanticized. In a "making of" documentary, co-director Lori Silverbush described it as a story about "the enormous tragedy of wasted human potential." And you can see what she means: these are bright, resourceful, resilient young women, women who, born into different circumstances, born across the river in one of New York's better neighborhoods, could have been formidable, accomplished people instead of mere survivors, which is about the best that anyone does here. At the end, Marisol is trading oral sex for cocaine, and Suzette violates parole and is on her way back to jail, hard and hardened. Only Oz seems to be poised on the edge of something better, throwing her stash into the river in what we presume is a commitment to stop dealing and to carve out a better life for herself. But, because it's not Hollywood, it's very unclear indeed whether she will succeed.

3 THE URBAN HELLSCAPE

Midnight Cowboy, Fort Apache the Bronx, Wolfen, Brick City

With films like *The Cool World* or *Killer of Sheep*, the Sixties could give us complicated portraits of poor urban communities that were stable and healthy at their core, even if there were signs of violence, dysfunction, and decay. But by the early 1970s, a national narrative of irredeemable urban decline had taken root, and that narrative was reflected on film: Cities were teetering on the edge of habitability, many thought, and the grim indicators were riots, poverty, exploding welfare rolls, the deinstitutionalization of the mentally ill, municipal bankruptcy, and white flight. Writing in 1974, Vincent Canby observed that "New York City has become a metaphor for what looks like the last days of American civilization." Pauline Kael, in a review of *The French Connection* (1971), thought that Mayor John Lindsay's successful efforts to increase film production in New York at this time had an unintended consequence and "usher[ed] in a new movie age of nightmare realism," in which New York became "Horror City" and the "urban-crisis city" of an "Urban Gothic period" (Kael, 1994, p. 389). This overwhelming sense of decay and disorder was the backdrop to many New York films like *Taxi Driver* (1976) and *Midnight Cowboy* (1969), and, a bit later, *Escape from New York* (1981), but it reached a kind of apotheosis in horror films in which the homeless man, largely absent since the Depression era, returns again to the screen. We'll turn to those films a bit later.

It wasn't only filmmakers who sought to draw out the connections between physical disorder and other social ills, however. First articulated in an article in *The Atlantic* (Wilson and Kelling, 1982), the "broken windows" conjecture suggested that signs of dysfunction and disarray—graffiti, trash in the streets, unlit streetlamps, abandoned buildings with broken and boarded-up windows, and so on—would communicate a message that such decline would be tolerated, and thus encourage people to commit crime. Order fosters order, disorder fosters disorder. The remedy was to focus police attention on small infractions, like people who were jumping subway turnstiles to avoid paying the fare, drinking alcohol in public, committing acts of petty theft, or smoking marijuana, to make it clear that all infractions would be punished, thereby discouraging more serious crime. Despite the fact that evidence for such claims has never been good (Shelden, 2004; Harcourt and Ludwig, 2006; Sampson and Raudenbush, 2001), and that it tends to interpret signs of poverty as signs of danger, this would quickly become conventional wisdom among politicians and police chiefs throughout the United States, aided by widespread media coverage, reaching its illogical conclusion in the saturation policing of poor neighborhood in later decades.

I should point out that some parts of New York *were* a bit of a nightmare, and not for nothing did New York City's population decline by more than ten percent between 1970 and 1980, according to Census Bureau data. Luc Sante (2003), author of *Low Life*, a history of the "underbelly" of nineteenth-century New York, offers this remembrance of the later Lower East and Upper West Sides:

> In the blocks east of Avenue A the situation was dramatically worse. In 1978 I got used to seeing large fires in that direction every night, usually set by arsonists hired by landlords of empty buildings who found it an easy choice to make, between paying property taxes and collecting insurance. By 1980 Avenue C was a lunar landscape of vacant blocks and hollow tenement shells.... I spent the summer of 1975 in a top-floor apartment on 107th Street, where at night the windows were lit by the glow of fires along Amsterdam Avenue. A sanitation strike was in progress, and mounds of refuse, reeking in the heat, decorated the curbs of every neighborhood, not excepting those whose houses were manned by doormen. Here, though, instead of being double-bagged in plastic, they were simply set on fire every night. The spectacle achieved the transition from apocalyptic to dully normal in a matter of days.

The intuitive power of Broken Windows, although empirically unsupported, is something even Santé (2003) seems to have recognized: "Almost everybody had a story about walking down the street smoking a joint and suddenly realizing they had just passed a uniformed patrolman, who could not possibly have failed to detect the odor but resolutely looked the other way. Casual illegality was unremarkable and quotidian." The forces of law and order themselves had abandoned civilized norms and surrendered to chaos. It seems fair to suggest that, in film, too, physically poor conditions were trying to tell us something about poverty and its relationship to crime.

Midnight Cowboy (1969) offers us one of these iconic cinematic visions of New York. Joe Buck (Jon Voight) is a troubled man who moves from Texas to earn a living as a hustler, and quickly finds himself without money or a place to stay. He's befriended by Enrico "Ratso" Rizzo (Dustin Hoffman), and shares his grim, unheated room in a condemned, abandoned building. Ratso's place "turns out to be the very embodiment of disconnection," as Sanders (2001, p. 393) put it: "not just poor but drained of all warmth and all life, a place that is the cold blue of death itself. It is one of the saddest, most miserable dwellings ever portrayed in the movie city, the symbol of those who live within the city's borders yet can find no way of attaching themselves to its currents." It's a good description.

They hustle and steal, and eventually Joe kills a man to acquire enough money to get him and Ratso on a bus to Florida. But it's perhaps most notable for its portrayal of Times Square (the vision that will appear even more fully formed in *Taxi Driver*). Again, this image was not crafted out of thin air but rooted very much in real developments: by the 1970s, billboards and theaters had gone dark, all-night newsstands became pornographic bookstores, and the theaters that remained opened went X-rated. Single Room Occupancy (SRO) hotels filled up with desperate people pushed from their homes by the collapsing local and national economy, while the sex trade burgeoned, and trafficking in illegal drugs moved in. *Respectable* people wouldn't go near "The Deuce" (42nd Street) or certainly not unaccompanied, given that rates

FIGURE 3.1 Ratso's place. *Midnight Cowboy*, MGM, 1969.

of crime, and especially violent crime, really were much higher there (see Berman, 2009, pp. 164–172). "Someday," Travis Bickle will say in *Taxi Driver* as he travels through Times Square, "a real rain will come and wash all the scum off the streets." That rain has come, and instead of junkies and dealers, pimps and prostitutes, SROs and pickpockets, Times Square is now a dazzling tourist attraction, with themed and branded stores, multi-story chain restaurants, and life-size costumed cartoon characters waddling through the street, available for you to be photographed with. Joe and Ratso wouldn't be able to live there now; they'd probably be homeless, or live in the South Bronx, to this day home to the United States' poorest congressional district.

Far north and east of midtown Manhattan, The Bronx may have been even more iconic as an image of the demise of Western civilization. Its decay was real, set in motion by factors that affected other cities—white flight, deindustrialization, and so on—but exacerbated by the construction of the Cross Bronx Expressway, a Robert Moses project, which razed entire neighborhoods, poor but often healthy and vibrant ones, driving out residents and businesses and wreaking havoc on property values and human lives (Caro, 1975). By the 1970s, the Bronx was literally burning, thanks to landlords trying to salvage value from their property via fire insurance claims, and residents who set a match to their own buildings in hopes of becoming eligible for better housing. The drug trade moved in, and gangs took over entire neighborhoods. The broader economic crisis facing the entire city meant that there were fewer police and firefighters just at a time when more were needed, and it became home to the nation's highest rates of murder, rape, assault, and arson (Gonzales, 2006, Chap. 7).

Fort Apache, the Bronx (1981), from the director of *Raisin in the Sun*, for what that's worth, begins with a disclaimer: "Because the story involves police work it does not involve the law abiding members of the community nor does it dramatize the efforts of the individuals and groups who are struggling to turn the Bronx around." This was a concession to the Bronx community organizations who complained about the film's unrelentingly dismal portrayal of their home (*New York Times*, 1981). The police here—and the filmmakers, too, it seems to me—are racist and homophobic, and for them the South Bronx is a lawless, bombed-out ghetto so beyond hope of redemption that the police largely avoid enforcing the law or trying to keep order until a new commander decides to gain control and, in the process, sets off what appear to be borough-wide riots. There's an *Escape from New York* meets *Mad Max* tenor to the film, and residents were right to complain: it ignores all those who were working hard, struggling to raise their families and survive but were trapped, unable to escape, and unable to hold back the mammoth forces laying siege to their city.

FIGURE 3.2 The rubbled landscape of the Bronx, *Fort Apache, The Bronx,* 20th Century Fox, 1981.

More than this, *Fort Apache* is clumsy, with little insight and little discernible point of view, except perhaps to say that the Bronx was terrible and people in it, cops included, were also terrible, without any evident opinion as to how or why that came to be and what might be done about it. It's the apotheosis, perhaps, of the "City Is Dangerous and Breeds Crime" strain we've witnessed since the silent era, but doesn't seem to have a point to make, while most of those earlier films did. It's not even, as is often the case, about those who make the best of a bad environment and rise above it against all odds.

There's a similar problem with *Wolfen* (1981). The evil lurking in this movie—not, as the film first leads us to believe, shape-shifting Native

FIGURE 3.3 The Bronx in *Wolfen,* Orion Pictures, 1981.

Americans but ordinary wolves after all—emerges from the worst parts of this same South Bronx, a desolate landscape that looks like Dresden after the bombings.

The first victims are a wealthy, prominent businessman, his wife, and their chauffeur. This is a theme of the 1980s, as we'll see when we look at films about homelessness in particular: There's evil rampaging through our hopeless, dying cities, rising up and attacking the rich and powerful, although in *Wolfen* everyone is at risk, and the next victim is an apparently homeless addict. Ancient wolves, it seems, have been hiding out in the "the new wilderness, your cities . . . the slum areas, the great graveyards of your fucking species . . . [and] your abandoned people became their new meat animal," as one of the wise Native Americans explains. The homeless become dog food, and The Bronx is their feeding ground.

There's another kind of urban dystopia evident in *Brick City* (2009), a five-part documentary showing us a year or so in the life of post-industrial Newark, New Jersey, another city with high poverty and unemployment that saw riots in the 1960s and which has been losing population since the 1940s. The film splits its focus between Mayor Corey Booker (whose first, losing election campaign was chronicled in *Street Fight* and who later became a United States senator), the Director of Police, and Jayda, a former gang member trying to clear up her criminal past while building a small not-for-profit organization to help other young women. There's much to admire in this effort, and it would be churlish not to be grateful at least for the fact of it, so unusual is it to see into a very poor American city beyond the salacious blare of nightly news headlines. By the final episode, there is a powerful cumulative effect, although the result is not a sense of hope but, rather, a grim realization of the scope and depth of the problems to be confronted and the obstacles faced by all those who would seek even modest change—not just for the mayor and the police department, but for the individuals and families and small groups and neighborhoods trying to improve the lives, and the chances of survival, for their own.

In this way and in others, *Brick City* brings to mind *The Wire*, and it is that inevitable comparison that makes this documentary account so much less three-dimensional, so much less rich, so much less affecting than that fictional one. One problem is that the narrowness of the frame in *Brick City* cannot give us more than a superficial sense of the city and its problems. This is most evident when a challenge to the Police Director from the Chief of Police for control over the department emerges more or less from nowhere. Because we've spent no time with the Chief, nor with any members of the department other than the Director (or with outside analysts, journalists, state politicians, and so on), we are left with little choice but to side reflexively with the Director (and the Mayor), since it is their story that we have been witnessing—and the Chief does looks a bit shifty. We don't get even a short interview with the Chief here, and that hints at the largest problem with the film: because it's so narrowly focused on Booker, and he is portrayed so consistently as heroic, even if he were a hero it's hard to believe it because it feels like such a relentlessly one-sided view. It's not a campaign advertisement, but it could serve as one, and that failure to offer perspective makes me reluctant to trust the entire enterprise.

There's a more peculiar and unsettling effect of this narrow frame: early in the first episode, when a child is killed by a stray bullet, in the context of this narrative the immediate import is to wonder what this will do to the Mayor's efforts to show lower crime rates. The small-scale family tragedy is, at best, secondary, and it feels jarring, shameful, to realize this. A surer hand would have made these tensions explicit and given them dimension (as *The Wire* often did with such occasions). And as the final episode unfolds and a gang war breaks out, the emotional arc is focused on what will be the effect upon the Mayor's determination to reduce the homicide rate, with no attention given to other matters, and no realization of how crass and callous and ugly this is. As with so many cinematic efforts to tackle "serious" subjects, what ought to be the subject here—Newark and its residents—is instead an excuse to tell a more traditional story of He Who Would Come and Save Them. Finally, to make Barack Obama's election night the emotional climax of the picture, as they do, is odd, given that we've been immersed in a local story. It's not a bad movie, and it's worth seeing, but it's a film of little insight beyond what it offers as a historical record. This matters, for it remains a key part of how poverty in cities appears on film—as dangerous, out-of-control realms, always a step or two away from needing to be walled of, as they finally were in *Escape from New York* or in the Parisian ghetto of *Banlieue 13*.

4 SOCIAL WORKERS AND CHARITY REFORMERS

The Reformers, Intolerance, Regeneration, It, Tomorrow's Children, Street Scene, Body and Soul, Ann Vickers, Chains of Gold, Entertaining Angels, Major Barbara, Don't Call Me a Saint, The Second Chance, Sister Act, Robin Hood

Social workers have historically gotten a bad rap, and this has some-times been deserved. In part this is because many have approached relief from a personal, moral, judgmental perspective, and whether it's the Friendly Visitors of an earlier era or the modern caseworker, first-hand knowledge of the lived experience of poor families has not always been in evidence.

It may be useful to think of the history of social work as split between two philosophies. The one that tends to dominate our thinking today is most readily associated with Settlement House leader Jane Addams, whose understanding of the roots of need and the most effective method of addressing it was complex, thanks to her having embedded herself in a poor immigrant neighborhood, seeing firsthand the multitude of factors that contributed to poverty there. Poverty was an industrial and political problem for Addams more than it was a personal one (although we should not overstate this—there was the moralist in Addams, too). The other stream of social work thinking is exemplified by Josephine Shaw Lowell, one of the founders of the Charity Organization Society (COS) move-ment, a nationwide effort to rationalize and restrict the distribution of social welfare assistance, which had a role to play, not only in the development of the profession and the elaboration of the case work method, but in the development of the academic disciplines of sociology and political science. For Lowell, poverty was a much simpler thing than it was for Addams, for throughout most of her life (before a late conversion of sorts), Lowell saw individual and family moral failure at the root of need, and identified relief as, except in unusual circumstances, likely to do more harm than good (Pimpare, 2004).

Social work tends to look toward Addams (or a sanitized version of Baltimore COS leader Mary Richmond) for its forebears, but Lowell was as important then (and ultimately perhaps more influential), and her strain is still in evidence—every time a case worker sniffs disapprovingly at how a client dresses, at their housekeeping skills, or their child-rearing techniques, every time she thinks, however fleetingly, that some woman's poverty is her own fault, she is calling forth the ghost of Lowell. Every time she too readily breaks up a family for its own good, she honors her. This is the image of social work that has dominated in American media, as those few scholars or critics who have sought out representations of them have discovered, much to their general disappointment.

Catherine Hiersteiner (1998), examining a handful of pre–World War II movies (including *Regeneration* and *Street Scene*, which we'll discuss shortly), complains about depictions of the social worker as a "condescending intruder," who is, she claims, "constructed from class and gender bias for dramatic effect," appearing as "big-bosomed, well-meaning nitwits" or "prudish recluses" (p. 320–322). One schematic review of late–twentieth century portrayals finds them represented on television as "uneducated and bumbling, if not outright laughable" (Gibelman, 2004, p. 332). Valentine and Freeman (2002) examine twenty-seven movies from 1938 to 1999 that portray social workers engaged in work with children, about forty percent of which show need that stems from poverty, and in almost every instance, the social worker is an obstacle to be overcome so that the "right" outcome can prevail. They are "agents of social control," Valentine and Freeman write, and more likely to victimize than protect children and their families. Freeman and Valentine's (2004) broader analysis of forty-four films from the same period (which included these twenty-seven) similarly found social workers "variously portrayed as dedicated, petty, idealistic, incompetent, rigid, bossy, judgmental, caring, competent, obsessed, sensitive, bureaucratic, kindhearted, hardhearted, and patient" (p. 154). In contrast, however, to their tentative willingness in their previous article to consider the possibility that there might be something to be learned from this, the authors here are surprised and even a bit indignant to discover that social workers were so rarely depicted as engaging in activities to enact structural or systemic reform, or fighting larger forces of social injustice—in film, they are *caseworkers*, not activists. All of these critiques assume that such unflattering representations are absurd without demonstrating that they are inaccurate, and often blithely assert the need for better media outreach, education, and public relations on behalf of the profession without bothering to explain what that might look like and how it might be done (see also Zugazaga, Surette, Mendez, and Otto, 2006).

And yet, although the Code of Ethics of the National Association of Social Workers (NASW) does indeed require that social workers engage in political advocacy and activities to further social justice (NASW, 2008), in the real world, just as on film, that obligation is typically honored in its breach. Social workers are, it is true, more likely to vote, write letters to their elected officials, contribute to campaigns, and talk about politics with their friends and neighbors than are the general public (which is a very good thing indeed), but those tend to be the limits of their activism, with very few participating in community-based organizations fighting for political and social change (Ezell, 1993; Mary, 2001; Hamilton and Fauri, 2001; Weiss, Gal, Cnaan, and Majlaglic, 2002). That is to say, most social workers do not behave as these authors want movies to depict them as behaving. This is not necessarily surprising since, like other professionals, social workers may have little time to spare for such work, and they may well believe that they don't need to do more since they "already gave at the office." Whatever its self-image, social work is a fairly conservative occupation inhabited by well-meaning but cautious, centrist liberals. The discipline has historically driven the genuine radicals from its ranks, even if it will come to celebrate them and reclaim them much later when it is safe to do so (Reisch and Andrews, 2002; Wenocur and Reisch, 2001). Furthermore, many clients complain that caseworkers are disrespectful, judgmental, ignorant of the reality of their lives, more concerned with bureaucratic procedure than administering aid, and more committed to diagnosing them and "fixing" what they think to be wrong with them than helping them to negotiate a world that has them pinioned, trapped among nothing but bad options (Soss, 1999; Sandfort, Kalil, and Gottschalk, 1999; Hays, 2004; Watkins-Hayes, 2009; Morgen, Acker, and Weigt, 2010, Chap. 5). Frances Fox Piven and Richard Cloward (1971, p. 176) noted long ago that the "lower the number of caseworkers with a professional orientation, the larger the number of poor using AFDC [Aid to Families with Dependent Children]." Social workers themselves may help keep relief rolls low. Another study from the early 1960s suggests that the less likely respondents were to have contact with either the county welfare agency or the Society of St. Vincent DePaul, the more favorable their impression of relief workers and their agencies, and blacks consistently reported worse experiences than whites (Shannon, 1963).

So, is it possible that the image of the social worker on film that these authors complain about is, in fact, a fair reflection? Although a regular feature of the lives of people living in poverty, social workers do not appear often in the movies. However, while uncommon, they have been around from near the start, and once again D. W. Griffith got there first. In *The Reformers* (1913), the League of Civic Purity (yes, there were such organizations) greets the man they've asked to stand as their "good government" candidate for mayor. As he scribbles down plans to "right the world," a man asking for work, food, or money, with his hat, quite literally, in hand, interrupts him. The supplicant is summarily dismissed, placing the film within an old tradition: at least since Mrs. Jellyby and Pardiggle in Charles Dickens's *Bleak House*, philanthropists and reformers are understood to be so busy gazing afar (disapprovingly, or with pity) that they cannot see what is directly before their blue, up-turned noses. While campaigning, the candidate stops a woman (a prostitute, perhaps?) from flirting with a man on the street, and when another comes to him to shake his hand in support, he confiscates his pipe. He goes into a saloon and lifts the beer mugs right from patrons' hands, shuts down a dance and a vaudeville show, and generally acts like an insufferable prig, all with a policeman in tow to enforce his stern judgments, although under what authority is unclear. He is the classic Puritan, haunted by the fear that someone somewhere may be happy, as H. L. Mencken put it (1949, p. 624), and a loathsome character.

Griffith will pick up the themes of *The Reformers* in the "modern" portions of *Intolerance* (1916), a four-story epic Kael (1994, p. 172) described as "the greatest extravaganza and the greatest folly in movie history." As an early title card tells it, "each story shows how hatred and intolerance, through all the ages, have battled against love and charity." Here, "in a western city we find certain ambitious ladies banded together for the 'uplift' of humanity." The scare quotes around "uplift" make clear—as it was in *The Reformers*—Griffith's disdain for these "vestal virgins," as he'll later describe them. That he also characterizes them as *ambitious* is of interest: the Progressive-era private charity movements were one of the few places where women could make a career for themselves, and for one with aspiration, it was a sensible choice. But Griffith's reformers are engaged in no more urgent work than moral policing, and there's no hint of the women who were in the slums agitating for better housing, clean milk and water, education and training, and more (although neither are they here the irredeemably corrupt social worker of *Trash*, whom we'll turn to later).

We meet Mary Jenkins, the "unmarried sister of the autocratic industrial overlord." Aging and vain, Jenkins is "intolerant of youth and laughter." A bitter old maid, she's a ripe target for these other plain, sanctimonious spinsters dedicated to enforcing their own stringent moral codes, women who later will be referred to as "modern Pharisees." (One of the three other stories told in the film is, in fact, of the original Pharisees—prideful, arrogant, and inevitably hypocritical men, "meddlers, then and now," busily rooting out "too much pleasure-seeking.") As in *The Reformers*, the women are plain and joy-less, their behavior explained in a title card: "When women cease to attract men they often turn to Reform as a second choice."

This is some of what we saw in Chapter 1 from the Children's Aid Society social workers in *Boy of the Streets*, or when Rocky in *Crime School* refers to Laury as "a snappy-looking dish .... for a sociable worker." And here, too, the men among the Uplifters—less common in film just as they are in the profession—are effeminate and mincing. Although this seems meant to be more than mere observation but an insult as well, it did reflect concerns of the time. As Illinois charity reformer Frederick Wines complained in 1889: "there seems to be a general impression that anyone interested in charitable work is more or less of a crank, and it is a common belief that our conference is composed largely of long-haired men and short-haired women" (Proceedings of the National Conference on Charities and Corrections, 1889, p. 264). One notable exception to this is the former settlement house worker played by Humphrey Bogart in *Crime School*; even the tough, determined clerics of *Boys Town* and *The Hoodlum Priest*, whom we might initially think of as exceptions as well, are not. They, too, are emasculated, given that, as Catholic priests, they are presumed to be celibate.

At the turn of the century, lurid, insinuating stories of the "perversions" and "dreadful" goings-on among settlement house women and suffragists appeared in Chicago and New York newspapers (Herring, 2007), and given that educated women who didn't want to marry men had few choices at the time, it might make sense that lesbians would be overrepresented in settlement houses and other charitable organizations: it was one of the few professions open to them, and without traditional obligations of husband, household, and children, they had more time to devote to social activism. Lesbians do seem to be well rep-resented among late-century reformers, including, of course, Jane Addams herself (Faderman, 1999). That is to say, these images of charity reformers as "deviant" were rooted both in a reality and in a popular conception of that reality.

Getting back to *Intolerance*: Jenkins cuts wages by ten percent so that he has more money available to give his sister for her charitable endeavors. This is not lost on the workers, who strike, saying "They squeeze the money out of us and use it to advertise themselves by reforming us." It's a fairly sophisti-cated complaint, one made by many radical reformers in the Gilded Age, and one that added to the upset about the film among some do-gooders of the day (Merritt, 1990). This critique still applies: many modern corporations have philanthropy programs that are administered through their public relations—that is, advertising—departments.

FIGURES 4.1, 4.2, 4.3, **AND** 4.4 Effeminate male social workers. *Regeneration*, Fox Film Corporation, 1915; *Intolerance*, Triangle Distributing, 1916; *Trash*, Filmfactory, 1970. And the exception to the rule—former settlement house worker played by Humphrey Bogart in *Crime School*, Warner Brothers, 1938.

The strike is likely doomed to fail, we see, for there are plenty of "hungry ones that wait to take their places," men who are too desperate for us to casually condemn them as mere scabs. When the militia fires blanks to try to disperse the strikers, Jenkins calls on his private security force, who know their business better and fire real bullets, killing some strikers, including the father of The Boy. (This kind of violence has been a commonplace in American labor history.) Orphaned and alone, The Boy heads to the big city in search of work,

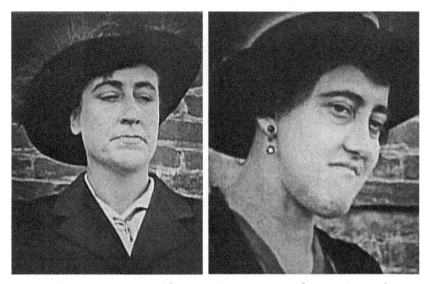

FIGURES 4.5 AND 4.6 Mannish, imperious women reformers in *Intolerance,* Triangle Distributing, 1916.

as do The Girl (sometimes referred to in the title cards as The Dear One) and her father. Unable to find employment, The Boy steals a wallet from a passed-out drunk and is soon "a barbarian of the streets," working for the Musketeer of the Slums, while The Girl's father dies from his "inability to meet new conditions." And the ever-dangerous Progressive-era city claims another victim.

The Boy and Girl get married, as we know they must, but The Boy, framed by The Boss when he tries to leave his life of crime, is sent off to prison; The Girl, with a newborn child, is wrongly judged by The Uplifters to be an unfit mother, and the child is taken away in a brutal scene in which they are monstrous villains. It all turns out well, however: The Boy is released from prison, and the baby is returned—a pat ending to this tale that Griffith deleted in a darker 1926 version, in which the child presumably remains under the cold care of the Uplifters (Merritt, 1990).

The conventional wisdom is that, stung by the charges of racism in *Birth of a Nation,* Griffith set out to redeem himself with *Intolerance.* Yet the sexism here is nearly as thoroughgoing as the racism of the earlier film, although apparently not sufficiently beyond the norm to be commented upon at the time. By contrast, there was a great outcry, especially in the black press, over *Birth of a Nation* (Everett, 2001; Bogle, 1973/2007). And while few mention *Birth of a Nation* today without reflexively noting its Confederate sympathies and pro-Ku Klux Klan propaganda, as they should, the sexism and homophobia of *Intolerance* don't seem to inspire the same kind of awareness.

FIGURES 4.7 AND 4.8 The reformers arrive to seize the baby. *Intolerance*, Triangle Distributing, 1916.

Raoul Walsh, who worked as an assistant to Griffith and played John Wilkes Booth in *Birth of a Nation* (Schickel, 1975), offers a different vision of the social worker in *Regeneration* (1915). Owen, orphaned at age ten, survives the abuse of his drunken, adoptive father to become a dockworker at age seventeen, one who fights in defense of a weaker boy. By twenty-five, he's a leader of a racially mixed gang. Meanwhile, the new district attorney announces a plan to clean up the city, and, wooing young Marie, takes her and her wealthy family to a nightclub where they can see real, live gangsters. Owen is there, has very dark circles under his eyes, drinks lots of beer, and looks drawn—utterly wasted. The crowd beats up the DA, causing Marie distress, but Owen breaks up the fight and escorts them all to safety. He has set a conversion in motion, for Marie decides then and there to become a settlement worker. Marie gets Owen and the boys to join the settlement's annual outing, and later asks Owen to help save a baby from an abusive father; he does, and as thanks she brings him a bucket of beer. Owen is slowly won over to "education, inspiration—and love," while another boy, Skinny, assumed leadership of the gang and then tries to rape Marie. Owen comes to rescue her one last time—only to see her shot and killed by Skinny. While Owen fights Skinny, a vision of Marie comes to him and makes him stop, and he falls to the ground weeping. At her grave, Owen speaks of the redemption Marie brought him.

This falls outside the typical pattern—here, it's the poor man who is ultimately redeemed by the reformer (although he inspired her conversion first). Whatever the implied moral, or the lesson we might draw from it, Walsh claims to have intended no deeper social message, and insists he was just trying to tell a good story (Brownlow, 1990, p. xxiii).

But the busybody social worker continues to be a recognizable villain. *It* (1927) is a story about Betty, a department store clerk played with exaggerated impishness by Clara Bow, and her efforts to seduce and marry the owner's son. (Reader, she succeeds!) In the course of the farce unfolding, we meet an apparently unmarried friend who is staying with Betty and caring for a newborn baby. After a title card that reads, "Poverty is no disgrace—until meddling neighbors hear of it," two social workers arrive to take the baby away to a more suitable environment. These are in essence the same women we met in *Intolerance*: sour, haughty, and mannish.

Just as *Intolerance* ascribes their vocational choice to their lack of feminine wiles, here Betty, throwing them from her flat, remonstrates: "If women like you would stay home and have babies of your own, we'd all be better off." It's hinting at a relatively common argument of the time: Lesbianism would lead to declining births among native whites while the immigrant hordes continued to pour in—it's "race suicide" (Herring, 2007). Claiming the baby as her own to shield her friend from these dowdy busybodies, Betty finds herself at the receiving end of their demand to know who her husband is and *where* he is, and they are aghast when she tells them that it's none of their business. They are ugly, utterly unsympathetic characters. A reporter happens to

FIGURES 4.9 AND 4.10 Prison matrons glare at the social worker who would disrupt their brutal regime, *Ann Vickers*, RKO Pictures, 1933 (above); and stern caseworkers from the Children's Aid Society stop a young girl from working to help support her family, making every one worse off, *Boy of the Streets*, Monogram Pictures, 1937 (below).

be present, and the headline the next day reads: "Girl mother battles bitterly for babe: Like Tigress at bay, routs welfare workers."

These harsh portrayals were not created out of whole cloth: since the founding of the Society for the Prevention of Cruelty to Children in the late nineteenth century, it was often referred to simply as The Cruelty, reflecting the esteem in which it was held by the poor families subject to its arbitrary power (Gordon, 1988). In *Tomorrow's Children* (1934), we see such power exerted in even more radical ways. In this bit of eugenicist propaganda, the father's an alcoholic who refuses to work. One son is in jail, two others are mentally

FIGURES 4.11 AND 4.12 Imperious welfare workers interrogate Clara Bow. *It*, Paramount Pictures, 1927.

disabled, and another is crippled. His wife, also alcoholic, has just given birth to a stillborn baby, and all concerned seem to think its death is for the best. The doctor, meaning to help, brings in the welfare department, who offer immediate aid to the family on the condition that all of the boys be shipped off to institutions and that the adults be sterilized, including their quite "normal" seventeen-year-old daughter. This was a common enough practice in poor neighborhoods and Indian reservations, even into the late twentieth century. Here the parents agree to the deal, as many did, because they needed the aid so badly, and while the film does capture some of the barbarity of the practice and the egregious use of state power over desperate, poor households, the ultimate message here seems be to only forcibly sterilize those truly in need of it.

The image of the social worker as unwanted intruder and soulless bureaucrat endured. Early in King Vidor's *Street Scene* (1931), an adaptation of Elmer Rice's Pulitzer Prize–winning play, a social worker arrives at a stoop looking for her widowed client and is told by the neighbors that she's at the movies. The poor woman arrives home, with her two children in tow, and is asked, with some disbelief, if she was really at "the moving picture show." She was.

"Where did you get the money?"

"It was only seventy-five cents."

"I suppose it came out of the money we gave you to buy groceries with!?"

The agent later reprimands a man who gives some money to the woman and her children: "It's bad for her character," she sniffs.

FIGURES 4.13, 4.14, **AND** 4.15 The social worker as judgmental scold, literally looking down her nose in *Street Scene*, United Artists, 1931 (*left*); *Claudine*, 20th Century Fox, 1974 (*center*); *Precious*, Lionsgate, 2009 (*right*): "Is that a new microwave oven?!"

This propels one man, leaning out a window, to offer a diatribe about the rights of the working class, their oppression by capitalists, and the evils of private property. Another launches into a complaint about the decline of morals and human values. With the sole exception of the caseworker, they all are asserting a right to more than mere subsistence, but to well-being, to dignity, to happiness, even. It's rare to find these claims in any context in the United States, especially on film—and note that the greatest resistance to this expanded notion of rights comes from the caseworker. Perhaps American political culture tends to ignore claims about higher-order human needs because the country fares so badly in ensuring basic ones, and those pressing demands for food and shelter rightly draw our attention before desire for pleasure, entertainment, or wish-fulfillment. Can you imagine a program of movie stamps to go along with food stamps? Meyer Levin, a critic for *Esquire*, made the case for just such a program, however, writing in 1936:

> Now, I know I'm not alone in feeling this hypnotic, habit-forming need for the movie. Sociologists, through the activity of social service workers, have in the past few years secured a fairly wide acceptance of the idea that the motion picture is a necessity, rather than a luxury, to the population. It's no longer a shock when a relief client confesses that a quarter out of the minimum-standard-food-budget allowance for the week is devoted to the purchase of movie tickets. (in Lopate, 2008, p. 103)

While this reveals some early strains of welfare-queen myth-making, given how unlikely it is that any significant number of families in need would spend that much of their food allowance on movie tickets, it recognizes, even if obliquely, the virtues of cinema, including an escapism that might be especially restorative for people whose daily lives are filled with incessant struggle (contradicting, yet again, Gilbert Seldes). Even the *New York Times* saw fit to complain about families being cut off the rolls when it was discovered that they traded their chickens for cash to buy movie tickets, for this was merely evidence of a "desperate need for release" of the kind that could only be supplied by a moving picture show (Robert Hartley quoted in *Experimental Cinema*, 1934, p. 42).

All the neighbors in *Street Scene* seem to think of the charity agent as a busybody, and one complains that her problem is that she lives alone "and hasn't got a sweetheart," echoing the perceived sexual aberrance of social workers. But in this movie, it's not just the social worker who's a busybody—everyone is. All the neighbors are into each other's business, and the film is scene after scene of gossip, flirtation, and argument, each resident judging the behavior of the others, while they, in turn, are judged. It's an incestuous, oppressive little place, rife with adultery and women in bad marriages susceptible to the entreaties of rogues who would purportedly better their condition. In fact, one of the young women regularly implores her parents to move away to Queens, or anyplace with some space and privacy.

The caseworker is a little better when she reappears some years later in *Body and Soul* (1947). Charley (John Garfield) becomes a professional boxer to earn enough money so that his mother (Anne Revere) will not have to subject herself to intrusive interrogations, even if the well-intended social worker is apologetic about the need for all her questions. "Get out!" he spits at her. "I don't want any handouts. . . . We don't want any help!"

As we'll see in Chapter 5, there's a worker of the same strain in *Claudine*, but there are a few exceptions to this general pattern. One we've discussed— the settlement house worker played by Humphrey Bogart in *Crime School*. Another appears in *Precious*, which we'll turn to shortly and discuss along- side *Claudine*. *Ann Vickers* (1933), about a social worker at the Corlears Hook Settlement, offers another exception. Ann is young, smart, attractive, and has suitors in abundance. As one man says, "Social worker, huh? Well, I wouldn't have guessed it!" She's duped by a soldier into thinking he's in love and wants to marry her; gets pregnant, has an abortion, and leaves the Settlement to work at a women's prison. She discovers that it's a cruel, brutal place, and writes a book-length exposé that leads to her own appointment as head of a reformatory, the Stuyvesant Industrial Home. And yet, it's clear that she's unhappy with her solitary life and envious of her secretary, who has a hus- band and child. Is this the inevitable fate of the professional do-gooder? Sure enough, she's soon happy and in love, but with a corrupt judge whose even- tual conviction causes her to abandon her own "social ethics" in efforts to secure his release, and while those efforts fail and cost her her job, she shows no remorse. Is the lesson that love conquers all? That all ethics are situational ethics? Her last words, once the judge is released from prison, are to talk of how his love freed her "from the prison of ambition, the prison of ambition for praise and success for myself!" What's settlement work or prison reform compared to the love of a corrupt man!

The film is based on a Sinclair Lewis novel in which Ann learns about prison by being incarcerated for two weeks after a suffrage meeting, and she concludes that the answer is to abolish prison (not the tepid penal reforms the film emphasizes). In the book, after her abortion, Ann remains at the settle- ment, no one the wiser, while the film feels the need to punish her for this transgression. When she does finally leave the settlement in Lewis's version, it's not because she must, but because she grows disgusted with its methods and its attitudes, and gives it up to manage the philanthropy of a rich widow, hoping to have greater impact. (She soon realizes, alas, that she's there to give the veneer of respectability to a project that's about public relations, not doing good.) As Lewis puts her critique in the novel:

> Ann questioned the value of settlement work. It was too parochial. It touched only a tiny neighborhood, and left all the adjoining neighborhoods that did not have their own settlements, which was most of them, without provision for such recreation, education, emergency relief, and advice as the settlement could give. It wasn't, Ann decided, much more valuable than its parent, the good old heart-warming and tear-bringing system whereby the elder daughter of the vicar (the one who had never married) amused herself by taking coals and blankets and jelly to such bedridden parishioners as were most slobberingly obsequious to the vicar and to the squire.... The settlement house ... smelled of the sour smell of charity.... At least organized charity was impersonal. It based relief not on the smiles and quaint friendliness of the victims, but on their need.... And it busied itself not with victims' desires to be better poets or cooks ... but with their need of food, shoes, and money for the rent (Lewis, 1932/1944, pp. 236ff).

The most notable exception to the typical portrayal of social workers is *Chains of Gold* (1991), a John Travolta vehicle intended for theatrical release, according to the Internet Movie Database (IMDB), but that went straight to cable television. Travolta plays Scott, a recovering alcoholic and a rule-breaking caseworker (it's set in Miami, for a change) who fights the soulless bureaucracy ("The bastard cares more about paperwork than he does about people!" he exclaims of his boss), bucks the system, and risks being fired as he struggles to rescue young Tommy (Joey Lawrence), who was a dealer and is now a captive of an evil drug lord (Benjamin Bratt). Most of the proceeds from Tommy's work go to his adult sister and mother (Conchata Farrell) who, although white, has been given something of a welfare queen vibe—she's obese, lazy, alcoholic, and willing to pretend she doesn't know where the money comes from. But soon thereafter Scott has to admonish his obese, sullen, insolent, black clients not to use their welfare checks to buy crack, so the stereotypical racial universe is set aright. That the social worker goes undercover to find the boy and bring down the organization tells you how seriously to take the effort, and it also tells you how concerned the film is either with

FIGURE 4.16 Just another day at the office for caseworker John Travolta, in *Chains of Gold*, Orion Pictures, 1991, as he is about to slide down a building; he will later fight off alligators.

poor, vulnerable children or with the adults who might try to help them. As far as I can tell, it is the cinema's only social worker/action hero.

I have largely set aside considerations of foreign films for this book, but it's hard not to talk about would-be do-gooders without at least a passing glance at *Major Barbara* (1941). It's a British film of a George Bernard Shaw play and, like *Pygmalion* (see Chap. 15), stars the wondrous Wendy Hiller as Barbara, a Salvation Army officer. As with *Pygmalion*, rich meets poor, and because Shaw wrote the screenplay, they talk smartly about class, poverty, and morality. "What kept us poor? Keeping you rich!" a man who was fired from his job says to Undershaft, the rich industrialist. The film wonders just who it is that Barbara and her Army are serving, since they are most interested in conversion, as is any missionary, and offering food and shelter are merely their way in. Two poor supplicants make it plain that they know their part in this game, pretending to be greater sinners than they are so that their feigned conversion is that much more valued and, therefore, valuable. It's also made clear, when a Salvation Army General is trying to convince Undershaft of the worth of the Army's work, that the institution knows that by providing food and cultivating the obedience that comes with "salvation," the rioter and protester are taken from the streets and rendered harmless. Relief is a good investment for the rich man, and a large check—though a pittance to someone like Undershaft—can ease his conscience and buy good public repute, as most industrialists came to learn. Only Barbara thinks this blood money should be refused, whatever the cost. At first, that is, for her ultimate realization is that her mission is not to save the poor, "weak souls in starved bodies, sobbing with gratitude for a scrap of bread and scrape," but to convert factory workers, "souls that are hungry because their bodies are full." That way she will no longer depend upon "the bribe of bread" to woo the heathen. Shaw's own preface to the play (Shaw, 1906) demonstrates more eloquently than I could the complexity of the social critique, the outrage at poverty, and the derision directed at those who would fail to acknowledge it or, worse, exploit it for their own ends. It is Shaw, so this is no surprise, but it does make me wonder if there is any American film about poverty or charity as sophisticated as this one. There is surely is nothing as funny and so angry all at once.

Charity serves many functions, both individual and social (see, for one accounting, Bekkers and Wiepking, 2010), as we've seen above. For the individual, motivations for giving can vary a lot. Some give out of altruism: they might genuinely and sincerely believe in the program and the need for it. Others may make contributions out of a self-interested altruism: a person might want to help because they would want others to help them if they were in need. This may help explain why low- and middle-income people generally give more to charity as a percentage of their total income than rich people do (Daniels, 2015). They might volunteer or make a donation because they want a tangible benefit—the Girl Scout cookies or the Public Broadcasting System (PBS) tote bag, say, or another kind of tangible benefit, like a tax deduction. Donors might seek an intangible benefit—to feel good or noble, or to relieve their own guilt about something. They might seek a social benefit, or use a donation to reinforce their social status: this is a means by which wealthier people solidify the perception among their cohort that they are good citizens; it may even be merely the act of comporting to class expectations. Some gifts are made out of ego: people want others to know how generous they are, or to see the plaque with their name on it, or the shiny new building named after them. Some give out of social obligation (it's just *what one does*), perhaps in the broader belief that they owe something back to the society that made them rich. This is *noblesse oblige*. Some giving is a networking opportunity—benefit galas, for example, function as a social and business network among the wealthy. There are *functions* of charity, too: Lowell (1884) argued that charity was the price society pays for its own security—a kind of bribe to placate the poorest classes and prevent them from revolting, just as Shaw saw, too (an argument extended and refined by Piven and Cloward in 1971/1993). And finally, some give out of religious obligation.

With that last item in mind, I want to turn our attention to instances of social workers or reformers working through religious organizations. I've already talked a bit about *Major Barbara*, and noted Shaw's complaint about the ways in which the Salvation Army used the enticement of food and shelter to recruit adherents and compel devotion—or at least the appearance of it. It is to this day not unheard of for some soup kitchens to require that people pray before they can eat.

Dorothy Day was her own kind of Major Barbara—a missionary who founded the *Catholic Worker* newspaper in the depths of the Great Depression and opened "houses of hospitality" for poor and homeless people. There are still some 200 today associated with her movement. But for Day, filling the stomach seemed often to take precedence over saving the soul (see Day, n.d.). In the biopic *Entertaining Angels* (1996), some of her political radicalism is present earlier in the film, but the last half sets aside politics in favor of portraying the day-to-day business of running her makeshift mission: keeping order, preparing food, tending to the sick, scrounging for money, and finding space for all the would-be lodgers. To the extent that religion figures in, it's a service-based New Testamentism that takes center stage, rather than her efforts at constructing a radical-socialist Catholicism. Perhaps by limiting displays of such tendencies to her youth, they can be written off as indiscretions, paving the way toward the more serious, mature work of ministering to the poor. System-challenging troublemaking among the middle-aged is perhaps more threatening, more complicated, and less safe for film. It's worth noting that the poor are objects here: they are the means by which Day achieves whatever greatness and nobility may be attributed to her. None is a three-dimensional character, which, to be fair, may be justified by the fact that it's a movie about Day, not them. But it is revealing nonetheless: devotion to Man is merely a means toward divine ends. That people are helped is incidental, even if that's welcomed. It's an awfully Protestant and Calvinist framing for a biography of a Catholic, but one that shows just how deeply resistant filmmakers are to trying to make sense of the world from the perspective of its most marginalized inhabitants. By contrast, *Dorothy Day: Don't Call Me a Saint* (2006), is a documentary that will give you a fuller sense of what made Day unusual, with special care taken here to distinguish between *mercy*, the benign, gentle form of charity that sits at the heart of *Entertaining Angels* (and most American movies discussed in this book), and the fight for *justice*, that more threatening and disruptive philosophy that, turned to action and indignation, made Day such a danger.

FIGURE 4.17 Dorothy Day with the United Farm Workers and police, *Don't Call Me a Saint*, One Lucky Dog Productions, 2006.

The Second Chance (2006) introduces us to Jake Sanders (Jeff Obafemi Carr), a radical, black, inner-city pastor in Nashville, and the occasional recipient of the largess of a large, rich, mostly white suburban mega-church. But his outspokenness may derail their plans to sell away his parish so that others can build a sports stadium. After he castigates the congregation on live television for writing checks rather than volunteering, Ethan, the preacher's son (Michael W. Smith), is called upon to monitor Sanders. He begins by asking Sanders to apologize.

"All right," Sanders says,

I'm sorry for associate pastors who got this all figured out because they spent an hour down here slinging potatoes. I'm sorry for rock stars who think they've lived the African American experience riding a tour bus with Tina Turner. And I'm sorry for whiteys who try and get their conscience fixed by coming down here and hanging with their homeboys in the ghetto once a year. How's that?

Sanders proceeds to educate Ethan about what life is like in this desperately poor community, and teaches him to see the residents as individuals, rather than as social problems. He teaches him respect for low-income people, and humility, too, in the face of their hard, complicated lives. There's more than a bit of social work philosophy in his approach: Sanders urges Jenkins to meet people where they are (in a dig at his father, who preaches far away, safely ensconced behind his pulpit). The rich white preacher's son does, inevitably, come to a new understanding (and to his own personal transformation). It's facile, but nonetheless manages better than most at offering informed and empathetic perspectives on a community of concentrated poverty. It would get even more credit if it had the courage to allow the church to be razed, as it would probably be in reality, instead of resorting to an eleventh-hour *deus ex machina* when Ethan's own father stops the demolition after undergoing his own transformation.

The Second Chance has some things in common with the much more popular *Sister Act* (1992) A church that has lost its way is brought back to its true mission by one charismatic person (Whoopi Goldberg), who inspires them to tear down the chain-link fence that separates them from the neighborhood, go out into the community, and, literally, meet people where they are and where they live, after which they set up daycare and emergency food programs and the like. It's a critique of a religion that preaches the gospel but fails to act upon it. Thanks to all these good works, and a newly invigorated choir, the parish thrives again. Yet it still offers another instance in which poor and homeless people serve as the fulcrum upon which the narrative turns and facilitate the redemption of the

FIGURE 4.18 The moribund parish comes alive thanks to the interventions of an outsider. *Sister Act*, Touchstone Pictures, 1992.

main characters (and, in this instance, the institution of the wayward church itself). Serving the poor in the movies is not typically about the poor, but about those who serve—a principle demonstrated even by Robin Hood.

The basic shape of that myth is well known: a dispossessed knight steals from the rich in order to give to the poor; he hides out in Sherwood Forest with his Band of Merry Men and does battle with the relentless (if sometimes hapless) Sheriff of Nottingham and with John, the ruthless usurper King. In the 1922 silent version, with Douglas Fairbanks as Robin, the rich-to-poor transfer activity is secondary to Robin Hood's principal motivation, which is terrorizing John and his supporters. In the film's 140 minutes, there are only three scenes (of under thirty seconds each) in which Fairbanks's Robin Hood delivers aid, first to a single family in need and later to a large group of people in the forest-village. Coins are literally tossed into the air, and Robin's men are nearly dancing in celebration as they distribute their bounty—with very little attention paid to the recipients of that aid, since they are not the subject. Robin and his men are the heroes of the tale, of course.

The exuberant 1938 version starring Errol Flynn (*Adventures of Robin Hood*), directed by Michael Curtiz (*Angels with Dirty Faces, Casablanca, Mildred Pierce*), sets up a starker contrast and a sharper political framework right from its start. A man who is threatened with execution by Prince John's men for killing a deer (so that he and his family might eat) is saved by Robin Hood and promptly joins the cause. Afterwards, we move to a grand banquet in the castle, where there is food in abundance and a dog feasting upon the fat carcass of another deer. The oath that Robin later asks his men to take articulates some of the principles of a modern welfare state: "You, the free men of this forest, swear to despoil the rich, only to give to the poor; to shelter the old and the helpless; to protect all women, rich or poor, Norman or Saxon." Even the gender bias characterizes most twentieth century welfare states as they would come into being in later years and decades: in the United States, for example, because they often tied eligibility and benefit levels to a person's work history and because women were excluded from the labor market throughout much of the twentieth century—and even when working, women have typically been paid less than men—social policies have often benefitted men more than women, intending that they be provided for indirectly, via fathers or husbands (Gordon, 1994; Skocpol, 1992).

The year 1964 brings us *Robin and the Seven Hoods*, a Rat Pack vehicle in which Robbo, a crime boss played by Frank Sinatra, gives $50,000 to an orphanage. The money was not quite stolen from the rich, but was given to him by a wealthy woman to kill the man who killed her father (someone else did the deed, but she credits Robbo). In part because of the publicity the act

FIGURE 4.19 A dog feasts on a carcass while people go hungry. *Robin Hood*, Warner Brothers, 1938.

brings him—and the need for more as he rebuilds his nightclub business— he hires a man (Bing Crosby) to manage further philanthropic affairs, setting up a soup kitchen, a free clinic, and more, all under the name The Robin Hood Foundation, anticipating a real-world Robin Hood Foundation founded

FIGURES 4.20 One of the charities Robbo sets up to improve his public image. *Robin and the Seven Hoods*, Warner Brothers, 1964.

in New York in 1988 by another kind of syndicate—hedge fund managers. This Robin Hood is a cynic and an opportunist, an anti-hero, we might say. And, unsurprisingly, the orphans and others in need are one-dimensional props to keep the story moving.

The 1973 animated Disney version foregrounds the idea that Robin Hood is engaged in a noble act, even if there are no actual poor people portrayed here (is it better that they are ignored instead of used as mere plot devices?). Early on, Robin and Little John, having just escaped the Sherriff and his henchmen, talk about what they do. Little John asks if their acts—"robbing the rich to feed the poor"—make them good guys or bad guys. Robin won't even concede that they steal: "Rob? That's a naughty word. We never rob. We just sort of borrow a bit from those who can afford it." To make the line bright, King John (Prince John, here), is found laughing while letting gold coins tumble through his fingers. He describes what he does through "Taxes! Taxes! Beautiful, lovely taxes!" as "rob[bing] the poor to feed the rich," although we could just as easily read the film as a bit of anti-tax propaganda as well. "What with taxes and all," reports the narrator, "the poor folks of Nottingham were starving to death," and the malevolent Sherriff is here also the tax collector, who takes a child's one-farthing birthday gift and empties the church's poor box. Contrast this with the Warner Brothers cartoon "Robin Hood Daffy" (1958), in which Daffy Duck as Robin Hood says, casually, "See yon rich, unwary traveller? I'll rob him of his gold, and give it to some poor, unworthy slob." *Poor, unworthy slob*—the derision of poor people is so casual and automatic that it probably goes unnoticed.

There are two more recent American adaptations of Robin Hood. One was directed by Ridley Scott (*Alien, Blade Runner*), starring Russell Crowe (2010), and deviates enough and in so many ways from the tale as it is usually told that there is not necessarily anything of import to the fact that among its omissions is the entire stealing-from-the-rich-to-give-to-the-poor thread. The other, *Robin Hood: Prince of Thieves* (1991), directed by Kevin Reynolds and starring Kevin Costner, has pretensions of being about religion, and has Robin's earliest inspiration emerge from the giving of alms to the poor in church. The earlier adaptations of the tale, by contrast, understood that what Robin Hood does is at heart returning to people what had been stolen away from them by the usurper brother to the rightful King. Here, it's just charity, the benevolence of the great white (Christian) savior. Indeed, some of the grateful peasants even say "God bless Robin Hood" when given bread. Beyond this, it's generally bad enough that Mel Brooks's satire, *Robin Hood: Men in Tights* (1993) feels superfluous.

From the social worker to religious leaders to Robin Hood himself, those who would help poor people are, on film, not to be trusted. Given the choice between siding with a poor person or a social worker, most films choose the would-be supplicant. But there are some exceptions, and we see a different pattern indeed when a woman on welfare sits at the center of the story.

5 WELFARE QUEENS

Trash, Precious, Claudine, Welfare, Mannequin, The Candidate

Much of the activity of social workers—in life and on film—has been focused on the reform and rescue of poor women with children. In the years after the 1935 creation of Aid to Dependent Children (ADC), those reformers would do more of their work for public agencies, established by state governments to administer, determine eligibility for, and manage the population of this new welfare program. ADC was relatively uncontroversial in its first decades—it was designed to offer aid to poor, white widows, and structured to make it easy for states to deny aid to populations it thought undeserving of assistance; many of those excluded from the rolls, despite their need, were black women living in the South. That began to change by the 1960s, as northward migration, publicly funded Legal Aid lawyers, welfare rights movement victories, and U.S. Supreme Court decisions, finally opened up the rolls to them. The subsequent "explosion" of the number of women on welfare soon became a rallying cry for conservatives looking for a (Democratic Party–identified) villain to mobilize against, and the Welfare Queen was born. She would become the embodiment of all that had gone wrong with America. But while the language is relatively new, there's something almost archetypal about this character.

The stereotype appears in the modern era, not first in a film from conservative Hollywood, but in an offering from the leading edge of the counterculture. *Trash* (1970) introduces us to Joe (Joe Dallessandro), who spends the movie looking for a heroin fix, and Holly (Holly Woodlawn), who is desperate for money. When her sister (Diane Podel) shows up pregnant, Holly decides to claim the baby as her own: "We could get on welfare.... You get extra for a baby. And they'll pay your rent.... Welfare can take care of us.... I need welfare, I deserve it! I was born on welfare and I'll die on welfare." Mr. Michaels (Michael Sklar), a caseworker, comes for a home visit and resists approving her claim for fear that the money

Average Monthly Welfare Recipients, 1936–2015

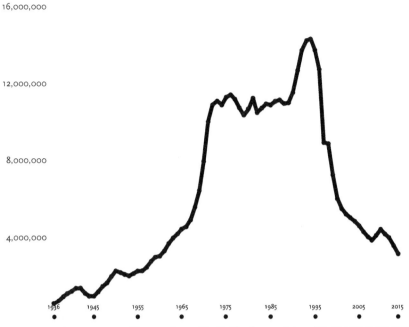

FIGURE 5.1 Average monthly number of individuals receiving ADC/AFDC/TANF benefits, 1936–2015.

Data Source: U.S. Department of Health and Human Services.

will be spent on drugs. But he finally agrees to look the other way and submit a fraudulent claim if she'll give him her shoes, which he has found to be irresistibly fabulous (you can see director Paul Morrisey's influence on John Waters here).

FIGURES 5.2 AND 5.3 Another effeminate social worker wants to trade welfare benefits for *fabulous* shoes; rebuffed, he turns vicious and vindictive. *Trash,* Filmfactory, 1970.

The caseworker asserts his power by saying "You may be entitled to [welfare], Ms. Santiago, but that doesn't mean you'll get it!" Later, he observes: "Look, I've dealt with the Negroes that crank out kids every five minutes . . . and I know that they get by, they get by with very meager existence. You're just going to have to get by without anything." She resists, and keeps insisting, "We're entitled to it! Just give us welfare! We're entitled to it!" But he too is stubborn: "You're garbage, you're all garbage, and you're not getting a dime." They are denied aid, and he leaves without her shoes. No one here is especially sympathetic, so this exchange might be understood to be one way of showing just how corrupt and irredeemable they are; but the welfare agent is corrupt, too, and articulates his own ugly view of his clients who are all, we could conclude from the film, welfare queens of one kind or another. But it's hardly the worst representation of either welfare recipients or welfare bureaucrats.

With domestic box-office receipts of some $50 million, *Precious* (2009) is the most extended encounter many contemporary Americans will have with black welfare recipients, and it reaffirms in every respect the most insidious stereotypes of the Welfare Queen and the rapacious black male. If we inhabited a media world in which images of welfare families and, more generally, poor people of color were common, then perhaps we could and should think differently about *Precious*. We could judge it based upon how well it captured something about this particular family, or of pre-gentrification Harlem in the late 1980s. We could focus, as many rightly have, on the extraordinary performance of stand-up comic Mo'Nique as one of the worst mothers you've ever seen on film, yet one we come to pity and even understand, if just a bit: she's a cruel, ugly monster, but Mo'Nique makes her a human one, not a caricature, and her more than two dozen Best Supporting Actress awards were earned. We could note the fine debut of Gabourey Sidibe and the wrenching tale of the title character she plays. Raped, beaten, and emotionally abused since age three by her father and mother both, at age sixteen she's about to give birth to her second incestuously conceived child. Virtually illiterate, homeless for a time, and HIV-positive, where most would surrender to the impossibility of it all, Clarisse Precious Jones somehow rises up to take control of her life: she enrolls in an alternative school and, thanks to dedicated teaching, sassy classmates, and her own hard labor, even wins a literacy award from the Mayor's office. With the help of a social worker played by Mariah Carey, she confronts her mother and separates from that toxic household for good; she flirts with a sexy nurse played by Lenny Kravitz; she reclaims her children (the eldest of whom has Down syndrome), and by the end of the film is on her way toward happiness and high school, though probably not the celebrity she yearns for in the film's dream sequences. The story is typical Hollywood fare, in its way, even if the setting is not.

But precisely because the central characters are black welfare recipients, it is not typical fare. American movies offer the public few images of the poor and welfare-reliant, and almost never as the main characters. Not since 1974's *Claudine*, which we'll examine next, has a relatively mainstream movie had a family on welfare at its heart (it's a curious absence, given how central the demonization of welfare has been to post-1960s backlash politics). Since these are families we so seldom see on film, and places, especially the welfare office, that movies rarely venture into—Frederick Wiseman will offer a rare exception—we have instead to ask if the director has a social responsibility to explain that the very dark image of poor women he presents is not typical. And it is a dark image, since there seems to be some correlation here between the lightness of character's skin and their positive virtue. I instinctively want to ask more of *Precious*, and want to impose upon it some duty, to burden it with more weight than it wants to bear, but I also suspect that it is unreasonable and perhaps even dangerous to do so. Almost all artists, after all, are of necessity representing a part rather than the whole. It is from all these parts that we then each assemble, in cubist fashion, our own interpretation of our own mediated world. It is the viewer who ultimately has the obligation to make sense of any act of artistic creation or interpretation.

And yet . . . as Martin Gilens (1999) and others have shown, relief programs and ideas about the work ethic are already racialized in the minds of Americans. What then is the impact of these 109 minutes of widely viewed, well-publicized, much-discussed film that could have first been pitched

FIGURE 5.4 Mary, Precious's mother. *Precious*, Lionsgate, 2009.

to the studios by anti-welfare eugenicist Charles Murray or the Heritage Foundation's Robert Rector? Here we have, after all, an obese, pregnant child living in a profoundly dysfunctional single-parent household and attending a raucous and undisciplined public school where she's earned As just for showing up. Her mother is on welfare and food stamps, collecting for both Precious and her grandchild, lying to maintain her benefits and staging domestic scenes so that it appears to the social workers that her grandchild lives with her and Precious instead of Precious's grandmother. Yet she seems capable of work, even if she's a foul-mouthed, foul-tempered, chain-smoking, lottery-playing layabout who spends her days and nights listless in front of the television, waiting for Precious to cook and serve her meals. Precious's father, who is also the father of her children, lives elsewhere and when present at all seems interested only in sex with the women of the household. About the only other men we see are hanging in the streets, causing trouble. And not to leave out even the hoariest of tropes, for breakfast one morning Precious not only steals, but steals a bucket of fried chicken. Betraying, perhaps, some of the politics of the filmmakers, one of Precious's first acts of defiance is to tell a social worker some of the truth of her home life, thereby getting herself cut off of welfare—which is portrayed as an act of heroism. Later, Precious's teacher points to the grave harm that welfare has done to the young woman's mother.

There are women on welfare in the United States who seem every inch the Queen, and there's no reason to accuse the author or filmmakers of invention out of whole cloth. But these are, at best, some small minority of recipients. Most women, as decades worth of social science research show, use relief for brief periods of time (about 18 months, on average) in ways most Americans seem to think appropriate—as a bridge between jobs, to escape an abusive relationship, to complete a college degree, as a means of accessing Medicaid for their kids, or to care for a newborn child or a sick family member (Edin and Lein, 1997; Hays, 2004; Seccombe, 2010). Given the pervasiveness of the stereotype, however, shouldn't a filmmaker—and especially a black filmmaker—seek to undermine it, not to reinforce it? Or is that asking him to sacrifice an artistic goal for a political one, or to tell a story I want told, instead of his own?

One of the reasons that 1980's *Cruising* spawned protests from gay men was that movies at the time rarely offered them as protagonists, and when they did, the characters were ineffectual fops, or, as in *Cruising*, psychopaths, sex addicts, and serial killers. But today, because film and television offer a much broader array of images of gay men and lesbians, we no longer worry quite so much that each portrayal has a duty to represent the whole, or to

FIGURES 5.5 AND 5.6 Two other Welfare Queens, from *Boyz N the Hood*, Columbia Pictures, 1991.

present a positive image. That's a mark of progress. No longer does one character need to represent the entire class of people. But there is no multitude of welfare types in the movies, and as a consequence, some (much? most?) of the audience surely will assume that this is a glimpse into the typical Harlem household, especially given that *Precious* so powerfully reinforces decades worth of malignant political rhetoric.

There's a 1949 essay by Ralph Ellison called "The Shadow and the Act." Ellison's subject is *Birth of a Nation*, one of the most influential—and racist— films in the American canon. As he writes:

> In the struggle against Negro freedom, motion pictures have been one of the strongest instruments for justifying some white Americans' anti-Negro attitudes and practices. . . . While the Negro stereotypes by no means made all white men Klansmen, the cinema did, to the extent that audiences accepted its images of Negroes, make them participants in the South's racial ritual of keeping the Negro 'in his place.'

Efforts to "deny the Negro's humanity" were hardly new, he said, but: "with the release of *Birth of a Nation* the propagation of subhuman images of Negroes became financially and dramatically profitable . . . the anti-Negro image is a ritual object of which Hollywood is not the creator, but the manipulator."

For Ellison (we can find this in Siegfried Kracauer's [1947/2004] writings on the political uses and consequences of 1920s German cinema, too) the racism of *Birth of a Nation* and other less well-known films of the era served a social and cultural function: this dehumanization, he argued, helped shore up the foundations, "legal, emotional, economic and political," of Jim Crow. Set aside the *intent* of *Precious*'s filmmakers—I am aware of no evidence to suggest any base motives on their part—doesn't the film risk making itself an ally of Reagan, Goldwater, Gingrich, and Rector?

One of the striking things about movies featuring homeless single men, as we'll see, is that while the (often, though not always, black) homeless man may appear to be the subject of the story, he almost never is: he exists, rather, as an object to be acted upon, as a means toward the redemption of another (who is often, though not always, white). *The Soloist* (2009), as I'll argue in Chapter 16, presents itself as a film about a black Juilliard-trained cellist, played by Jamie Foxx, who struggles with mental illness and homelessness, but it's really about the white reporter, played by Robert Downey, Jr., and his efforts to reclaim meaning in his work and save his marriage. Ellison makes a kindred observation about the movies he's examining: "Obviously, these films are not *about* Negroes at all; they are about what whites think and feel about Negroes." He asks us to note the "profuse flow of tears and sighs" from white audiences; it's a sentimentality that takes the place of a clearer-eyed examination of social trauma and political wrongs, yet serves its function—self-congratulation. This was surely at work when audiences went to see *The Soloist* or, in much larger numbers, *Slumdog Millionaire* (2008). Many went not to see the film, but to have seen it, so that they would be able to report having seen it and to note the Very Important Issues it raises; perhaps, even, they went to be redeemed in some small way. *Precious* fulfills some of that function, too: the act of seeing the film substitutes for action directed at the problem and, comfortingly, confirms the futility of trying to solve it, since most of these characters seem irredeemable and designed to engender disgust or, at best, pity.

The racial politics—and the class politics, too—are complicated here by the fact that the author of the book upon which *Precious* is based (Sapphire 1996/1997), the screenwriter, the director, and two of its most notable producers, Oprah Winfrey and Tyler Perry, are black. Winfrey and Perry are among the wealthiest and most well-known African Americans alive, and their involvement is further complicated: both are childhood abuse survivors, and both have told interviewers that it was the story of Precious herself they focused on.

It was her struggle and her eventual survival, if not triumph, that drew them to the movie. As Winfrey told *Entertainment Weekly* (Nov. 6, 2009):

> I realized that, Jesus, I have seen that girl a million times. I see that girl every morning on the way to work, I see her standing on the corner, I see her waiting for the bus as I'm passing by in my limo, I see her coming out of the drugstore. And she's been invisible to me. I've done exactly what the people in this film did to her. I've seen her and not seen her. And I thought, That will never happen to me again.

Perry told the same reporter:

> I was watching, like, 60 or 70 percent of my life played out on screen in front of me. I was sitting in *my* house, in *my* screening room, taken back 25 years to my childhood, looking at Mo'Nique's character and knowing that that was my father, and still to this day, it's the same way. So I was like, "People have got to see this."

What responsibilities do these (exceedingly wealthy) celebrities bear for the dissemination and, thanks to their imprimatur, legitimization, of the most invidious stereotypes of poor blacks?

Yet, in addition to its many film festival and critics' organization honors, *Precious* won directing, screenplay, and best film awards from the National Association for the Advancement of Colored People (NAACP), the Foundation for the Advancement of African Americans in Film, and the African American Film Critics Association. If prominent organizations of African Americans valued *Precious* enough to single it out for so many honors, who am I, a professional-class white male, to pass judgment on the manner in which it represents poor, black women? But I will, nonetheless: *Precious* is a beautifully realized portrait of survival, and a nasty and pernicious piece of work.

Claudine (1974) is the antidote. Claudine Price (Diahann Carroll) is on welfare while simultaneously working off the books as a maid for a suburban family and trying to raise her six children alone in Harlem after what she describes as "two marriages and two almost marriages." She's hard-working, and a caring and attentive, if sometimes impatient, mother. The kids are a mix, as kids are, some better behaved and more responsible than others. While these are generally positive portrayals, they are not one-dimensional ones: The film shows us people, not caricatures or stereotypes. It also does as well as anything before or since in capturing what we know about life on AFDC: Claudine works because welfare never paid enough to care for a family,

FIGURES 5.7 AND 5.8 Claudine Price meets her caseworker. "Mrs. Price, you know I'm your friend," and hiding Rooper. *Claudine*, 20th Century Fox, 1974.

but she does so surreptitiously because the program was structured in such a way that the financial penalties were so great that it made no sense to report income (see Gustafson, 2011, on the bind this put poor women in). The program did treat recipients like criminals or children, rhetoric about "responsibility" notwithstanding, and surprise home inspections were a common event, designed to enforce narrow conceptions of appropriate sexual behavior (especially as it pertained to black women), to monitor household "deservingness," and to ensure that clients were abiding by the government's Calvinist notions of frugality. The scenes in which Claudine's family prepares for and deals with the visits from the (white) welfare worker are especially good. They hide their iron, coffee pot, toaster, and small living room rug, for fear they will be cut off the rolls for wastefully spending "public" money, and Claudine gets asked directly whether she's been working and whether a man has been visiting, as a neighbor evidently reported (these are not the neighbors of *Street Scene,* who might come to the poor woman's defense). Later, there will be an unannounced visit when her new boyfriend, Rooper (James Earl Jones), is over, and she'll have to hide him, too. Her eldest son refers to the whole process as "sitting around beggin' when the welfare ladies come around."

This dynamic of neighbor-reporting-neighbor is another way in which such state surveillance has historically functioned—it is a way for one person to do battle with others, using the welfare office as their weapons. This is well known among welfare scholars, recipients, and some caseworkers, but it's a bit shocking to see find its way into film. The film is even self-aware enough to comment on common conceptions about black women and about women on welfare. When Rooper asks Claudine how, at age thirty-six, she could have six children, she snaps:

> Haven't you heard about us ignorant, black bitches, always got to be layin' up with some dude, just grindin' out them babies for the taxpayer to take care of?! I get thirty bucks apiece for them kids! Oh, I'm livin' like a queen on welfare, you know. . . . I get that shit all the time from the welfare, always asking me to apologize for my kids. I don't have to explain that to nobody. Now, you just pushed the wrong button.

When asked later whether she loves Rooper, she replies, "Love is when a man brings the groceries, instead of eating yours." It's an echo of the lament made by Johnnie Tillmon, a leader of the National Welfare Rights Organization, when she spoke of welfare as "like a super-sexist marriage. You trade in *a* man for *the* man" (Tillmon, 1972). Claudine even refers to herself as "married to the man, the welfare man," for what amounts to "starvation money." It's an impossible bind, as she observes to Rooper: if she doesn't care for her children, she'll be charged with child neglect; if she gets a job, she's cheating the system and breaking the rules; and if she stays at home, she's lazy. "You can't win," she says. "Mr. Welfare? That is the nosiest husband in the world. Mr. Welfare: I'd do anything to divorce that bastard."

Later, Rooper argues against moving in with Claudine and her kids for fear that he'd become subject to the intrusion of welfare—"looking up your asshole to see if you've got a dime hidden up there." Claudine says that she has to put up with it, why shouldn't he, to which he responds, "You have to put up with it. You're a woman. You had the kids."

FIGURE 5.9 "I didn't make the rules, Sir, I'm only doing my job!" *Claudine*, 20th Century Fox, 1974.

And that's the way the program has always worked (and still does)—some of which we can see in Frederick Wiseman's documentary look at a range of social service offices in New York City. David Denby says this of the people portrayed in *Welfare* (1975):

> They want money and shelter, but they also want something that they cannot articulate; dignity or sympathy, perhaps, but also a reasonable explanation of their "case." But this is precisely what the staff at the center—timid, self-obsessed, and obtuse, and themselves victims of the rigid and absurd rules of the welfare system—cannot possibly provide. (Denby in Lopate, 2008, p. 583)

Wiseman's film captures, as no other account does, how much of what happens in such offices is the frustrating, overwhelming, incomprehensible movement of people and paper, a Byzantine bureaucracy in which caseworkers are not necessarily any better at knowing how to get the system to function than clients or would-be clients. It does offer evidence in support of radical claims that the dysfunction of the system is, in its own way, functional. And while the myth is of the able-bodied men and women who are merely too lazy and dependent to work, Wiseman shows a welfare office overwhelmed with the old, disabled, sick, addicted, mentally ill, poorly educated and inarticulate, and otherwise fragile and vulnerable, uncomprehending and often incomprehensible. It's welcome to see on film the things that are common in such offices: people so frustrated that they hover constantly on the verge of tears; others angry but afraid to speak their minds lest they risk losing the money they need so badly; caseworkers more committed to procedure than well-being; and a dense, opaque bureaucracy that can appropriately be compared to something out of a Kafka tale, when it's not being gratuitously cruel and looking for small ways to express the petty powers it has available to it.

The way we treat relief recipients is why poor women, in film as in life, have gone to great lengths to escape the need for it or to hide its use. *Mannequin* (1937) gives us one extreme example. "Leaky faucets. Dirt. Smells. What a place to live! What a place for human beings to grow up in!" exclaims Jessie (Joan Crawford), an exhausted and frustrated clothing factory worker whose brother and father seem to vie for who can most effectively waste away her scant salary while she and her mother struggle to make it possible for them to eke by in their East Side tenement. "I'm gonna get out," she vows to her mother, "I've got to get out before it's too late!" And soon enough she marries her shady beau (Alan Curtis) to escape the tenement. Although she seems genuinely in love, she finds herself being wooed by a shipping magnate (Spencer Tracy). Rebuffing his advances at first, she later turns to him to borrow money to bail Eddie out of jail (he's there for unpaid gambling debts). Meanwhile, her family is preparing to apply for relief, and her mother mournfully urges her not to suffer her own awful fate. Jessie's scheming husband suggests they divorce so that she can marry the millionaire, and then take as much money as she can before, in turn, divorcing him. She leaves Eddie, appalled by the suggestion—or perhaps appalled that she's considering it—but soon enough falls in love with the millionaire and marries him. When he's rendered bankrupt by a strike, she stays with him, though broke, and vows to help him start fresh. There was nothing romantic about the poverty she first escaped, but there is to this poverty she finds herself in at the end. It's almost as if the film wants to construct a hierarchy of dependence.

In *The Candidate* (1972), Robert Redford plays Bill McKay, the son of a senator and a smart, hard-working Legal Aid lawyer who is seduced into running for his own Senate seat. The movie chronicles his steady slide from idealistic, radical reformer fighting for the environment and low-income people to practical, compromised, run-of-the mill candidate by the time he wins, a sad necessity in American campaigns, the film tells us. Here's what's relevant for us: his opponent, Sen. Crocker Jarman (Don Porter), says this in his stump speech: "I remember my mom and dad went through the 1930s without welfare, without poverty programs. Why, none of us kids even had a social worker!" he adds wryly. "How did we do it?" When McKay is asked how *he* feels about welfare, he replies, "We subsidize trains. We subsidize planes. Why not subsidize people?" He talks about health care, hunger, public transportation, birth control, problems in the ghetto, all of which, his advisors tell him as it starts to look as if he could win, are losing issues unless defanged and rendered in less threatening blandishments. There's no constituency for that, is the message, certainly not among the money men. The moral is that welfare is useful and sensible, but that defending it is political poison. It's a lesson politicians seem not to need, since it's rare to hear them come to its defense. *Claudine*, *Welfare*, and, perhaps, *The Candidate* show us a relatively radical vision of poor people and the programs that might help them, although it's an awfully small universe of films that even bother to turn their gaze in that direction. But, thinking of *Precious*, that image is too often all Welfare Queen when a larger audience tunes in.

6 TEACHERS TO THE RESCUE

Blackboard Jungle, To Sir with Love, A Piece of the Action, Up the Down Staircase, Conrack, Stand and Deliver, Lean on Me, The Principal, Dangerous Minds, Music of the Heart, Freedom Writers, Hardball, 187, The Blind Side, High School High, Half Nelson, Entre les Murs

There's another set of movies that embody a different kind of reform philosophy, one that harks back to the nineteenth-century child-saving project we've discussed. But in this case, the implication is that, if we can't remove children from the evil influence of the city, since there are no modern Orphan Trains—that we can't reform the city is almost always assumed—we'll have to change the children instead: make them stronger and smarter and surer and better able to resist the pernicious influences that surround them. We must *educate* them.

The Blackboard Jungle (1951) is the first of what will become a long line of films that hew to the following pattern: A noble young teacher arrives at a dysfunctional and dangerous inner city school naïve and optimistic, reluctant to believe the discrete, veiled warnings they've been given about what they're in for. They are soon shocked to discover the utter chaos of the school and the impossibility of any actual education given those conditions. But, stubborn, earnest, and determined, even in the face of physical violence and other setbacks, they persevere, winning over the children and giving them hope for a better life while, in the process, realizing or reaffirming their own commitment to teaching. It is the redemption of the teacher that is at the heart of the narrative.

Blackboard Jungle and its descendants have something in common with the Dead End Kids line of films, but the punishment vs. reformation divide here is between hardened, cynical teachers who think that the only approach is to maintain discipline and cultivate students' fear—or to simply surrender to them—while others, including new teacher Mr. Dadier (Glenn Ford), believe that they can be reached if one can only figure out how: The children are a

FIGURE 6.1 Students as caged animals. Notice the placement of the coke bottle on the right, and the implicit threat. *Blackboard Jungle*, MGM, 1955.

puzzle to be solved. He refuses to press charges against the students who brutalize him and another teacher in an alley in the belief that turning them over to the criminal justice system "will do more harm than good," just as Bogart in *Crime School* or Spencer Tracy's Father Flanagan might have said. But the kids here possess genuine menace, unlike those in most of the Dead End sagas and in the later teacher-to-the-rescue movies we'll turn to next. The students in *Blackboard Jungle* are capable of rape, physical violence, and a kind of cruelty that suggests the genuine sociopath. Christensen and Haas (2005, p. 118) report that the film was even "condemned as Communist propaganda because it presented a negative picture of the United States." And yet all that's required, as the genre will seem to dictate, is that the teacher find some clever teaching tool—a cartoon of Jack and the Beanstalk, in this case. Then, the students are inspired, a bond of trust is formed, and the process of real learning has begun; and once the worst troublemakers are removed from the class, the other students are revealed to want to learn after all.

These films echo some of the most pernicious myths of public education even today, evidenced in the 2010 documentary *Waiting for Superman*, which concludes that better teachers and stern principals can solve much of what supposedly ails U.S. education. It's a *leadership* problem. If we could only have more of them in the school systems (which means, conveniently, scrapping teachers' unions), everything else is possible. That's the idea at the heart of corporate-centrist education reform and movies about teaching "troubled" children alike. Good teaching is possible and it matters, make no mistake, but the problem with these films, like contemporary education reform, is that it focuses on what happens in the classroom at the expense of everything else, much of which matters more (see Dodson, 2009, Chap. 5, on the actual challenges of teaching poor children).

In *To Sir, with Love* (1967), a dozen years after he played one of the young toughs in *Blackboard Jungle,* Sidney Poitier returns to school, now on the other side of the desk. Although here the students are merely ill-mannered and disruptive rather than an actual threat (and they're British, rather than

American), it's the same story: Idealistic new teacher confronts a classroom filled with hopeless misfits from rough, poor, and working-class homes, but once the key moment of pedagogical insight is acquired—in this case, treating the East London students like adults, calling them Miss and Mister, and opening up classroom discussion to the topics that interest them most—they are won over, inspired, and transformed. In the end, the teacher, ready to give up and move on to a better school (*Blackboard Jungle*) or an engineering job (*To Sir*), concludes that he can make a difference in the classroom and decides to stick it out. And thus the protagonist finds meaning in his life through the poor kids he can remake. It is worth noting that, unlike many of its imitators to follow, we have here a black man (from British Guyana) teaching a mostly (but not entirely) white class. Poitier will play this role one final time in *A Piece of the Action* (1977), in which he and Bill Cosby portray thieves who are blackmailed into finding jobs for disaffected ghetto youth. They do, naturally, following essentially the same model as these other teacher-to-the-rescue films and, naturally again, decide at the end to remain and give over their lives to rescuing the young from crime, unemployment, and despair.

Up the Down Staircase (1967), released in the same year as *To Sir, with Love*, tells another version of what is essentially the same story, although the determined young teacher is white and female, the setting is New York instead of London, and the focus is as much on the mismanagement of the school and its embrace of rigid and pointless bureaucracy in lieu of education as it is on the undisciplined, troubled students. It captures this in the opening—crowded, chaotic hallways and offices, jostling and noise, while a school administrator yells, "ignore the bells, disregard all bells!" which seem to be going off indiscriminately, adding to the confusion. That it's Sandy Dennis (as Sylvia Barrett) the camera follows—perhaps American cinema's leading lady of anxiety and angst—only makes it that much more disorienting. The stultifying bureaucracy doesn't mean the school is well managed, of course, nor is it well funded. Barrett, an English teacher, has been provided with a form to requisition basketballs, but she can't get more than a single piece of chalk. It has more in common with Season 4 of *The Wire*, in this regard, than it does with many of the other films in this chapter. There's an obsession here with cataloguing each administrator's own peculiar fetishization of record-keeping, form-filling, and procedures—sometimes achieving a truly grim humor—which can reduce the System to a simplistic caricature. The soulless administrator will become a stock character in these movies (and in Frederick Wiseman's documentary, *High School*). What it hints of in the students' home lives is abuse or indifference, homelessness, late-night jobs, or petty crime.

While Sylvia works to rescue her charges, as the genre requires, it's done with a shade more subtlety and attention to character than we'll come to expect. And there's one stand-out scene. It's her walk down a nearby block with a fellow teacher, alongside the burned-out shells of buildings that typified the worst of the postwar Bronx. Her colleague points to the poverty and despair and says, "This is what we're up against." She notes that their students spend eighteen hours a day on those streets, while they only have them in school for six. "Eighteen to six," she observes, "almost insurmountable odds." But "notice that I said *almost*," she adds. "You can't give them up, because they've been given up by too many." This is still how many educators describe the difficulties facing schools in high poverty areas, and how difficult the task is: Eighteen to six.

Based on a memoir called *The Water Is Wide* (1972) by novelist Pat Conroy (who wrote *The Prince of Tides*), *Conrack* (1974) is unusual in some ways. It is a teacher-to-the rescue story set, not in the inner city, but on a small, isolated island off the coast of South Carolina, in the spring of 1969. It's a two-room schoolhouse, perched precariously on stilts, with a few dozen students, not a large, boisterous, unruly school with hundreds or thousands. Conroy, who is white (he's played by Jon Voight) has about twenty or so fifth- through eighth-graders, all of whom are black. They are quiet, well-behaved kids (the pathologies of the city have been abandoned), but they know almost nothing: Many can't count, recite the alphabet, or spell their own names; they can't name the country they live in or the nearby ocean; and they've never been off the island. But modest differences in setting aside, there are, alas, the usual tropes. The principal (Madge Sinclair) is an awful woman who berates and humiliates the students, calls them "babies" and "slow" and "lazy," and, as is often the case with such types, consistently makes one wonder why she embarked upon a career in education to begin with (although the sheer physical brutality she displays in the book has been considerably softened). There's another

FIGURE 6.2 *Up the Down Staircase*, Warner Brothers, 1967. "Just think of the odds. Eighteen to six."

thinly drawn villain in the guise of the cruel superintendent (Hume Cronyn). The film charts the journey of Conroy (the children can only pronounce it "Conrack," hence the title) as he struggles to find new, exciting, unorthodox ways to ignite their imaginations, so that they might finally fulfill their deep-buried potential. As the formula demands, the more they learn, the greater the principal and superintendent resent it, eventually getting the teacher fired. Conroy does, nonetheless, prevail, for the poor black children must be rescued by the decent white man, even if all he can do is awaken them and light the way forward. This is what an emancipatory message looks like when filtered through a colonial mind, but it's especially absurd here. To "turn around" the lives of young people living, as generations of their predecessors did, on a small, incestuous, isolated island without electricity or a steady connection to the world beyond might require more than merely the inspirational lessons of one man, it would seem to me. There is a self-awareness about this very dilemma on display throughout Conroy's memoir—"Only a thoroughbred do-gooder can appreciate the feeling, the roseate, swanlike, and nauseating glow that enveloped me.... I had found a place to absorb my wildest do-gooding tendency" (Conroy, 1972, p. 22)—but that self-awareness is mostly stripped from the film, making it look a lot like the rest when it could have been so much better.

In *Stand and Deliver* (1988), Edward James Olmos plays Jaime Escalante, hired to teach computer science to high school students in a low-income-neighborhood school that doesn't have computers. He winds up teaching math. Menaced by would-be toughs, who are one-dimensional, racist, Latino-gang stereotypes, he reaches out using his own special brand of tough love, and manages to overcome all the impediments erected by their home lives: dilapidated and overcrowded housing, threadbare budgets, full-time jobs, and caregiving responsibilities. The message once again is that poor students—even poor Latino or Hispanic students—only need an inspirational teacher, for they merely lack motivation. Once given that, the rest will follow.

As the opening crawl tells us, *Lean on Me* (1989) is a story of "the battle of one man, Joe Clark, to save East Side High School" in Paterson, New Jersey. *One man. Save.* It's a principal this time, instead of a teacher, although the opening scene shows him (played by Morgan Freeman) decades earlier as a teacher of mostly white, well-dressed students in the same school. Flash forward to 1987, where the wood-paneled halls are graffiti'd over, drugs and guns are sold openly, students fight and break windows while teachers stand helplessly by (and those who don't are beaten nearly to death), and to make sure we don't miss the point, Guns N' Roses' "Welcome to the Jungle" blares on the soundtrack. The students are now overwhelmingly black and Hispanic, and the scene is so chaotic that it suggests that the last vestiges of civilization are slipping away, if they're not already gone. Even with a black principal as the lead, it's a racist vision. When he addresses a group of parents angry that he's expelled the most disruptive students, he lectures them: "If you want to help us, fine. Sit down with your kids and make them study at night. Go get your families off welfare. Give our children some pride." It's what we'd today call a *respectability politics* vision of social problems (lack of middle-class values) and their solutions (moral uplift plus pulling up your damn pants). He's a petty despot, relying upon public humiliation and imperious proclamation. Instead of the usual model of these films, in which students must be inspired, somehow, for their reform to proceed, here the vision is turned upside down, at least at first. Students must be intimidated, belittled, hectored, and taught blind obedience to arbitrary rules (much as the principal thought in *Conrack*). The Guns N' Roses song was right—it is a *jungle*, and these are mere animals. After firing a talented music teacher for nothing more than daring to disagree with him, Clark seems to betray a disdain for the project of liberal education itself: "What good is Mozart going to do a bunch of children who can't go out and get a job?"

That said, there is at times here the kind of realization that *Up the Down Staircase* has about the real impediments to education, and to aid an especially promising student, Clark offers to help her mother find a job and a better place to live. He later suggests that they open up some of their remedial sessions to parents who may have reading difficulties, too. But the usual clichés do ultimately prevail, especially in a montage in which, teacher by teacher, classroom by classroom, we see students suddenly smiling and engaged and eager to learn while prepping for the standardized test that will save the school from a state takeover. Instead of one teacher finding the magic pedagogical tool, they all do.

Although *The Principal* (1987) comes off as a knockoff of *Lean on Me*, it was released some two years earlier. The formula is much the same: Principal restores order to out-of-control inner-city school by behaving like a bully, demonstrating that all that was needed was discipline. The problem with education is, we are meant to believe, the lack of a firm hand. But this film really has no pretentions, unlike most of the others discussed here—it's a gang movie, at best, with an especially ugly worldview: low-income neighborhoods of color are populated by dangerous men and slutty women, who have an utter disregard for the norms and behaviors of "civilized" society. They are "animals" and "trash," and must be treated as such—thrown away or broken down and trained.

Instead of "Welcome to the Jungle," *Dangerous Minds* (1995) opens with Coolio's "Gangster's Paradise," but over a graffiti-covered streetscape, with burnt-out, abandoned buildings, homeless people bedding down on the street, drug deals on the corners, and, finally, teenagers boarding a school bus that, as we get closer to school, slowly brings the screen from black-and-white to color. But once we get into the school, it's the usual—tough but ultimately misunderstood kids who need only someone to care and discover how to reach them. There will be some setbacks, including fights with a detached, officious bureaucracy, and a threat to quit, but the teacher (Michelle Pfeiffer this time) will prevail. As with *Blackboard Jungle*, there's one recalcitrant student, a leader of sorts, and when he's brought along, the rest follow. "I'll help you," he says snidely to Pfeiffer when she asks why he's so angry. "I come from a broken home and we're poor, okay? I see the same fucking movies you do, man." He goes on, much angrier: "How the fuck you gonna save me from my life, huh?" The self-awareness—of the student and of the film itself—is unusual. "Why don't you go find some other poor boys to save," she's later told by a parent who pulls her children out of school because she objects to them learning poetry. Also unusual for this genre is that the teacher's exertions extend beyond the classroom. She visits students at home to speak with them or their parents, and we get small glimpses of poor neighborhoods that are, to the film's credit, merely rundown and overcrowded, not some Hollywood vision of an otherworldly hellscape. It does, in truth, pay more attention to where the students come from and what they're up against than is typical, and is less facile and clumsy about it than we've come to expect. She fails here—on more than a few occasions: she fails a student who is pulled from class by his mother; she fails a pregnant girl who leaves school; and she fails the recalcitrant-leader student, who is shot and killed. She doesn't save him from his life after all.

Music of the Heart (1999) give us a music teacher this time, with little experience, desperate for work after a divorce, who finds herself in a poor, public school in East Harlem. The battle, as it often is, is with the bureaucracy as much as it is with the students, who are younger than is typically the case. But there is here also more self-awareness of the clichés than is typical, too. One black parent confronts Roberta (Meryl Streep) early on: "Look, I've seen this before. You white women come up here and think you can rescue our poor inner city children, who never asked to be rescued in the first place." Roberta responds, truthfully, that she didn't come to Harlem to rescue anyone, but that she was a single mother who needed a job. And she really isn't engaged in the White Man's Burden shtick that can anchor these movies. She loves music, she has experience (having taught her sons), and this is better than the department store job she had. Also unusual, the film is as much about the rest of her life—her boyfriend, her sons—as it is about the classroom and her students. When she buys a house in the neighborhood, it's rather matter-of-fact: I work in the neighborhood, she says, and I want to live here, too. There's no sense that she's saving anyone. Moreover, there are no dramatic transformations, no epiphanies, fewer of the usual tropes. And for the most part, the students are people, not abstractions. The "based on a true story" aspect of this may be part of the reason, continuing the pattern in which material about poor people and poor neighborhoods can sometimes be less contrived, with fewer forced dramatic turns, and boasts better-drawn characters when it's rooted in actual knowledge of the places and people being portrayed. But that's no guarantee—*Stand and Deliver* and *Lean on Me* were both based on memoirs, after all.

In *Freedom Writers* (2007), Erin (Hilary Swank) was going to go to law school until she found herself in front of the television watching the violent protests that occurred in Los Angeles in 1992 after a jury acquitted the police officers who mercilessly beat black motorist Rodney King. "I thought, God, by the time you're defending a kid in the courtroom, the battle's already lost. I think

Glenn Ford, Blackboard Jungle

Sidney Poitier, To Sir With Love

Sandy Dennis, UTDS

Jon Voight, Conrack

Edward J. Olmos, Stand and Deliver

Morgan Freeman, Lean on Me

Jim Belushi, The Principal

Michelle Pfeiffer, Dangerous Minds

Meryl Streep, Music of the Heart

Hilary Swank, Freedom Writers

Keanu Reeves, Hardball

Samuel Jackson, 187

Ryan Gosling, Half Nelson

Francois Begaudeau, The Class

FIGURE 6.3 Teachers to the rescue.

that the real fighting should happen here, in the classroom." She's even more naïve than most of the teachers in the genre, and the school's even worse, with students bussed in ninety minutes away from their gang-controlled, violence-soaked neighborhoods. These are the streets of *Boyz in the Hood* and *Menace II Society*. Almost all the students are black and brown, and she, there to save them, is a white girl from Newport Beach—wearing pearls, no less. A fight breaks out in class on her first day, and one student is ready to pull out a gun if the need arises.

There are dilapidated, dangerous schools, make no mistake, and no shortage of violence in low-income communities—although it has been on the decline for some time now, remember—but so many of these films seem to be communicating a message that kids from low-income neighborhoods are little better than animals, and driven by animal urges and instincts. They are in need of civilizing. And it is often (though not always) the white hero who will civilize them. The hero is always Kipling. The savages always need to be brought to Christ. These are, in that way, very old stories celebrating the need to tame the foreign, the other, the brown and the black. That the filmmakers seem to think they are engaged in a liberal project of opening minds makes it worse. That it reinforces generations of racist stereotypes makes it insidious.

That said, *Freedom Writers* is ostensibly told in part from the viewpoint of one of Erin's students, Eva, a gang member who is in school only because her probation officer insists upon it. Had her brother not been killed in a gang rivalry and her father sent to prison for retaliating for his murder, she might have grown up to be a very different kind of young woman—more like Erin herself, we are led to believe. There are some variations on the theme, but it still follows the well-trodden path: After much struggle with students and resistance from an assistant principal played by Imelda Staunton—who will, appropriately enough, play Delores Umbridge in the *Harry Potter* movies— Erin finds a way to engage the students and gain their trust, and part of how she does so, although clichéd in the usual kinds of ways, is a strength of the film. By playing a classroom game in which she seeks to show the students, divided by race and ethnicity (blacks against Latinos against Asians against whites), what they have in common, the film shows these gang members and thugs, not as perpetrators of violence, but as victims of it—almost everyone in the room lost at least one friend to violence, and half lost three or more. It's emotionally manipulative, but it does seem to be communicating an important message: What are the odds that these kids, given the very particular worlds they inhabit, could grow up to be much other than what they are? What are the odds that they will survive to adulthood and grow up at all? Like the eighteen-to-six scene in *Up the Down Staircase*, it's a moment of insight and shows a kind of empathy that, taken seriously, would negate the very premise of the film: that one teacher can make a difference, and that what's most missing from these children's lives is inspiration and motivation. This point is made even more clearly when she gets the students to begin keeping journals and we hear some of their stories. There's violence in their homes to match the violence on their streets, begging for change to put food on the table, juvenile hall and prisons, eviction and homelessness, trauma and anger and defenses erected to safeguard what's left.

"What're you doing in here that makes a goddam difference in my life?" asks one student, echoing the challenge in *Dangerous Minds*: "How the fuck you gonna save me from my life?" Toward the end, Erin observes: "When I'm help-ing these kids make sense of their lives, everything about my life makes sense to me." There is again the essence of the genre—the redemption of the white, middle- or upper-class protagonist by the poor, black, and brown students.

Although not set mainly inside a school, *Hardball* (2001) follows the pat-tern. To pay off gambling debts, Conor (Keanu Reeves) agrees to teach baseball to a group of Chicago kids from, as he puts it, "the shitty housing projects," where he'll be "coaching the crack babies," as a friend says. The kids use the word "bitch" a lot, can casually identify the make of a gun when they hear it fired nearby, and live in fear of gangs. The kids are, naturally, incompetent, undisciplined misfits on the field, but while we might expect that Reeves will teach them lessons about baseball that are, inevitably, also Life Lessons, and ones he needs to learn, too, he mostly just watches them play and takes them out for pizza when they win. Stuff happens, none of it matters, and there's not only no reason that this particular story needs to be set in the projects, it's not ultimately affected by that setting in any appreciable way, with the exception of the youngest and most self-consciously adorable team member being caught in the crossfire of a gun battle. But it's a death not earned. It's manipulative and not especially affecting, in the way of most of such cheap Hollywood sen-timentality. The poor ravaged children of the ghetto are the means by which this typical Hollywood offering tries to bestow seriousness upon itself—they are, as is so often the case, the means toward someone else's end, exploiting them under the guise of honoring them.

One Eight Seven (1997) offers the usual, with a twist or two, managing to set its story in both Los Angeles and New York, where so many of these films place their tales. Trevor Garfield (Samuel Jackson) is a Brooklyn teacher who, after having been stabbed by a student, moves to Los Angeles, where the students turn out to be no less menacing and no more interested in instruction in the physical sciences, though they are Latino rather than black. While all these films tend to feature the one student who must be won over to bring the rest along, in this case it becomes a much more brutal grudge match, as the student's violence escalates from destroying the classroom and lab to killing a dog Garfield is caring for. Garfield attacks and mutilates one of the students, and kills another, and the film looks on that with sympathy, as popular film often does with vigilante justice. After Garfield and his nemesis are both dead, another student explains Garfield's actions by observing, "You can push a good teacher too far." And a caption before the end credits notes: "One in nine teachers has been attacked in school. Ninety-five percent of those attacks were committed by students.... A teacher wrote this movie." The message would appear to be that, if attacked, teachers can and should kill, assault, and mutilate their students.

The Blind Side (2009) is a much more familiar and simpler kind of movie. The narrative tends to unfold in predictable fashion, but, economically enough for recessionary times, it offers not the usual classroom full of children to be saved, but just one. As I've complained at length, in most movies that seem to feature poor people of color, it's the redemption of the middle-class or well-to-do white protagonist that really sits at the heart of the narrative. The means to that end is an African American teenager named Michael in this version, and he's more or less a football-playing cipher: Large, passive, quiet, protective, he's a force to be acted upon, not to act. *The Blind Side's* particular take on this tale is no better but probably no worse than most of the others, even if it is based on real events. Sandra Bullock has her charms, and country singer Tim McGraw turns in a creditable performance as the hapless, supportive husband. Through him, we are further meant to admire the determination of privileged Bullock to do the right thing, even when her rich friends raise their professionally plucked eyebrows over her latest do-gooder crusade (that is, the remaking of Michael). But they love her for it, with a little shrug and a hint of affectionate eye-rolling. Noblesse oblige lives gallantly on, in soft Southern accents and smart outfits.

High School High (1996) tries to make a joke of these conventions, as some of the most exploitive films about homelessness will. The neighborhood is so poor that it has not only 99¢ stores but 25¢ and 5¢ stores, too. There are literally explosions in the burned-out, graffiti'd school building (named Marion Barry High). There are reserved parking spots for S.W.A.T and the National Guard, the classroom has holes in the floor and walls, teachers wear bulletproof vests, and there's a malt liquor machine instead of a soda machine. Instead of just being merely disruptive and unruly on their first day, the students start a fire. But none of it is pushed far enough, and there's no cleverness or real satire here—it's a stream of lazy jokes common to parodies that have come after *Airplane!,* the original of the genre. There's a *Mad TV* skit from 2007 (Season 12, Episode #1215)—called *Nice White Lady*—that offers a much more pointed and funny commentary.

Half Nelson (2006) pushes against the conventions. It's not set in high school (joining *Music of the Heart* and *Conrack*), but the eighth grade. The teacher doesn't stay up late at night grading papers or making lesson plans, but going to bars, clubs, and his drug dealer. He teaches history rather than English. The students aren't dramatically violent or despairing or, well, dramatically much of anything—they're a normal classroom full of public school students, some asleep, some eager and engaged, most just ordinary. They are decent kids of varying abilities. He coaches girls' basketball, but doesn't use the game to impart Important Life Lessons. They just play basketball. A student discovers him smoking crack in a bathroom, and they develop a friendship. There is no grand narrative, no dramatic events that change everything: Just a handful of lives, closely observed. And if there's anyone who needs saving, it's the teacher, not the students.

And, once again, I'll turn to a foreign film as a way to highlight what's possible. To call *Entre les Murs/The Class* (2008) "social realism" is to do it an injustice, because that would suggest that it's didactic and somber. Instead, it's a wondrous glimpse into the day-to-day interactions in a classroom. Part of why it feels so real and so fully realized, as we learn from Brigitte Tijou's "making of" documentary (*Une Année Entre les Murs*) is that it emerges from a series of improvisations with actual students, and an actor, played by François Bégaudeau, who is himself a former teacher and who wrote the novel that serves as the inspiration for the film. It's a different kind of project, to be sure, but it puts its American cousins to shame—it doesn't use the students as objects but as full subjects, and, as someone who's taught for many years now (although never the thirteen- to fifteen-year-old students portrayed here), it's as real a depiction of what actually goes on in the classroom as I've ever seen on film. And yet it's powerful and dramatic and entrancing and charming all at once. All of what I have identified as the typical tropes of the Hollywood version of this film are absent: There are no heroes, no villains, no sudden transformations or epiphanies, no notion that all that's required is discovering the magic key to unlocking hungry minds, no cartoon bureaucracy to battle against. It's a multi-racial and multi-ethnic classroom, with more than a few students who are first-generation immigrants (from Africa, the Caribbean, and China, at least), but they are not marked out as *poor* or *ghetto* children in the way they are in the American versions. Poor children of color in the American versions are poor and of color first—these are the things about them that matter. *Entre les Murs* shows us the much more interesting possibilities available by treating them as children engaged in trying to make sense of the world and their own lives, rather than vehicles for their instructor's growth.

7 THE ARCHITECTURE OF POVERTY

One Third of a Nation, The Landlord, The Super, A Tree Grows in Brooklyn, The Fight for Life, Angela's Ashes, In America, Candyman, The Architect, Little Shop of Horrors, Hoop Dreams, Finding Forester, Public Housing, The Corner, The Pruitt-Igoe Myth, Complex, Women of Brewster Place

One Third of a Nation (1939) opens in the shadow of the Brooklyn Bridge with children playing on a crowded street; later, they are swimming in the river. It could be a block away from where *Dead End* is set, and it even has a cop shaking his nightstick at a group of boys playing in the spray from an open fire hydrant and calling them "hoodlums." It takes a grimmer and more gruesomely earnest turn than we find in the films about ghettos and gangs, when a fatal fire in a dilapidated tenement brings together a young salesgirl, Mary, whose father is on relief, and Peter, her handsome absentee landlord, who rescues her brother and volunteers to pay his medical bills before he realizes that it's his own building.

The film becomes an indictment of the substandard construction and lax maintenance of the tenements, in which shoddy buildings "go up like matchsticks," plumbing rarely works, stairways and floors have gaping, treacherous holes, trash accumulates in the basements, "roaches and bedbugs and fleas!" abound, and the fire escapes are all but useless. The whole building has "the poverty smell," Peter's spoiled sister would say. But these residents are not alone: Peter owns many, many such buildings, as do others of his kind elsewhere: "You turn any city in this country upside down like a rock, and you'll find us underneath: the poor, like grubs," says one resident. This is a story about institutions, about structures—physical structures and social structures alike—rather than behaviors, and that's a large part of what binds together the films in this chapter. While movies are typically set in a particular place, that location and its geography are not necessarily central to the narrative; but given that there is a significant

FIGURES 7.1 AND 7.2 A poor woman, just hit and thrown to the floor by her abusive husband, is caught in a tenement fire (*above*) and bodies of the dead lined up on the sidewalk (*below*). *One Third of a Nation,* Dudley Murphy Productions, 1939.

body of evidence that shows how the concentration of poverty, the isolation of poor communities from the rest of the city, and the physical state of those neighborhoods matter (Kneebone, 2014), we should note the films that betray a similar kinds of awareness about the settings of their stories and of the particular ways in which place matters.

Thus, *One Third of a Nation* can tell us something about the politics of poor places, given that the grim state of housing there is possible because, as it notes explicitly, regulations and laws were written to exempt older buildings, "the very buildings that need it most!" in the words of one shocked investigator. Worse, the understaffed and underfunded Tenement Buildings Department would need three years to inspect the buildings under its jurisdiction just one time each. Heavy-handed though it can be, the film serves as a reminder that some forty years after Jacob Riis helped draw attention to the living conditions on the Lower East Side of New York, conditions in the slums were still dangerous and deadly.

But the movie nonetheless works hard to absolve landlord Peter of responsibility for the fire, going so far as to have the apartment building itself become a character that speaks in voiceover, boasting of having killed thousands of its poor inhabitants over the years with cholera, fire, and more. It's as if *The Shining*'s Overlook Hotel had a speaking part. And yet the film still offers an extended disquisition against inherited wealth, and Peter not only assumes responsibility for his tenements, but goes further by vowing to sell

FIGURE 7.3 The tenement taunts the boy it crippled. *One Third of a Nation*, Dudley Murphy Productions, 1939.

FIGURES 7.4 AND 7.5 Tearing down the tenements (*left*) and the vision of what's to replace them (*right*). *One Third of a Nation,* Dudley Murphy Productions, 1939.

his properties to the city in exchange for a handful of bonds and a commitment to build affordable housing in its place, against the increasingly strenuous objections of his family, who at first succeed in putting a stop to the plan.

But when Mary's now-crippled brother tries to burn the place to the ground and dies in the process—he was spurred on by continuing delusions, if that's what they are, of the apartment building speaking to him and taunting him with its victims—Peter vows to redouble his efforts, and in the end we see bulldozers "ripping these old rat-boxes right to the ground," followed quickly with a scene of brand-new flats with a courtyard, trees, a playground, and a nearby public pool and park. Urban renewal wins out, and little Joey did not die in vain. Moreover, once again, the rich (white) man is the hero, and his determination to do good saves an entire block of poor and working-class families and, in the process, gives his own life new meaning and provides him with the useful occupation he's always wanted but never been able to have for fear that his family would disapprove. The ghetto has taught him to be his own man.

But the ugly irony is that what the film shows as a hopeful coda was, in actuality, the beginnings of slum clearance—the destruction of low-income neighborhoods and the often thriving, vibrant, social and economic networks within them to make way for an auto-friendly urban infrastructure—think Robert Moses and the steam-rolling of the Bronx—and for the modern high-rise housing projects whose failure and ultimate destruction we'll see in other films.

Peter's narrative brings to mind two later movie landlords. In Hal Ashby's first film, *The Landlord* (1970), a spoiled, rich, white man (Beau Bridges) buys a tenement building in the then-poor neighborhood of Park Slope in Brooklyn to convert it into a bachelor pad. Most of the tenants are well behind on their rent, and all are black. His mother (Lee Grant) derides this as his "poverty program." He begins to repair the building, essentially taking over as its super, while hoping to find a way to evict them all and take over the building. That goal is abandoned as he finds new friends and lovers among the residents. It's smart and ambitious and doesn't pathologize the residents, even if it's not much interested in describing or explaining their circumstances. By contrast, *The Super* (1991) is glib and shallow. Here, too, a rich man (Joe Pesci) moves into his own rundown Brooklyn tenement, only this time it's as a court-mandated punishment for housing code violations. Because it's black and poor, the film also feels it necessary to make the neighborhood loud and dangerous. There's no sign this landlord feels much of anything but contempt for the residents, whom he mocks as "assholes stuck in a shithole." He's an irredeemable monster of a kind, and yet he completes the repairs, gets the girl, and is hailed as a hero. What both movies have in common is that, at the end, the selfish, ignorant, rich, white men are redeemed. And it sometimes seems that there is no character so vile, if he is white and wealthy, that he cannot be transformed and held up as an example to the audience. This is perhaps part of how white supremacy is maintained.

Pare Lorentz's slow and didactic *The Fight for Life* (1940) offers long, lingering shots of grim, teetering, Chicago houses in the slums, displaying what can feel like a voyeuristic, even prurient gaze. The film is notable for the location alone, however, given that the only other time we see this place—where Saul Alinsky did much of his organizing work—is in *Call Northside 777* (1948), which has a few short shots of the Back of the Yards neighborhood. But Lorentz's film has its own awareness of where the residents come from, pointing out efforts to lure workers to the city without any attendant efforts to ensure that they would have safe, clean, affordable housing as well. That so many in poor neighborhoods are sick is no wonder, Lorentz observes, while tracking the efforts of obstetricians struggling to improve the health of poor women and their newborn children, an effort that can seem hopeless. It harks back to Progressive fears of the dangers of the city itself—it's a dirty, crowded, breeding ground for disease and despair.

A Tree Grows in Brooklyn (1945) brings us to tenements in pre–Depression era Brooklyn. We witness the daily grind of the Nolans, who are struggling to get by and managing only by watching every penny (despite spending fearful sums for burial insurance, as many did), and their struggle is complicated by the fact that Johnny, the father, works irregularly at best and is an alcoholic. He eventually dies of pneumonia, making his family better off, arguably, freeing his wife to marry the police officer who has become enamored with her. Some of the darker elements of Betty Smith's (1943) novel have been pushed aside—in a screenplay co-written by Tess Slesinger, who wrote *The Bride Wore Red* (see Chapter 15)—but it remains a closely observed tale of life on the margins and the women who are the center of the household and of the household economy. Manny Farber (in Polito, 2009) was right when he observed, "It is one of those rare Hollywood films which earnestly endeavors to show the drabness and unhappiness in an American family and in a section of American society." For example, it offers a rare instance in which the impending birth of a child is not a cause for celebration but, as it often is in the real world, a tragedy that will drive the family even deeper into penury. Farber is also on to something when he complains that

> the most destructive element in the film is its photography, which blankets the poverty in lovely shadows and pearly sentimentality.... Its material is mostly confined to showing how the life of poor people is dominated by the scrabble for money, and only in a scene of childbirth is there any real terror or hardness in the faces and gestures, any drabness in the photography and any complexity of thought and feeling (pp. 224–226).

Angela's Ashes (1999) gives us another view of Depression-era Brooklyn, albeit a brief one. The film begins there in 1935, but after the first death of a child—two more will follow—the poor family moves back to Ireland, winding up in a Limerick ghetto that seems almost medieval. There are dark, wet stones and narrow, rutted streets of mud and water and human waste. The children are hungry and always filthy. Everything is gray and as bleak as the blue-black stones. The tenements of Brooklyn seem modern by comparison, dirty and cramped and fetid though they, too, were. Here, the family abandons the ground floor of their small stone hut for months at a time because it's flooded. The father can't find work (it is a Depression there too, of course, and he's drunk whenever he can be), but he's too proud to beg, so the begging is left to the mother, who lines up to plead for furniture, clothes, and food from the haughty, scolding relief agents. We see their disdain for the women who seek help, and see how the women are forced to supplicate in a way that is both true to how such charity can function and rare to find on film—perhaps accounted for by the fact that the film is set almost entirely in Ireland, has a British director, and hews so close to the source material, Frank McCourt's memoir. No film of 1930s America, *Grapes of Wrath* included, is so grim and dire, yet *Angela's Ashes* has no facile moralizing, contrived plot devices, cheap sentimentality, or romanticizing of poverty. There's a lesson here in just how little most filmmakers comprehend what a life in poverty actually looks and feels like. Instead, we get cartoons, or copies of copies—faded ideas drawn from other faded, clichéd stories. McDonald (1969, p. 142) captured this well:

"One mark of a bad movie or play is that the characters exist only as functions of the plot, which means that they have lots of Big Moments, but no small ones. Real people, however, exist all the time.... Their small moments, or everyday life, count as much as the big ones and perhaps more, since there are many more of them."

Joe Queenan (2009, p. 45), in a memoir about growing up poor, reacts even more strongly:

> No afterglow accompanies these experiences. Nothing good ever came out of living in that [housing] project. One might argue that the degrading experience of poverty taught me to be ambitious and self-sufficient, but it would be more accurate to say that it taught me to be ruthless and cruel, indifferent to other people's feelings, particularly if I was writing about them. I never had any warm memories of the project; it gave me nothing, taught me nothing. The rich old men who run Hollywood have long been smitten with the romance of indigence, zealously manufacturing life-affirming cultural pornography that appeals to middle-class people who quite fancy the poor but only in an innocuous celluloid incarnation. Up close and personal, the poor are less appealing: They wear bad clothes and use bad language and do bad things, and have guns. They make excellent fodder for films but even better fodder for cannons. They are fascinating when seen from a distance, less fascinating when they move in next door. They make unsatisfactory dining companions; they are too busy being desperate to be idiosyncratic or clever.

By contrast, *In America* (2002) is about an Irish family that emigrates illegally and finds themselves in the kind of apartment building that only exists in movies. It's a dilapidated, once majestic, nineteenth-century relic with wide staircases leading to high-ceilinged, thin-walled apartments, peeling paint, broken windows, erratic water, and a too-colorful cast of characters as neighbors. It's exotic and romantic and *grand*. *Kill the Poor* (2006), in which a young man and his pregnant wife move into a Lower East Side squat *cum* co-op, offers a similarly contrived kind of environment, filled with a carefully constructed assortment of character types. That film wants to be about gentrification and class, but we don't see or even hear about any poor people who are pushed out of the neighborhood—indeed, we don't really see much of the neighborhood or any of the people who should be in it. It's an empty landscape, but it doesn't feel intentionally empty. *In America* misses its putative target in a similar way: Poverty here is trying, but never too trying, making its

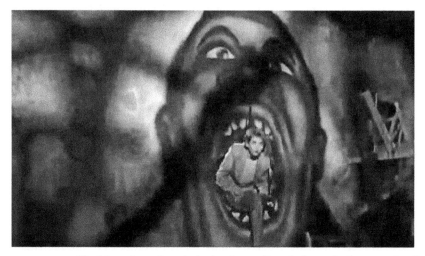

FIGURE 7.6 Climbing through a hole in the wall and through the mouth of *Candyman*, Propaganda Pictures, 1992.

appearance when needed for the story but otherwise forgotten. It is an especially unconvincing portrayal when compared with the relentless, real poverty of something like *Angela's Ashes*.

Candyman (1992) is a common horror tale in some ways—call his name five times in a mirror and Candyman (Tony Todd), with a hook for a hand and an unquenchable blood lust, appears and slaughters. But there's something deeper at work. Helen (Virginia Madsen) is a graduate student researching urban legends, "the un-self-conscious reflection of the fears of urban society," her husband (Xander Berkeley), a University of Illinois professor, calls them. She hears that Candyman now inhabits the public housing projects of Cabrini-Green, and will come to learn that the monster was a former slave who was tortured, killed, and set afire for falling in love with a white man's daughter, his ashes spread over what would become the projects. They are thus literally built upon the graves of slaves. While researching the case, Helen discovers that her own apartment building was intended to be public housing, too, but when they realized that "there were no highways or El train to keep the ghetto cut off" from the Gold Coast, as there were with other sites, they sold it off as condominiums. That's a pretty sophisticated urban-geography critique of the ghetto for a mainstream film. And yet, as she and her classmate (Kasi Lemmons) head to Cabrini-Green to interview its residents, they are terrified, carrying mace and a Taser, and there are, indeed, menacing drug dealers who try to prevent them from entering the building, and only leave them alone because they think the students are cops. They meet a young

FIGURES 7.7 AND 7.8 *Candyman*, Propaganda Pictures, 1992, emphasizing the isolation of the projects from the city proper *(left)*; and *The Architect*, Magnolia Pictures, 2006, showing us their otherworldly, inhuman scale.

woman who is suspicious, even more so when she learns that they are doing a study: "What'chu gonna' study? That we bad? Hmm? We steal? We gangbang? We all on drugs, right? We ain't all like them assholes downstairs, you know?" The film ultimately lends some credence to the idea that radical critiques can best find their way into mainstream cinema when hidden within genre films no one expects to have deeper meaning—this is what scholars have said about the relationship between film noir and the Cold War.

While *Candyman* focuses its attention on the intentional isolation of public housing from the rest of the city, *The Architect* (2006) is more concerned with how its own construction and design injure its residents and isolate them from each other. *The Architect* offers two settings: one is a housing project on Chicago's South Side, where Tonya (Viola Davis) is

FIGURE 7.8A Arguing about the gulf between the Architect's vision for public housing and the reality of it. *The Architect*, Magnolia Pictures, 2006.

an organizer fighting to have her complex torn down and rebuilt. As she explains early on, the very architecture of the buildings make them dangerous, unwelcoming, depressing, and unhealthy: They are susceptible to gangs, allowing them to easily control the exits, entrances, and elevators; the absence of bathrooms on the ground floor makes for more public urination; they lack air and light; and areas intended for grass collect water and turn to muddy fields.

The other setting is a home in the well-to-do Chicago suburbs, where the original architect of Tonya's complex (Anthony LaPaglia) lives with his unhappy wife (Isabella Rosellini), alienated son, and conflicted daughter. That these two worlds will meet is obvious, and how they do is predictable in many respects, but there are ways in which this is more sophisticated and thoughtful than typical Hollywood fare, in part because of the (sometimes heavy-handed) way in which physical aspects of the built environment are used as metaphors throughout, as with *Candyman*. The film alters the David Greig play upon which it is based (Grieg, 1996) in a number of ways, shifting the location from a Glasgow council flat to Chicago public housing, and elevating the secondary character of the public-housing advocate into a central one, thus taking what is merely a metaphor for failure in the play and turning it into a more immediate meditation on how spaces used by actual people may not comport with their designers' visions, how an aesthetic that thinks about how buildings will look from above utterly fails to accommodate the need for them on the ground, and how ignorance of people's lives results in efforts to help that may not, in fact, be helpful. The connection between these films goes back even to the Grieg play and the Clive Barker short story *Candyman* is based on (Barker, 1987). Grieg's "Playwright's Note" cites as inspiration for the play urban legends about architects of public housing projects being so distraught at what had become of their grand visions that they killed themselves in despair; such stories circulated, he thought, because residents wanted them to be true, "they wanted punishment. Communities seemed to be taking collective psychic revenge on the designers of the environment." Barker, similarly, opens his story this way:

> No doubt the estate and its two companion developments had once been an architect's dream. No doubt the city-planners had wept with pleasure at a design which housed three hundred and thirty-six persons per hectare, and still boasted space for a children's playground. Doubtless fortunes and reputations had been built upon Spector Street, and at its opening fine words had been spoken of its being a yardstick by which all future developments would be measured. But

FIGURES 7.9 AND 7.10 Public housing as enclosure, *The Architect,* Magnolia Pictures, 2006 (*left*); and *Little Shop of Horrors* (*right*), Warner Brothers, 1986.

the planners—tears wept, words spoken—had left the estate to its own devices; the architects occupied restored Georgian houses at the other end of the city, and probably never set foot here.

In some ways, the villain is the same one in *One Third of a Nation*: poorly designed and badly maintained housing that *created* communities of concentrated poverty and trapped people within them. They show us what ill-conceived policy looks like in its physical form.

From the beginning of *Little Shop of Horrors* (1986), the setting matters, even if Skid Row is little more than a place to escape from. When admonished to stop loitering on the street and to "better yourselves," the young women respond: "Better ourselves? Better ourselves?! Mister, when you're from skid row, ain't no such thing." It's hopeless, which an entire song ("Skid Row") and production number proceed to emphasize.

FIGURE 7.11 Even the choreography emphasizes the isolation and despair of Skid Row. *Little Shop of Horrors.* Warner Brothers, 1986.

This opening number also recognizes something else about the geography of poverty: that the people who live there don't work there, but uptown. This is where they come home to, because it's all that they can afford, no matter how hard they work:

Uptown you cater to a million jerks

The jobs are really menial, you make no bread

And then at five o'clock, you head Downtown.

Later, Audrey, who's in an abusive relationship (and regularly appears with bruises and black eyes), dreams of leaving skid row to go "Somewhere That's Green." Here, too, we see the dangerous city contrasted with the wholesome lands outside it, although here it's the suburbs rather than nature.

Hoop Dreams (1994) is a documentary set in the actual Cabrini-Green public housing projects on the north side of Chicago, which have since been destroyed, the same place *Candyman* and *The Architect* are meant to takes place, and it, too, is a story of the ways in which geography is, with very rare exception, destiny. William Gates (age fourteen when the film begins) and Arthur Agee (also fourteen) are two young black men who see basketball as their only way out of that ghetto and as a way toward something more than mere escape—it's a path toward a mythical, wondrous life. They are recruited to play for St. Joseph's High School, where William thrives academically but Arthur struggles, in part because Arthur's life is complicated by the fact that his family is paying half his tuition (William got grants to cover the whole amount), a burden they cannot meet. Arthur has to drop out in the middle of the school year, which puts him behind. By junior year, William is being recruited by colleges across the country, until a knee injury sidelines him, and his grades begin to drop, too. Arthur, back at his local public high school, has made the varsity team (a losing one for most of the film), while his family's financial position is even more precarious after his father goes off for a stint in prison and an injury pushes his mother out of work onto the disability rolls and then welfare, where the strict enforcement of arbitrary rules causes them to go months at a time without electricity and gas. A pretty familiar story, as these things go: disability, physical illness, and mental illness are prevalent in poor households—they are both a cause of poverty and a consequence of it—and the incarceration of one individual can drive their whole family further into poverty (American Psychological Association, 2000). All of those factors hinder children's ability to get to college in the first place and then to thrive once there.

There's much that's powerful here, but perhaps nothing more than Arthur's mother, preparing a cake for his eighteenth-birthday celebration, pointing out what an important milestone it is: "Another thing to be proud about [is that] it's his eighteenth birthday," she beams. "He lived. To get to see eighteen, that's good!" She says this in the same tones others use when talking about what an achievement it is to reach eighty or ninety or 100. One recent study found that people in Chicago households with annual income below $25,000 lived fourteen years less than those in households with incomes over $53,000 (Joint Center for Political and Economic Studies, 2012). Other research found life expectancy of black men in another poor neighborhood in the 1990s, Harlem, to be lower than for men in Bangladesh (Sen, 1999). Shortly after the birthday party scene, Arthur's mother, explaining that now that Arthur is eighteen her welfare check will be reduced to $286, asks whether people don't wonder just how it is that she cares for a family on that meager amount—and indeed, this is the kind of question that was almost ignored by scholars until Edin and Lein (1997) documented just how it is that household get by on such stingy benefits and erratic income.

Finding Forrester (2000) introduces us to Jamal Wallace (Rob Brown). He's sixteen, lives in public housing in the Bronx, plays basketball, hangs with his friends, reads voraciously, and writes. Jamal's friends are good, funny kids who just don't care much about school. Just like the young men in Hoop Dreams, he's recruited by a tony Manhattan preparatory school, at least as much for his basket-ball ability as his test scores, and is treated poorly by some students and teachers who feel his presence is unearned. Meanwhile, Jamal befriends a reclusive nov-elist (Sean Connery), who helps him with his writing and, ultimately, defends him when falsely accused of plagiarism by a teacher (F. Murray Abraham) who cannot believe that a black basketball player from public housing in the Bronx is capable of such exceptional work. The director is Gus Van Sant, and it's hard not to feel the echoes of the more sure-footed Good Will Hunting here. Still, there's no prurient gaze cast upon the poor neighborhood, and it upends a few of the usual tropes: William Forrester, the novelist and ersatz teacher, doesn't try to save young Jamal so much as Jamal tries to save Forrester, prodding him to end his reclusive life and, finally, write a new novel. Most important, the projects are not some hellscape, or some deep tragedy, or the grimmest of social facts, or the embodiment of social decline or familial dysfunction—it's just a place where some of these characters live. It's not, to be sure, the Upper East Side, where the prep school sits, but it's not some other world, either. It's nice to see so many ordinary people living in poor neighborhoods.

Frederick Wiseman's documentary Public Housing (1997) also offers us ordinary people in very poor places. Like Welfare, it takes its camera—without voiceover, without interviews, without the apparatus of most documentaries—and observes, at great length. Here, it's the Ida B. Wells housing complex in

Chicago. The film opens with something we see in *The Architect*, and rarely otherwise—a resident activist and tenant advocate, here fighting with the city to get empty apartments inhabitable and to find a home for a young, pregnant girl. Later, we see a meeting of Men of Wells, another community service and advocacy group, then a residents' meeting with city and union leaders, and meetings with family preservation advocates. There's nothing unusual about these organizations or these kind of struggles by residents to make their homes and neighborhoods better—they are an ordinary part of life in many public housing projects. What's unusual is to see this kind of activity on film, even in documentaries.

Although the canvas of *Public Housing* is broader than in *Welfare*, one theme it has in common with the latter is the arbitrary use of power. In the first ten minutes, we see police harassing a young woman for loitering—that is, being idle in a public space—and then delivering a lengthy, pompous, condescending lecture about how she should live her life. Such scenes reoccur. These are common crimes in poor neighborhoods, but essentially unheard of in other places. We also see the ways in which fears, rational and irrational both, structure neighborhood institutions—a small store in which everything is behind bulletproof glass, and customers have to point to or call out the items they want.

What we also witness is the ordinariness of life in the projects—talking with the exterminator about strategies for keeping rats and roaches away; hanging out at the grill; kids playing ball and riding their bikes; community yard sales; repairing and washing cars; playing cards and talking good-natured trash; fighting addiction and alcohol, some succeeding, others failing; the old and sick struggling especially hard; people complaining about their jobs, or the lack of jobs; the daily work and chat of the barber shops and beauty salons; kids in school; women in a sewing club; a community garden; cops and residents working together to improve safety; a client being interviewed at length by an addiction counselor about his income, work history, and his drug and alcohol use; a workshop with women on welfare; and another on birth control and sexually transmitted disease (STD) prevention. What Wiseman's camera shows us is the many people in the projects working actively to improve their living conditions, their own lives, the lives of their neighbors, and the life prospects of their children. And it is this ultimate banality that makes this a radical portrait of the ghetto. It's not a foreign land, not inhabited by a race of aliens, and not exotic. It's desperately ordinary, and often even dull.

The Pruitt-Igoe Myth (2011), another documentary about public housing, seeks to answer an ostensibly simple question: What went wrong?

Pruitt-Igoe, like many projects of the 1950s and beyond, was meant to solve the problem of urban poverty and substandard housing, but by the early 1970s, it was deemed a failure and torn down, as many others would be in subsequent years. This is a film about larger issues of policy rather than the small-bore observations of *Public Housing*. It quickly reviews the usual explanations, some of which we've seen offered in other films, fiction and documentary alike: The architecture itself, many have argued, was in large part to blame, the argument at the core of *The Architect*; the welfare state was to blame, others have said, breeding dependency and fostering the dysfunctional families and communities that overwhelmed Pruitt-Igoe; or, still others posit, the rural residents were unprepared for urban living, and that it was thus a failure of education and integration. Instead, director Chad Freidrichs focuses our attention on the political economy of post–World War II America, highlighting the ways in which cities first funneled migrants into downtown slums, then, when it wanted to reclaim those spaces, cleared the slums and pushed residents further out of the cities via public housing, simultaneously creating segregated communities of owners, too, with the help of city planners and the federal government under the auspices of the Federal Housing Administration. The projects, fresh and gleaming when new, weren't maintained because there was no federal funding for maintenance once construction was complete, and they quickly began to deteriorate, as any large apartment complex with tens of thousands of residents would without steady upkeep. The exodus of working-class and middle-income families from the city meant fewer local taxes dollars were available to provide services to those in need.

Meanwhile, the badly designed rules of the ADC/AFDC cash welfare program, which forbade two-parent households, broke apart families—or forced them to lie and deceive, as we saw in *Claudine*—while employment discrimination made matters still worse, even on the occasions when jobs were available within the city. And as the resident population became poorer and the city's tax base declined, rents were raised again and again to try to cover costs, further impoverishing the tenants. Crime flourished among young kids with few options and little to fear. It's a lot of moving pieces for a documentary, but it manages them exceptionally well, and highlights just how unusual it is to see this micro-macro dual focus anywhere beyond academic analysis. It's got many of the same concerns as *Candyman* and *The Architect*, but it provides an even more critical view, one that helps us make sense of what we see in *Public Housing*.

The Corner (2000) also gives us real, three-dimensional people inhabiting confined, concentrated areas of poverty. Based on the book by David

Simon, who would become creator of *The Wire,* and Edward Burns, it's set in the same Baltimore, although *The Corner* is much more narrowly focused geographically—it's a small group of drug dealers and users and their families and friends and foes. This is a six-hour HBO miniseries, so, like *The Wire,* it might be better thought of as a TV serial rather than a film, and thus, perhaps, ought to be excluded from my analysis; but a few words in passing seem in order.

The world of *The Corner* is a grim one. Gary (T. K. Carter) is a heroin addict who spends most of the day looking for his next hit. He's fallen far, having once had a range of decent jobs, and some very good ones, too, until he became addicted to crack cocaine. He forages for scrap metal to sell (as do the children of *A Tree Grows in Brooklyn* and *Chop Shop*), going as far as to taking working pipes from occupied buildings, and even stealing refrigerators out of people's apartments, for which he periodically serves some time. His fifteen-year-old son DeAndre (Sean Nelson), smart, charming, funny, and handsome, deals drugs on the corner (but doesn't use them himself—not at first), for which he gets put out of the house and goes to jail. DeAndre's mother, Fran (Khandi Alexander), tries to keep him off the corners, although she's pretty beat down and used up, and an addict herself. Her efforts to find a space in rehab feel a bit like the challenges that Tupac Shakur faces in *Gridlock'd*—those moments when she's brave enough or fed up enough to seek treatment are not the moments when treatment is available (we will see this a bit in *MacArthur Park,* too). She does get clean, for a while. DeAndre tries to get right, as well: He gets off the corners, goes back to school, gets a "real" job, and tries to be a father to his child, but that, too, is difficult, and ultimately fleeting. Why? Why is it so hard to get clean, or to go legit? There are no easy answers here, but one problem DeAndre and Fran both face, as do all addicts, is how to become new people while remaining in their old world, surrounded by the old influences and pressures; and then overcome the very real physiological urges that propel and sustain any addiction.

It's a story about climbing up out of the ghetto, against all odds, and then slipping back in, with drugs being the key protagonist along with the Corner itself, hovering as a physical presence, the source of all hope and all despair. In one of the mock interviews that frame the episodes, a cop who's been around a while responds to a question about why the corner kids think the younger cops are more brutal than the older ones. The cop suspects it's because he saw what the neighborhood once was, and is able to see the residents as more than criminals and dope fiends. He knows about the ones who work, the ones who are struggling to improve the neighborhood, who are trying to provide better options for kids. It's not an insight we're accustomed to seeing on film. Likewise, we see the men, and to a lesser extent, the women, who are harassed and humiliated by the police, and submit in silence—knowing the price for talking back, resisting, demanding to be treated like something other than a criminal. It's a pose that lots of people—mostly men of color—have to learn if they are going to survive, and also vanishingly rare to see on film (*Public Housing* marks one of the few other exceptions).

A contrast to these thoughtful portrayals is offered in *Complex: Life Inside a Section 8 Apartment* (2005), a documentary that follows eight federally subsidized residents of one building in Seattle. It takes a traditional format, offering interviews with residents, each of whom tell their stories, and with the landlord, too, who is alcoholic, angry, and unsympathetic to residents' circumstances, and trying to evict them. The residents are a complicated mess, variously disabled, mentally ill, pedophiles, addicts and alcoholics, and victims of abuse. It's a prurient glimpse into a collection of people you wouldn't want to live with, even if you might have some sympathy and empathy for them. There's little insight, but a voyeuristic thrill, and thus it is a more common kind of endeavor.

While there are lots of smaller dramas within this made-for-television melodrama, in *Women of Brewster Place* (1988), the central narrative concerns one poor neighborhood that is literally walled off from the rest of the city. Some years ago, the city needed to close off a street to control traffic flow, we learn, and all the other streets were better organized or had rich and middle-class people better able to resist. Mattie Michael (Oprah Winfrey) says that she could tear down the wall with her bare hands, and they'd just build it right back up the next day, so what's the use of trying? Yet the movie ends with Mattie doing just that, and going at the wall with a tire iron. Other neighbors join in, and they begin to literally pull bricks from the wall. It's perhaps an unsubtle metaphor, but there's something to this. What is a ghetto, after all, but a container, an enclosure, and, as sociologist Loic Wacquant (2008) and others would tell us, how far removed in function from a more literal prison? And isn't this the literal configuration of the street in *Dead End*, after all?

We've travelled a long way from the cramped, fetid black-and-white ghetto lanes of Pig Alley and the like to the multi-story, sprawling complexes of the post–World War II ghetto, but in cinematic terms, the inhabitants would have much in common throughout the twentieth century. But that so many of these films focus, not on removing people from the ghetto but on razing it—in the sequel to the French film *Banlieue 13*, called *B13*, the prime minister launches missiles to obliterate the ghetto so that it can be built anew—perhaps tells us something not only about how Americans have come to think of their poorest places, and what hope we might have for them, but perhaps how people in other countries might be despairing about them as well.

8 ESCAPING THE CITY

RURAL POVERTY

Grapes of Wrath, Tobacco Road, How Green Was My Valley, The Southerner,
Sounder, Sunday Dinner for a Soldier, Bound for Glory, Stroszek, The River, Places
in the Heart, Country, The Dollmaker, Gummo, George Washington, Frozen River,
Ballast, Winter's Bone, Rich Hill, Coal Miner's Daughter, Wendy and Lucy

As we've seen so far, American movies have set most of their stories about poverty in the ghetto—in urban areas of concentrated
poverty. You would be forgiven for thinking that that's where most
poverty is. In fact, in recent decades, a relatively small percentage
occurs in places where forty percent or more of all people were poor,
which is generally how scholars define a "ghetto." Fourteen percent
of poor people lived in such places in 1990, 9.1 percent in 2000,
and 10.5 percent between 2005 and 2009 (Kneebone, Nadeau, and
Berube, 2011). Even in the decades before, although rates of concentrated poverty in metropolitan areas doubled from 1970 to 1990
(Jargowsky, 1997), there were fewer people there than you might
think. The overwhelming majority of poor people, then and now,
do not live in areas of concentrated poverty. They don't even mostly
live in the city. Poverty outside of metropolitan areas has historically been higher than within them, as much as eighteen percentage points higher in 1959, and still 2.4 percentage points higher by
2011 (U.S. Department of Agriculture Economic Research Service,
2013). Poverty has just as consistently been highest in the South, not
the North, despite what you might conclude, given where poverty
tends to appear on film. Moreover, with a 2010 population of just
over eight million, and a poverty rate of just under twenty percent,
perhaps 1.6 million poor Americans were to be found in New York
City, or at most four percent of the total (which was about 46 million nationwide in 2011). Films about poverty set in New York and
other big cities exist radically out of proportion to the actual poverty
we find there. Perhaps this is part of why so many think of poverty
as a principally urban phenomenon.

FIGURE 8.1 AND 8.2 *Grapes of Wrath*, 20th Century Fox, 1940.

But the movies have shown us rural poverty now and again (even if suburban poverty is still almost entirely absent), and while it's the ghetto that dominates, what is probably the most famous representation of poverty on film is, in fact, about rural poverty (and arguably about homelessness, too).

The Grapes of Wrath (1940) begins its long, grim trek with Tom Joad arriving home, freshly paroled from prison. The landscape isn't far off from what we'll see decades later in *The Road* (see Chapter 17), and here, too, there has been an apocalypse of sorts, leaving the land brittle and bare.

In both instances, the disaster is part of what makes it possible for poverty to be grand and pitiable and noble: There is no mental illness, no alcoholism, no idleness or nonconformity at the root of their misery, just Nature and the Bank, forces beyond their control or, for that matter, their understanding. This is the essence of the history of the American tramp: Disaster strikes, driving people to the road in search of work. The scale of the Great Depression marks it in our minds as a signal event, but its scale may be the only difference—Americans are always being driven from their homes and from their lands. *Grapes of Wrath* is unusual not just because it is a Depression-era film that's not set in the city; it's also rare in films of the era to see entire poor families. Rich families abound (as in *My Man Godfrey*, for example), as do poor single men (and occasionally women), but not poor families.

What verisimilitude the novel has Steinbeck (1939) came by honestly, having spent some time in his youth as an itinerant laborer, and in his early married life he was poor enough to seek government cheese, steal produce from nearby farms, and wrap a manuscript with pieces torn from the roof of his tar-paper shack—and yet still be without enough money for postage to mail it. After success came with *Tortilla Flats*, he worried that he might lose his insight and vantage point into the lives of poor people, and he was a bit shocked and haunted by the begging letters that began to pour in. He reported on the migrant labor camps before turning to the novel, and his encounter with Tom Collins, manager of the Arvin Sanitary Camp, would

FIGURE 8.3 The Joads, pushed out onto the road, *Grapes of Wrath*, 20th Century Fox, 1940.

FIGURE 8.4 Meeting the kindly Camp Manager, and not quite believing it can be as good as he says. Note the resemblance to FDR. *Grapes of Wrath*, 20th Century Fox, 1940.

provide the model for the benevolent camp manager in the film; it is there that Steinbeck may have met the family that would become the Joads, and Collins's reports were the inspiration for many characters and scenes. Collins subsequently served as a consultant on the film, and portions were filmed at his Weedpatch camp at Arvin (Benson, 1984; DeMott, 1989; Nealand, 2008). This gives us more evidence that films written and directed by people with first-hand knowledge and experience of poverty might be more likely to give us representations that better reflect what we know about actual poor places and poor people.

John Ford's film is a sentimentalized and softened version of the novel (especially in the foregrounding of Tom's relationship with his mother and the unforgivable excision of the novel's final scene), but it's one that nonetheless retains some sheer radicalism, even if Andrew Sarris, among others, hated it (see Sarris, 1996, 1998). James Agee (2000) dismissed the picture with a few derisive lines and scoffed at Hollywood's efforts to portray "common people."

FIGURES 8.5, 8.6, AND 8.7 *"Who runs this place?"* "The government." *"Ma's sure gonna like it. She ain't been treated decent for a long while."* Grapes of Wrath, 20th Century Fox, 1940.

By contrast, Otis Ferguson (in Wilson, 1971, pp. 282–285) wrote: "If there is anything more poor, scuffed-out, and plain no-good than these homes, trucks, clothes, and every patched-up detail of equipment; or anything more real in squalor than the Okie camp, the pickers' shacks, etc., I wouldn't know it." Pare Lorentz raved about it, too, claiming that it had a scrupulous fidelity, "a peculiar newsreel quality" (which he meant to be praise), and he cites it as the only Hollywood movie since the Crash "that deals with a current social problem" (Lorentz, 1975, p. 185). Perhaps this is to be expected, since John Ford had been influenced by Lorentz's *Plow That Broke the Plains* (Parini, 1995, p. 200). Steinbeck and Lorentz were friends, and Lorentz's *The River* probably had some influence on Steinbeck; visually (Benson, 1984), the influence of Lorentz seems unmistakable in the film version.

I think Ferguson and Lorentz get the better part of this argument, and the film holds up exceedingly well. Steinbeck extracted a promise from studio head Darryl Zanuck that he wouldn't compromise the book in making the movie, and the author was ultimately pleased with the results: "Zanuck has more than kept his word," Steinbeck wrote. "He has a hard, straight picture in which the actors are submerged so completely that it looks and feels like a documentary film and certainly has a hard, truthful ring" (Benson, 1984, pp. 409–410). He even said he thought the film was harsher than the book, although that seems wrong to me. But it did retain some of the novel's power to shock. Much as the book had been the subject of obscenity charges, burnings, and banning (even today), the film was denounced as Communist propaganda, and Motion Picture Association of America president Eric Johnson proclaimed: "We'll have no more *Grapes of Wrath*. We'll have no more films that show the seamy side of American life. We'll have no pictures that deal with labor strikes [or] ... the banker as villain" (in Morone, 2003, p. 389; Christensen and Haas, 2005, p. 90; Benson, 1984).

Tobacco Road (1941) might be thought of as a companion piece to *Grapes of Wrath*. As Sarris (1998, p. 195) put it, "Whereas *The Grapes of Wrath* extolled the nobility of the deserving poor, *Tobacco Road* exploited the nuttiness of the undeserving poor." Based on Erskine Caldwell's novel and then Jack Kirkland's stage adaptation, with a screenplay by Nunnally Johnson (he wrote the screenplay for *Grapes of Wrath*, too), it's set in Georgia in the decaying remains of once-grand plantation homes on dried-out, dead land, inhabited by people who, on one hand, are poor because they are determined to remain on the property of their forebears—and thus possess a kind of honor—but on the other hand are the rankest kind of undeserving poor: Lazy, toothless, thieving hicks salivating at the prospect of a mere turnip; abusive men with thirteen-year-old child-brides; simple-minded, busybody religious zealots;

cruel, reckless, wasteful men repulsed by the very idea of bathing; and women with so many children they've literally lost count. They are ignorant, mostly unlikeable people, although desperate and hungry. As bad as things are, they get worse when the bank shows up, and unless the old couple can come up with $100, an impossible sum, they are bound for the poor farm. There is a soft and sympathetic moment late in the film, when they survey what little they have that might be worth taking with them as they prepare for eviction, but it's ruined when Jeeter, the old man, pimps out their daughter to the brute down the road, whose current wife escaped literal bonds (of rope) and ran off to Augusta. About the best that can be said of it is that Ford offers as powerful a sense of the land and the landscape as he did in *Grapes of Wrath*, and what occasional pity we may have for the characters might be entirely absent in less sure hands. Something Manny Farber (Nov. 8, 1952, in Polito, 2009, p. 417) wrote of another film is apt here: "It tends to reiterate the twisted sentimentality of left-wing writers that tries to be very sympathetic toward little people while breaking its back to show them as hopelessly vulgar, shallow, and unhappy." But while the images here are negative, just as the film stereotypes of poor urban blacks are, it may be that sympathy Farber's referring to that makes all the difference.

In *The Southerner* (1945), from another Nunnally Johnson screenplay, the hard life is stationary, with tenant farmers living crop to crop, instead of from check to check, as poor people do today. They work hard, suffer setbacks, periodically go hungry, overcome obstacles, work hard some more, and survive. What the urban and rural poor have in common is that their lives are ones of constant insecurity, always a crisis away from insolvency and despair. In this case, it's a terrible rainstorm that destroys their very first crop. Almost ready to give up, move to the city, and take factory jobs, they decide instead to stick it out—this is indomitability of the human spirit stuff, clothed in a lecture about the city's need for the farm and the farm's need for the city (a counterargument to the one Griffith makes in *A Corner in Wheat*). It's Renoir's loving attention to the daily tasks of taming the land that stands out, although too few of the lead actors seem at home as farmers, and it's all a bit thin, a bit pat. Agee (2000, July 9, 1945, pp. 155–157) thought it ultimately apolitical (which it is), patronizing, and typical of Hollywood's efforts. "Most of the players are wrong," he wrote. "They didn't walk right, stand right, eat right, sound right, or look right. . . . Beulah Bondi [who plays a *very* cranky old woman], an actress I generally admire, demonstrates merely how massively misguided, and how swarmed with unconscious patronage, the whole attitude of the theater has always been toward peasants." Thanks to the work that culminated in *Let Us Now Praise Famous Men* (1941/2001), Agee knows whereof he speaks on this count. I'm not sure the movie is patronizing, as he complains, but it is surely over-earnest, naïve, and feels as if it's striving for a Pare Lorentz-ified version of Soviet realism.

The third in the John Ford triptych of Depression-era pictures is *How Green Was My Valley* (1941), with the setting moved to a mining town in Wales, and the subject the struggles of the Morgan family. The mining company plays the role the banks do in *Grapes of Wrath*, leaving the landscape just as scarred as the Dustbowl does, and here, too, a family is broken up and torn apart by man and nature alike. It's radical, I suppose, in that it treats striking workers sympathetically, and gives voice to their arguments for a union, but it covers its bases by making the family patriarch, who is sympathetic and pitiable, the chief opponent of the union. But when all is said and done, this is another instance in which it's probably not useful to think of these families as poor—they live relatively simple lives and work hard for what they have, but there is work, shelter, food, and leisure for most. Breadlines and unemployment intrude, from stories of Cardiff and elsewhere, and the elder sons leave for fear that they, too, will soon be out of work. But it's an episodic melodrama, told through the eyes of the youngest child, and unlike *Angela's Ashes*, say, privation and misery and want are not the subject here: It's a story about how the world changes around you.

Edward R. Murrow's, *Harvest of Shame* (1960), a more recent exposé of poor, exploited, migrant farm workers, both black and white, was meant to be a "1960s *Grapes of Wrath*," he said. The film strives to humanize the workers and to empathize with them, spending a lot of screen time focusing on their children. "We should like you to meet some of your fellow citizens who harvest the food for the best-fed nation on earth," Murrow says at the beginning. It's not Pare Lorentz or Dorothea Lange, but their influence is hard to escape, as is the concern with mundane details of daily life and privation so central to *Let Us Now Praise Famous Men*. "As primitive as man can live," observes Murrow. What's worth pondering is that this documentary did not mark the beginning of a long line of films about poverty in the United States, even as Kennedy and then Johnson tried to draw national attention to the problem. The Great Depression and New Deal era abounded with poor and homeless people on film, as we'll see, but the Great Society period inspire no such outpouring, perhaps because in the 1930s suffering was widespread, and the solutions were bold, whereas the War on Poverty occurred during a time of general prosperity and, apart from Medicare, generated more modest programs targeted at a much smaller share of the population.

At about the same time the fictional Joads were driving west to California, Woodie Guthrie was riding the rails in the same direction, hoping to find work to support his family back in Texas. Who and what he would become is well known, and much of the biopic *Bound for Glory* (1976) tracks a familiar path: He hops freights, tries to escape the bulls, scrambles to find work (even if only enough to earn a meal), visits soup kitchens staffed by pretty, earnest charity ladies, and encounters haughty moralizing preachers and decent, at-the-end-of-their tether folks eager to share what little they have, just as he is. He finds himself in a migrant labor camp, where we might find the Joads themselves, gets himself a guitar, and soon is on a path that forces him to choose between his radio jobs, with their corporate sponsors, and his radical lyrics. It's nicely done, if much overlong, and unabashedly, if a bit safely and abstractly, pro-union. Still, along with *Corner in Wheat, Grapes of Wrath*, and *Harvest of Shame*, it's unusual for movies to present the viewer with poverty that is rooted in the rank exploitation of workers.

Sunday Dinner for a Soldier (1944) takes us to Florida, an unusual locale for films about poverty, and offers us a struggling family preparing to host a United Service Organizations (USO) sponsored dinner for an enlisted man. Tessa (Ann Baxter) manages the household, and she spends a great deal of the film worrying about money and her father's carelessness with it. She sends her younger brother with him to town to make sure he gets the full sixteen cents each for the crabs they have caught and that he doesn't buy anything foolish, but it's all for naught. He gives away the crabs (they're stolen, actually, but he thinks he's given them away) and buys an expensive dress for Tessa. When she finds out about the crabs, she explodes: "You gave them away?! I showed you my budget—so much for food, so much for payment on the place. You seemed to understand that we could just about make it this month if we were careful!" But's it's all forgotten so quickly that it's hard to believe that their circumstances are made all that much more dire. She's frustrated and increasingly tempted to escape via marriage to a man she doesn't quite dislike, but doesn't love, either—it's the fate Kay confronts in *Dead End*—and describes where they live as a "filthy shack," and their clothes and bedding as "rags." The jury-rigged pipe they get their well water from barely functions, and so on. Yet even when things are at their worst, she sighs and laughs a carefree, resigned, exaggerated laugh. It's not a brave or noble or heroic struggle, though: any time the film edges toward real privation or suffering, it backs off. It's sentimentalized, and self-consciously precious—the lovable but irresponsible grandfather is called "Grandfeathers," for example. And to make matters worse, Tessa and the family are saved from both poverty and loveless marriage when the Soldier does finally arrive, and he and Tessa fall instantly in love. Poverty here is occasionally inconvenient and makes one just a shade tense now and again, but little more. We see again how rare it is for films to try to show either the grinding, repetitive, daily, exhausting struggle that poverty often is or the genuine pain that can accompany it. When the day is done, a woman in poverty can readily escape it, as long as there is a man handy. Agee (2000, Feb. 3, 1945, pp. 126–127) liked it even less than I did:

> They are represented as nice people, but very poor and, in their poverty, ever so whimsical and lucky.... The confused but genuine sweetness of their intention is as visible through all the mawkish formulas.... I cannot bear to say in detail why I found the film so distasteful. To do so would be like spending a self-controlled day with an innocently awful family, then sneering at all that was painful to you but dear to them.

Stroszek (1977) offers another unusual location, and though in color, it's a bleak, washed-out landscape. A couple emigrates from Germany, and lives a threadbare, working-class existence in rural Wisconsin until they can't keep up with the payments on their mobile home, and it's repossessed. The woman resumes earning a living through prostitution, while the man commits suicide on a ski lift after visiting a quarter-slot sideshow that has a dancing chicken and a piano-playing duck. The moral? It's a Werner Herzog film, so you can't be sure. And while their life in America is grim, it's arguably better than what they left behind, and their expectations were never grand or terribly naïve, as they would be in more facile films.

Seconds into *Places in the Heart* (1984), as the credits are rolling, amidst quick scenes of small-town country life, we see a shot of an old woman living out of her car, a sign in front reading: "I have been thrown out of the home where I lived for 17 years. This is WRONG. I will stay right here until they let me back into my HOME. PS. I am Not Crazy." It's Waxahachie, Texas, 1935. For much of American history, women have had few options for survival apart from a man; and, indeed, they were, as a rule, expected to marry, raise children, and tend the home, while their husbands earned the money for all of their support. But if he should die, what was left of the family would be in dire straits. Edna (Sally Field) is one such woman, left widowed and facing foreclosure. Enter Moze (Danny Glover), who offers to help her turn the land toward a productive and profitable cotton crop, which he does, only to be driven off by the Ku Klux Klan. It's about a small, unlikely group of decent people thrown together, including a blind boarder pawned off on Edna by the bank manager, who wind up forming a family of sorts. But without them, she would have lost the house, and probably would have had to split up the children, sending

FIGURE 8.8 *Places in the Heart*, TriStar Pictures, 1984.

them off to separate relatives or the poorhouse, and then moved in with her sister, if she'd have her and could afford her.... That's how precarious women's lives were then. They are as precarious now, for many—it's why poverty remains highest among female-headed households.

The year *Places in the Heart* gave us a Depression-era widow trying to save her farm, *The River* (1984) and *Country* (1984) offered contemporary versions. In the first, Mel Gibson and Sissy Spacek play Tom and Mae Garvey, hard-working farmers barely hanging on, over-mortgaged to the bank, when a flooding rainstorm destroys their crop. The bank won't lend them more. They sell off some furniture and some equipment, and there are hints of a larger crisis: On the way to the auction, they pass by families living in encampments that could be late twentieth-century Hoovervilles. When Mae wonders where they are all coming from, Tom quietly observes that a lot of them look like farmers. Later, the camera pans by closed factories, abandoned buildings, and people living in teetering shacks. Soon enough Tom and Mae have nothing left to sell, except the land, and are running out of options. Tom gets a job at an ironworks, only realizing when it's too late that he's a scab; when he confronts his cousin who got him the gig, the latter shrugs: "It's the only jobs there are." The film ends more or less where it began, with a storm that threatens to wipe them out. But this time, he swallows his pride and calls for help and, in what must be a nod to Lorentz's *The*

River, they join together in common cause, in ever growing numbers, and hold back the river. The villains here are other local, larger, farmers, who want Tom's land so that they can flood the valley it sits in, build a dam, and create a reservoir. Nowhere is there a hint of federal farm policies of the 1980s and how they fit into this family's dilemma, unlike in *Country* (1984), where those policies are front and center. Indeed, *Country* documents a very similar kind of struggle for the survival of a small family farm, with Sam Shepard and Jessica Lange playing the struggling couple this time, but here their misery is created by government, not by nature, with the foreclosure-hungry (and now-defunct) Farmers Home Administration playing the role the banks did in *Grapes of Wrath*.

These films mark an unusual period in U.S. history. The American farm economy began a precipitous decline in the 1970s, and reached something of a nadir in the Reagan years. The final retreat from 1930s grain policies and the redirection of federal funds to larger and larger operations, the lingering effects of the oil and grain embargoes, high interest rates, declining land values, overproduction, the hollowing-out of price supports, and more, came together in a wave of bankruptcies and foreclosures among small- and mid-size American farms (Pollan, 2006; Manning, n.d.). *Country* ends with a glimmer of hope—the announcement of a moratorium on foreclosures by the the agency responsible for most farm loans. But that would be a short-lived reprieve, and after this brief spate of films drew our attention to the problem, Hollywood, never especially worried about the well-being of rural Americans or too concerned with the on-the-ground effects of national agricultural policy, seems to have turned away again.

FIGURE 8.9. The bank refuses another loan. *Country,* Touchstone Films, 1984.

From that same year, we should also note *The Dollmaker* (1984), a TV movie starring Jane Fonda as Gertie, a stubbornly resourceful, hard-working, poor, salt-of-the-earth Kentucky farm woman who is uprooted, unwillingly, and moved to Detroit so that her husband can take a factory job. (There's a brief cameo by Studs Terkel as a cab driver.) It becomes a bit of a fish-out-of-water story of the "hillbilly in the city," as we see this strong, smart, capable mother suddenly befuddled by all around her. She economizes and tries to save up to buy a home when, she hopes, they move back, but she has to spend it on a funeral for her young daughter. Mostly, she just longs for home. It's a bit like Loretta Lynn's life might have been without her singing. But there is victory here of a sort, as they all, at the end, return to Kentucky.

Gummo (1997) is set in an ugly, rural Ohio town that's never recovered from a devastating tornado, and it tracks the daily doings of this very poor, white community. They appear largely uneducated, and it's always unclear what people do for work. The kids kill cats and sell them to a man who, in turn, sells them to local restaurants, and they ride bikes, sniff glue, and have sex with women who are pimped out by their own husbands. It's meant to be some kind of cinema verité, a mock documentary slice-of-life look at these odd and dysfunctional people, but it's trying too hard to be edgy and odd. Other than offering more evidence for the claim that the rural poor are disproportionately white in film, while the urban poor are black, and perhaps another instance in which marginal populations are made foreign and "other," it offers little. It's voyeuristic, off-balance, cruel, and is especially bad if we hold it up against a film like *Winter's Bone* (which we'll turn to shortly), which does care about its characters and where they live, and offers a real sense of what life is like in that brutal, bleak landscape, making the pretentiousness and self-consciousness of *Gummo* obvious. And yet, as ugly and prurient and voyeuristic as *Gummo* is, it does wind up putting on film people rarely put on film and, like *Winter's Bone*, uses non-actors for many of its parts, giving us a range of portraits of badly nourished, worn-down, drug-addled, and ill-educated rural white Americans, and highlighting how badly skewed are our cultural images of need, of hunger, of destitution, and of insecurity.

George Washington (2000) is a bit like *Gummo*, although more assured and more competent. It's a slow-moving, observational, slice-of-life portrait of a down-and-out rural community, focusing mostly on the mostly black kids there, following them throughout their mostly ordinary days. Ordinary, that is, until one young man is accidently killed, and his friends, afraid, hide the body. This North Carolina town is less utterly devastated and less cut off from the world than the Ohio town of *Gummo*, but it's still dark and dirty, a decaying industrial landscape filled with abandoned cars and homes, piled with trash, overgrown with weeds, and filled with talk of dead animals. It's less interested in shocking us, not as concerned with being weird and self-consciously clever as *Gummo* is (though it also has such moments, like showing us a hat made from a dog), and it seems to want to show us something about, not just these young boys' present, but the kind of future they might have, too. Which is not much at all, even without the threat of going to prison. Also, like *Gummo*, it feels improvised, and as if the actors are novices, which they are. As a result, it too is showing us people seldom seen on film.

An African American family living in rural Mississippi in the wake of a suicide sits at the center of *Ballast* (2008). The dead man's son gets himself indebted to local drug dealers. When things get desperate, he tells his mother than he needs $100. She looks at him utterly dumbfounded: "James, I ain't got that kind of money!" He has already stolen all the money in his uncle's wallet: nine dollars. They scrape by, talk little, and tread quietly around each other. It's a lean and exhausting life, and filmed so that we feel that we're getting a glimpse of it in real time. It's meditative, and even this description makes it sound a shade more dramatic than it is. There are almost no other people in it, and yet it seems also to suggest how many other gray, draining stories could just as easily be told about this sparse, gray land. It's a beautiful example of a filmmaker showing us people and giving us a glimpse into their lives without telling us what to think about them or it. Perhaps because there's so little space, still, for movies about African Americans, only the very best ones see the light of day, perhaps helping to account for why *Ballast* and *George Washington* are so good. Yet there are not the only realistic portraits of rural poverty to be found.

We know from the start of *Frozen River* (2008) that things are not going well for Ray (Melissa Leo). When we meet her, she's barefoot, in her bathrobe,

FIGURE 8.10 *Ballast*, Alluvial Film, 2008.

FIGURES 8.11 AND 8.12 Our first glimpses of Ray (*left*) and Ree (*right*). *Frozen River*, Sony Pictures, 2008; and *Winter's Bone*, Roadside Attractions, 2010.

sitting outside her battered trailer, smoking and crying. Her husband has run off with the $4,000 she's amassed to make a balloon payment on a new trailer, and when they arrive with the first half of her new home on a flatbed truck, they refuse to leave it, and tell her she'll forfeit her $1,500 down payment if she can't come up with the next payment by Christmas, a week away. Although once hopeful that she'd get promoted to full-time and an assistant manager position in the dollar store where she works, that doesn't happen. Her rent-to-own TV is about to be repossessed, she pays for gas for her car with coins a few dollars at a time, the pipes in her house freeze solid, and there's nothing there for food but popcorn and Tang. Desperate to keep herself and her boys fed and housed, and unwilling to let her fifteen-year-old son drop out of school to take a job, she joins a poor woman who lives on the nearby Mohawk reservation to smuggle Chinese and Pakistani immigrants across the Canadian border into New York. She gets caught and goes to jail for a few months, but she gets her new trailer, too, thanks to the smuggling money. When she gets out, we're left to assume that her life might get a little bit better, but it's not likely to be too much different, and will, inevitably, continue to be grueling and threadbare.

As with *Frozen River*, *Winter's Bone* (2010) is the story of a poor, white, rural woman, the man who abandoned her and her family, and their grim struggle to keep their home. Ree (Jennifer Lawrence) is a teenage girl who has, it would appear, had to drop out of high school in order to care for her mother, who's mentally ill and fairly helpless, and her younger brother and sister. They live in a small, broken-down house on a small piece of land in the Ozarks. Ree says she's seventeen, but it feels like she's lying and is probably a year or two younger. There's never much food, except for potatoes, the occasional squirrel, and what is offered by a generous if taciturn neighbor. Ree has already asked her to take in their horse to save the expense of hay. Her father, who's been arrested in the past for cooking methamphetamine, has put up the property as collateral on his bail, and, with his court date coming up, is nowhere to be found. It's a world in which all women seem preternaturally exhausted, worn and beaten down (sometimes literally) by a world dominated by men. Everything is scarce. Ree spends the film searching for her father, trekking across a landscape as hard and cold as the people living on it. She finds him, eventually—he's dead—and she keeps the house along with the cash balance of the bail, but there's no happy ending here, no end at all, really. They'll continue on, her siblings will grow older, and they'll lead lives much like everyone else's. This failure to force a tidy resolution is part of what allows both *Frozen Winter* and *Winter's Bone* to offer portraits of cinematic poverty that better reflect what we know of actual poverty: Most Americans who are born poor will die poor, and constant struggle and scarcity are the norm for many. Moreover, if you are poor in a big city, there's a chance you might get some useful and consistent assistance from local agencies; that's less likely in rural places, since there's less help available, and what help there is is often far away.

The landscape of *Winter's Bone* echoes that in *Coal Miner's Daughter* (1980), a biopic of country singer Loretta Lynn, with Sissy Spacek in the title role. "If you're born in the mountains, you've got three choices: coal mine, moon shine, or movin' on down the line" says a moonshiner. There really are few options for men in this small Kentucky mining town, and even fewer for women. While we don't see Loretta's family struggling to survive—they seem to be housed and clothed and fed and warm—it's a spare life, where the decision to turn on the radio is made with care, so as to preserve the batteries. When Loretta marries Doolittle (Tommy Lee Jones) and he decides to set off west, she follows because she's his wife. Were it not for him buying her a guitar and then pushing her to go on stage, her life would have been much like her mother's. It's a rags-to-riches tale, but there's no moral here, neither one about the virtues of diligence and persistence, nor one about the indomitability of hard-working "real America." She had talent, she was persistent, she got lucky, she succeeded. Once again, as I seem to keep saying, poverty that emerges from personal accounts and memoirs usually differs in important ways from most other accounts—it's not there to drive the narrative or to frame a message, but as events and conditions, as things that were, as just the stuff of life.

In the same year in which *Slumdog Millionaire* earned $24 million in just its first seven weeks, and would go on to win eight Oscars, including Best Picture (see Chap. 17), *Wendy and Lucy* (2008) gives us a smaller and surer story of poverty, with a much smaller audience, alas, earning under $900,000 during the entire twenty weeks of its theatrical release. Wendy (Michele Williams) is on her way to Alaska with her dog, Lucy, in hopes of finding work. Early on, we see her in her car, where she lives and sleeps, totaling her money: it comes to $525. In a lovely touch, we regularly see Wendy adjusting the total amount she has available on this scrap of paper, each deduction a small terror. Millions of people live just like this, tracking every dollar as if their survival depended upon it, because it does. Then the car breaks down. She collects cans to redeem, and shoplifts dog food, getting caught by a pompous little grocery boy, who says, "You people who can't afford dog food, you shouldn't have a dog." (For why poor and homeless people do keep pets, see Leslie Irvine's [2013], *My Dog Always Eats First*). He calls the police, she's arrested and pays a $50 fine, but by the time she gets back, Lucy is gone. The bulk of the movie is her search for Lucy, but also, obliquely, a tour of a poor former mill town, a story of decline, made most poignant when the security guard who befriends her presses money upon her as she's ready to finally leave town, money he clearly can't afford to give away. It's seven dollars. The irony of the shop boy's tirade is that, after learning that her car is broken beyond repair (and would cost $2,000 or more to fix), and after finally finding Lucy, she does choose to leave her behind, presumably because she thinks the dog will have a better life with the family who's taken her in than with her. She sets off on foot, and hops onto a boxcar.

Wendy and Lucy is cousin to *Frozen River* and *Winter's Bone*. They are somber, slow, observational films directed by women, and, like the best TV movies about homeless women, they spend time helping viewers understand the reality of lives lived under harsh, brutal, insecure circumstances. I'm not sure how much of this is a product of gender, how much is the fact that both are modest-budget, independent films, and how much is the fact that they're the product of their times. It is tempting to talk about these last string of independent movies as reacting in some way to the Great Recession, but *Frozen River* and *Wendy and Lucy* were filmed before the official start of the crisis in December of 2007. Perhaps it's simply that there's an inverse correlation between the sophistication of the portrayal and the size of the audience that a film is trying to reach: there may be greater space to be more subtle because there's less pressure to appeal broadly.

There's an even more recent movie that might serve as a fitting way to conclude this review of rural poverty. By car, Rich Hill, Missouri, is about an hour and twenty minutes from Kansas City. According to the Census Bureau, its 2012 population was 1,341. Median household income was about $29,800 (about half of what it is for the Kansas City metropolitan area), and its poverty rate was just over twenty-seven percent—nearly double the level for Missouri or the country, but about the same as the U.S. rate for African Americans or Hispanics; the difference is that ninety-eight percent of this

FIGURE 8.13 "We're not trash," says Andrew. *Rich Hill*, The Orchard, 2014.

poor town is white. That's the setting for Andrew Droz Palermo and Tracy Droz Tragos's 2014 documentary, *Rich Hill*. First we meet Andrew. "We're not trash. We're good people," says the teenager. He recounts his family's many recent moves (they'll be uprooted three more times before the film is over), and introduces us to his younger sister, whom he dotes on, and his parents. His mom may be developmentally disabled, and she's missing most of her teeth. Andrew works when he can with his father, who does "oddball jobs and stuff"—mostly yardwork, by the looks of it. His dad is pretty good-natured about it all, or at least inured to it: "You learn to survive," he shrugs. When Andrew's dad dreams, he dreams small, imagining a summer with enough work that he can "take the kids down to Wal-Mart, or the dollar store, and let 'em buy whatever they want . . . in a reasonable amount . . . about $400 apiece worth of stuff." He laughs as he says the last part, as if excited at the prospect but a bit ashamed that he'd even imagine it possible.

Appachey is a bit younger. We meet him as he comes home to a dirty, crowded house, and lights a cigarette from the coils of a beat-up toaster. He tells us that his father disappeared one night when the boy was six, and never returned. Appachey's been diagnosed with obsessive-compulsive disorder (OCD) and attention-deficit disorder (ADD), and he may have Asperger's, says his mom, who, lying in bed with a cigarette and a Big Gulp, appears initially to be hard and lazy in contrast to the sweet, simple temperament of Andrew's mom. But as we hear more from her, it feels as if she's just *worn*, and disappointed by her life: She never had a chance for one of her own, she says, going straight from her mother's house to marriage at seventeen and caring for a growing number of children. Appachey is angry, cruel to his siblings, and looking for trouble. He's soon enough in juvenile court, and sentenced to a detention facility by the film's end.

Harley, the third teenager featured, tells us that he's on medication to control his temper while we watch, warily, as he shops for a hunting knife. His mom, a waitress, is in prison, and she, too, has just had the last of her teeth pulled. He lives with his grandmother, who is supporting them with the help of a small food stamp allowance. Harley will tell us that he was raped by his stepfather, whom, we'll learn, his mother then tried to kill—it's why she's in prison. Harley's always on the verge of erupting in frustration and rage.

Everyone here seems exhausted, more than anything, and resigned to their fate. In truth, there's a reason, given that even those who seem to have some hope, like Andrew, barely have a chance, so deep and broad are the forces arrayed against them: a child born poor in the United States is likely to remain poor; and depending upon where you live, the odds of escaping such circumstances are incredibly low (Economic Policy Institute [EPI], 2013). People try as best they can, but trying doesn't correlate with success. And that's the crucial lesson.

Much of what many will see here as "culture" is actually structure, the product of decades of disinvestment that's befallen many such areas, which leaves behind a depressed, isolated, local economy with no jobs, a dwindling tax base, and nothing to attract business or new residents; aging, dilapidated housing stock; underfunded, inferior schools; little or no access to health care and other social services; and few people around who aren't as poor as you are. This segregation of poor people matters, producing what social scientists call "concentration effects" (Dept. of Housing and Urban Development, 2011). Thus, disability, physical illness, and mental illness are more common in poor families and in poor places, and the fact that there are lots of people medicated in *Rich Hill*—Andrew's mom (who dies from an overdose of sleeping pills), Appachey, and Harley, at least—shouldn't surprise us. Even those in *Rich Hill* who are not on prescription drugs self-medicate, especially by smoking: cigarettes have short-term calming effects and might serve as a substitute for more expensive remedies. This may be why rates of smoking today correlate with education and income levels. You might judge this behavior to be foolish (it's so unhealthy!) and wasteful (it's so expensive!), but consider the pleasure it might bring when everything feels awful and beyond your control.

Nor should it surprise us that so many in *Rich Hill* have bad teeth or no teeth at all: this may be the clearest physical marker of poverty in the United States, and another way in which disadvantages accumulate: If you're too poor for dental care and are missing teeth, you'll have a much harder time finding work, which makes you less likely to secure the income or insurance that might prevent you from losing yet more teeth and your children from losing theirs.

There are other ways in which *Rich Hill* offers useful insight. Like the struggling families depicted here, most poor people in the United States are or have been married (Fremstad, 2012). Contrary to the simplistic rhetoric of many conservatives, marriage is not a magical ceremony with anti-poverty powers. There are higher rates of unintended pregnancies among poor women (Guttmacher Institute, 2016), but that's not because they're irresponsible, it's because they're poor—contraception is expensive and may require a doctor's supervision, two potentially large obstacles.

Most of the poor adults here work, and those who don't are often looking for work, disabled, or caring for children or grandchildren—who may themselves be sick or disabled. But even working and working hard won't get you out of poverty if your wages are low, and in 2011, one-quarter of all male workers and one-third of all female workers were employed in poverty-wage jobs (EPI, 2013, Table 4e).

Finally, U.S. prisons are filled with poor people, just as they are in the film, and women are the fastest-growing segment, although at twice the rate for black women as for whites. Mass incarceration is a consequence of poverty and a cause of it: having an incarcerated parent makes children poorer, but also increases the likelihood that they will have their own early encounters with the criminal justice system. That reduces their chance of completing high school, which increases the likelihood that they will be poor and incarcerated as an adult, which makes them more likely to remain poor, given the difficulty ex-offenders have in getting hired. Our criminal justice system is a massive engine for making people poor, sick, and angry, and if there is any such thing as a "cycle of poverty," it's built and maintained by public policy.

And perhaps that's the lesson to take away, not just from this film, or the films in this chapter, but, perhaps, from so many of those we've discussed so far—poverty is often created or exacerbated by public policy, a product of politics and power, but, with some exceptions, on film, and in the public imagination, too, it's personal moral failure that best explains need. This pattern will be even more evident as we turn our attention away from how the places that house poor people are portrayed in the movies toward how they show us people without homes at all.

II ON THE STREET, ON THE ROAD: POOR OUT OF DOORS

9 THE FIRST TRAMP

City Lights, Kid Auto Races at Venice, Mabel's Strange Predicament, Between Showers, In the Park, A Film Johnnie, The Gold Rush, The Police, The Tramp, Face on the Bar Room Floor, The Pawn Shop, A Dog's Life, The Idle Class, The Kid, The Circus, Payday, Modern Times, The Great Dictator

There are three ways people explain homelessness, sociologist Teresa Gowan (2010) argues. *Sin-talk* emphasizes the moral failure of the individual and the bad behavior that led them into crisis. *Sick-talk*, by contrast, understands homelessness to be the product of addiction or mental illness. *System-talk*, finally, focuses on the social and economic forces that limit opportunity. More succinctly, in her words, it's "homelessness as moral offense, homelessness as pathology, and homelessness as the product of systemic injustice or instability" (p. xxi). I've come to a slightly different conclusion, although one consistent with Gowan's observation. There are, it seems to me, four patterns to the way American movies approach the homeless man (we'll turn to the women in due course). He is a Vaudevillian (to be laughed at), a Villain (to be feared), a Victor (to be celebrated and held up as a hero), or a Victim (to be pitied). Let's begin with the vaudevillians, and the most famous vaudevillian of them all.

In the third movie to appear featuring Charlie Chaplin, *Kid Auto Races at Venice* (1914), a formative version of the character we will come to know as the Tramp appears to the public. He's not so clearly poor as he is in some films, and he's self-assured, almost cocky, with none of the self-abnegating charm of the later Tramp. Chaplin's Tramp is almost always at the center of the story only by accident, through mishap or misunderstanding, but in *Kid Auto Races* he's fighting for our attention—quite literally, as a crew films a car race and the Tramp tries to get on camera.

The Tramp shows up next in *Mabel's Strange Predicament* (1914). He's still smoking furiously, has a wider and bushier mustache,

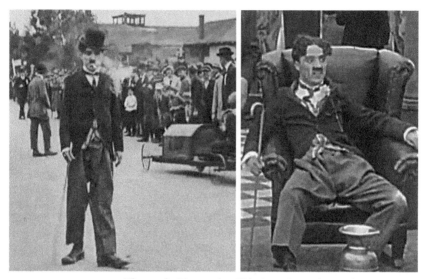

FIGURES 9.1 AND 9.2 The early Tramp in *Kid Auto Races in Venice,* Keystone Studios, 1914 (*left*); and *Mabel's Strange Predicament*, Keystone Studios, 1914 (*right*).

and is drunk. Here, too, the vulnerability we will come to associate with the Tramp is not present, and while his antics are funny, he's not an attractive or sympathetic character. Indeed, in *Mabel's Strange Predicament*—which, while released after *Kid Auto Races,* was probably made before it, and is probably the actual first appearance of the Tramp (Robinson, 1985/1994, p. 113)—he's an object of ridicule and a man not to be trusted. The dignity that is at the core of the Tramp, the hint of a fallen man with a tragic past, or of the humble man with aspirations of gentility, is not yet evident.

To complete the catalog of early appearances of the Tramp: In *Between Showers* (1914), another tramp gets caught in the middle of a fight Charlie's having, and the other tramp gets hit in the head by a brick and knocked into a pond. With *In the Park* (1915), a more poorly dressed tramp repeatedly tries to pick Charlie's pocket, with Charlie always coming out on top of the encounters. In *A Film Johnnie* (1914), as the Tramp tries to get into a movie studio, he's told, "I don't want any bums around here," by the security guard—one of the few times the character's outcast state is explicitly referred to. (Another is in *The Gold Rush* [1925], where a girl will pick him out of the crowd as "the most deplorable looking tramp in the dance hall.") Finally, *The Tramp* (1915) gives us the fullest sense yet of the character he would become. In the first scene, walking down a dirt road toward the camera, covered by dust from passing automobiles, he pulls a whiskbroom from his clothes and carefully brushes himself off. Such efforts at maintaining his dignity and his public appearance will be a regular trait of the character. We first see a battle between the Tramp and a group of dangerous hoboes (for more on the historical distinction between tramps and hoboes, see Pimpare, 2004, Chap. 6) who are trying to steal a young woman's money. These men are dirtier than Charlie, with bad teeth, hardened features, more disheveled clothing, and none of the innocence or charm of the Tramp, and they are clearly a threat. The Tramp rescues her, and for his bravery, the girl, with whom he's now smitten, invites him home for a meal and to work on her family's farm. He's not very useful, it turns out, and we are likely to find him playing around instead of working. Still, he defends her family from a renewed attack of the hoboes, suffering injuries in the process. While he is recuperating, the young woman's boyfriend appears, and with a forlorn look at his own ragged clothes, the Tramp realizes his own unsuitability for her, and leaves, having refused an offer of money.

So, by the end, he's back on the road, alone, in what will become the iconic image of Chaplin as the Tramp: Dejected, solitary, walking away from the camera (there's a poignant echo of this in *Monsieur Verdoux*, as Verdoux heads off to his execution). But while the walk begins forlornly, as he recedes from view, we see him kick up his heels and then pick up his pace. He's already made his peace with the outcome, perhaps knowing that he can expect little else, and is moving on to his next adventure. Likewise, in 1916's *The Police*, after being released from jail for some unspecified crime, the Tramp finds himself at a cheap lodging house with a grotesquely over-made-up collection

FIGURE 9.3 *The Tramp*, Essanay Studios, 1915.

of bums. They have ragged, torn, stained clothing, and their faces are blackened with dirt. One has a grim cough that suggests tuberculosis. Lacking a dime, Charlie is refused a bed, and yet, too poor even to afford the dosshouse, he seems unperturbed and to take it all in stride.

The Tramp is something of an enigma, and one of the goals of this chapter is to try to make sense of that character and to see if we can understand where he came from and why he seems to have had such a hold, not just on American movie audiences, but on people around the world. By 1915, the Tramp could already be found in cartoons, comic strips, songs, and poems. There were dolls, toys, figurines, books, and in France, a dance called the Charlot One-Step. There were look-alike contests, and an urban legend has it that Chaplin himself entered one and came in third (Robinson, 1985/1994, pp. 152–153; Sobel and Francis, 1977, pp. 142–143). He had, with shocking speed, become the first global celebrity—by playing a homeless man.

Not all reviews were favorable, even in the early years before Chaplin's own politics were a subject of debate and, eventually, the cause of his exile from the United States. As *Variety* sniffed in 1915, "Never anything dirtier was placed upon the screen than Chaplin's Tramp" (in Sobel and Francis, 1977, p. 146). The Tramp is elsewhere referred to as *tawdry, cheap, vulgar, unmanly, crude,* and *obscene* (Sobel and Francis, 1977). Some of this, Sobel and Francis suggest, may be resentment at Chaplin's sudden success. Some may reflect the bias against the cinema that was evident among many critics, who thought it unworthy of any but the lower classes. But some of this antipathy must surely have had something to do with the long-standing, widespread negative associations that came with tramps and their hobo brethren. The puzzle is why these reactions weren't more widespread, and why film audiences would come to love so dearly a vagabond who assiduously avoids work, doesn't concern himself much with the well-being of others, and has middle-class pretensions. How does he wind up being sympathetic?

Part of the answer is that the Tramp has a kind of courtliness. He is gracious and polite (to a point), a man of refined manners who, were it not for the other indicators of his condition, one might think had some breeding. When discovered sleeping in the arms of a statue at its unveiling in *City Lights* (1931), for example, he faces the surprised crowd and demurely doffs his hat and tries to climb down, sheepish but not ashamed, looking as if he just doesn't want to be in anyone's way. The comportment of this man does not gibe with the stereotype of the Tramp: He is no threat, no danger, no bum. How he arrived in this position we do not know, and one of the few times we get a hint of the Tramp's past is in *Face on the Bar Room Floor* (1914), where we see the Tramp before he's a tramp: He's a portrait artist, commissioned by a wealthy woman to paint her husband. He falls in love with her, and she flirts with him, but rebuffs him. Inconsolable, he's soon telling his sad tale in a bar, and then sleeping on park benches. It is fitting that love made him a tramp, since so much of his subsequent life is spent falling in love with women who do not love him.

The Tramp's dignity is more than a façade: when he is mocked by two newsboys in *City Lights*, he stops to reprimand them, looking neither angry nor particularly hurt, but as if he were trying to teach them simple manners, as if the man he was reproaching them for taunting were someone other than himself. Only a few minutes into the film, and this Tramp has surprised us and revealed something about his character. This is why so many for so long have been so ready to label Chaplin a genius: his gift is not that he is funny, though he is that, but that with a few gestures and a few subtle narrative clues, an empathetic human appears on the screen. He's not quite a three-dimensional man—we know almost nothing about him, after all—but is one who nonetheless seems so fully realized that it touches something within us. It is this *grace* that makes the Tramp so beloved, so universal. Chaplin once described it to a magazine reporter as being "desperately serious in my attempt to appear as a normal little gentleman" (in Robinson, 1985/1994, pp. 202–203). That he is a homeless man is all the more remarkable, given how rare it was and still is to see a poor person depicted on screen (or in our broader political culture) as something other than an object of fear or maudlin pity.

There's also something poignant about the Tramp's middle-class pretensions. When we first meet him in *The Kid*, he opens a cigarette case made from a sardine tin that's filled with the butt ends of cigarettes and cigars. He carefully chooses among them, closes the tin, and then taps the cigarette on the lid, as if he were extracting a fresh one from a silver case. When he removes his gloves, he does so in studied fashion, pulling one finger at a time. This is a common behavior for him: Extracting the whisk broom from his clothes in *The Tramp* (1915), using a handkerchief to sweep of a bench before going to sleep on it in *City Lights*, using a piece of old pipe as a muff in *A Dog's Life* (1918), employing a trowel to clean underneath his fingernails, and then using sandpaper to buff them in *Work* (1915). Indeed, the Tramp's clothes suggest a man of some means who has come to fall on hard times. He is, in the title of a 1975 biopic, *The Gentleman Tramp*.

But not always. For all the adoration audiences have had for the Tramp, he's no paragon. There's another side to his eventual love for the child in *The Kid* (1921), for example. After first finding the baby, he tries to give it to a woman pushing a perambulator, thinking it must be hers. When she refuses to take it, he is prepared to leave it back on the ground here he found it, and

FIGURE 9.4 The Tramp contemplates ridding himself of the baby by putting it in the sewer. *The Kid*, Charles Chaplin Productions, 1921.

as he's about to walk away, abandoning it to its fate, he is stopped only by a policeman. Later, he tries to trick another poor-looking bum to take it. That having failed, he contemplates leaving it in the sewer. He is, in these scenes, cruel and selfish, looking for every chance he gets to abandon the helpless infant to the mercy of whoever stumbles upon it next.

In *The Circus* (1928), the Tramp is hanging "around the side shows, hungry and broke," and is sufficiently hungry to take food from a baby. And there's something unkind about the Tramp's seduction of the Flower Girl in *City Lights*. She thinks he's a wealthy man, and seems to have hopes he'll make a new life for her, and he continues to allow her to believe it long after he could have cleared up the confusion. If *City Lights* were made in the usual Hollywood fashion, Chaplin would fall for the girl before realizing that she was blind, and then continue to love her nonetheless. Instead, his infatuation doesn't seem evident until he recognizes her state. Perhaps it makes him even more human by making him a bit shallow. Or is it that he, an object of pity, is glad to find someone that he can pity?

FIGURE 9.5 City Lights, *United Artists*, 1931. Is it possible she really loves him?

The Tramp's occasional indifference to others doesn't extend to animals. *A Dog's Life* (1918) opens with the Tramp trying to sleep along a fence in a yard, with a small wooden barrel as a pillow—he'll later use the dog—and a length old pipe as a hand muff, as I've noted. It reminds us that rarely do we see the Tramp "roughing it," as in *City Lights* when he seems to be about to retire for the night to his bench along the river. We see the Tramp stealing food, first from a hot-dog vendor's box, and then from a lunch cart, where the dog grabs a link of sausages and the Tramp surreptitiously eats rolls, one after another. What are we meant to think about the obvious parallels between the Tramp's status and that of the dog, which Chaplin admitted were intentional (Chaplin, 1964/2003, p. 208)? For Robinson (1985/1994, p. 231), "Chaplin discovers here something universal, in the mysterious doorways, the loitering bums, the loungers at corners, the sitters on doorsteps, the traders with their flimsy stalls only waiting for pilferers or for the small daily catastrophe which will upend them with avalanches of fruit and vegetables." He had tapped into this before, with *The Champion* (1915). The first title card reads, "Completely broke. Meditating on the ingratitude of humanity," and we see the Tramp sitting on a stoop with a bulldog, sharing what appears to be the last of his food.

The Tramp can be kind on other occasions, too, especially when there's a pretty girl involved. In *The Circus* (1928), hungry and poor, he nonetheless lets the abused daughter of the circus owner have his last slice of bread and gives her the egg he recently purloined. But he's not generous only when there's a pretty girl, as we see in *The Kid* (1921). The Tramp can sometimes seem dim, but we here see evidence of his cleverness and resourcefulness when the need arises. He has improvised a crib and an automated bottle feeder, and makes diapers out of what appear to be old bed sheets. Because it's so clear that he has come to love the child and is working hard to care for him, we feel affection for him. When we flash forward five years, the well-fed child, played by Jackie Coogan—who will play Oliver Twist (see Chapter 11) and many years later, Uncle Fester on *The Addams Family*—is sitting on the curb outside their building. He's carefully cleaning his nails, having adopted the habits, and the pretentions, of his adoptive father. When he comes in for dinner, his nails are inspected and the Tramp washes the boy's face and buffs his neck as if it were a shoeshine. When the child falls ill, the Tramp calls for a doctor, who, upon learning of the circumstances of his parentage, threatens to have him taken away so that he can receive "proper care and attention." The County Orphan Asylum truck arrives, and the social workers wrench the child away from the Tramp. Father and adopted son are hysterical and distraught. The Tramp rescues the boy, and they flee to a flophouse, only to have the proprietor take the child and turn him in for the reward money. But as the film hurtles toward its close, the boy's mother is reunited with her long lost child, and the Tramp is brought to her doorstep and invited in. (Unlike in other Chaplin films, there has been no romance, or even the vaguest hint of one, between the mother and the Tramp). At the movie's opening in Paris, Jackie Coogan hosted a separate premiere for orphans at the Cinema Madeleine, and according to Robinson (1985/1994, p. 265), "Chaplin himself was among those who felt that the vast, universal response to Jackie's image was in part due to his function as a symbol of all the orphans of the recent war."

While he is only sometimes indifferent to the well-being of other people, the Tramp is almost always indifferent to work, a trait that on one hand reinforces the stereotypes of the lazy bum, but on the other hand may have resonated with Chaplin's working-class audiences. After all, the kinds of jobs that were typically available to the Tramp and those who watched him on screen required hard labor at long hours for low pay, as in *Work* (1915), where he's whipped like a mule while pulling his boss's cart. Who wouldn't want to avoid that if they could? *Pay Day* (1922) is another occasion when Chaplin plays the Tramp as a working man, and also a rare case of a later film in which he drinks to drunkenness. Perhaps it's that he can be sober as the carefree Tramp, but needs to be drunk as a laborer? Or perhaps it's just that Chaplin missed the fun of playing a drunk: he was famous for it in the Sennett era, and on the stage before that.

The most famous exception to the idle Tramp is *Modern Times* (1936). Here, the character has advanced from the lowest classes: "A Tramp" is now replaced in the credits with "A Factory Worker." But after a "nervous breakdown" and a stint in the hospital, the Factory Worker emerges as a tramp, offering another story about where the Tramp might have come from to go along with *Face in the Bar Room Floor*. But soon enough, for the love of a woman, he vows to rejoin the working class again: "I'll do it!" he pledges. "We'll get a home, *even if I have to work for it*." The Tramp is often shown to live up to the stereotype of the bum who shuns labor, and only when truly pressed will he condescend to work, like when things get desperate in *The Champion* (1915), or when he's determined to come to the aid of the girl in *Modern Times* or *The Tramp* or *City Lights*, or, sometimes, if there's another reward. In *A Dog's Life*, he and the other unemployed men seem little interested in a call for "Strong Men for Sewer Work," but then fight each other for a job in a brewery. Often when he does work he winds up being ill-suited to it. In *The Pawnshop* (1916), he plays a clerk trying to determine the value of a clock—he examines it as if he were a doctor looking for a heartbeat in a patient, using a stethoscope and all—and in the process destroys it, handing it back to the poor man in pieces, leaving him worse off than when he came in to pawn it.

To return to *Modern Times*: Reading a headline in the newspaper about factories reopening, Chaplin bounds from his chair and heads out. There's a mixed message here—the soulless factory is nonetheless all that a man can depend upon for dignity and for sustenance. Once he's back to work, a strike puts him out of work yet again. He gets a job as a security guard, and on his first night surprises three burglars. Their leader recognizes him from working in the steel mills, and, telling him that they are not really burglars but merely hungry, breaks into tears. Hunger forms a theme in this picture, and over and over again, it's what motivates the characters. Food is the difference between employment and unemployment. But every time he gets a job and a place to live, something goes wrong, so that by the end, he and they girl are once again on the side of the road, with her tying a bindle together, and they both walk off out of the picture, two Tramps now instead of one.

Chaplin opens his autobiography (1964/2003) with a scene of him at age twelve, returning home to the "small garret" he shared with his mother and half-brother Sydney. "The house was depressing and the air was foul with stale slops and old clothes." Times were harder than usual. Sydney was off at sea, and his mother's sewing machine, from which she earned her meager living, had been repossessed. And yet, notes Chaplin, "I was hardly aware of a crisis because we lived in continual crisis." But as it had before, his mother's mental illness would take her away to the asylum. In between descriptions of the shoddy room and the privation is the warm memory of waking to a fire in the "tidy little room," Mother in cheerier times, toast on the way. It's a scene that seems to have haunted Chaplin a bit, and this small grim flat at 3 Pownall Terrace is a place he would revisit—world famous, impossibly wealthy—on visits back from his new life in America. It's trite to suggest that Chaplin never forgot his own poverty, but that does not make the claim false. Yet neither does that mean that his remembrance turned into activism, or to outrage over economic injustice. His political engagement, which mostly consisted of speechmaking, was more likely to be focused upon international affairs, and the Red-baiting that finally refused him reentry into the United States in 1952 began with a fairly innocuous speech urging support of Roosevelt's calls for the opening of a Second Front to aid the Soviet Union, then our ally, in World War II. Though he was never subpoenaed to appear before the House Un-American Activities Committee, Chaplin imagined turning up to testify in the Tramp costume "to make a laughing stock of the inquisitors" (Robinson, 1985/1994, p. 547). It's possible that what makes the middle-class pretensions of the Tramp so poignant was that they reflect Chaplin's own unease among the wealthy and well-educated, something evident in his constant efforts at self-improvement: reading ponderous books, memorizing new vocabulary words, carefully planning ahead so that at parties he would have something to say. As when the Tramp is playing golf at a country club in *The Idle Class* (1921), he can seem most happy when he is "passing" for a member of another class.

Chaplin's mother was an aspiring singer who struggled to earn a living after losing her voice. She sold what little she owned in order to survive, including what remained of her stage costumes—the rest she made into clothes for the boys, which were a source of mockery and fistfights at school for Sydney. Chaplin rarely saw his father, an alcoholic who died at thirty-seven and whose financial contributions to the household were sporadic at best. "Picasso had a blue period," writes Charlie. "We had a grey one, in which we lived on parochial charity, soup tickets and relief parcels" (Chaplin, 1964/2003, p. 23). As he would write of later years, "I was well aware of the social stigma of our poverty. Even the poorest of children sat down to a home-cooked Sunday dinner. A roast at home meant respectability, a ritual that distinguished one poor class from another. Those who could not sit down to a Sunday dinner at home were of the mendicant class, and we were that. Mother would send me to the nearest coffee-shop to buy a sixpenny dinner (meat and two vegetables). The shame of it—especially on Sunday!" (Chaplin, 1964/2003, p. 50).

When the boys were older and Sydney was working during the week, in uniform, as a telegraph boy, Hannah would pawn his suit clothes every Monday and retrieve them the next weekend, that small float of money making the difference in cash flow. And yet, "in spite of the squalor on which we were forced to live, she had kept Sydney and me off the streets and made us feel we were not the ordinary products of poverty, but unique and distinguished" (Chaplin, 1964/2003, p. 285). Indeed, Robinson (1985/1994) writes that there's evidence that Hannah Chaplin may have "kept the worst from her children," including a grandmother who "declined into alcoholism and vagrancy" (pp. xii–xiii).

His mother's health was in steady decline and, in 1895, when Chaplin was age seven, this close family of three entered the workhouse. Charlie and Sydney were soon transferred to the Hanwell School for Orphans and Destitute Children, where the brothers, in separate wings, would live for over a year before returning, once again, to the workhouse (Chaplin, 1964/2003; Robinson, 1985/1994). The worst poorhouses, workhouses, and orphanages at the turn of the century were cruel, dirty, dreadful places, but while Chaplin reports that "we were aware of the shame of going to the workhouse" (Chaplin, 1964/2003, p. 26), their experience at Lambeth and then at Hanwell doesn't seem to have been as bad as it could have been, although Chaplin inhabited more institutions, and moved between them more frequently, than his autobiography reveals. "Although at Hanwell we were well looked after, it was a forlorn existence. Sadness was in the air; it was in those country lanes through which we walked, a hundred of us two abreast. How I disliked those walks, and the villages though which we passed, the locals staring at us! We were known as inmates of the 'booby hatch,' a slang term for the workhouse" (Chaplin, 1964/2003, p. 29). But the children were publicly beaten—*flogged* sounds too gentle for what Chaplin describes—with a birch stick for offenses real and imagined.

Soon thereafter, as reluctant guests of his father and his new wife, life was little better. His stepmother clearly resented the children's presence, even though they spent at most two months there (Robinson, 1985/1994, pp. 26–27). Hannah was released from the asylum to which she'd been transferred from the workhouse, and they were back together in a cheap, small room near a pickle factory. But back to the asylum she would go, and the next time, with Sydney away again at sea, Charlie would live alone, hiding from the landlady for fear he would be carted off to an orphanage or workhouse. He was probably never homeless, but often on the edge of it, and Payne (1952, p. 82) suggests there was a brief period of sleeping on park benches.

It is tempting to read into this background the genesis and continued presence of the Tramp character who would make Chaplin rich and famous, but there are other explanations that are at least as plausible. First, tramps of one sort or another were stock characters on the London stage during Charlie's boyhood and before (see *Charlie* [2003]; Robinson, 1985/1994, p. 114), and on the American vaudeville stage, too (Payne, 1952, pp. 87–88), including a tramp juggler played by W. C. Fields that may have had more than passing influence on Chaplin (Cresswell, 2001, p. 134, citing Nicole Vigouroux-Frey). Even before Chaplin's Tramp became ubiquitous in popular culture, there were stock tramp and hobo characters in the comic strips (Cresswell, 2001, p. 139). Furthermore, the part of the Tramp that was a clown has roots in the *commedia dell'arte* stock character Harlequin (Sobel and Francis, 1977, p. 109) and, perhaps, Pierrot (see Payne, 1952), and, just as *Saturday Night Live* features sketches with the same familiar characters over and over again, so, too, did the English music hall feature actors who became identified with a single, familiar role. Given this tradition, the recurrence of the Tramp in Chaplin's work is consistent with the form (Sobel and Francis, 1977, p. 55), something Chaplin acknowledged many years later in *Limelight* (1952), where he plays a character named Calvero, a one-time "Tramp Comedian," as a publicity poster calls him, something of a singing and dancing circus clown working on the vaudeville stage. Calvero is clearly not *The* Tramp, however.

We don't know what forces of psychology were at work when Chaplin first cobbled together the Tramp costume for Mack Sennett, but it was done on the fly, at least as Chaplin tells it:

> I had no idea what make-up to put on ... on the way to the wardrobe I thought I would dress in baggy pants, big shoes, a cane and a derby hat. I wanted everything a contradiction: the pants baggy, the coat tight, the hat small and the shoes large. I was undecided whether to look old or young, but remembering Sennett had expected me to be a much older man, I added a small moustache, which, I reasoned, would add age without hiding my expression. I had no idea of the character. But the moment I was dressed, the clothes and the make-up made me feel the person he was. I began to know him, and by the time I walked on the to the stage he was fully born.... [As I explained the character to Sennett]: 'You know, this fellow is many-sided, a tramp, a gentleman, a poet, a dreamer, a lonely fellow, always hopeful of romance and adventure. He would have you believe he is a scientist, a musician, a duke, a polo-player. However, he is not above picking up cigarette-butts or robbing a baby of its candy. And, of course, if the occasion warrants, he will kick a lady in the rear—but only in extreme anger!'... As the clothes had imbued me with the character, I then and there decided I would keep to this costume whatever happened.... My character was different and unfamiliar to the American, and even unfamiliar to

myself. But with the clothes on I felt he was a reality, a living person. In fact he ignited all sorts of crazy ideas that I would never have dreamt of until I was dressed and made up as the Tramp.

But the character type had been in Chaplin's mind before: here he is relating his dissatisfaction, at age twelve, with working in an eight-boy troupe of clog dancers:

My first impulse to do something other than dance was to be funny. My ideal was a double act, two boys dressed as comedy tramps. I told it to one of the other boys and we decided to become partners. It became our cherished dream. We would call ourselves "Bristol and Chaplin, the Millionaire Tramps," and would wear tramp whiskers and big diamond rings. It embraced every aspect of what we thought would be funny and profitable, but, alas, it never materialized. (Chaplin, 1964/2003, p. 44)

FIGURE 9.6 Charlie Chaplin, circa 1920. Image published in the U.S. prior to 1923 and in the public domain.

Robert Payne (1952, pp. 121–122) tells another genesis story, one that Chaplin does not recount in the *Autobiography*:

> Quite accidently he met a hobo in San Francisco. The man was down and out, hungry and thirsty.... Chaplin took him into the barroom for a drink and some food, and suddenly the man began to talk of his own irresponsible joy in living the life of a hobo. It was a life lived to the uttermost.... Chaplin was delighted with the man, with his gesture, his expressions, his good talk. "He was rather surprised when we parted, because I thanked him so much," Chaplin said later. "But he had given me a good deal more that I had given him, though he didn't know it."

There's nothing implausible in this account, and I'm not sure it matters too much where the Tramp came from. But a previously lost Chaplin short from 1914 that was found in 2010, *The Thief Catcher*, seems to show, suggests Richard Roberts, that the essence of the character had been around for some time before the supposed "on the fly" creation (Zongker, 2010).

Chaplin remembers his mother reading aloud to him from the Bible, and emphasizing its admonitions to care for the poor and weak, and he recounts a public scene in which she "stopped to upbraid some boys tormenting a derelict woman who was grotesquely ragged and dirty." When it turned out that his mother knew the woman from her days on the stage, Chaplin confesses, "I was so embarrassed that I moved on and waited for Mother at the corner." He reveals his disgust with the woman, and the "horror" when his mother, after a trip to the public baths, brought her home. But he voices no regret over these feelings, no shame. That does not mean that he did not feel remorse, but it does seem curious to report such strong feelings of antagonism to this actual homeless woman without reflecting upon it (see Chaplin, 1964/2003, pp. 56–57). Years later, in an event not recounted in the autobiography, he reports that "there was an old woman about seventy [sleeping outside]. I gave her something. She woke up, or stirred in her sleep, took the money without a word of thanks—took it as though it was her ration from the bread line and no thanks were expected, huddled herself up in a tighter knot than before, and continued her slumber. The inertia of poverty had long since claimed her" (in Robinson, 1985/1994, p. 285). Her *ingratitude* is what rankles Chaplin. But perhaps this was all merely an awkward and unconscious reflection of a fear that that those women could have been his own mother, and that he would have been helpless to stop it.

Yet, he was so "illumined with kindly light and a fervent goodwill" after his first date with Hetty Kelly, his first real love, that he "distributed among the derelicts who slept on the Thames Embankment" the last of the money he had withdrawn for the date (Chaplin, 1964/2003, p. 105). He makes a point of describing his first trip to New York and the parts of the city where "poverty was callous, bitter and cynical, a sprawling, yelling, laughing, crying poverty piling around doorways, on fire escapes and spewing about the streets. It was all very depressing and made me want to hurry back to Broadway." Here again, Chaplin notes poverty, and is depressed by it, not spurred to action, not outraged. But that is not to say that he forgets it, or failed to have learned from it. As he wrote, "Unlike Freud, I do not believe sex is the most important element in the complexity of behavior. Cold, hunger, and the shame of poverty are more likely to affect one's psychology."

Thomas Burke (1932, p. 150) reported the following reaction from Chaplin to the crowds that would come to surround him wherever he went:

> Oh, God, Tommy, isn't it pathetic—isn't it awful? That these poor people should hang round me and shout "God bless you, Charlie," and want to touch my overcoat, and laugh, and even shed tears—I've seen 'em do it—if they can touch my hand. And why? Why? Because I made 'em laugh. Because I cheered 'em up. Cheered 'em up! Ugh! Say, Tommy, what kind of filthy world is this—that makes people lead such wretched lives that if anybody makes 'em laugh they want to kiss his overcoat, as though he were Jesus Christ raising 'em from the dead? Eh? *There's* a comment on life. *There's* a pretty world to live in. When those crowds come round me like that—sweet as it is to me personally—it makes me sick. Because I know what's behind it. Such drabness and ugliness, such misery, that simply because someone makes 'em laugh and help 'em to forget, they ask God to bless him!

Burke (1932) claims that Chaplin's story about his childhood changed frequently, and that he was terrible at remembering dates and addresses. David Robinson, however, was able to corroborate almost every salient fact of Chaplin's *Autobiography* and confirmed that his "memory for sums of money seemed infallible" (Robinson, 1985/1994). So, it's probably wise to take the statement Burke attributes to Chaplin with some skepticism. On the other hand, Chaplin's well-documented scorn for those who would romanticize poverty or the slum is consistent with this outburst, and Burke relates other stories told to him by Chaplin that themselves reappear, with the salient details, in his autobiography some thirty years later. Moreover, Robert Payne (1952, p. 293) tells a similar tale:

> Chaplin is inevitably the child of paradox. He will say, for example, "Why shouldn't I mock poverty? The poor deserve to be mocked. What fools they are!" He will say this savagely, the face becoming a mask of horror-stricken accusation. "Why don't they rebel against poverty? Why do they accept it? It is the ultimate stupidity to accept poverty when there are all the riches of the world—every man should have them." The next moment, confronted with human misery, knowing that it is there, knowing that there is almost nothing he can do about it, he will say, "The whole world is full of poor devils caught in the trap. How will they ever get out? I've tried to help them forget the trap in my films, but the trap is still there."

Here Chaplin responds to speculation from Somerset Maugham that he "suffers from a nostalgia of the slums":

> The attitude of wanting to make poverty attractive for the other person is annoying. I have yet to know a poor man who has nostalgia for poverty, or who finds freedom in it. Nor could Mr. Maugham convince any poor man that celebrity and extreme wealth mean constraint. I find no constraint in wealth—on the contrary I find much freedom in it.... I found poverty neither attractive nor edifying. It taught me nothing but a distortion of values, an over-rating of the virtues and the graces of the rich and the so-called better classes. Wealth and celebrity, on the contrary, taught me to view the world in proper perspective, to discover that men of eminence, when I came close to them, were as deficient in their way as the rest of us (Chaplin, 1964/2003, pp. 266–267).

On his trip to the United Kingdom to promote *City Lights*, Chaplin reports having said to the prime minister,

> Since my first visit there was a great change for the better. In 1921 I had seen much poverty in London, grey-haired old ladies sleeping on the Thames Embankment, but now those old ladies were gone; no more were derelicts sleeping there. The shops looked well stocked and the children well shod, and that, surely, must be to the credit of the Labour Government. (Chaplin, 1964/2003, p. 338)

But of course the derelicts could still have been there, and merely moved out of sight, as American cities have come to do before events that bring attention to them. On the same trip, a meeting with Lloyd George had him "enthusiastically developing a plan for clearance of the London slums" (Robinson, 1985/ 1994, p. 424). Later, in 1931, he would tell a reporter, "Something is wrong. Things have been badly managed when five million men are out of work in the richest country in the world," and that the changes he most wanted to see were "shorter hours for the working man, and a minimum wage for both skilled and unskilled labor, which will guarantee every man over the age of twenty-one a salary that will enable him to live decently" (Robinson, 1985/ 1994, p. 457). While promoting *City Lights* in Britain in 1931, Chaplin told an "old Victorian" who was complaining that "the dole is ruining England!" that "without the dole there'd be no England" (p. 359), just as J. K. Rowling, nearly as famous but even richer than Chaplin, and a former relief recipient herself, defended the dole more recently and even more vigorously (Rowling, 2010).

However, in his autobiography there is almost no discussion at all about the Great Depression, and the Tramp was seldom used to make a point. He was a means toward an end, but that end was comedy, not education. Note, for example, the manner in which Chaplin describes *The Idle Class* (1921):

> The plot was simple. The tramp indulges in all the pleasures of the rich. He goes south for the warm weather, but travels under the trains instead of inside them. He plays golf with balls he finds on the golf-course. At a fancy dress ball he mingles with the rich, dressed as a tramp, and becomes involved with a beautiful girl. After a romantic misadventure he escapes from the irate guests and is on his way again. (Chaplin, 1964/2003, pp. 258–259)

It's not a film about class or wealth or homelessness; it's about contrasts. As he told a reporter for the *New York World* in 1931, "I am always suspicious of a picture with a message. Don't say that I'm a propagandist" (in Robinson, 1985/1994, p. 458). That does not and should not preclude our own readings of Chaplin's films and of the Tramp himself.

There are more critical appraisals of Chaplin's life. For a contrast to *The Autobiography*, Robinson's diligent biography that confirms most of it, Agee's effusive reviews, and Payne's hagiographic account—Charlie is "half god, half man, and always vagabond, brother to St. Francis and the moon, the loveliest things that ever graced the screen," he wrote (Payne, 1952, p. viii)—there's Sobel and Francis (1977; esp. Chap. 5). They find greater fault with Chaplin's memory and make much of his omissions and contradictions, including on the genesis of the Tramp. They criticize his failure to acknowledge the contributions made by the technicians who worked on his films, recount the jokes and bits of business that may have been stolen from other comedians, suggest there's something a bit venal about Chaplin's willingness to throw out a scene if it fared poorly with a test audience, find his politics amorphous and shallow, and, echoing Burke (1932), suggest there was little he cared about other than notoriety and financial security. But they may prove too much. For example, they write that "Poverty, when it came [to Chaplin], only lasted three or four years, after which he was in almost continuous work. Even the workhouse and orphanage he was sent to would have been nothing like as terrifying as at the beginning of Victoria's reign. They supplied meat and fresh milk every day and provided a balanced diet many poor people nowadays would be grateful to receive." Even if we see Chaplin's childhood through Sobel and Francis's lens, however, we might wonder what the effects of *only* three or four years of poverty might mean to a child, or what incarceration in an institution, no matter how supposedly benign, might portend. But they continue: "Of course, there must have been periods of near-starvation when his mother was in the asylum and his brother at sea; moments of despair, of loneliness, hopelessness, of biting shame." That these events were fleeting, as they emphasize, does not necessarily tell us that they were not important to who Chaplin would become or how he would think and act. As they themselves note:

> The periods of poverty, short though they may have been, left their mark. The progressively worse slums he had to live in, the abjectness of relying on parish relief, the clinging taint of the soup kitchen, the disease and malnutrition that glared out of the mutilated faces of some of the people he worked with, the torpor of unemployment—all fused into the blazing belief that poverty was the ultimate fall from grace and wealth the golden redeemer. (Sobel and Francis, 1977, p. 75)

In the autobiography, Chaplin does not reflect much in his later years upon the poverty of others, or set about to reform workhouses, or even to advocate for better mental health services. He does, however frequently marvel at how far he had come, and feel grateful for the comfort in which he lived. Chaplin was never extravagant, despite his enormous wealth. And, especially in his early years of film success, when he seemed fearful that it could all end at any moment, he assiduously squirreled away as much of his salary as possible and seemed to recognize how much of his initial opportunities in the theater owed as much to good fortune as to hard work or talent.

Sobel and Francis (1977, pp. 159–161) also complain that the Tramp is insufficiently degraded to be the real thing: too clean and clean-shaven, too often housed and employed, too easily able to interact with members of the other classes. I am sympathetic to this complaint. But Chaplin is not playing a tramp, a hobo, or a vagabond so much as he is playing the *idea* of one. The Chaplin Tramp is a tramp in the most essential sense—he is rootless, he is a transient, arriving someplace anew at the beginning of the film, causing mayhem, falling in love and, that love unrequited, shuffling off down the road and on to another adventure. It's the romance of the hobo lifestyle and, importantly, the freedom that creates for Chaplin, since the character can be anywhere at the start of a new film, and he never has to worry about living with the consequences of his actions. The poverty of the Tramp is only at issue when Chaplin needs it to be to set up a scene or to pull off a joke, and it is not necessarily his poverty that is essential, but his relative powerlessness. The Tramp's attacks are upon authority and upon those with power, because, as Chaplin himself observed on many occasions, jokes at the expense of those who are weaker are not funny. We might also read the Tramp's reflexive avoidance of the police as an indicator of his class and status; the poor, and especially homeless men, have had particular reason for such fears.

While we may take pleasure in the Tramp because he gets the better of his supposed superiors, the audience is, in turn, the Tramp's superior—perhaps the great wellspring of affection for the Tramp comes from a place near to where we keep fondness for puppies and children: They are impetuous and unpredictable, but they are dependent upon us. We are, in the end, possessed of more power over our lives, however tenuous, however fragile that power may be, than they are. Perhaps this also tells us something about why only children, dogs, drunks, and the blind are the Tramp's true friends.

There's no evidence to suggest that Chaplin meant for the Tramp to communicate a political point or to make a statement about poverty. It's then left for us to determine whether people read a political commentary into the films and, if so, to try to understand why. Because no message or meaning was intended does not mean that there was no meaning or message. As Chaplin himself wrote, "There are more valid facts and details in works of art than there are in history books" (Chaplin, 1964/2003, p. 320). There's at least a class consciousness at work in many of his films. The millionaire the Tramp rescues from suicide in *City Lights* (1931) is, as others have observed, happy to call the Tramp a friend so long as the millionaire is drunk. Once sober, he is, in the words of the title card, "a different man," and literally does not recognize the Tramp—he almost does not even see him. Once drunk again, he returns to his old affection for his savior and playmate. As in many movies of the 1930s, the rich are not evil, but ridiculous and oblivious to the kinds of lives that are not their own.

Creswell argues that Chaplin's portrayal of the Tramp helped turn the public from a fear of and contempt for the dangerous hobo to some sympathy for the homeless man. But we have to reconcile such claims with the fact that the word "Tramp" remained an epithet through the 1930s and 1940s. Besides, the Little Tramp seems to exist in his own class, apart from all the other hoboes and bums and bindlestiffs. He doesn't see himself as a danger, and since the movies are from his perspective, neither does the audience. Charlie's not like all the other tramps, so affection for him, or concern about his plight, won't necessarily translate into a more general concern for all homeless men. The Tramp is a stand-in, many critics have nonetheless suggested, not just for all tramps, but for all the dispossessed and the downtrodden: He's an Everyman. In *The Great Dictator* (1940), as a Jewish barber, he carries this conceit to its most tragic extreme. Chaplin said the barber was not meant to be the Tramp (Bourne, 2003), but this seems a suspect claim: examine the moustache, the clothes, the walk, the demeanor. They all echo the Tramp. That the Tramp, in the guise of a Jewish barber, is mistaken for and takes the place of Hitler is out of character in that the Tramp, while he has always aspired to wealth, has never aspired to power. But here, when he gets it, he offers a paean to fellowship and a tirade against technology and greed. Never too terribly concerned about others, the Tramp, in what is arguably his final appearance, becomes the ultimate humanist.

What distinguishes Chaplin from D. W. Griffith is precisely that humanism. Griffith's films are spectacles, and they are about events on a grand, historic, scale. Chaplin's movies are smaller in every respect, but most importantly, they are about people, not events, even when they are set against the rise of Adolf Hitler in Nazi Germany. It's striking how natural and naturalistic so much of the acting in Chaplin's films remains, even the early ones, especially when contrasted with the histrionics of a D. W. Griffith melodrama. This is part of why Chaplin's films still seem fresh and funny and engaging, whereas D. W. Griffith's movies are of interest as historical artifacts and for their grand set pieces, like the ride of the Klan in *Birth of a Nation* or the spectacle of Babylon in *Intolerance*. Griffith's characters feel like characters, whereas Chaplin's characters, even to modern eyes, seem like people.

10 THE LAST FREE TRAMP AND THE HOBO PLAYED FOR LAUGHS

Boudu Saved from Drowning, Down and Out in Beverly Hills, Lady and the Tramp, Billion Dollar Hobo, The Jerk, Life Stinks, Carnivore, Hobo with a Shotgun, Bum Man: Hero of the Homeless, Hancock, Bindlestiffs, Easter Parade, Zoolander

Chaplin would not be the last to try to wring humor out of homelessness and vagrancy. In *Boudu Saved from Drowning*, Boudu (Michel Simon), a homeless man living in Paris, loses his dog. Those he asks for help look at him with a mixture of disgust and fear and scurry off, while a police officer tells him to move along or he'll be arrested. Meanwhile, a wealthy woman has lost her valuable purebred, and the same officer promptly enlists two others to join in a search. Not subtle, but the point is made. Distraught and despondent, Boudu throws himself into the Seine, only to be rescued and taken in by a bookseller who lives above his shop with his wife and a servant girl who is also his mistress. Boudu is not sympathetic—he's rude and ungrateful, thoughtless, ugly, dirty, and eats with his hands; he disrupts the household so much that his benefactor, at wit's end, concludes that "one should only come to the aid of one's equals." Yet both the servant and wife are bedded by Boudu, and he wins the lottery and weds the girl. But he seems happy, in the end, only after he has run away and gone back to living alone—homeless and carefree. A "savage," the wife ultimately calls him. Director Jean Renoir reported in an interview that accompanies the Criterion Collection version of the film that the police shut down *Boudu* after three days, so appalled was Paris—and especially Parisian women—to see such uncivilized behavior on screen. Yet Simon would gain respectability nonetheless, and go on to advertise cigarettes as Boudu for the French National Tobacco Company.

While there's nothing ennobling or redemptive about the effects Boudu has on the bookseller's world, in an American film

FIGURE 10.1 Michel Simon exploits the popularity of Boudu to advertise cigarettes for Tabac Clo-Cloche.

we would expect him to teach Important Lessons to those he encounters, just as we would expect the bookseller's home to be transformed or liberated by him. But, other than revealing the relationship between the husband and servant, little seems to have been altered by the homeless man's presence. No lessons were learned, no morals imparted, no horizons opened. He came, he created chaos, and he went back to where he began, still without his dog. (We're so used to the conventions of modern U.S. cinema that it is shocking that the lost dog does not reappear when Boudu finally returns to his bench in the park.)

Down and Out in Beverly Hills (1986) is Paul Mazursky's remake of *Boudu*, and it differs in revealing ways. In *Boudu*, the dog simply disappears, not to be seen again. In the updated version, the dog first follows a woman who has a bag of food (donuts, perhaps?); she assumes it's lost, since it has no collar. The dog looks at the Boudu character, now called Jerry (Nick Nolte), who is asleep, looks back at the woman, then looks back again at Jerry, before heading off with her, happily trading his homeless life for regular food and some security. Already the film is struggling to make commentary, while *Boudu* was content to let behavior unfold and for most of its import to be ambiguous. What's more, Mazursky is working to make Jerry sympathetic in ways that Renoir made sure that Boudu was not. Here, the homeless man is a statement and a symbol, rather than merely a man. Similarly, well before the rescuer, a rich clothes-hanger magnate called Dave Whiteman (Richard Dreyfus), meets

FIGURE 10.2 A passer-by looks down, literally, at Boudu and his dog. *Boudu Saved from Drowning.* Les Établissements Jacques Haïk, 1932.

Jerry, we are told—twice—that he feels guilty about his wealth. Ambiguity about motives is dispensed with even before the plot is fully wound up.

In American movies, homelessness and poverty need to be explained. Dave asks, moments after he rescues Jerry, "What happened to you? I mean, you're obviously a very intelligent guy." Jerry then tells an elaborate (and at

FIGURE 10.3 Jerry and his dog eat from the trash. *Down and Out in Beverly Hills*, Touchstone Pictures, 1986.

least partially fabricated) story of a failed relationship, a sister who died of tuberculosis, jail, alcohol, and drug abuse. While Boudu has no past, Jerry has many. The film, to its credit, has some awareness about our expectations of such men and seems to know that homeless people will exploit those expectations, which Jerry does when he constructs a narrative that casts himself as a worthy tramp rather than an undeserving hobo (Lankenau, 1999).

Dave soon goes with Jerry, who has been bathed, groomed, and dressed in clean clothes (Boudu never was), to visit Jerry's friends on Venice beach. Dave gets drunk and stays the night, presumably as a way to escape his privileged but dreary life. "They live like animals, but they have a great capacity for love," he reports. "I ate garbage last night, Barbara," he tells his wife, "and I loved it!" These are the sentiments of a man who is slumming, experiencing a night of poverty as if it were an amusement park ride. Later, after Jerry sleeps with Barbara (Bette Midler), she is reborn—released from nine years of grim, orgasm-less marriage in which she substituted shopping for sex and withdrew further and further from the world. Jerry awakened her, performing what I argue is the principal function of the homeless man on film—to transform and redeem others, a trope that reaches absurdist heights here when he also helps their son come out as gay, befriends an alienated neighbor child, radicalizes the maid, saves the dog from depression, cures Dave's daughter of anorexia (then seduces her, too), and teaches Barbara's friends to walk on hot coals.

FIGURE 10.4 A homeless dog sees how the other half lives. "Huh. Snob Hill. I'll bet they've got a lid on every trash can, and a fence on every tree." *Lady and the Tramp*. Walt Disney Productions, 1955.

Chaplin's Tramp often acted much as Boudu does, coming into to a dull, routine world, introducing chaos into it, and then leaving. But Jerry, unlike The Tramp or Boudu, doesn't go away, doesn't go back to where he came from—he stays. Boudu and the Tramp feel a kind of freedom with their vagrancy, but Mazursky seems to find that unimaginable; as would most American film-makers. We even see the pattern in a Disney cartoon movie, *Lady and the Tramp* (1955). Tramp is a homeless mutt who sleeps by the railroad tracks, begs for food at local restaurants, and says he's free and happy, which seems to be the case. He meets Lady, a dog from a well-to-do household—Snob Hill, Tramp first calls it. But after a few escapades, they settle down in her home and have puppies. It seems inconceivable that there could have been a happy ending in which Lady joins Tramp by the tracks, living rough, rather than Tramp being adopted by Lady's rich family and living in comfort, which is how the film ends.

There are a few other American films that try to play homelessness for laughs. The first words of *The Jerk* (1979), played by Steve Martin, are "Huh? I am not a bum. I'm a jerk," spoken directly to a camera that has shown us an alley and a small group of homeless, drunk men. "I once had wealth, power, and the love of a beautiful woman," he continues. Prompted to tell his life story, the white Martin begins: "It was never easy for me. I was born a poor black child." The joke is that's he's so dumb that he doesn't even realize that he was adopted by the African American family that raised him. He sets out on his own, and after stints at a gas station and in the carnival, strikes it rich thanks to an accidental invention. His life as a wealthy man is just as absurd and frivolous as his previous one, and after losing it all, he finds himself back in the alley where we first met him. There's a happy ending, however, as his Mississippi family comes to rescue him, having wisely invested the money he had been sending home. The lesson is not obvious, if there is one. But there are more than a few funny bits, unlike *Billion Dollar Hobo* (1977).

That film gives us a supposedly self-made billionaire, a Depression-era hobo who once rode the rails with only his dog for company, who is now getting ready to pass along his empire to his only surviving relative, nephew Vernon (Tim Conway). To demonstrate his worthiness, the magnate insists that Vernon travel the country by train, just like his uncle did. But after get-ting off the freight train after only a few miles and a few minutes of film—he realized that he was heading in the wrong direction—Vernon becomes an unwitting accomplice in the kidnapping and ransom of a valuable Sharpei, and various unfunny hijinks ensue, nowhere near the rails and utterly aban-doning the set-up, which, if nothing else, at least promised a regular change of locale. Other than to observe that the magnate thought that his time as a hobo taught him "self-reliance, self-confidence, resourcefulness, ingenuity," as he put it, there's little here of note.

In *Life Stinks* (1991), Mel Brooks plays another billionaire, Goddard Bolt, who accepts a bet that he couldn't survive thirty days alone, without money, in the ghetto he intends to raze. Bolt panhandles, washes car windows, and steals; he's mugged for his shoes, urinated on, goes to a soup kitchen for food, visits a grim flophouse he can't ultimately afford, sleeps in boxes, and is covered in rats. He meets Molly, a cynical, bitter, homeless woman. It's not exactly unsympathetic to the people Bolt encounters, but they are tools to advance the plot, such as it is, not fully realized humans. That said, the non-homeless characters are one-dimensional, too, so perhaps we shouldn't read too much into that. There's no coherent message here (and it is a Mel Brooks movie, after all), although there is a moment when a fellow "derelict" is found dead in the gutter and the music swells to indicate that we are witnessing a tragic, dramatic moment, one that offers a revelation to Bolt about the worthiness of even these people. What's consistent is the pattern it holds to: A bitter, empty man is made human, empathetic, and ennobled by his experience of poverty and his encounters with "authentic" people. In that respect, it's the same old story, and *Life Stinks* is not a send-up of the redemption genre, as it wants to be, but an example of it.

However, in a short documentary included with the DVD release ("Does Life Really Stink?"), Brooks says this of the pitch for the film made by Rudy DeLuca and Steve Haberman:

> It's always nice to say something about the social dynamics of a time instead of merely having fun with human foibles. . . . Reagan had closed down clinics and hospitals that took care of the mentally imperfect, and there was no shelter for them, and LA and New York were being overrun by these begging zombies . . . a case of incredible social injustice . . . and I thought it would be a kind of Rembrandt and Breughel backdrop to play a comedy against. . . . We could have a lot of fun with this and also maybe say a little something about what was going on during a hard time.

But what is it that the movie actually says? Some bums might be people worthy of sympathy or pity? Rich men can be callous? Even if Brooks's intention here was to humanize, he failed, perhaps because even with good intentions, most Hollywood writers, directors, and producers know little about such realities. I do not, for one example, know anyone who studies, lives with, or works on behalf of homeless or mentally ill people in need who would refer to them as "begging zombies."

This may be the place to comment briefly on a film that never got made. The Wachowskis' first script (predating their *Matrix* movies and *V for Vendetta*) is a dark comedy called *Carnivore*. It's about a soup kitchen that feeds their clientele human meat. When a man named John arrives at the mission, he first refuses help, as many heroes do to demonstrate their worthiness: Rejection of assistance when in need is an indication that one has not fallen beyond redemption, a Victorian-era notion of worthiness that we can't seem to shake (Pimpare, 2004).

"I don't need any charity," says John.

The proprietor, Mundi, replies, "I am not offering charity. Charity has no place here."

John's confused: "I thought this was a soup kitchen."

Says Mundi, "Oh it is. But it is not run out of charity. There is a bargain, a contract if you will. I offer a bowl of stew in exchange for an appetite. This is my mission, you see. To teach those that will listen that no one need ever be hungry."

Which he does by killing and butchering other people. As another man notes: "There is one basic rule of thumb. The richer they are, the more they eat, the better they taste." As Mundi says in the screenplay's most polemical section: "Two percent of the world's population controls ninety percent of the world's wealth. . . . What is it that they whisper to each other when they open a closet full of fur coats. . . . deep down the rich know exactly what I know. They know that this world is cruel. It is unfair and uncaring and its single guiding principle is dog eat dog." It calls to mind a sign you could see at Occupy Wall Street protests in 2011 and 2012: "Soon the poor will have nothing left to eat but the rich."

Hobo with a Shotgun (2011) began life as a two-minute mock trailer in Quentin Tarantino's *Grindhouse* (2007), but the one-joke premise can't be sustained. Rutger Hauer arrives by rail in Scumtown, a decaying, dog-eat-dog civilization that is occupied by ruthless sociopathic villains, and has descended into the early stages of Mad Maxdom. It's a sister to *Street Trash* (see Chapter 14) as much as anything, filmed in a faux Technicolor that makes this dystopian future a 1970s urban nightmare. And, as with *Street Trash*, it feels futile to search for meaning—hidden or explicit—because it also feels as if that would be giving the film more thought than its makers did. For example: Perhaps we could make more of the fact that the Chief of Police calls Hauer "street trash" and literally tosses him into a dumpster. But virtually everyone is treated as garbage here, homeless or not. What's important for the story is not that Hauer is homeless but that he's a stranger in town, seeking to right the wrongs that he finds there, to impose order where there is only lawlessness and brutality and raw power: It's a Western, that is to say. The hobo is not only the protagonist here, but the hero, albeit a ruthless vigilante as bloodthirsty as those he kills, a hero who suggests that the solution to the town's problem is to load up dump trucks full of criminals and bury them in a mass grave. And, even if he is not mentally ill, he regularly murmurs in a manner to suggest part of him is locked in some past events. There are occasional efforts at humor: after Hauer begins his law-and-order rampage, for example, a newspaper headline reads: "Hobo Stops Begging, Demands Change." But this may well be stolen from a 2008 *Onion* headline about then-candidate Barack Obama that read: "Black Guy Asks Nation for Change."

As part of an effort to kill Hauer, who's been interfering with his plans, a gangster commands the public to kill all the homeless people or he, instead, will kill all of their children, having demonstrated his seriousness by burning alive a bus full of them already. "Death to the Homeless" is spray-painted on a dumpster, and many are killed in a brutal, graphic, and hyper-bloody fashion that is wantonly cruel and ultimately misanthropic (again, much like *Street Trash*).

Bum Man: Hero of the Homeless (2007) tries for a similar joke, and it also fails. A distant planet exiles Bum Man to Earth for failing to contribute to their society—he's lazy, drinks to excess (he's drinking even at his trial), smells terrible, and refuses to work. We learn later that it was, in fact, his alcoholism that caused his demise. A fellow panhandler tells his own story, and for him the lure of the road drove him to becoming a hobo, and then a "common bum," though he still aspires to be a "great hobo" one day. "Gutter Girl" was once a "respectable citizen," too, with a husband and children, until one day her "mind just snapped," as she tells it. It's a typical range of explanations for how people become homeless in the movies.

It seems unwise to reflect too deeply upon *Bum Man,* a film that looks as if it was made by some not especially talented kids who borrowed their parents' video camera (IMDB reports its budget as $3,000). But it becomes notably implausible when a developer and the Mayor conclude that a television report about the homeless men who will be evicted from an alley once their new project begins construction will stop their plan. "This report is going to make it politically impossible to destroy that building, because there's no one who's going to want to see those bums lose their home." It clearly wants to make a larger point, as evidenced by a conversation between the TV reporter and the developer, Mr. Rich (ahem), in which she accuses him of caring about nothing but money and not realizing that the gap between rich and poor is growing and that even middle-class households are having a hard time. Rich replies with the Heritage Foundation's perennial claim that poor people in

America today aren't really poor because they have televisions and VCRs and cell phones and so on. But it's ham-handed and juvenile, ultimately, with the occasional rote catchphrases of liberal nostrum inserted to give an air of seriousness to a trivial project. It's in its own way as rank an exploitation of poverty and homelessness as fouler enterprises like *Street Trash*. When it's revealed that the developer is actually an alien preparing for an invasion of Earth, Bum Man saves the day by using the lethal power of his flatulence and body odor. Because these would, presumably, be the powers of a homeless man.

The obvious comparison is *Hancock* (2008), in which Will Smith plays an inept, alcoholic superhero who, although not strictly homeless, we first meet passed out on a bench. He's unwashed, constantly drunk, unconcerned with others and, as others in the film regularly observe, something of an asshole. But the salient features of his character are his addiction and his attitude. Unlike Bum Man, the joke is not built on his poverty or homelessness—in fact, we see the trailer in which he lives. He's not lazy like Bum Man, merely apathetic. But in reviews at the time in major newspapers, he was referred to variously as "homeless," "a super-gifted bum," "a homeless guy sleeping on a bench," "a homeless drunk," "a bum," and "a surly SuperDerelict with a drinking problem." More accurately, but using the same language, Hancock is referred to as "an alcohol-soaked curmudgeon with a bum's wardrobe," as a man who "appears virtually homeless." It seems an important social fact: Although the film makes it clear that Hancock is not homeless, because he is drunk and dirty and angry, he is nonetheless read by the audience as homeless.

Another recent effort uses a homeless woman as a central gag, in an ugly way. In *Bindlestiffs* (2012), three high school students are suspended and decide to use the time to get a hotel room and try to lose their virginities. One of them gets drunk and winds up having sex on a bench with a drunk homeless woman—we never see her face, which is obscured by dirty, long, gray hair. She then becomes a running gag. Another of them thinks he's accidently killed her, and they are prepared to toss her into a dumpster. She's not dead, but then vomits blood and worse all over the bathroom, while the young man who slept with her nonetheless holds her hair while she spews, then kisses and has sex with her. It's meant to be disgusting and shocking, and is, but much of the humor is meant to be derived from the fact that she's a homeless woman. She's a prop, a joke, and barely treated as human. Indeed, before she's brutally killed later on, she's treated, in effect, as a pet.

There is more difference in degree than in kind in the way homelessness is played for a joke in *Easter Parade* (1948). Fred Astaire and Judy Garland, dancers in a variety show, enter the stage dressed in black-tie-and-tails, which

FIGURE 10.5 "We're a Couple of Swells." *Easter Parade,* MGM, 1948.

are exceedingly dirty, tattered, and torn. Garland is missing teeth. They straighten their cuffs, check their ties, and pull out handkerchiefs to dust imaginary chairs, and launch into song: "We're a couple of swells / We stop at the best hotels / But we prefer the country far away from the city smells." Despite the lyrics, the Vanderbilts really haven't asked them up for tea, of course, and they're not Wall Street bankers who've merely lost the key to their safe. They are merely pretending to be swells. But instead of the poignancy

FIGURE 10.6 *Zoolander,* Paramount Pictures, 2001.

Chaplin wrings from similar acts, this is mere mocking. The basis for the joke is that it's inherently ridiculous for homeless people to pretend to be rich, and unlike Chaplin, it is without empathy or affection them: Bums and tramps are to be laughed at.

Zoolander (2001) may be the only instance in which this kind of joke works. In this satire of models and the fashion industry, we find a couture line called "Derelicte," described by its designer—and the movie's villain—as "a fashion, a way of life inspired by the very homeless, the vagrants, the crack whores that make this wonderful city so unique." At a runway show—for which the narration over the music intones "I am vile spew of the wretched masses . . . I am really, really dirty . . . I am Derelicte!"—a refrigerator box turns into a dress, others are made from discarded condoms, scraps of fabric, and cans, and so on. The joke is that the industry will exploit anything for its own purposes, and what would be more tasteless than making fashion out of the trappings of homelessness and vagrancy? Part of why it works is that it's not implausible: Some years later, a Dior spread in *W Magazine* featured a model, dressed to the nines, posing as an urban refugee sleeping on a park bench and lolling about in an alley, presumably hoping for spare change (Blay, 2009).

Most of these post-Chaplin films that seek to find humor in homelessness fail because there is something mean-spirited in the approach—these people are meant to be looked down upon, with pity or derision. Chaplin succeeds because the objects of humor in his films are typically the Tramp's social and economic superiors, and the Tramp himself never fails to regain his dignity, even when it's lost for a time. With Steve Martin's Jerk, there's an empathy, even an affection, we're meant to have for this man—which makes the viewer disappointed when he becomes a boor. By contrast, in most of the other comedies discuss above, and in the films to follow in the next chapters, the homeless men are *objects* rather than *subjects*.

11 IMPOSTOR TRAMPS

From the Submerged, My Man Godfrey, Merrily We Live, Sullivan's Travels, Gold Diggers of 1933, None But the Lonely Heart, Oliver Twist, My Own Private Idaho

Mel Brooks in *Life Stinks* offered a recent example of a peculiar pattern to be found in the Depression era: movies about men who at first seem to be homeless, who present themselves as those whom Franklin Roosevelt, in the 1932 campaign, called "the Forgotten Man" (Hiltzik, 2011, p. 5), but turn out to be wealthy men in disguise. The Forgotten Man is often just a costume put on by the rich so can we can see their good nature and their *noblesse oblige*. Even in the earliest years of commercial cinema, there's the faux hobo.

The first imposter tramp, as far as I can tell, appears in *From the Submerged* (1912). In this eleven-minute short, a man wakes up having slept on park bench, and is saved from killing himself by a working-class woman who is passing by. Later, he faints while waiting for food at a breadline. But, called home to his dying father, he inherits his fortune and soon rejoins the upper class. When he goes on a "Slumming Party" that includes the same breadline, his companions find it "funny" that he was once among the supplicants there. Taken aback, or perhaps just nostalgic, he sets off looking for the woman who rescued him, now finding her in distress; it is his turn to convince her to live, and they marry. The lesson here, such as it is, seems to be about the fluidity of class and wealth—or that the best way to avoid long-term homelessness is to have a rich family.

My Man Godfrey (1936) opens with men picking through the trash at a Hooverville along New York's East River, one that's a bit grungier and less established than the one in *Man's Castle* (see Chapter 12). After one man complains that if the police weren't so attentive, there wouldn't even be the need for "relief and all that stuff" (since, if they were left alone, there would be enough in the trash for the poor to survive?), Godfrey is singled out by an

FIGURES 11.1 AND 11.2 *From the Submerged*, Essanay Films, 1912. Fainting in the breadline (*left*); and the Slumming Party returns to mock the hungry men (*right*).

imperious rich girl looking for a "forgotten man" as part of scavenger hunt. He's indignant and snide, and drives her off. The rich are made to seem frivolous, silly, and stupid even ("empty-headed nitwits," in Godfrey's phrase), as they are with some frequency in movies of the 1930s. Chaplin thought he understood why: "One of the things most quickly learned in theatrical work is that people as a whole get satisfaction from seeing the rich get the worst of things. The reason for this, of course, lies in the fact that nine tenths of the people in the world are poor, and secretly resent the wealth of the other tenth" (in Robinson, 1985/1994, p. 203). There's truth here, I suspect, but there's more to it, for while people may resent the rich, they also often aspire to be among them (Newport, 2012). That said, it is unusual to find homeless men who are allowed to be as angry as Godfrey, who are so self-assured and self-possessed, or who hold the wealthy in such active, eloquent contempt. In the movies, homeless men may be worthy of pity, but they are rarely worthy of respect. But Godfrey is not homeless, or even poor, we'll learn; he's a wealthy,

FIGURES 11.3 **AND** 11.4 Hooverville in an East River dump. *My Man Godfrey,* Universal Pictures, 1936.

Harvard-educated man in disguise—he's Godfrey Parks, "one of the Parks of Boston," an old friend notes. Having gone down one night, heartbroken, to the East River to kill himself, he found something noble in the poor men there, deciding not only to live, but to join their fraternity. His homelessness is voluntary. I wonder if it would be possible to have an actually homeless man portrayed as this wise, adept, and worldly?

Godfrey allows himself to be taken in by the woman's sister, who thereby wins the game, and is soon hired to be the family's butler, demonstrating talents we might associate with P. G. Wodehouse's Jeeves (in fact, early in his employment, Godfrey makes a Jeeves reference, simultaneously foreshadowing his role and revealing his cultural literacy). Merriment ensues. Later, when he returns to the riverside dump, he says of one of the men there that "when his bank failed, he gave up everything he had so that his depositors wouldn't suffer." He may be living in a dump, the message is, but he is noble, he is to be counted among the "deserving" poor. As Godfrey says, "The only difference between a derelict and a man is a job." Godfrey eventually saves the family from financial ruin, and then builds a wildly expensive job-training and housing program at the site of the dump, as the wealthy come to the rescue of the passive poor.

The poor songwriter in *Gold Diggers of 1933* (1933) is also an impostor. In the midst of a Broadway show's opening musical number, "We're in the Money"—which insists, in song, that "Old man Depression you are through / We never see a headline 'bout a breadline"—bill collectors arrive and close it down, taking the scenery and props to satisfy the creditors. Soon enough, the producer, searching for something to build a new show on that might catch the public's attention, wonders if there might be a show to be made about the Depression.

The musician tentatively offers: "I have something about a forgotten man, but I don't have the words to it yet."

"Play it, play it!" pleads the producer.

"I just got the idea for it last night," he says, as he starts to play. "Was down on Times Square, watching those men on the breadline. Standing there in the rain, waiting for coffee and doughnuts. Around the soup kitchen."

PRODUCER: That's it! That's what this show's about. The Depression! Men marching, marching in the rain, doughnuts and crullers, men marching, marching, jobs, jobs, and in the background will be Carol, [as the] Spirit of the Depression, a blue song, no not a blue song, but a wailing, a wailing, and this woman, this gorgeous woman, singing this song that tears your heart out, the big parade of tears. Work on it! Work on it!

And so he does. Meanwhile, the composer puts up a large sum of money to back this new show, something he can do because he is, in fact, a rich man's

FIGURES 11.5, 11.6, AND 11.7 The final production number of *Gold Diggers of 1933*, Warner Brothers, 1933.

son who is incognito because he has been forbidden to associate with theater folk. The middle act of the film is an entirely typical mistaken-identity sex farce, bracketed loosely by that more somber opening and a genuinely haunting closing number, which finally gives us that endless marching, with men first seen in uniform, fighting at war, and then, having come home to a world without jobs or hope, in a soup line. This is an unusually sympathetic portrait of men in need, but perhaps we can explain that by noting that these men are traditionally counted among the "deserving" poor, having "earned" their relief through national service.

Preston Sturges's *Sullivan's Travels* (1941) might itself be read as a commentary on Hollywood films of the Great Depression and of how poverty is portrayed. It is about John Sullivan, a director who wants to make a movie about poverty and human suffering. Realizing that he doesn't know anything about either of those things, he disguises himself as a hobo (a bindlestiff, to be precise), just as Sturges himself did when he accompanied John Huston and William Wyler for a research trip to Los Angeles flophouses (Jacobs, in Pittenger, 2012, p. 105). Getting ready to set off, Sullivan's butler—who has a bit of Jeeves in him, too—assumes his employer must be dressed for a costume party, and notes that he finds caricaturing the poor distasteful. When the butler learns the real reason for the disguise, he wonders what the audience is for a film about poverty:

THE BUTLER: If you'll permit me to say so, sir: the subject is not an interesting one. The poor know all about poverty and only the morbid rich would find the topic glamorous.

SULLIVAN: But I'm doing it for the poor!

THE BUTLER: I doubt that they would appreciate it, sir. They rather resent the invasion of their privacy. I believe quite properly, sir. You see, sir, rich people and theorists, who are usually rich people, think of poverty in the negative . . . as the lack of riches . . . as disease might be called the lack of health . . . but it isn't, sir. Poverty is not the lack of anything, but a positive plague, virulent in itself, contagious as cholera, with filth, criminality, vice and despair as only a few of its symptoms. It is to be stayed away from, even for purposes of study. It is to be shunned.

SULLIVAN: Well, you seem to have made quite a study of it.

THE BUTLER: Quite unwillingly, sir. Will that be all, sir?

Note the critique about the voyeuristic nature of Hollywood portrayals of poverty, and of how little Hollywood's image of poverty and need comports with the perspective of those, like the Butler, who have actually experienced it.

The canvas in this film is broader than usual. Through Sullivan's eyes, often riding the rails, we see charity missions, lodging houses, and

FIGURE 11.8 Sullivan is gently berated by his butler for his scheme to study the poor. *Sullivan's Travels*, Paramount Pictures, 1941.

Hoovervilles, accompanied by slow, sad camera pans and mournful music. And yet, as is true of most movies of the 1930s (and of most movies in all periods), *Sullivan's Travels* shows us a tragedy without causes: the politics and history that might explain what we see and add dimension to the lives of those we are meant to pity are stripped out. And it is pity and sympathy we are meant to feel, not anger or outrage or indignation. But, whatever Sturges's intent to dig more deeply or to reveal the facile manner in which so many films of the Depression dealt with need, the movie isn't about poor and hungry and homeless men, it's about Sullivan, a Hollywood movie director, whose journey a publicist describes as "almost the greatest sacrifice ever made by human man."

With *Merrily We Live* (1938), like *My Man Godfrey* and *Sullivan's Travels*, we again have at the center of the film a "tramp" who is not actually a tramp at all. In this case, he is a famous novelist. Again it is set largely in the household of a very rich and very silly family, complete with put-upon servants, an eldest daughter who falls for the would-be tramp, Rawlins (Brain Aherne), and a dim-witted matriarch, played with giddy charm by Billie Burke (whom you're more likely to remember as Glinda the Good Witch in 1939's *The*

FIGURE 11.9 Sullivan in a soup kitchen. *Sullivan's Travels*, Paramount Pictures, 1941.

Wizard of Oz). Wade Rawlins finds his way to the Kilbourne home after his car breaks down. We have learned that Burke's Mrs. Kilbourne is wont to take in tramps in order to "save" them; the most recent has absconded with the silver, as the film opens. Rawlins wants only to use the phone, but, mistaking him for yet another tramp, Mrs. Kilbourne finds him a room, insists he take a job as chauffeur, and promptly gets him in uniform. He plays along, and no one seems to notice his well-cultivated speech or accent, and, indeed, later on he will be mistaken for a guest at an important party Mr. Kilbourne is hosting to court a senator from whom he needs a favor. At that dinner, the Senator mentions to Mrs. Kilbourne the rumors of "a very eccentric woman in the district" who "has a hobby of inviting hobos into her home and trying to reform them."

MRS. KILBOURNE: What's wrong with that?

SENATOR: What's wrong with that?! Supposing one were sitting here right here. Now, what would be the topic of his conversation? What would *he* say? What would *we* say?

RAWLINS: Well, it's hard to imagine, unless the tramp, or the hobo as you call him, was a victim of circumstances.

FIGURES 11.10 AND 11.11 Before and after, Rollins mistaken for a tramp and conscripted into serving as a butler. *Merrily We Live*, Hal Roach Studios, 1938.

SENATOR: A tramp is a tramp. He's what he is because he wants to be. He's indolent, and menace to society.... (to Rawlins) You believe that a tramp, if given the opportunity, would give up what he calls his comforts, and accept a job that requires the use of his brain, or hands?

RAWLINS: Well, of course.

SENATOR: Aach, I doubt it.

ROLLINS: Oh, but I'm sure of it. Now, for instance, take me....

At which point the family interrupts him—not out of concern for Rawlins, but for fear that he will reveal himself to be a tramp, offending the Senator and ruining the whole affair. What's interesting about this scene is that we, like the family, are meant to still think Wade Rawlins a tramp, and to have grown to like him—he is, after all, handsome, funny, and charming—so we are not likely to be taking the Senator's side. It might be misunderstood as a noble and forward-thinking position for the film to take, until we remember that the man we might want to defend against scurrilous stereotyping is neither poor nor homeless. It is perhaps a gesture toward seriousness, toward making a "social problem film," but is no more than a gesture. The movie concludes with one final tramp joke, as the butler, finally having had enough of this family's antics, appears with a bindle, ready to head off and become a tramp himself.

None But the Lonely Heart (1944) shares some of the problems I have attributed to *The Blot* (see Chapter 1). Although filmed on an RKO backlot in California, it is set in East London, between the first and second world wars. Clifford Odets directed his own screenplay, adapted from a novel by Richard Llewelyn. Ernie Mott (Cary Grant) comes homes after a period of tramping around and, we presume, causing trouble. Upon hearing that his mother (Ethel Barrymore) is sick and dying, he decides to remain to help her run her used furniture *cum* pawn shop. And that's the funny thing. While critics like Manny Farber (in Polito, 2009), James Agee (2000), and Robert Warshow (2002) have all written about the poverty portrayed here—and disagreed about its authenticity—the Motts are not all that poor. They own a shop, one that we'll learn has been serving as a place to fence stolen goods. Upon Ernie's return, Ma Mott goes out and buys him suits of new clothing and shoes, and there's no hint that the cost was a burden. The kitchen is well-appointed with china, and neither Ernie nor his mother, nor most of the rest of the cast, look or sound as if they've spent much time in a slum. Agee (2000, Dec. 2, 1944, pp. 114–116) thinks this is one of the film's virtues:

> I suppose I should be equally impressed by the fact that the picture all but comes right out and says that it is a bad world which can permit poor people to be poor; but I was impressed rather because Odets was more interested in filling his people with life and grace than in explaining them, arguing over them, or using them as boxing-gloves.

Now, Ma herself talks of their poverty, if indirectly, deflecting Ernie's question about whether she loved his father by observing that "Love's not for the poor, son. No time for it." And Ernie complains about breakfast in this way: "Sheep's heart again? Are we that poor, to be eating the inside of sheeps and cows day in and day out?" When his mother tells him that millions are worse off, he sneers and sighs a bit: "Poor, putrid millions." He's shocked when a young girl tells him she saved up for twenty-seven weeks to buy a pair of new boots. But perhaps it's simply the atmosphere that communicates poverty to those critics: It's all dark, wet stones, like *Angela's Ashes*, but in the chiaroscuro of black and white, heavy with shadows and portent. It's *gloomy*, Leila Rogers told the House Un-American Activities Committee, as evidence for why the film was treasonous (Warshow, 2002, p. 98).

Dickens's Oliver Twist (1938) is another kind of impostor tramp, since this much-abused orphan boy, bounced from poorhouse to workhouse to imprisonment with a criminal gang, turns out not to be just another street urchin, but a young man of noble birth who comes with his own inheritance. Oliver's goodness, his sweetness, his refusal to do harm to commit crime are not, then, visions of how a dirty waif might still be good and noble. And while the middling- and upper-class men and women of the novel and its many adaptations are often awful humans, most of the poor ones are dreadful, too—thieves, liars, cheats, and murderers. The silent version with *The Kid's* Jackie Coogan as Oliver and Lon Cheney as Fagin (1922) hews closely to the novel, even if it skirts the extent of abuse that Oliver suffers. David Lean's 1948 British adaption, by contrast, takes mild liberties with the novel, but better captures the routine of the workhouse, the cruelty of the Poor Laws, and their self-important, overfed administrators. Perhaps no American has enough experience or cultural memory of the workhouse to have such strong feelings about it as Lean does. The children seem shockingly undernourished; they are sallow-cheeked and frail, with dark, sunken eyes, looking more than a bit like concentration camp survivors—and given the period in which the film was made, it's hard not to suspect that this echo is intentional. Lean gives the poorest parts of London a dark, oppressive feel, with close quarters and winding stone stairs that feel as if they might be borrowed from *The Cabinet of Dr. Caligari*. Roman Polanski's 2005 adaptation adds nothing to Lean's, while borrowing liberally from it, but it makes one notable choice: Oliver is just another street urchin in his version, with no noble parentage, although he will end up living a soft, comfortable life nonetheless, no thanks to any of his own labors.

There's even a documentary version of this impostor tramp trope. In *Skid Row* (2007), Pras Michel (from the hip hop/reggae group *The Fugees*) spends nine days homeless on the streets of Los Angeles, armed only with a tent and nine dollars. And a camera crew. And the knowledge that he could leave whenever he wanted. As with Food Stamp challenges, in which celebrities and politicians live for a week on a food stamp budget, I appreciate the effort at some level, but am ambivalent about the usefulness or meaning of it. Those who are most in need of education about SNAP recipients, the program, and what life in poverty is like are the least likely to take the challenge, and there's always something self-serving and self-referential about endeavors like Pras's. It's a movie about *him*, ultimately, whatever its rhetoric about offering insight into "the homeless" or its efforts to offer some political, economic, and even historical context. In this way, even this documentary fits into the larger pattern—there are relatively few films about homelessness or about homeless people, but many that pretend to be.

Take *My Own Private Idaho* (1991), to offer one final example, a film that spends a fair bit of time with homeless street hustlers in Seattle and Portland.

But one of the two main characters, Scott (Keanu Reeves), is in fact the son of the Mayor and soon to come into an inheritance. He's merely biding his time, and is only too glad to abandon his supposed friends for his chance to assume a place in respectable society once it presents itself. Since *From the Submerged*, we've accumulated a 100-year tradition of men in homeless drag, either for a joke, or to make Important Statements about Life.

12 FORGOTTEN MEN

Beggars of Life; Halleluiah, I'm a Bum; A Man's Castle; Swing It, Professor!;
Heroes for Sale; I am a Fugitive from a Chain Gang; Fifth Avenue Girl; The Great
McGinty; Meet John Doe; Our Daily Bread; Mr. Deeds Goes to Town; It Happened
on Fifth Avenue; Washington Merry-Go- Round; Gabriel Over the White House;
Stand Up and Cheer!; Beggars in Ermine; Emperor of the North Pole; Pennies from
Heaven; Ironweed; Cinderella Man

The first Americans who wandered the nation in search of work during the Depression era were doing so before the Crash of 1929, which exacerbated what were already terrible conditions for many in the 1920s. So, 1928's *Beggars of Life* gives us Jim (Richard Arlen), who comes to a screen door looking to work for food, and discovers that the man of the house is dead—killed, we learn, by his adopted (orphaned) daughter Nancy (Louise Brooks) while defending herself from rape. Pretending to be brothers on their way to visit their sick mother, Jim and Nancy (in drag) hop a freight train to escape the law—there will soon be a $1,000 reward posted for her capture— although the ruse doesn't work too well, and they're tossed off by the first bull (a police officer for the railway) who comes across them. As they settle down for the night in a hollowed-out haystack, we learn that Jim is heading to Canada where, his uncle assures him, there's land available for homesteaders. As they drift off, he takes comfort in the idea that even people settling down in warm beds aren't ultimately satisfied: "We're all beggars of life," Jim says in the title card. "Some beg for one thing, and some for another." Nancy says she knows what *she* wants, something she says she's never had: just a place in which to be warm and clean, "a place to call home." It's somehow poignant rather than maudlin: We get the sense that she really has had an awfully rough life so far. By morning they're off again. Wellman's camera has a habit of lingering now and again on a low shot of legs walking—it's how the film opens, with the legs that we'll come to know as Arlen's trundling toward the fateful breakfast table and the events that would set the story in motion.

FIGURE 12.1 Hopping a train. *Beggars of Life*, Paramount Pictures, 1928.

This device repeated has the effect of emphasizing the distance to be traveled, the monotony of the journey, and the anonymity, or perhaps interchangeableness, of the men (and women) tramping the nation in search of something better, themes Wellman will return to in *Wild Boys of the Road* and *Heroes for Sale*. They come upon a hobo jungle—Jim describes it in just those words—and the menacing Oklahoma Red (Wallace Beery). Nancy is quickly discovered to be female, and it's nice to see this *very* old device fail, as it probably would in the world, although female tramps did often travel in men's clothing to try not to draw attention to themselves. The police show up looking for her, but the gang ties up the cops and helps her escape with them. Their motives are probably selfish, however, for she would have been raped by them had events taken a slightly different course, and Oklahoma Red expects her to sleep with him in gratitude for their rescue. In short order, Red has an improbable conversion and allows the couple to take his car and escape, while he uses another body and a train wreck to convince the police that the fugitives are dead, getting himself killed in the process. Thus, even the most hardened soul and the most vile and ruthless man can be touched and do good as a result.

Halleluiah, I'm a Bum (1933) is an odd film. Based on a Ben Hecht story, with music by Rodgers and Hart, it gives us Al Jolson as Bumper, "The Mayor of Central Park," a kind of King of the Hoboes, whom we first meet vacationing in Florida with his (effeminate, black, Step-n-Fetchit-type) male

FIGURE 12.2 Bumper and Acorn prepare for the day, a reminder of how rare it is to see on film homeless people deal with daily hygiene. *Hallelujah, I'm a Bum*, Lewis Milestone Productions, 1933.

companion (Edgar Connor). Back home, he is greeted by the other Central Park bums with a song singing his praises ("My Pal Bumper").

He's soon in a confrontation with a park worker picking up trash, who calls them all "Scum!" insisting that "If a man doesn't work he ought to be dead." Bumper, in turn, calls him a "radical," an "egghead," and says "you talk like a Red." Then, in song, Bumper defends his life:

> *I love to feel the air and feel I'm free*
> *I don't give a stitch if I never get rich*
> *Not a soul I know ever owed me dough*
> *When a bank goes crash I don't lose my cash*
> *I find great enjoyment in unemployment*
> *I'm the only man the World Depression can't overcome*
> *In other words, gentlemen, Halleluiah, I'm a bum.*

But the park worker warns him:

> *The workers will rule the world someday,*
> *and all of your kind'll be wiped away.*
> *Your socks and pants may have holes,*

but you're plutocrats down to your souls! . . .
You're slaves and white trash . . .
Parasites living off parasites!

Bumper finds a wallet with a $1,000 bill (!) in it, and sets off to return it ("Money is a curse!" he says), while all the bums fight to get a share. He's offered the bill as a reward for returning it, and when he tries to refuse, he's called a socialist. So, he gets it broken into smaller bills and distributes it to passers-by while wandering through the park, again singing the praises of being a bum. But soon enough, he falls in love, and after he asks the Mayor to help him get a job to support the woman, the Central Park bums sing their outrage at the prospect, while the trash collector congratulates him for abandoning the "shirkers" in favor of the "workers." At the end, he nonetheless ends up in the park, lying back, content, as the trash man rolls by, contemptuous. The politics here places the working class in opposition to the idle classes, to the rich on one hand, and tramps on the other.

Instead of a rich man playing at being a tramp, in *Man's Castle* (1933), we have Bill, in tuxedo and tails (Spencer Tracy), who appears to be rich to the audience and to Trina (Loretta Young), but who we soon discover lives in a Hooverville by the East River. When he explains to the manager of the restaurant they've just eaten in that he has no money, and offers an indignant diatribe about hunger and injustice and the failures of government, it somehow feels like a cop-out to have him dressed as a rich man. It softens the indictment, even if it simultaneously legitimizes it—whether here or in the films discussed above, the harshest complaints come out of the mouths of rich men disguised as tramps or ersatz rich men being played by tramps. The poor man never gets to be angry or outraged as himself.

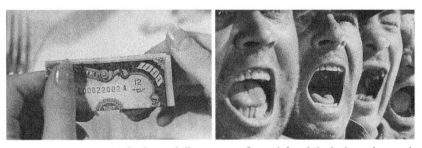

FIGURES 12.3 AND 12.4 The $1,000 bill Bumper refuses (*left*), while the homeless mob demand a share (*right*). *Hallelujah, I'm a Bum*, Lewis Milestone Productions, 1933.

FIGURES 12.5 "You can afford one on the house once in a while!" *A Man's Castle*, Columbia Pictures, 1933.

Trina, we learn, has been out of work for a year and is homeless and desperate, having considered both prostitution and suicide. She moves in with Bill, and soon enough is pregnant and turning his shack into a home, a poor girl having again been rescued by an abusive man. A film that could have been about the Depression becomes a film about love, wanderlust, and a woman's yearning for a new stove. There's a romanticizing of life in this shanty, and we get many scenes of Trina cooking dinner, hanging curtains, washing clothes, and ironing—and she is doing these things just as she would in a tenement flat. There's no effort to convey how dirty, wet, cold, and harsh such lives were in reality, nor any sense that the entire community could be torn down and torched by the police, should they decide to, as they sometimes did. Critic Dave Platt (1933) complained that the Hays Office sought to ban the film "because one of the characters in the film lives with a girl out of wedlock" but was certain that it was "because the Hays organization wants to keep off the screen all vital references to unemployment and the crisis." He notes, by contrast, the "salacious liberties" Mae West was permitted. But "the moment a film dealing with a subject like unemployment makes an appearance, the slightest pretext is found to stop it from being shown." Platt's accusation is plausible, even if I find the capitalist critique in *Man's Castle* to be brief and gentle.

Designed initially to fend off government censorship of content and growing protests from Catholics and their League of Decency, the Hays Office (with

Joseph Breen at its head from 1934–1954) and the Production Code (in effect from 1930–1968) enforced orthodoxy of all stripes throughout the mid-century. As Doherty writes (2007, p. 117), "When a studio, usually Warner Bros., ventured into controversial thickets and dared to manipulate melodrama to denounce lynching, union busting, or fascist militarism, the [Motion Picture Producers and Distributors of America] 'on behalf of the industry' acted to stifle the preachments." Indeed, he continues (Doherty, 2007, p. 232), while pre-Code Hollywood gave us *Heroes for Sale* and *Wild Boys of the Road*, later social problem films "almost never had anything to do with money." We do know that, according to the Hays Office's own figures, the "social problem" film declined from twenty-one percent of the total in 1947 to 9.5 percent by the early fifties (Neve, 1992, p. 85).

Swing It, Professor (1937) gives us genuine tramps in what is, of all things, a pro-swing music propaganda film, featuring a young music professor who is fired for being old fashioned. After tramping around the country a short bit, but never getting the least bit scraggly, he comes upon a group of (anti-swing music!) hobos, gathered round a fire, eating and singing. The Professor must, literally, sing for his supper, which he does:

> *Open your eyes and you will see*
> *the world's at your command*
> *The best things in life are free*
> *and that's why I feel so grand*
> *I've got the sun above, the earth below*
> *the summer breeze, the winter snow*
> *O, what more could I ask for*
> *I'm richer than a millionaire*

Other lyrics extol the virtues of having "the time to roam," and note that "the world's a home to me / but I don't pay the rent." It's a romanticized, idealized scene (they have a piano with them in the woods, after all), and filmed in soft light. In the morning, the Four Singing Tramps ("As Themselves," as they appear in the credits) have taken up the Professor's song, in sweet soft harmonies, as they do the washing up after breakfast. The Professor promptly joins their "colony" (as they call it), and one of them soon takes him "off to work," where they play and sing on the street for change.

And that's the last we see of the tramps: the Professor, as one does in such movies, pretends to be a nightclub owner and then actually becomes one, getting the mobster's girl in the process, but his newfound friends disappear from the picture, which presents a curious missed opportunity. Late in the film, the Professor needs a crowd to help him reclaim the nightclub and the girl from a rival gangster, and he sets out to gather people for the task. I assumed that he would go back to his friends in the colony, and that they would come to the rescue. But instead, he steals a cab and, simply by honking his horn and waving at other cabbies to join him, amasses a convoy to bring to the nightclub. The initial storyline disappears, the tramps fade from view, and the Forgotten Men are forgotten once again.

Heroes for Sale (1933) is an origin story, showing us where the Tramp comes from (this need to explain homelessness is common, as I've noted; Chaplin's Tramp and Boudu will remain exceptions). As the theatrical trailer asked, over battle scenes from the trenches of World War I: "Yesterday's Hero: Is He Today's Forgotten Man?" The answer is yes.

Tom Holmes (Richard Barthelmess) is shot and wounded capturing a German soldier, but another soldier, Roger (Gordon Westcott), gets the credit. After the war, Tom gets a job in the bank Roger's father owns, but is fired when they discover his morphine addiction, which he acquired in the hospital while recovering from his injuries—"A loathsome, cowardly habit!" spits the pompous father. Roger fails to come to Tom's defense and allows his father to think Tom crazy when Tom insists that *he* was the hero. (A more typical movie hero would never have tried to claim those heroic acts for himself. Tom is more flawed, perhaps, or more desperate.) He's committed to six months of rehabilitation, and the day after his admittance, his mother dies. The work Wellman is doing to make Tom sympathetic—or downright pitiable—is not subtle: how much more compelling, and authentic, might the film be if this addict and eventual hobo were not a war hero, although that's probably asking too much of Hollywood in general and of Wellman in particular. Manny Farber (in Polito, 2009, p. 487) once complained that "in any Bill Wellman operation, there are at least four directors—a sentimentalist, deep thinker, hooey vaudevillian, and an expedient short-cut artist whose special love is for mulish toughs expressing themselves in drop-kicking heads and somber standing around." All are in evidence here, with the sentimentalist dominating.

After his release, Tom finds his way to a coffee shop that bears a prominent sign saying, "Stop and Rest. This Is Not a Flop House, but You Can Have a Nap." A father and his daughter, Mary (Aline MacMahon), run it. Mary sometimes complains, gently, about her father giving away too much food. Tom joins their small group of tenants, including Max, a German anarchist who spouts revolutionary rhetoric and suggests that well-placed bombs might be the best answer to poverty, hunger, and the exploitation of workers. That he is constantly at work tinkering in his room, "inventing," he says, makes his threats doubly portentous. Or so we think. In truth, Max has created a

FIGURE 12.6 Women turned away when the soup kitchen runs out of food. *Heroes for Sale.* Warner Brothers, 1933.

new industrial laundry machine, which he and Tom manage to sell to Tom's employer. Max becomes rich in the process, but Tom, thanks to the automation he helped usher in, is fired. While trying to prevent an angry, unemployed mob from smashing the machines—they are genuine Luddites—Tom is arrested and sentenced to five years in the state prison.

Meanwhile, Max, having amassed a fortune, has abandoned his radicalism: "There's only one thing important in the world," he tells Tom shortly after his release in 1932. "To have money. Without it, you are just garbage. With it, you are a king." Later, he sneers as he and Tom watch the men in the soup line Mary has established (she's now a full conspirator in her father's benevolent ways). "You mean she gives food away to these tramps? Feed them once and you have to feed them all the time. Charity! Feeding a lot of lazy moochers. Poor?! Needy?! A cancer on civilization."

It's curious that this most hard-hearted of all the characters in the film (with the possible exception of the laundry owner who laid off most of his workers) was, at first, its most radical. He himself attributes his change in attitude to finally having money, but there's more at work here than this, for Tom will demonstrate that merely having money does not make one cold, callous, or cruel: $50,000 in royalties accumulated for him while he was in prison, and he gives Mary every last cent of it so that she can keep her soup kitchen open

FIGURES 12.7 AND 12.8 Tom passes beneath a large billboard displaying an image that would come to be commonly called upon to illustrate stories about the Depression (*left*). *Heroes for Sale*, Warner Brothers, 1933; and a publicity still for the film (*right*).

twenty-four hours a day. It may be just this sort of scene that Sarris had in mind when he claimed that "most of the cinema of the breadlines looks excessively mannered" (Sarris, 1996, p. 75), but to my eyes, much of it effectively captures what we know of the mood of the time.

Tom is soon visited by police officers from the Red Squad, who drive him out of town (along with many other supposedly dangerous men). He tramps his way back and forth across the Midwest in search of work; he tries to ride the trains and is thrown off, responding indignantly to the bulls: "Who you calling hobo? We're ex-service men." The bull looks skeptical, perhaps hearing this a lot: "Maybe you are and maybe you ain't," he says, suggesting that perhaps some bulls were liable to be more lenient to those they thought more "deserving." We see this in *Blues in the Night* (1941), the story of a blues/jazz ensemble—neither poor nor homeless—that travels from gig to gig by riding the rails; one stationmaster tells them how nice it is to see them, making no effort to throw them off the train, and we're led to believe he does this for others, too. But would he have treated Tom and his fellow tramps the way he does these musicians?

Tom soon runs into Roger, who has since served two years for stealing bank customers' deposits, huddled beside a fire. Roger's father, caught as well, killed himself. "You started out way up high," Tom observes, "and I started out pretty low, and we end up here in the rain, together." The Depression is a great leveler, Wellman means to tell us, but by working so hard to make Tom so sympathetic—right down to having his mother die the day after he's unjustly imprisoned—he winds up with a story about the "worthy" poor, and of how even a hard-working family man of good character can find himself at loose ends, leaving room for us to conclude that someone less noble might deserve the same fate.

I Am a Fugitive from a Chain Gang (1932) gave us a similarly sympathetic veteran, who tramps the country in search of work more satisfying than the dull factory job that awaited him on his return, but fares badly and tries to pawn his war medals. The pawnbroker won't give him anything, though, showing him a glass cabinet filled with the medals of poor, desperate veterans (they have always been disproportionately homeless, a fact that, now and again, finds its way onto the screen).

Fifth Avenue Girl (1939) is not quite a female version of Gregory La Cava's *My Man Godfrey*, but there are echoes, although here the political statements are explicit, and even didactic. Mr. Borden (Walter Connelly), the chief executive officer of Amalgamated Pump, is in the midst of a conversation in his office about unions threatening to strike, and it is clear that his own business is in some trouble. Arriving home, he comments to Mike, the chauffeur (James Ellison), that there "seems to be a touch of spring in the air," to which Mike replies, a bit sardonically, that that's "something even the poor people can enjoy." That's only a hint of the class-based anger Mike will express in the film. Soon he'll be sparring with Borden's daughter in clunky but nonetheless radical language, railing against capitalists (he means capitalist "scum," the daughter helpfully offers). He complains at length that "the rich can afford to be rude … never mind; one day the dictatorship of the proletariat will arise and lean against the columns of this temple and the walls will come tumbling down." Indignant, Michael notes that there are forty million Americans whose annual income is less than the cost of the dozen cases of the champagne the girl is carrying off to her friends. (Later, one character will observe that "horses have better breeding than the people that ride them.")

Borden's Fifth Avenue home is large even by Hollywood movie standards—and his daughter's friends, presumably also rich, spoiled, and accustomed to grand houses, will even comment on it, and we've already seen something of his character—or think we have—when, being kind, he compliments a tie given to him as a birthday gift as quite *conservative*. But all's not well, and he worries that he frightens his family, having grown a bit estranged from them. Later, he'll portray himself not as an oppressor but as "a victim of the capitalistic system," since, through no fault of his own, the pump he invented made him wealthy. "I never wanted all this…. All I wanted out of life was to have some fun and a family."

Upon the urging of his butler—who confesses that he enjoys his work in part because "we servants enjoy the luxuries of the rich and have none of the responsibility"—he goes for a walk in Central Park, where he meets Mary Grey (Ginger Rogers). Grey, unemployed, her rent paid only for another week, and down to her last five dollars, complains about all the "sour" people who live on Fifth Avenue and fail to appreciate all they have. As is the way with bona-fide stars (the Astaire-Rogers films were mostly behind her), there is little outward indication of Mary's poverty; her clothing is a bit plain, but is nonetheless impeccable. They chat for a bit, and Borden, desperate for someone to share his birthday and intrigued by her animosity to his class, invites Mary to dine with him at the Flamingo Club, where "we'll have lots of fun, insulting the rich." They do have lots of fun, dancing and buying champagne for everyone, though Mary's politics intrudes as she snaps at a nearby table to "lay off the government" when a man complains about there being too much of it in business (and too much business in government). Charmed by Mary, whom he enlists in a plot to make his wife and children jealous, and influenced by her talk, Borden refuses to lay off any of his workers, although he has been old he must do so to save the firm. Instead, he leaves it to the ministrations of his once-feckless son (played by Tim Holt, whom we'll meet again in *Treasure of the Sierra Madre*), who turns out to have a knack for it.

There's no mistaking the radical language of the film, especially in the words of the chauffeur. Michael, an avowed Socialist, is handsome (sexy, even), passionate, and smart; though pedantic and bombastic, he's mostly sympathetic, and his tirades against injustice and the depredations of the rich are surely meant to resonate with Depression-era audiences. There's even something of the proud mother in the cook's gentle digs at Michael's constant talking and impenetrable vocabulary. Yet late in the film, he's dressed down, and harshly, by Mary, who accuses him of not having the courage to be a capitalist and contenting himself with trying to bring everyone else down to his level: she makes him suddenly seem pompous, blind, and arrogant—a poseur. And, indeed, he will wind up marrying Borden's daughter and opening up a shop of his own, blithely joining the ranks of the bourgeoisie by film's end, while Mary will marry Borden's son, clearly set to take over Amalgamated Pump and the enormous Fifth Avenue mansion.

Mary, perched on the edge of homelessness when we first met her, is now saved: not by government and the New Deal, not by charity, not even by dint of her own hard work, but by marrying a wealthy man. Michael, instead of setting off to foment revolution—or at least to agitate for social policies that might make life better for poor and working people—also marries rich, and sets off to open up a business of his own. Borden's business is saved by a scheme his son designed to secure loans to farmers so that they can afford to buy (irrigation?) pumps, thus making a virtue of the business itself. And Borden himself, unlike the silly rich people who populate *My Man Godfrey*, is revealed to be a hapless victim of wealth who is at heart a simple man who wants only a nice bowl of stew and to be reunited with his wife.

Like in *Godfrey*, we see a dysfunctional, perhaps *degenerate*, household of enormous wealth and privilege in need of rescuing. In *Godfrey* it's the homeless man who does the rescuing, and it's the nearly homeless woman in *Fifth Avenue Girl*. There's something here of the Nobility of the Poor, perhaps: It takes good, plain folk to apply common sense to solve problems, substantive and trivial ones alike. It smells of condescension and admiration, as if the Poor were clever children. But the nobility of poverty has its limits: Mary Grey doesn't go back to it, and Godfrey never came from poverty to begin with. We may admire the poor and the working class, in an abstract kind of way, but we aspire to be rich; even if that means we'll be a bit callous and frivolous.

By contrast, there is little effort to make poor men seem good or noble in Preston Sturges's *The Great McGinty* (1940). Outside of a soup kitchen sponsored by the Mayor, we meet Daniel McGinty, looking down and out in the way that homeless men do in the movies of the period. He has a few days growth of beard (stippled-in with make-up), is dirty and unkempt, with rumpled clothing (but not *too* dirty, *too* unkempt, or *too* rumpled), and has a defeated countenance. He's told that he can get two dollars if he will go vote for the Mayor under someone else's name. He does it thirty-seven times, and is soon hired by the party boss to collect from businesses who are resisting paying into the Mayor's protection racket. McGinty collects a substantial sum and is told to keep it. "Yesterday you was a hobo on the bread line," the Boss

FIGURE 12.9 *The Great McGinty*, Paramount Pictures, 1940.

says; "today you've got a thousand berries and a new suit. I wonder where you'll be tomorrow? This is a land of great opportunity!"

McGinty—amoral, mercenary, ruthless, and cynical—moves up quickly to Alderman, then Mayor and, finally, Governor. Along the way, he marries to improve his electoral chances, and when his wife tries to persuade him to use his power to do something about the tenements, McGinty brushes it off: "Don't you know those people just want to be let alone? They want to be dirty. They don't like people fooling around with them. Give them a bathtub, they keep coal in it." But she finally persuades him, and when he threatens to work toward reform, the Boss spits, "You're spouting like a woman!" and gets him arrested. He escapes and winds up alongside the Boss as a bartender in some "banana republic," now fighting, quite literally, over small change. McGinty's redemption is only partial, at best, since he only threatens to become a reformer and is deposed before he can actually do any good. But Sturges's attitude seems to be best given voice by a singer who refers to McGinty as "the kind of tramp . . . that anyone would be glad to get rid of." It's a reminder that even in the 1930s, not all images of homeless men were sympathetic ones.

A year later gives us an anti-McGinty. *Meet John Doe* (1941) introduces us to Ann Mitchell (Barbara Stanwyck), a desperate reporter about to be laid off, who makes up a story about a depressed, unemployed man who is planning to kill himself on Christmas Eve. In response to her story, the Mayor and others promise this John Doe a job to keep him from despair, and the newspaper offices are flooded with scraggly looking men claiming to be Doe. "One of those men is your John Doe," says the editor as the scheme to give life to her fiction takes shape. "They're desperate and they'll do anything for a cup of coffee." Stanwyck sets about picking one to become her Doe, and once again the homeless man is a cog in someone else's elaborate machine.

We see a short parade of tramps and bums, until we get to Gary Cooper. He won't claim to have written the letter, as others do, but says that he thought if there was one job available, then there might be more. Quickly having established that he's honest and wants to work—director Frank Capra has made sure to make him one of the deserving poor—we learn that his name is Long John Willoughby, a former baseball player headed to the major leagues until he suffered an arm injury. Again, his deservingness is underlined: he's unemployed not through laziness or insolence, but from a genuine physical disability. After looking longingly at a sandwich on the nearby desk, he faints from hunger; we learn that he's been tramping for at least two years, and most recently has been sleeping under a bridge.

Despite protestations from his buddy (Walter Brennan, as the Colonel), John agrees to take part in the charade, thanks in part to the promise of a doctor to fix his bum arm. The Colonel wants none of it and refuses to stay in the hotel room the newspaper procures, insisting that when you are without money or possessions, no one wants anything from you; when you are truly homeless, he says, you have no obligations, and, as a result, are more free.

Mitchell, writing as Doe, puts out a series of columns entitled "I Protest." We get flashes of what Doe protests: "corruption in local politics," "county hospital shutting doors to needy," and "graft in state relief." This dig at Poor Relief will become a recurring theme in the film. Circulation skyrockets, and people begin taking to the streets of their own accord to march and protest under Doe's name. The newspaper owner sees Doe as a path toward building circulation and, we will learn, toward achieving influence and political power, so they put Doe on the radio next. His talk is pure, soporific Capra populism: It's not a call to action, not a call for resistance or rebellion, not an indictment of corruption and undemocratic powers, but a plea for cooperation, to be more neighborly. Thanks to the generous funding of the newspaper owner, John Doe clubs begin forming throughout the country, some of which sport "Be a Better Neighbor" buttons, no doubt meant to echo the real-world John Reed clubs of the 1930s.

FIGURE 12.10 John Doe Convention, *Meet John Doe,* Warner Brothers, 1941.

Willoughby/Doe meets a founder of one club, who describes what he and his neighbors did to help a man they once thought was "the worst no-account in the neighborhood." But it turns out he "lives out of garbage cans 'cause he won't take charity [and] ruin his self-respect!" So, says the President of the club, they all got together and got him a job, which they then did for six others. "And they've all gone off relief!" the man exclaims. This a deep antipathy to government aid: Here a man is held in high regard because he chose to eat garbage rather than seek help. And the naïveté of Capra's politics becomes apparent, too. Simply by joining together as neighbors, these folks were evidently able to manufacture jobs where there were none before. The message is not necessarily that the unemployed are lazy, but that there is unemployment only because people don't work together to solve problems that, we must believe, government cannot solve. If Capra were alive today, he'd be espousing the laziest kind of Beltway centrism. He'd be David Brooks, filmmaker.

Capra removes the conflict—that is, the politics—from his politics. Instead, we get cheap populism, made easier by the one-dimensionality of the villains. As the newspaper owner says to John when John threatens finally to fight back against his own manipulation and, in turn, his manipulation of others: "May I remind you that I picked you up out of the gutter and I can throw you right back there again? You've got a nerve, accusing people of things! These gentlemen and I know what's best for the John Does of America, regardless of what tramps like you think." As in *Pretty Woman*, another retrograde film that pretends to have emancipatory politics, a Tramp will always be a Tramp, just as a Whore will always be a Whore. And when Doe is ultimately revealed in public for the fraud he is, one voice from the crowd shouts, "Back to the jungle, you hobo!"

While I'm complaining about Capra, there's an earlier Depression-era film of his that is worth a passing glance. *Mr. Deeds Goes to Town* (1936) is the story of a simple farmer—although, as the form demands, he is wise in his way—who inherits a large fortune, and then is the subject of plots to steal it. Wrapped up in gauzy pieties about the nobility of simple, country men, it is another kind of New Deal wish-fulfillment movie, culminating in something of a Forty Acres and a Mule program for (deserving, white) farmers. Brian Neve (1992, p. 45) is right about the inherent conservatism of the film: "Deed's values are activated only when he encounters an unemployed farmer and is shocked into social responsibility.... Deeds in no sense responds to collective action by farmers, only to the one farmer who is driven by his circumstances to threaten him with a gun." That said, it does offer a sympathetic portrait of people in need—of people who are in need through no fault of their own, that is—which does indeed seem easier to come by in the 1930s.

FARMER: What do I want? A chance to feed a wife and kids! I'm a farmer. A job! That's what I want!

LONGFELLOW: A farmer, eh! You're a moocher, that's what you are! I wouldn't believe you or anybody else on a stack of bibles! You're a moocher like all the rest of them around here, so get out of here!

FARMER: Sure—everybody's a moocher to you. A mongrel dog eating out of a garbage pail is a moocher to you! ... You never gave a thought to all of those starving people standing in the bread lines, not knowing where their next meal was coming from! Not able to feed their wife and kids.... Losing your farm after twenty years' work—seeing your kids go hungry.... Standing there in the bread lines. It killed me to take a handout. I ain't used to it.

While this may appear to be a diatribe in sympathy with poor people trapped in the Depression, and to some extent it is, it is also rooted in that same conservatism—notice how hard the script is working to ensure that we know that this farmer, brandishing a gun and threatening to kill Deeds, is nonetheless among the worthy poor. There is no room for ambivalence or ambiguity here. It's white hats and blacks hats, a one-dimensional fable that, somehow, manages to align itself with institutions of power, and reinforces the idea that although we must maintain the status quo, we might need to soften its edges by taking power from the corrupt and granting it to simpler, nobler men. As Manny Farber (in Polito, 2009, 6/10/1950, pp. 332–334) complained, Capra is:

> always in favor of copybook maxims (Be Kind, Love Thy Country, The Best Things Are Free).... Hollywood's best-loved preacher should please anyone who goes for obvious social consciousness, character-building, and entertainment.... As in all Capra films, the world is given to the underdog ... but the sleek, pampered technique ... subtly eulogizes the world of power and wealth ... [and] his smart aleck jibes at artless, hard-working waiters or farmers invariably win sympathy where Capra intends you to snicker.

As Ferguson noted (in Wilson, 1971, p. 273), Capra "started to make movies about themes instead of people." Indeed, Capra himself later admitted that *Mr. Deeds* was, as he put it, "the first film I made in which I consciously tried to make a social statement" (in Schickel, 1975, p. 73).

Finally, there's *It Happened on Fifth Avenue* (1947), a post–World War II movie, but one that still feels like a late-Depression film about homeless men.

"The most celebrated, richest avenue in the world," says the guide from atop a tour bus as the film opens. "It's the street where the original 400 built their houses." As his voice continues on, we see a man in typical bum's attire, carrying his small dog, whistling; he dodges a cop, slips through a fence and then into a sewer, emerging under the grand staircase in the foyer of a Fifth Avenue mansion. Familiar with the place, he turns on the lights, winds the grandfather clock, and rigs the fuse box so that the lights shut off when the front door opens. He takes a bath, and dresses.

Meanwhile, across town, Jim Bullock (Don DeFore), a World War II veteran, is being evicted from his apartment building, which is being torn down to make room for an eighty-story skyscraper to be built by Michael O'Connor (Charles Ruggles), the second-richest man in the world. Bullock resists as best he can, calling it "fighting tyranny" and vowing revenge, but he loses the battle and winds up out in the cold, sleeping on a park bench (though his protest does make the newspaper).

The man who slipped into the mansion, Aloysius T. McKeever (Victor Moore), now in full gentleman's regalia, comes upon Bullock and invites him back to the mansion—O'Connor's home, we learn. Meanwhile, O'Connor's daughter Trudy (Gale Storm) has run away from boarding school and comes home to New York to find Bullock and McKeever in her house, McKeever revealing to Bullock that for the past three years he has inhabited it from November to March while O'Connor is away at his winter retreat (he's been doing it in other places for a total of twenty years). Trudy overhears and plays along, pretending to be a poor girl escaping an abusive, alcoholic father, while they pretend to be guests of the owner. Bullock runs into two old army buddies and their families who are living out of the back of a car and invites them to join them in the mansion. Trudy then convinces her father to pretend to be homeless, and gets him invited into the mansion so that he can meet Bullock, with whom she's fallen in love. While in the park, the father, who has become yet another Impostor Tramp, is rousted by a cop: "If it's a place to sleep ya want, try a flophouse; if you're hungry, try the soup kitchen. But no loafing in the park! Now go on, beat it!"

We learn that, like the wealthy business man in *Fifth Avenue Girl*, O'Connor and his wife came from modest beginnings, their early years spent in a small railroad flat. At the end, McKeever defines real poverty as being without friends, and as McKeever walks off, O'Connor says, "You know, Mary, there are richer men than I." The film ends with McKeever walking happily away, dog in his arms, whistling and looking content. But he's not. He's confessed to being lonely, and to having what may be many regrets.

The homeless man, as we see in this set of films (and others), is generally passive—he's a beggar, shuffling from place to place, despondent. But the history of the New Deal era can't adequately be told without the massive protest movements—the Bonus Marchers and the marches of the unemployed—that pushed Roosevelt into action. And they do occasionally appear in the movies.

Our Daily Bread (1934) shows us what happens when people actually do leave the ghetto to make a better life and is one of the few Depression-era films to imagine a new economic world. According to director King Vidor (1953/1981, Chap. 6), the studios were uninterested in the film because it lacked "glamor," and securing loans to make it himself was hindered by the fact that "when a banker reads a script in which a bank forces a sheriff to make a foreclosure sale which a disreputable-looking group of neighbors won't permit, he doesn't feel kindly toward your venture." It was ultimately made only thanks to Chaplin's help, Vidor would later claim (in Schickel, 1975, p. 149). Upon its release, a Moscow film festival jury called it "capitalist propaganda," though they awarded it second prize (it won a League of Nations award, too, Vidor notes), while a Hearst review called it "pinko," and the *Los Angeles Times* refused to accept advertisements for it.

"Inspired by Headlines of Today," is the subtitle, and as the film opens, a bill collector, whistling and singing, is coming to collect past-due rent from Mary (Karen Morley) and threatens eviction if it's not paid soon. John (Tom Keene), her husband, returns from a day of looking for work: "Same old story, a hundred guys and only one job," he laments. He rummages through the apartment for something left to pawn so that they can buy food for dinner. Her uncle soon gives them a small parcel of land, and tells John and Mary that if they can make a go of it, it's theirs. They do, but only by realizing the virtues of "a cooperative community," as John calls it, "where money isn't so important . . . where you help me, and I help you." Comparing their project to the first migrants off the *Mayflower*, John importunes, "What did they do, stand around and beef about the unemployment situation and the value of the dollar? No! They set to work, to make their own employment. To build their own houses, and grow their own food. . . . If they got along without landlords and grocery bills, then so can we." They pool their assets and resources, build a commissary, appoint a treasurer, acclaim John leader (rejecting both democratic and state-controlled socialist models), and set to work plowing the fields and building houses, culminating in the digging of an enormous ditch to save the crops. It is, if nothing else, something rare: a portrayal of successful collective action in American film. As Christensen and Haas put it (2005, p. 280), "Despite our democratic ideals, when people get together in American

FIGURES 12.11 **AND** 12.12 *Our Daily Bread*, United Artists, 1934.

movies, they are more likely to be condemned as a lynch mob than to be praised for their collective endeavor. The exceptions are few and far between."

The paucity of Great Depression–era movies that reimagine the social or political landscape seems curious. There's plenty of Busby Berkeley escapism, lots of fancy New York night life, but we don't find many "radical" perspectives. There are almost no films of the 1930s that are utopian, offering visions of a new world, a new economy, or a new society; there is almost no re-envisioning of a nation in turmoil, and there are not even science fiction films that would fit the bill. Movies of the 1930s did not ignore the Great Depression, but neither did they offer insight into its causes or suggest alternative visions. The Hays Code probably played some role in this: while we are likely to remember its regulations regarding sex (and its infamous requirement that if a couple was on the bed, three feet must be on the floor at all times), it was also understood to require the regulation of political content, as we've seen, with a special eye toward limiting portrayals of class conflict. Anti-Communist hysteria further discouraged studios from making pictures that might be construed as "radical" (and discouraged anyone from writing or proposing them in the first place), while the studios' own struggle against unionism in the industry may also have contributed to an unwillingness to fund more reformist visions; though the studios were, to be sure, not without politics. As Buhle and Wagner write,

> The studio chiefs decreed that every employee join the drive against Upton Sinclair, best-selling Socialist novelist who captured the Democratic nomination for Governor with his End Poverty in California (EPIC) platform. Many studios demanded employees' financial contributions for his Republican opponent and even distributed their own short features during the election season spuriously associating the novelist with riots and rabble.... The calculated attack upon Sinclair, a rare decent political figure, offered proof as to why the protections allowed by unionism and an associated political movement of some kind were desperately needed. (Buhle and Wagner, 2002, p. 62)

In contrast is Jack Warner's famous allegiance to Roosevelt and the New Deal, even going as far as to include pro–National Recovery Act signs in musical numbers. There were some modest efforts by the Communist Party to teach those in Hollywood to "be more confident that they could present progressive ideas, one way or another, in any phase of their work as writers, actors, directors, even technicians," recalled Party organizer John Weber, a former "mobilizer of hunger marches and assorted demonstrations" (Buhle and Wagner, 2002, p. 100). And, drawing on Victor Navasky's *Naming Names*, Christensen and Haas (2005, p. 43) add that: "The Communist Party had made the industry a special organizing target in 1936, a move that reflected Lenin's belief in the power of cinema. Proclaiming that movies are 'the weapon of mass culture,' the party organizers urged their recruits to at least 'keep anti-Soviet agitprop' out of the movies they worked on." But in general the Party made little real effort, for "films, especially Hollywood films, were so far up the superstructure, and so suspect as escapist products of bourgeois culture, that control or even serious influence upon film content was never seriously contemplated" (Buhle and Wagner, 2002, p. 101).

So, in the 1930s, we often see on the screen mere escapism into an idealized New York nightlife, and when we do see waifs and tramps and panhandlers and other down-and-outers, they exist in a world without causes—there are no real politics or economics, just, at best, conditions that, if one is very plucky, one can rise above. Sarris notes, I think rightly, that for all the efforts to find meaning in the screwball comedies of the Depression era, there is "surprisingly little awareness in the characters of either an 'economic crisis' or 'a threat of approaching war'" (Sarris, 1998, p. 94). But is it too much to suggest that that itself might be their meaning? As Bergman (1971/1992, p. 120) notes, "The movies always knew that the Depression was there. What they didn't know, and didn't want to know, was why." But as I've said, there are some notable exceptions.

In *Washington Merry-Go-Round* (1932), a newly elected U.S. House member arrives in Washington, D.C., determined not to heed the instructions of the wealthy man who bought him his seat. Meanwhile, the Bonus Armies have gathered, here portrayed none too sympathetically. As Dave Platt wrote in the *Harlem Liberator* (Platt, 1934), the film "suggest[s] that the bonus marchers, the same ones who were driven out of Washington by bayonets and tear gas, came to Washington not to demonstrate for back wages due them but to panhandle easy money from gullible citizens of the capitol." As the sanctimonious Congressman Brown says to them, "What do you do? You all march out here like a bunch of panhandlers, begging for a handout, like so many blind men rattling tin cups. . . . Why don't you help your government instead of hindering it! Go on back home!" He's meant to be idealistic, but not in a way that's ultimately celebrated by anyone in the film, even as he loses his seat thanks to a recount orchestrated by the money-powers he's rebuffed. It's a less politically sophisticated *Mr. Smith Goes to Washington*, if you can imagine such a thing, right down to a ponderous visit to the Lincoln Memorial to commune with the spirit of Abe. The Congressman winds up joining forces with the Bonus Marchers—who admit that he was right to condemn them as misguided (!)—in order to stop a man who would, he says, become our own Stalin or Mussolini. In a final victory for clean government, the still sanctimonious leader convinces the corrupt would-be despot to kill himself.

Gabriel Over the White House (1933), directed by Gregory LaCava (who also directed *Fifth Avenue Girl*), is another political wish-fulfillment film, one financed by William Randolph Hearst, reports Robert McConnell (1976). The credits say "from the anonymous novel" of the same name, but while the book was published anonymously in the United States, it was released under Thomas F. Tweed's name in Britain, the *New York Times* reported in its review. (Tweed, curiously, was a British citizen who was an advisor to Prime Minister Lloyd George and may have been inspired, in part, by ideas that he heard from department store magnate Gordon Selfridge [McConnell, 1976]). Neither Roosevelt's name nor much commentary on the film's politics appears in the *Times'* review, which merely describes it as a "melodramatic" but "interesting" story (Hall, 1933).

Here's the plot: A new President (Walter Huston) is sworn in during the Depression. We soon see his hard character: he requires the press to submit all of their questions to him in advance, and even then rarely allows them to quote him. He refuses to meet with the leader of the unemployed, John Bronson, dismissing their concerns by insisting that unemployment is a local matter. In response to a reporter's blistering tirade about the sorry state of the nation, President Hammond offers platitudes and a suggestion that prosperity is "just around the corner," as Herbert Hoover infamously said in 1932. Thus, without its being said too explicitly, we have a glimpse of a fictional world in which Hoover, or someone very much like him, was reelected while, as the novel put it, the world inside and outside the United States "seemed to be moving toward complete and final chaos" (Tweed, 1933, p. 43).

Thanks to reckless driving—perhaps as reckless as his passive governance in the midst of crisis—Hammond is in an automobile accident and thrust into a deep coma, expected by doctors soon to die. But there's a breeze at the window, an odd change in lighting, and he awakens possessed—his personal assistant and paramour will later speculate that it's the archangel Gabriel. He is a man transformed, and transformed, it is not unreasonable to speculate, into Roosevelt. He now refuses to call out the armed forces against the unemployed armies set to march on D.C. (one million strong, they are clearly meant to be Bonus marchers), and requires his Department of War to provide food, supplies, and medical care to them, for this, too, "is war, and the enemy is starvation." He then muses: "Tons of food rotting. Millions of people starving. What's to prevent us from putting the food into the mouths of the hungry?" He even starts talking straight to the press. Beekman, his aide (Franchot Tone), marvels that "the way he thinks [now] is so simple and honest, it sounds a little crazy." The personal assistant responds: "If he's mad, it's a divine madness." It's not terribly subtle, but propaganda rarely is.

Having seen this peaceful industrial army briefly at camp, we then see them marching, orderly column after column, and full-frame close-ups of some of the men looking determined and proud. There's even a black face in the mix. The scene has clear roots in the novel:

There came stalwart bronzed men, few of them unshaven, marching in reasonably good military formation. Instead of sullen hatred they had laughter in their eyes and many of the detachments were singing. There was none of the crushed look of beaten men, Each head was held high and from each face shone courage and good cheer. (Tweed, 1933, p. 111)

Hammond goes to Baltimore to meet the marchers, who chant "We want work, we want work, we want work." He proposes an Army of Construction

FIGURE 12.13 "We want work, we want work," the unemployed chant to the President. *Gabriel Over the White House*, MGM, 1933.

in a speech in which even the timbre of his voice seems to the echo the peculiar pinched, patrician quality of Roosevelt. He fires his entire cabinet, who were plotting to undermine his efforts, and when Congress, in the midst of a debate about impeaching him, rejects his proposal for four billion dollars for "immediate and effective action," he threatens to impose martial law and render them impotent unless they formally grant him emergency executive powers. They do. When accused by one Senator of imposing a dictatorship, Hammond replies that it is the kind of dictatorship that Thomas Jefferson himself might have conceived, one dedicated to "the greatest good for the greatest number." It's a measure of how gauzy the view is here that he can't even rise to plausibility by citing Hamilton, rather than Jefferson.

He suspends all mortgage foreclosures, creates deposit insurance, provides emergency farm relief, and vows war against gangsters and bootleggers, the last of which is begun with a repeal of Prohibition and the opening of U.S. Government Liquor Stores. When the first of them is bombed, Hammond forms a special federal police force to capture the guilty mobsters, who are brought before a military tribunal presided over by Hammond's aide, and summarily executed, the Statue of Liberty standing proud in the background. Finally, the President turns to foreign affairs and the debt owed the United

States by other nations. He demands payment, and when rebuffed (*how can we*, they ask?), he suggests that massive worldwide disarmament will provide all the money needed. To demonstrate his sincerity, he bombs and sinks two American battleships. Soon after signing the global treaty, he dies, and whatever supernatural force was inhabiting him wafts away.

Tweed's novel differs in some interesting ways, although, for the most part, the film is faithful. Perhaps not surprisingly, given how Hollywood films strip away complexity, Hammond is not quite so one-dimensional before his conversion—he's a much shrewder and more self-aware man in the book, if perhaps a more cynical one, given Tweed's suggestions that much of his public persona might have been shaped to appeal to party leaders and voters, and not be a full reflection of his beliefs or desires. This lays some groundwork for explaining his conversion, which, we'll see in the novel, is not supernatural but medical—it's a lesion on his brain, not, as in the film, an angel. And after an assassination attempt, Hammond reverts to his old self, appalled by his own actions, calling them "outrages against that spirit of individualism and national independence which is our proudest attribute," and railing that "liberty has been destroyed and the Constitution I swore to uphold has been practically scrapped" (Tweed, 1933, pp. 291ff). But he dies of a heart attack—as the Cabinet plots against him—before he can renounce his previous actions.

It's not explicit in the novel that the unemployed marchers are veterans—perhaps a change made in the film to make them more sympathetic, though in the novel one of the movement leaders is, in fact, a war hero. The breadth of Hammond's action is clearer in the book: he creates a Department of Education, which functions as a Department of Propaganda (see also *Stand Up and Cheer!*); expands the Supreme Court from nine to fifteen justices; nationalizes the railroads; takes the United States off the gold standard; implements widespread electrification projects; builds canals, dams, and irrigation projects; nationalizes the manufacture and sale of alcohol; outlaws guns; federalizes every police force in the nation; enacts a NAFTA-like trade agreement with Canada and Central and South America, and then a WTO-like global free trade pact; strips states of their autonomy under the Constitution; disbands all militaries, replacing them with an international police force administered in International City through the new World Council; and turns Ellis Island into a "concentration camp," in Tweed's words, for those arrested by the new federal police force. The novel admits he's an "autocrat," although he does later come to propose sixteen Constitutional Amendments to codify his actions. Ironically enough, the title of the book may have come from Father Charles Coughlin, who, before he turned against Roosevelt, assured his radio listeners that "Gabriel is over the White House, not Lucifer" (Leuchtenburg, 1963/2009, p. 101).

Louis B. Mayer and Hays "were appalled, not because of the film's fascist implications, but because it seemed pro-Roosevelt and they were staunch Republicans," write Christensen and Haas (2005, p. 79). "Mayer took the film in hand, reshooting some scenes and toning others down. . . . Some members of Congress complained, but President Roosevelt enjoyed the film and saw it several times" (see also McConnell, 1976).

Stand Up and Cheer! (1934), a Shirley Temple vehicle, is another political fantasy. It's the depths of the Depression, and the President appoints Lawrence Cromwell to be the first Secretary of a new Cabinet-level agency, the Department of Amusement, which has a first-year appropriation of $100 million, which would be about $1.7 billion today. An early musical number sets the tone, as all kinds of downtrodden Americans from all walks of life (though an unusual number of them are employed) sing "I'm laughin' though I got nothin' to laugh about / If I can stand this daily grind, then brother so can you!" While Cromwell sets about scouring the country for the most uplifting talent, an evil cabal of businessmen profiting off of the Depression conspires to ensure he fails, for fear that if he succeeds in lifting the public mood, the Depression will end. Even for Hollywood it's incoherent. But this is all mostly irrelevant, for the plot is merely an excuse for a procession of song and dance acts and the occasional big production numbers, like the fantasy sequence that constitutes the finale, "We're out of the red," which celebrates the end of the Depression and, we're meant to assume, the ultimate victory of the Department of Amusement. In this worldview, economic depression is no different than emotional depression.

There's also, finally, the oddity of *Beggars in Ermine* (1934), in which tramps build their own Social Security program. Flint Dawson (Lionel Atwill), a benevolent steel mill owner, loses his legs in an industrial accident, the result of a plot to steal the mill from him. Left destitute and alone, he meets up with a blind beggar in a charity ward that he himself, in better days, founded and funded; together, they set up something of a Penny Provident fund, building an investment portfolio from the savings of other disabled street beggars and providing, out of the proceeds, discounted or free housing, food, medical care, legal assistance, and help with securing licensing for whatever they may peddle; his only assistance to the able-bodied is an employment service. With the help of his army of beggars, their funds, and fifteen years' of interest and investment returns, they acquire a majority share of the company, and Dawson is reinstated as CEO. We don't spend much time with the poor men who form the core of this cooperative, but they are almost all obviously and physically disabled—missing arms and legs, blind, mute, deaf, and the like—the classically "deserving" poor. That the answer is what is essentially social insurance, in 1934 no less, is telling. These kinds of programs have a long history, first as voluntary associations and then, in the decades prior to the film, as state-run unemployment and widow's pension programs, which will become enshrined in national law a year later with the Social Security Act. Without government aid, the consequences could be dire, a fear carried to extremes with Chaplin's *Monsieur Verdoux* (1947), where, after the Crash, a man fired from the bank where he's worked for thirty years seduces, marries, and then kills middle-aged women of means to support his invalid wife and child. The Depression turned the Tramp into a monster (as he will be *en masse* in the 1980s and 1990s).

The most heartbreaking case of pre–Social Security insecurity is *Make Way for Tomorrow*. An old couple gather their children to tell them that the bank's taking their home (the man's been out of work for four years), and the elderly husband and wife each go off with a separate, selfish child, each of whom is looking for a way to get rid of their burden. Finally, the couple spends one last day together in New York before he goes off to California to live with a daughter, and she is sent off to an old age home. It's utterly wrenching, in part because right up until it happens you do not believe that they will really be separated and destined to die apart. In an interview on the DVD, Peter Bogdanovich says Orson Welles called it the saddest movie ever made, and it's surely a contender.

We can compare these images of homelessness created during or shortly after the Depression itself with later efforts that take the era as their setting. How do the Depression and its tramps look with hindsight? The first post-Depression film that spent significant time in the period appears to be 1973's *Emperor of the North (Pole)*. The opening cards read as follows:

> 1933. The Height of the Great Depression. Hoboes roamed the land, riding the rails in a desperate search for jobs. Spurned by society, unwanted and homeless, they became a breed apart. Nomads who scorned the law and enforced their own. Dedicated to their destruction was the Railroad Man who stood between them and their only source of survival—The Trains.

Ernest Borgnine is that Railroad Man, Shack. In the opening scene, he sees a tramp climb aboard, finds him eating a sandwich in between cars, and hits him over the head with a large hammer; the poor man falls beneath the train and is cut in half. It's gruesome, and quite shocking. So notorious is

Shack that the Holy Grail among rail-riders is to arrive on the Nineteen, his train, as one hobo does. This evolves into a contest to ride the Nineteen all the way to Portland, and is what sets the rest of the film in motion. But it's not a contest of rich against poor, or the little guy against the soulless railroad, but mostly rooted merely in the fact that pretty much everyone hates Shack because he's a nasty son of a bitch. His peculiar obsession with never allowing anyone to ride his train is never explained, which tends to make the film seem like an extended series of chase set pieces without much emotional impact or investment.

But the hoboes are the heroes, here, or at least the protagonists, and the periodic foray into hobo jungles shows them as mostly harmless, struggling to get by as best they can, and doing so as a community that looks out for their own. Those in for the most derision are Shack and, by extension, other bulls, the police, and church men. One hobo eventually throws Borgnine from the train, having first cut off one of his hands with an axe. The Depression does intrude here—an extended bit of Roosevelt on the radio, two trainmen expressing gratitude at being able to eat standing still, and then being grateful for being able to eat at all—and a subplot that's set in motion when a tramp and two children try to steal a live chicken. But it nonetheless seems not so much a movie about the Depression as one merely set in the Depression. A year later, perhaps with recession, the oil embargo, and municipal bank-ruptcies in mind, we get *Brother Can You Spare a Dime* (1974), a pastiche of 1930s films and documentary footage, but one without narration (or any indi-cation of which film is which).

Much better are *Pennies from Heaven* (1981), which Pauline Kael called "our communal vision of the Depression, based on images handed down to us" (Kael, 1994, p. 919) and another gauzy reflection on the era, Woody Allen's *Purple Rose of Cairo* (1985). *Pennies* is a remake of the British miniseries, and it may in its own way be even darker, a Depression tale told through the eyes

FIGURES 12.14 AND 12.15 Cecilia arrives in the movie, where she's dreamed of escaping to (*left*); and Cecilia realizes she has been left behind, and that she cannot escape her life (*right*). *Purple Rose of Cairo*, Orion Pictures, 1985.

of a naïf and a dreamer. As going to the movies will serve as the escape for Cecilia (Mia Farrow) in *Purple Rose*, songs are the escape for Arthur (Steve Martin) in *Pennies*. For Cecilia, a character steps off the screen—literally—and transforms her life, before she, for one evening, enters a movie herself.

The lesson is that films can serve as a wondrous escape, but when the last reel ends, your life remains, unchanged. Perhaps the bravest thing is that there is no happy ending. In *Pennies from Heaven*, it's much the same: trapped in a bad marriage (though Arthur has a sour and inattentive spouse rather than the abusive one that Cecilia does), struggling to earn an income selling sheet music, at especially grim moments (and others, too), he and those around them burst into song. Mostly it's Arthur's wish fulfillment, while at other moments the songs are deeper, unspoken hopes or feelings (as when his wife, suspecting infidelity, menacingly sings "It's a sin to tell a lie"). These movies can surely be read as commentaries on and critiques of Great Depression–era escapist movies and songs themselves, although this is more palpably true for *Pennies* than for *Purple Rose*. There's something much more pessimistic and cruel in *Pennies* than in most Depression films, something dangerous and ugly and desperate lurking throughout, erupting in the murder of a blind girl for which Arthur is accused and hanged. There is no lasting escape, despite momentary flights of fantasy (like the homage to "We're in the Money" from *Gold Diggers of 1933*), and the happy ending that's tacked on in a self-consciously self-aware way, winking at us, telling us that while we know that the real ending was the one with Arthur at the gallows, convention requires the happy, dancing finale, one great last Busby Berkeley–style number.

Perhaps the most fully realized of modern films set in the Depression era are *Cinderella Man* (2005) and *Ironweed* (1987). In the latter, Jack Nicholson and Meryl Streep play Francis and Helen, two homeless alcoholics in 1938 Albany. The cause of their desperate situation is unclear. There is little world here in this grim city beyond its poorer inhabitants, a church-run mission, and a bar. Francis is a former baseball player who once killed a scab during a trolley strike and dropped his own newborn son on the floor, possibly while drunk, killing him, too. He hopped a train and was gone for some twenty years, doing what, we don't quite know, and is now back for reasons that are also unclear. Francis, like Albany itself, is at most an echo of what he once was, all lost promise and faded hope. Dirty, weak, sick, foul-smelling, with bad teeth and broken shoes, he's haunted (literally) by the men he has killed and other dead men he once knew. Mission scenes, like so much of the film, ring true: this "brotherhood of the desolate," as William Kennedy calls them in the novel upon which his screenplay is based (Kennedy, 1979/1984), must pray before being fed, and they play along.

FIGURES 12.16, 12.17, **AND** 12.18 *Pennies from Heaven*, MGM, 1981.

FIGURE 12.19 "Never mind the blood," says Francis about the words of the hymn, "just pass the soup." *Ironweed*, TriStar Pictures, 1987.

The Minister won't allow anyone in if they are drunk, like Sandra, whom Francis, his new friend Rudy, and Helen come across passed out on the sidewalk. "She a bum or just on a heavy drunk?" asks Francis.

RUDY: She's a bum
FRANCIS: She looks like a bum.
RUDY: She's been a bum all her life.
FRANCIS: No. Nobody's a bum all their life. She hadda been somethin' once.
RUDY: She was a whore before she was a bum.
FRANCIS: And what about before she was a whore?
RUDY: I don't know. She just talks about whorin' in Alaska. Before that I guess she was just a little kid.
FRANCIS: Then that's somethin'. A little kid's somethin' that ain't a bum or a whore.

Even more so than with Francis, Helen's past is obscure, but it haunts her time on screen, too. She's hollowed out, a remnant of something that once was, however minimally, more than just the bum she is today. But how she came to this state is not clear, and is not meant to be clear; there are no pat

FIGURE 12.20 Helen. *Ironweed,* TriStar Pictures, 1987.

answers offered to the viewer, no comforting parable or morality tale about how people fall to ruin, how they become bums, something that distinguishes the portrayal of homeless men and women here from most movies, which typically go out of their way to offer the audience a reason for a homeless character's descent, as I've noted. That Sandra was once something and someone else feels like the most salient fact. Maybe she was brought down by the Depression that's never mentioned, or by grief or loss (like Francis), or by bad luck or by drink. But she was something before becoming just one more bum in a city that seems full of them, though she'll die in the street, her flesh gnawed on by dogs.

Helen, unwilling to take more than coffee from the mission and proud that she's never had to sleep out in the weeds, later goes to the library to escape the cold, and falls asleep; she's awakened by a librarian, who sweetly hands her a magazine and tells her she can stay as long as she reads. It's a scene we wouldn't find in most movies—the librarian is neither a callous villain, expelling Helen out into the cold, nor a gauzy, noble hero. Just someone being casually decent to someone else. The homeless men and women of *Ironweed* are not archetypes or stereotypes or plot devices, just people at the end of a line. It's too late, too late for all of them, despite Francis's brave claim that "there ain't no difference" between "swells and bums."

There's much to admire about *Cinderella Man* (2005), too, a fact-based tale of a down-and-out boxer *cum* dockworker struggling to support his family during the Depression, despite its clear place within the "indomitability of the human spirit" genre of Hollywood dramaturgy and the fact that we know how it must end, even if we don't know the actual history. Russell Crowe, as Jim Braddock, does give us something of an idealized figure, to be sure, but there is an earnest effort to convey a sense of the daily grind of life and a decent portrayal of the ambivalence with which people then (as now) approached the need for and dependence upon (or refusal of) relief. Constant in the background are Hoovervilles, soup and relief lines, men desperate to be among the five or so chosen daily for work at the docks, crowding around fifty deep, struggling to get the attention of the boss, some families breaking down billboards to burn for fuel, others filling pails from fire hydrants.

A utility company employee tells Braddock's wife that he has to turn off their gas and electricity or he'll lose his job: "They already let two guys go," he says, and we know it was because they relented to some other mother's desperate pleading. "Lady, I got kids, too." And we feel for both of them. Braddock himself, counting change to try to gather enough to pay the past-due bill, says, "If I work 26 out of every 24 hours, it still won't add up." The family breaks up, scattered with relatives in an attempt to survive. Sufficiently desperate, he goes to the relief office and, in an act of public humiliation, with his hat literally in hand, begs the men who manage Madison Square Garden for the balance he needs to turn the heat back on. He succeeds, and brings his family back home. Braddock knows where to place the blame for the Depression, responding to a plea for organizing against the government by asking what they'd be protesting: "Bad luck? Greed? Drought? We'll work our way through this. FDR, he's gonna handle this."

FIGURE 12.21 At the relief office. *Cinderella Man*, Universal Pictures, 2005.

When Braddock gets a second chance to enter the ring, it becomes in some ways just another movie about an athletic contest, building to the inevitable final fight, but what makes this a bit different is that Jim is fighting, not for honor, restored glory, or for ego, but for his family's economic survival, making the stakes high indeed—in one bout, exhausted and near collapse, he flashes on images of past-due notices, the grim rooms where his family lives, and his wife's worried face. He rallies, and wins. Later, when asked why he suddenly seems to be a better fighter, he replies that he has something to fight for now: *milk*. Still later, as he prepares to battle the champion, he becomes a popular hero, invested with the hopes and fears of others struggling to survive—and as is too often the case, his victory too lazily suggests that, somehow, all will be better. After all, as the announcer proclaims, "just a year ago, he was standing in breadline!"

Once the prize money has started to come in, Braddock goes to the relief office to pay back every cent he received—smiling with satisfaction as if he's regained some pride, too. It's a measure of how debased and narrow our attitudes toward relief are that this scene even exists at all (or that the real Braddock may, in fact, have paid back, with interest, the aid his family received). The message is that to have received assistance in the first place is confirmation that he had failed himself, his family, and perhaps even his country—a message that is, alas, consistent with American politics and movies both.

13 THE DEPRESSION THROUGH THE EYES OF A CLEVER CHILD

Paper Moon, Kit Kitridge: American Girl, The Journey of Natty Gann, Two Bits, From This Day Forward, King of the Hill, Annie, The Little Princess, A Little Princess, Wild Boys of the Road

There's a final Depression-era pattern, one peculiar to films that are about the Great Depression but were not made during the Great Depression (with one exception, as we'll see): films that have strong, even mature, children at the center of a story about surviving economic calamity.

First up is *Paper Moon*, from 1973. It's the depths of the Depression, and Moses (Ryan O'Neal), a con-man, and young Addie (Tatum O'Neal)—who may or may not be his daughter—grift their way from Kansas to Missouri in crisp black-and-white. Addie is the shrewder of the two, but she has a soft spot: while perfectly content to judge one woman as well-to-do and a mark for more money, she's prone to take pity on the poor and steer Moses away from taking what little they have. As they drive across the Great Plains, we see glimpses of families, all that they own strapped to a car, making their way toward what they hope will be a better life. Addie wants to stop and give money to one family that's broken down by the side of the road. "But they're poorly," she complains when Moses refuses to stop. "The whole country's poorly," he responds. Addie still protests, "But Frank Roosevelt says we gotta look out for one another!"

In *Kit Kitridge: American Girl* (2008), Kit (Abigail Breslin) is another whip-smart young woman, a ten-year-old Cincinnati girl hoping to be a reporter, whose family seems to be thriving, despite the creeping effects of the Depression that are in evidence all around. But her family also feels the effects when her father loses his business and sets off to Chicago in search of work. It's a sweet story, with Kit at the center, one that offers a rich and sympathetic portrait of Depression life. We enter soup kitchens, see hobo jungles (and even get a brief lesson in hobo signs and markers),

FIGURE 13.1 *Kit Kittredge,* New Line Cinema, 2008.

witness families taking in boarders, planting gardens, raising chickens to sell eggs, and doing all that can be done to fend off the final trip to the poorhouse. The voices of those who still think poor people are lazy and undeserving, who fear hoboes, or who judge poverty as moral failure, are present throughout, but the film always makes them small, petty, cruel, pitiable, and ultimately even villainous people. Kit solves a mystery, absolving hoboes of thefts they've been wrongfully accused of, and her father returns home, still

FIGURE 13.2 Kit sees her father lining up for food at a soup kitchen. *Kit Kittredge,* New Line Cinema, 2008.

unemployed but determined that they will all struggle together. If there's a lesson here, it's to judge people by their deeds and their intentions, not their appearance or their economic state; or, perhaps, to evaluate people as a child would, as Kit does.

The Journey of Natty Gann (1985) offers another Great Depression tale told mostly through a child's eyes, and another way in which we can see how need in the 1930s is sometimes thought of as something different from need in other periods. Men search for work, to no avail; people sell what they can, trying to keep upbeat about it; other children are evicted from their homes, along with their families, and the villains are the landlords and their allies, the police, who come across as dangerous, cold-hearted thugs. Natty's father finds work, but it takes him out of town, leaving her alone with their rooming house matron, who's interested in the money she will get for caring for Natty (Meredith Salenger) while he's away, but not much in the girl herself. Overhearing plans to pass her off to the child welfare authorities, Natty escapes and tramps her way across the country in search of her father. She hops freights and is chased by bulls, eats out of the trash, interrupts a brutal dogfight, survives a train wreck, stumbles into a teenagers' hobo jungle (and reluctantly helps them steal, which brings her to a harsh reform school, from which she escapes), befriends a one-eyed

FIGURE 13.3 Natty Gann does what she needs to do to survive the Depression and her cross-country search for her father. *The Journey of Natty Gann*, Walt Disney Pictures, 1985.

blacksmith, fends off a sexual assault, wanders through a Hooverville, which she sees destroyed by locals, and is left alone again after a young man she's been travelling with finally gets a job, thanks to the Works Progress Administration (WPA). The film seems eager to show us as many different facets of Depression-era America as it can, as this set of movies often does. Natty is reunited with her father, but there's nothing to suggest their lives will be any easier.

Two Bits (1995) brings us to Depression-era Philadelphia. Gennaro (Jerry Barone) is a twelve-year-old who wants nothing more than a quarter so that he can go to the opening day of the brand-new movie theater. He asks his mother (Mary Elizabeth Mastrantonio), who says she has no money to give him. In fact, she continues,

> That welfare lady came by last week, and I asked her, please, is there any way we can get a few more dollars just so that the check lasts from one week to the next. And she looked at me, in the way that she does, and she said, Mrs. Spirito, a lot of people are using their checks to play the numbers, people are taking trains to the shore, or they're going to the movies, and she said the Board is so upset they're thinking of giving us less money every week. I said, well that's terrific, that's just what we need around here, less money! That way we can starve to death all at once rather than one at a time. She laughed. She wasn't a bad lady.

This child is also on something of a quest—not to find his father (like Natty Gann) or solve a crime (as with Kit Kittredge), but to raise the two bits necessary to attend opening night. As with the others, most of the people he encounters are doing their best under very bad circumstances, and some do even better, like the proprietor who resigns himself to people stealing groceries from his store. There's a similar kind of scene in an earlier film: *From This Day Forward* (1946) shows us Bill Cummings (Mark Stevens) a World War II veteran just back from the war, looking for work, and thinking back upon his life since his marriage in the late 1930s. After Bill has been laid off from his job and unemployed for some time, his nephew Timmy says he can help get him a meal. He does it for his parents sometimes: he goes to the butcher and asks for a bone for his dog, and then his mother makes soup from it. Bill, both touched and a bit humiliated that the boy is worried about whether he has enough food, asks whether the butcher ever catches on. "Nah," says Timmy." But he pauses, and hangs his head down a bit. "Anyway, he knows." Bill prods, "He knows what?" "I ain't got a dog." It's unusual to see the worry of a child in this way, and it's an especially graceful way to show how members of the community, often if not always, would discreetly try to offer help in such a way as not to injure people's pride. It's a lovely touch.

King of the Hill (1993) gives us a struggling family who send their youngest to live with his uncle to save the dollar per week they reckon his care costs, leaving his brother behind. They're still perched on the edge of eviction, and hiding their car for fear it will be repossessed. Soon enough, his mother, who is apparently tubercular, is sent off to a sanitarium, leaving the boy, Aaron (Jesse Bradford), with his father, who is not quite neglectful, but is surely inattentive. He's a travelling salesman of useless devices waiting on a WPA job (which is anachronistic: the film is set in 1932 and 1933, but the WPA didn't come along until 1935). But Aaron is smart, resourceful, diligent, and charming—there's a Ferris Bueller quality to him, and they share talents as fabulists. Much of the film charts his adventures in the fading hotel where he lives and throughout St. Louis, including in the homes of the very well-to-do. It's dark, but never quite grim, and does an admirable job of showing the ordinary, daily challenges—difficult and unrelenting but seldom dramatic— that come with a life lived perched on the edge of total penury. It's filled with people whose backs are up against the wall and about out of options, and the camera regularly finds opportunity to pan over nearby shanty towns, showing where the next step is for many. Aaron is constantly on the hunt for food after being left on his own when his father takes a job selling watches out-of-state. He overhears other kids at school complaining that there's always "a poor kid," and that he gets special treatment (Aaron doesn't), and he's eventually evicted from the hotel. As the manager tells it, it's not him, but the bank—"it's the money. All they care about is the money"—and not long after, we see the police, seeming to enjoy themselves, brutally evicting residents from one of the Hoovervilles, then destroying it. These are all, to a person, the deserving poor, but not in the maudlin or patronizing way it can be in other films. If director Steven Soderbergh offers what can sometimes be a soft-focused view of the Depression, he does nonetheless capture the basic truth: most poor people are poor despite their efforts, not for lack of them, and this is doubly true in periods of widespread economic decline. In the end, the WPA job comes through, paying a princely sum of $65 per month that allows them all to move back in together, into a proper apartment; but it's a measure of how deeply Aaron has been scarred, despite his apparent resilience, that he doesn't trust that it will last. It's a lovely movie, and among the best of the Depression portrayals.

From the comic strip ("Little Orphan Annie") and then the Broadway musi-cal comes an often (but not always) dreary, treacly film, *Annie* (1981). What's startling is the manner in which it makes light of the abusive conditions in the

FIGURE 13.4 A family of beggars. *A Little Princess*, Warner Brothers, 1985.

orphanage where Annie lives, overseen by wantonly cruel, drunken matron played by Carol Burnett. And what of the fact that the film treats so casually the notion that a billionaire borrows an orphan for a week as a publicity stunt? It's supposedly set during the Great Depression, but apart from a cameo by Franklin (Edward Herman) and Eleanor Roosevelt (Lois De Banzie) that makes "The Sun'll Come Out Tomorrow" a New Deal propaganda song, you'd never know. *The Little Princess* (1939) and its remake *A Little Princess* (1995) have a bit of Annie in them: a young girl is sent off to a group home ruled over by a cruel mistress. Poor and seemingly alone, she nonetheless winds up wealthy and with a loving father, just as Annie does. Perhaps the lesson is that grown women can escape poverty through marriage, while young girls must do it through adoption.

There's one exception to this pattern of films about homeless children in the Great Depression being made long after the Depression was over—setting aside the Dead End Kids movies we've already discussed, since those kids were not homeless—and that's *Wild Boys of the Road* (1933). (1940's *Wild Girls of the Road* appears to be about adults, but is among the films I've not been able to screen.)

FIGURES 13.5 AND 13.6 Kids ride the rails, searching for work and food; and, later, battling to save their Hooverville. *Wild Boys of the Road*. First National Pictures, 1933.

Eddie and Tommy, well-dressed, clean-cut teenagers, talk after having been thrown out of a dance for sneaking in without paying the admission fee, and one confesses to the other that his family is getting food from the Community Chest. The other offers to help, but goes home to find that his father has been laid off. We flash forward, and the formerly dapper boys are now walking in beat-up old clothes. To be less of a burden on their families, they hop on a train in search of work and eventually find themselves part of a large group of boy and girls in similar straits, riding the rails and trying to survive. They kill a bull (after he raped a girl travelling with them), build their own shantytown, panhandle, fight with the police, are driven off, and build a new Hooverville in a garbage dump. (A still from the film was used by one newspaper as propaganda against Upton Sinclair's campaign for California governor, an effort to show that if his "End Poverty in California" plan were to pass, the state would be overrun with people seeking handouts [Ceplair and Englund, 1983, p. 92]). For a sense of what such a life was like, see the documentary *Riding the Rails* (1997), which has at its core interviews with men, and one woman, who had travelled the country as children and teenagers.

After Eddie gets conned into unknowingly robbing a movie theater, he is arrested, and the whole gang gets hauled in. Described by the judge as "an enemy to society," Eddie speaks:

> I'll tell you why we can't go home, because our folks are poor. They can't get jobs, and there isn't enough to eat. What good will it do you to send us home to starve? You say you've got to send us to jail to keep us off the streets. Well, that's a lie. You want to send us to jail because you don't want to see us, you want to forget us. Well you can't do it, because I'm not the only one. There's thousands more just like me. There's more hitting the road every day. You read in the papers about people getting help: the banks get it; the soldiers get it; the breweries get it; they're always yelling about giving it to the farmers. What about us? We're kids! I'm not a bad boy. Neither is Tommy. Us three kids have been traveling around the country looking for work. You don't think we like the road, do you? ... When a guy gave me a chance to make five bucks, sure, I took it. Wouldn't you? Wouldn't anybody? ... Go ahead, put me in a cell, lock me up. I'm sick of being hungry and cold, sick of freight trains. Jail can't be any worse than the street, so give it to me.

The judge takes pity on them, and dismisses the case. And that's the finale, with no happy or pat ending, but with an acknowledgment that these children surely can't be blamed for their state. That simple notion—that circumstances beyond an individual's control might lie at the heart of their poverty or rootlessness—would become a rarity, as films later in the century were much more likely to see the tramp as deviant and dangerous.

14 THE MODERN TRAMP

VILLAINS

Scanners; C.H.U.D.; Prince of Darkness; Street Trash; Night of the Bums; The Vagrant; Down, Out and Dangerous; The Stray; Up Your Alley; Acid Rain; The Purge; The Purge: Anarchy; Soap Dish; Suspect; Surviving the Game; Extreme Measures

There's a cycle to media coverage of homelessness during any given year, increasing during the Thanksgiving and Christmas holiday period, and sharply declining thereafter (Bunis, Yancik, and Snow, 1996; Shields, 2001). But there's a longer-term pattern that's more important for our purposes. As Barrett Lee, Kimberly Tyler, and James Wright (2012) sum up their findings:

> News stories during the early 1980s portrayed the homeless as a diverse group challenged by circumstances beyond their control and hence deserving of aid. This positive picture has given way to somewhat harsher coverage over the past two decades, with more stories on the deviance of homeless persons, the disorder they create, and the steps being taken to deal with them. (see also Buck, Toro and Ramos, 2004)

Perhaps because the stories media told about people in need changed in this way—although I see evidence of this even by the early 1980s—policy changed as well; or did the tone of stories change because policy did? Regardless, there appears to be a relationship between the ways in which media have framed their coverage of poverty—the extent to which people are portrayed as underserving, lazy, and dependent—and the relative generosity of means-tested social welfare programs at the federal, state, and local levels (Rose and Baumgartner, 2013).

This is consistent with other findings. Joshua Guetzkow (2010), looking at the rhetoric used during congressional debates, shows that there was something distinct about the Great Society period of the 1960s. Then, poor people were, by and large, understood to be poor as a consequence of forces beyond their control, when such thinking was at the heart of programs like the Job Corps (modeled on the New Deal's Civilian Conservation Corps) on one hand, which sought to "cure" poverty by removing people from the ghetto (it's that old story), and Community Action on the other, which was to provide resources for local mobilization, organization, and community and individual empowerment. Much of the effort remained on changing the individual, we should note, even if the individual was not necessarily understood to be at fault, either by removing him or her from the ghetto or changing the role they played in it. By contrast, if we turn our attention to the 1980s and 1990s, the individual is more likely to be judged as culpable and, therefore, the remedies were punitive and coercive, from the Family Support Act of 1988, to the Violent Crime Control and Law Enforcement Act of 1994, to the repeal of AFDC in 1996.

As elite debate shifted, with Democrats and Republicans both becoming more likely to blame poverty and homelessness on laziness or bad behavior, we should expect to find that consensus reflected in public opinion (Zaller, 1992). And we do. By 2007, according to one large, multi-city survey (Gallup and Fannie Mae, 2007), the single most common explanation for homelessness

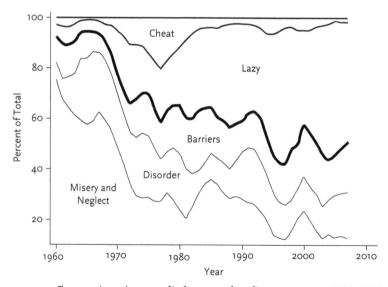

FIGURE 14.0 Frames American media have used to discuss poverty, 1960–2010. Source: Rose and Baumgartner, 2013, Figure 2. Reprinted with the permission of John Wiley and Sons.

FIGURE 14.1 "I've never seen anything so disgusting in all my life." *Scanners*, Avco-Embassy Pictures, 1981.

among survey respondents was drug abuse, followed by mental illness. They were, moreover, likely to underestimate the number of poor families and to overestimate the number of single men among the overall population of people without a home of their own. It is not too hard to see, as a consequence, how the ideas for the following films might have been generated, and why they are framed in the way that they are: they reflect the zeitgeist.

Scanners (1981) begins with a man we are meant to identify as homeless coming into the food court of a mall. Two women stare, disapproving, and one comments: "look at that fellow over there. I've never seen anything so disgusting in all my life.... I don't know how they let creatures like that in here." He glares back at her, seemingly causing her to have a violent seizure, before he's chased and shot with a dart gun. When he wakes, he's clad in white and strapped to a bed, "You are thirty-five years old, Mister Vale," a man says. "Why are you such a derelict? Such a piece of human junk? The answer is simple. You're a scanner, but you don't realize. That has been the source of all your agony. But I will show you now, it can be a source of great power."

We learn that scanners, "telepathic curiosities," in one bureaucrat's phrase, were part of a government weapons program; rival companies are now fighting to control them. The conceit here is that many mental patients or homeless men who hear voices or suffer aural delusions are not, in truth, mad, but simply telepathic and telekinetic supermen (and women), the result of technology gone awry. The mentally ill homeless man had made his modern debut, and he is dangerous, whatever the roots of his condition. In its own way, *Scanners* is doing some of the same work television, newspapers, advocates, and scholars were all beginning to be engaged in—to explain the growing presence of this new, and much more troubling, tramp.

There's an underground community of homeless people in *Scanners* that's similar to the real one we find in Marc Singer's *Dark Days* (2000), a documentary about an encampment of men and women living in Amtrak's tunnels. "You'd be surprised what the human mind and the human body can adjust to," notes one of them. There's another documentary like this, inspired by Jennifer Toth's sensational book *The Mole People* (1993), called *Voices in the Tunnels: In Search of the Mole People* (2008), but it's framed from the viewpoint of the filmmaker as a myth-busting kind of exercise—do the Mole People really exist? They are exotic and pathologized, even for homeless people: Their initial meeting with people in the tunnels is given the title card "First Contact."

C.H.U.D. (1984) carries this danger to new, and somewhat absurdist, depths. In the 1980s, homelessness was more than just a crisis, but was a sort of urban Rorschach test, representing a greater fear about economic and social

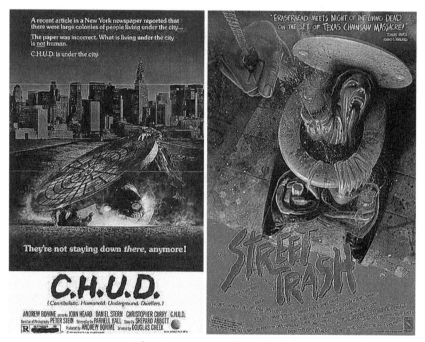

FIGURES 14.2 AND 14.3 Advertising posters for *C.H.U.D.*, New World Pictures, 1984; and *Street Trash*, Synapse Films, 1987.

insecurity, escalating class divisions, and national decline. This is seen most clearly in an ad for *CHUD*: "A recent article in a New York newspaper reported that there were large colonies of people living under the city.... The paper was incorrect. What is living under the city is *not* human.... [And] they're not staying down *there* anymore." The film begins at night, on dark, wet streets, with a woman walking her dog, pulled through a manhole cover by a creature we don't quite see. We learn about a conspiracy to cover up the illegal dumping of toxic waste, and discover that the homeless people who have been contaminated by it have become monsters ("Cannibalistic Humanoid Underground Dwellers") who prey upon the public, killing them as they did this poor woman. Variously referred to as *bums, sewer people, derelicts, bag ladies, undergrounders*, and *Bowery bums*. whatever the cause of their *illness*, as in *Scanners*, homeless people are victims but, more importantly, a threat to be eliminated.

In *Prince of Darkness* (1987), an apocalyptic God versus the Devil tale, homeless people are also infected—by a green, gooey primordial matter that comes from Satan himself—and then become threats, serving as hosts to ants, worms, maggots, and beetles, indiscriminately killing anyone who would stop the Devil from rising again. As one character explains, making sense of why it's the homeless people who serve as the first hosts, "*He* controls simple organisms easily." Homeless people are thus not merely made dangerous, but are, quite literally, dehumanized in the process.

Street Trash (1987), something of a minor cult classic, is yet another film very much in this vein. It's set mostly in the junkyard of a desperate urban landscape on the border of Brooklyn and Queens, and centered around the effects of Tenafly Viper, cheap liquor found buried behind the wall of a package store and sold to the desperate for a dollar a bottle. One swig, and the consumer literally melts away, as if showered in acid (or as if one were a Nazi witnessing the opening of the Ark of the Covenant in *Raiders of the Lost Ark*). The homeless men here (and all are men except for one desperate, abused, and sex-starved woman) are dirty, rank-smelling, violent, thieving, alcoholic, stupid, and often insane. They are objects to be feared, ridiculed, or held in contempt. In one scene early in the film, a well-dressed couple is assaulted by homeless people, one of whom pulls the driver from a car and slams him through the windshield, killing him. More than merely making you uncomfortable by asking for money, these people are literally a threat to your life. (Another man is *punished* by the police by being showered and dressed in clean clothes.) And this is their behavior before the effects of the demon rum. These are one-dimensional characters and mostly interchangeable (except, perhaps, for the most violent of the group, a homeless Vietnam veteran, subject to murderous rages and periodic flashbacks; he uses a sharpened human bone as a weapon).

Perhaps the only (arguably) sympathetic portrayal is that of Kevin (Mark Sferrazza), a teenager living in the junkyard with his brother, Fred, who is not quite as degenerate as the rest, although hardly a hero. The boss's secretary asks him, at one point, "So, what brought you to this?" But he is pulled away before answering. In another movie, this oblique recognition of its own failure to give these men histories or to explain how they arrive at such a terrible pass might be its own kind of commentary. But *Street Trash* is not interested in explanation or analysis—the homeless people here are contemptible and expendable, and their infection and destruction by Tenafly Viper is, it seems fair to say, meant to be entertaining and, to some degree, a just punishment for their degradation. It is, in fact, such an ugly worldview that it inspired a scathing review by Walter Goodman (*New York Times*, Sept. 16, 1987), which begins, "*Street Trash*, now befouling the Eighth Street Cinema, is the stuff that civil-libertarian nightmares are made of. It claims no redeeming social value, and you don't have to be a Supreme Court nominee to question whether the Founders could have foreseen anything like it when they wrote the First Amendment."

All that said, it is probably unfair to make too much of the fact that homeless people are treated so unsympathetically or one-dimensionally here, since everyone is treated unsympathetically and one-dimensionally. Nor is it likely to be useful to single out the film for being anti-homeless, since it is also misogynist (a gang rape is played for laughs), racist (it singles out Italians, "gooks," and "slopes," for special derision, and says about one character: "He's black. No one gives a shit about him: there's enough of them already"), and homophobic ("fag" and "homo" are used regularly as epithets). It's violent and vulgar (at the end of fights, people are urinated or vomited on; after a castration, the penis is played with by the junkyard denizens as if it were a football) and in addition to bodies melting or exploding, there's an assortment of beatings, stabbings, and mutilation. But, unlike *C.H.U.D.* or *Scanners*, these homeless men don't turn into homicidal monsters—they are that already—they just die, graphically, gleefully, and extravagantly. There is a relief, a catharsis, in their demise, as their deaths each make the streets just a little bit safer.

The theatrical trailer for the film seems to have its tongue more firmly in its cheek than the movie itself, suggesting, in the Announcer's voice, that if you are tired of your boss, your wife, and your kids, you could "Drop out and join the ranks of the few, the filthy, the trash.... Where else can you live for free and eat for even less? [clip of a character shoplifting in a supermarket] ... But be forewarned. Freedom has its price. Yes, there's always a snake in the garden of Eden," as they show a bottle of Tenafly Viper. But it's the tag line that may be most revealing: "Street Trash: It's easy to find us. We're all over the place." This echoes all too clearly the growing obsession with homeless men and "squeegee guys" in big cities throughout the nation—a problem that would come to be treated as one of crime and public order, rather than of mental illness, unaffordable housing, or failed social service programs.

In the documentary *The Meltdown Memoirs* (2006), *Street Trash* director James Muro is asked: "Why'd you make a film about bums and winos?" His reply: "Because, you know, bums are inherent in my family, unfortunately. Bums are an integral part of New York City, and nobody ever makes films about them. But, I love bums. I mean, it's something you see every day on the street." Producer Roy Frumkes, discussing the release of the film, noted: "The Coalition for the Homeless took out radio time and told us off. I was thrilled. I was only disappointed they didn't get a bunch of derelicts to picket the theater." One of the film's actors, James Lorinz, further observed:

> There are crazy homeless people [in the film]. I mean, you know, and it's not their fault. But on the other hand, you had these people that were governing themselves, and they lived in their own little culture, and had their own community, and people knew each other, so . . . and they were happy. You didn't see anybody complaining, or sick, they were happy, you know, about being homeless, they're drinking, and having a good time. [He pauses, with a twinkle in his eye]: But I do give to the homeless funds . . . I do some volunteer work as well. [to the camera] Did you get that?

The message seems to be, "Hey, relax, it's a movie, for heaven's sake," even if these comments also seem defensive. Yet these images of the homeless man as a threat to public order reflected a genuine public concern, typified by a *New York Post* editorial (Nov. 19, 1999): "It's time to end the madness. It's time to get the dangerously deranged off the streets for their sake and ours. . . . There are crazies among us. Some of them are dangerous. A few of them are murderous. Get them off the street. Now!"

Night of the Bums (1998) is very much in the spirit of *Street Trash*, as wine poisoned by witches turns "bums" into flesh-eating zombies. The film opens with a montage of homeless men, played by people who were genuinely homeless, according to the director, drinking, loitering, harassing passers-by, vomiting, eating dog food, and so on. One of the witches leaves bottles scattered in streets and alleyways throughout the city, which are then drunk greedily by the homeless men. They rampage, murdering, beheading, dismembering, disemboweling, and, being zombies, eating the flesh of their victims. "It appears," says the Mayor, "that the bums are multiplying like rats. They're taking over the city." But they are soon all killed, and, once again, the movies find a solution to the "homeless crisis" where public policy cannot.

The lone murderous homeless man would also become a reoccurring character. *The Vagrant* (1992) gives us a "vile derelict" who relentlessly stalks a new homeowner, making him wonder if he is losing his mind. As he says to a friend: "God, he's disgusting, Chuck. I mean, filthy. He's got this mangled eye, and this sick smile, like he's deranged, or had some kind of head injury or something.... He's clever and he's dangerous—I can see it in his eyes." We learn that the Vagrant is a disgraced doctor who has apparently been using the man for a psychological experiment. The Vagrant is ultimately killed, however —twice: first by the homeowner, or so it appears, and then by the police, after he has reappeared, in horror-film fashion.

Down, Out and Dangerous (1995) offers more of the same. Tim (Richard Thomas) is a panhandler who berates and kills a man who refuses to give him money and then works his way into Brad's (Bruce Davidson) life, where he kills one of Brad's neighbors and his assistant, setting Brad up to take the blame while trying to convince his wife he's having an affair (we'll learn that Tim previously killed his own wife and business partner and escaped from prison). Tim manages to cancel Brad's credit cards and to get him fired; Brad, unable to get any money, finds himself begging for change on the street to make a phone call. Brad eventually kills Tim; the police say he won't be charged, though, and his wife, now fully aware of what has gone on, comes home from the hospital with their new baby. So, they live happily ever after, with the panhandler dead at the end, as it would appear he must be.

FIGURES 14.4 AND 14.5 *Vagrant*, MGM, 1982; and *Down, Out and Dangerous*, Wilshire Court Productions, 1995.

Similarly, we have *The Stray* (2000). Ben, a cop, and Kate, a wealthy restaurant owner, are dating. In the opening scene, Ben's chasing a masked bandit. The next day, Kate accidentally hits a man with her car. The man, Gil Draper (Stefan Lysenko), has no memory of the accident, he says, and the doctor reports that he's apparently been living on the street for some time, with no immediate family they can find.

Kate asks, "If he's homeless, where's he going to go?"

The doctor responds, "Our homeless population is too large for us to have a welfare shelter; there are places he can go, but we leave that up to the patient."

Kate wants to meet the unfortunate man, but Ben scoffs: "I know what you're thinking; I deal with these kind of people all the time, and most of them wish you would have backed up that car and finished the job ... I've seen a lot of homeless people, you know; they've got nothing to lose, and they're just waiting for someone like you to come along." Brushing aside his warnings, determined to take the man in, she makes a space for him in the garage. We're meant to think her kindhearted, yet she lives in an enormous house—we might even call it a mansion—and her act of nobility is clearing a small space in a dark, dirty, dusty, junk-filled garage that has at least one pigeon in it. Why not a room in the house? Yet he expresses his gratitude, and pledges to "prove my worth."

When Kate was a girl, she recounts, a dog got stuck in one of her father's raccoon traps, and they took him in and cared for him. "That was just a dog," she says to Ben, who thinks she's lost her mind, and we know that Kate will be the one caught in the raccoon trap, not this homeless "stray." And soon enough, Gil leads Ben off into the woods, where a friend, the masked bandit we met in the first scene, tries to shoot him. Murder and more mayhem follow, and it turns out that Kate and Gil were childhood friends, but his father was rendered bankrupt by her father; this was Gil's revenge. But he, too, ends up dead.

Worse is *Up Your Alley* (1989), which gives us a large, slow white kid—in spotless clothing—pushing a shopping cart, presumably with all his possessions in it. A gang of "toughs" (ruffians? hooligans?) is potentially a threat, but he gives their leader a sweater (handmade by his mother, who died two months earlier), and, thus the leader (J.J.) tells his "gang" to leave the boy alone. J.J. warns the kid (Sonny) to be wary of the "street killer." Sonny is then chased by a man with knife, but he runs into David, another homeless street denizen, who brings Sonny to the Midnight Mission, where, for some reason, they sleep out in the back alley. The film doesn't seem to have much of a point of view—there's not even anything coherent or consistent about the portrayal of the skid row residents. But it does end as we might now predict: Sonny hits the killer over the head with a rock.

Worse again is *Acid Rain* (1998). The opening shot moves from the Brooklyn Bridge to Times Square, where a large black man in a torn black T-shirt rips the arm off of a street performer (though this is neither funny nor scary), as a tourist traveling with her husband and young son notes that she has a bad feeling. There are then many shots of homeless people living on the street, with mournful music. A blind (black) homeless man hears a prophetic voice, which tells him that the end of the world coming in three days, and he can suddenly see. Presumably, in this way of thinking (such as it is), the least likely candidate to receive a message from God is a blind, homeless, black man.

The Purge (2013) presents another kind of dangerous, homeless man. The film shows us an America with a one-percent unemployment rate and virtually no crime; this is because, many believe, once each year, for a twelve-hour period, all crime, including murder, is legal. The official government line is that this allows humans, naturally violent, a regular opportunity to "purge" their aggressions, leaving a tranquil populace for the remainder of the year. How this is meant to result in full employment is not explained. An alternative theory, given voice in the film by a sociologist, is that the purge is "actually about the elimination of the poor, the needy, the sick—those unable to defend themselves. The eradication of those so-called non-contributing members of society, ultimately unburdening the economy." This explanation is plausible, at least, if the culling is large enough to eliminate those without jobs.

When the rich family at the center of the story reluctantly gives shelter to a man in danger, the people hunting him and demanding his release refer to him as "a dirty, homeless pig; a grotesque menace to our just society." They are led by a preening young man who is a gross caricature of a spoiled, entitled product of generations of ultra-wealthy inbreeding, and to drive home the never-subtle point, he describes killing the "homeless pig," the "filth," as a right, even an obligation. That the hunted man is black could make this as much about his race as his class, but that possibility is not explored even in the clumsy way the film tries to comment on class relations (and on violence, for that matter). Here the horror is not caused by a homeless man, but by choosing to care about him.

The 2014 sequel, *The Purge: Anarchy*, offers a similar critique: "Who dies tonight?" asks one activist as the annual purge is set to begin. "The poor," is his answer: "We can't afford to protect ourselves." We learn that the wealthy now purge by "buying poor and sick people, and they take them in their homes and they kill them where they're safe." Later we see an auction in which patrons in black tie and evening gowns bid for the privilege of hunting and killing people captured off the streets. But this year, the poor are fighting back. "Fuck you, fuck your money, and fuck the purge!" Carmello yells as he leads an assault on the charity auction. "Change only comes when their blood spills," he adds. "Get ready to bleed, rich bitches! This is our time now!" In an age of record inequality, it's tempting to read these films, and some of their contemporaries like *Upside Down* (2012) or *Elysium* (2013), as efforts at social commentary. Perhaps the *Purge* films are complaints about a world in which the poor exist merely as fodder to "cleanse the souls" of the rich and powerful, and perhaps the dual dystopian-utopian science fiction landscapes of *Upside Down* and *Elysium* are commentaries on social and economic inequality, the predations of modern global capitalism, and the cruelty of power. But I think not. These films are all ultimately not interested in ideas so much as wanting to be perceived as being interested in ideas, as if Meaning might redeem these otherwise run-of-the-mill slasher or sci-fi flicks (see further discussion in Chapter 15).

Another homicidal homeless man appears in *Rail Kings* (2005). A spoiled rich kid is accused of killing his parents, so to find out who actually murdered them and why, he tracks down the "hobo uncle" he remembers his mother having mentioned. Improbably enough, he finds an old hobo called Steamtrain—played in a short scene by Ernest Borgnine, a nice counterpoint to the bull he played in *Emperor of the North Pole*—via an internet bulletin board called *Hobo News,* run, apparently, by the National Hobo Association (which is an actual organization founded by the film's director). Preston, the young man, sets off in search of his uncle, beginning with a hobo jungle conveniently located down the road from where he lives; he first observes the residents while crouched behind a tree, as if stalking wild animals. They know the uncle (because of course they do) and point Preston to where they think he is. And he is found. As he talks with his uncle, we learn that Preston has come to believe that the murderer was a hobo who subsequently escaped on a freight train (and who, in 2005, still talked of "hobos" and "tramps" as the people here do?). The uncle (played by the director) makes a living by extorting money from people after threatening to burn down their homes, at least once killing one when things went wrong. When at home, he seems to be living a pretty ordinary married-with-three-kids middle-class lifestyle, down the road from where his sister lives, though his kids didn't know about her and Preston only vaguely knew he had an uncle at all. None of this makes much sense, but taps into the filmmakers' apparent interest in hobos, having made a middling documentary called *The American Hobo* (2003), with Ernest Borgnine as narrator, which focuses almost exclusively on the romance of the road—adventure, freedom, autonomy, excitement, "colorful characters"—with almost no critical analysis but lots of palaver about "the hobo that lives in us all." And, curiously, it has scenes from *Rail Kings* periodically cut in as background footage.

The very first rail riders Preston and his uncle run into have, for no especially good reason, a good idea of who the killer is, someone who goes by the name of Phantom 13. They move off in a slow, meandering pursuit, with no sense of urgency at all despite the fact that Preston has only two weeks before his trial date. Phantom turns out to be the Uncle himself, who turns out to be Preston's father. It continues to make no sense. The film ends with Preston becoming a "hobo," too, with a voiceover about learning his uncle's/father's lesson about each man becoming a hobo for his own reasons. But he's not some romantic figure making his own way in the world, as the film would have it, he's a fugitive from the law for his role in a murder that one of their own committed.

Perhaps the fact that so many of the films that offer a homeless man as a homicidal maniac are so bad is not mere happenstance: *Soap Dish* (1991), a much better movie, offers a lesson. The producer of a daytime soap opera (Robert Downey, Jr.) complains to the casting director (Carrie Fisher) that there's a problem with their "socially relevant storyline," as he calls it: "We need new homeless. But good-looking homeless. This batch are disgusting. You could have picked them up off the street." They have written homeless people into their scripts to lend seriousness to their efforts, and since the film is a comedy and a satire, it is offering its own kind of commentary about such cynical efforts to create the appearance of substance where there is none. Perhaps that's why so many of these movies were made when homelessness was a widely covered public issue—it was the social problem du jour, and sufficiently in the air, and thus what writers grabbed at as an easy way to demonstrate their "seriousness."

The idea of the homeless man as Other, and as a danger, is common even in better crafted, bigger-budget dramatic films. In *Suspect* (1987), for example, a homeless man (Liam Neeson) who lives in a drainpipe is arrested, having been found with a murder victim's wallet and the nine dollars it contained. The motive—killing a man for nine dollars—is plausible precisely because of his status, as his court-appointed attorney, Kathleen Riley (Cher) will later admit.

From her opening statement to the jury:

Carl Wayne Anderson isn't a decent, hard-working citizen.... On the contrary, Carl Anderson is the personification of the American nightmare. He's one of the nameless, faceless derelicts who wander aimlessly through the streets of our country by the thousands every day! We step over them in doorways. We cross the street to avoid actually coming into contact with one of them. We look through them with a mixture of pity, contempt and fear! We choose not to see that under their ragged blankets and filthy clothes, behind their mutters and their shouts is a frightened, lost human being. A human being just like you and me with a name and a history. They were somebody's child, somebody's sweetheart, and someone's mother or father! These people weren't born the way we see them today. Carl Anderson wasn't born a vagrant living in a drainpipe. He grew up, went to school and got married! He was a soldier in Vietnam. Not a hero, just a dog soldier who believed in and fought for his country. He suffered the trauma of that war. And when he tried to regain his identity and self-respect in a Veterans Hospital, he contracted spinal meningitis that made him deaf and caused a traumatic speech loss. We will show that Carl Anderson was cold and hungry. That he lived in a drainpipe because the shelters were too full.... Please don't judge him by your fears or your prejudices. For who among us cannot say, "If not for the grace of God, there go I?"

The juror who comes to investigate the case on his own (Dennis Quaid), passing along the information he gathers to Riley, finds himself in an encampment of homeless people: he wanders in, and the scene is dark with scattered fires, and the sounds of breaking glass. There's a fight taking place, and the

FIGURE 14.6 Carl Wayne Anderson. *Suspect*, Tri-Star Pictures, 1987.

whole atmosphere is menacing. These are dangerous, desperate people, we are meant to know.

Kathleen says the following to Carl, when he's on the witness stand, after she recounts some of his personal history:

> It's been rough. You've had your share of problems. You've been kicked around pretty good. Am I supposed to feel sorry for you? There's plenty of people who've been kicked around. Plenty of people who had their noses rubbed in it for one reason or the other. You know the difference between you and them? They have dignity. They don't lie in the street wrapped in a blanket. They don't eat out of trash cans. They don't piss in people's yards. They take showers. They change their clothes. They don't walk around feeling sorry for themselves. They get jobs and have children and take care of their lives. They don't sleep in people's cars! They don't steal nine dollars from anybody!

She then asks if he killed the victim, and he struggles to speak aloud his denial. It's a smarter screenplay than many with homeless people at the center (the writer here, Eric Roth, also wrote *The Onion Field, The Insider,* and *Munich,* among others) but it ultimately differs little: pity is the guiding emotion, and Carl is sympathetic precisely because he didn't do anything "wrong" to wind up in his state, but is there because of his service in Vietnam. Yet, since only about eleven percent of homeless adults are veterans, the economic conditions and political power structures that account for most homelessness are ignored, as they almost always are.

The idea that homeless men are animals gets carried to its logical extreme in *Extreme Measures* and *Surviving the Game. Surviving the Game* (1994) opens with Jack Mason (Ice-T) picking through the trash for food. Mason is later caught stealing meat, which he brings back to a junkyard where he lives and feeds the other men there. We learn that Mason's wife and young child died in an apartment fire; he had tried to get the city to pay attention to unsafe conditions, to no avail. He is being set up as sympathetic so that we know that he is homeless for a *legitimate* reason. His dog and best friend die in quick succession, leading Mason to try to kill himself, but Walter Cole (Charles Dutton), from the Seventh Street Mission, stops him. Mason ultimately accepts his ministrations and then his offer to be a "survival guide" in the wilderness, and is brought to Hell's Canyon, where we learn that hunters have paid $50,000 each to stalk and kill humans. Mason will be the prey, not the guide. This homeless man is the animal. (Would this movie work if Ice-T were white? Is it important that Dutton is black, too?)

FIGURES 14.7 AND 14.8 The hunters (*left*), and the hunted (*right*). *Surviving the Game*, New Line Cinema, 1984.

The handsome young son of one of the hunters, brought along for the first time, is resistant: "We're not really going to hunt him, are we?" He pleads, "No, no, no. . . . He's a human being!" To which his father responds: "He's a homeless piece of shit. He's nothing. He's less than nothing." Is Mason truly "Nothing, less than nothing"? *No*, we are meant to say, along with the handsome young son, he's a man, with a tragic past.

The hunters (Gary Busey, F. Murray Abraham, John C. McGinley) are initially portrayed as ugly, crazed, odd, and evil: they are unhinged, brutal sociopaths. But the film eventually works to humanize them, too. As one reveals: "You, Mason, are a waste. . . . Someone like you, just like you, followed my daughter to school one day. The police report said that she tried to get away from him. Nobody ever caught him. And for all I know it was you." And so this hunter also gets a past that is supposed to complicate our appraisal of him, perhaps offering a justification for his behavior, and while the film pretends to be opposed to treating homeless people like animals, that's a pose; there's a relish to this hunt, it seems to me, and I wonder how much of this sadism is meant to attract us, and how much to repel?

There are some similarities with *Extreme Measures* (1996), in which Gene Hackman plays Lawrence Myrick, a gifted doctor who has been using homeless men as experimental subjects to try to cure paraplegics with spinal cord injuries, events with some analogues in history (see, e.g., Kolata, 2013). "These men aren't victims, they're heroes," insists Myrick, "They have nothing; no future; no family, nothing. But here, with us, here they're performing miracles." We are apparently meant to ask if it is worth it to use homeless men to save others—and to answer *No, of course not*. But we are not asked to question why these men and women are homeless in the first place, or the justice of that, or what can and should be done—merely to agree that they should not be used as subjects for medical experiments against their will, even if we might quietly wonder if they would have more value as lab rats. The ostensible

FIGURE 14.9 Homeless men escape from the lab where they have been experimented upon. *Extreme Measures*, Columbia Pictures, 1996.

hero of the film, another doctor, Guy Luthan (Hugh Grant), is noble precisely because he cares about what has happened *even* to a homeless man.

After his death, Myrick's wife brings his research to Luthan: the implied dilemma is, should he use it? It's the film's central question: can a "worthless" life be used to aid others with more value to society? Or as Myrick asked of Luthan, "If you could cure cancer by killing one person, wouldn't you have to do it?" That the film concludes by asking the viewer to consider this question again tells us that the filmmakers think it's a difficult choice, and it's meant to be difficult precisely because of the dubious benefit of the "one person" who would be killed in Myrick's hypothetical. Homeless men have become so vilified and dehumanized, their moral worth so routinely called into question, that whether we should torture and kill them if it would help us and others like us is meant to be a provocative question and a difficult choice.

FIGURE 14.10 Should Grant use the data from Hackman's experiments? *Extreme Measures*, Columbia Pictures, 1996.

15 THE MODERN TRAMP

VICTORS

Trading Places, The Prince and the Pauper, Pygmalion, The Bride Wore Red, Pursuit of Happyness, Homeless to Harvard, Upside Down, Elysium

There is another approach to dealing with homeless men beyond the victim and the villain: the Victor. The man (it is almost always a man) who rises up against all odds and succeeds, offering us all important life lessons and, in the process, reinforcing the notion that, with self-discipline, hard word, and pluck, homelessness can be overcome. This point is made explicitly with *Trading Places* (1983), a movie we'll turn to next, after noting a few of its precursors.

Curiously enough, a movie much like *Trading Places* was nearly made by Charlie Chaplin. Here's his description of an abandoned subplot for *City Lights*:

> Two members of a rich man's club, discussing the instability of human consciousness, decide to experiment with a tramp whom they find asleep on the Embankment. They take him to their palatial apartment and lavish him with wine, women, and song, and when he is dead drunk and asleep they put him back where they found him and he wakes up, thinking it has all been a dream. (Chaplin, 1964/2003, p. 322)

Trading Places, in its own way, improved upon Chaplin's scenario by complicating the experiment on the tramp to see if they can make him, Pygmalion-like, into their own upper-class creature and by simultaneously conducting another experiment to see if they can turn a spoiled, wealthy stockbroker into a bum. But even before Chaplin's notion (and Shaw's *Pygmalion*), we see something of both plots in Mark Twain's *The Prince and the Pauper*.

Twain's original story (1882) was simple enough—two young boys, one a much-abused beggar, "born in a hovel, bred in the gutters of London, familiar with rags and dirt and misery," the other heir to the British throne, wind up meeting. They exchange clothing on a lark, and are each mistaken for the other and thrust into leading the other's life. Poor Tom Canty, although he takes some acclimating, is soon enough playing the part of Prince and then King, so enamored of the role that he doubles his wardrobe and trebles his retinue and becomes quite adept at issuing edicts and brooking no dissent. The young Prince has a harder time of it and never quite makes peace with his new station, always insisting that he is, in fact, the true heir and King. But while Tom governs with generosity and mercy, and is possessed of a certain kind of folk wisdom, upon Edward's return to his rightful place, he, too, governs wisely and justly, thanks to his experience: "What dost *thou* know of suffering and oppression? I and my people know, but not thou," he proclaims. There is wisdom in poverty, and redemption to be had in it. There have been stage plays and comic book adaptations of the tale, cartoons and television series that riff on the premise, after-school specials and miniseries, video games, and Japanese and Indian adaptations, among others. Perhaps its appeal is part wish-fulfillment—how many people wouldn't like to be king for a day, or a month?—and part what Chaplin described as the natural desire to see the wealthy get their come-uppance. Moreover, like many of Shakespeare's comedies, well plotted mistaken-identity stories, can make for entertaining yarns, as Twain's surely does.

The only extant American interpretation that was made for the big screen (two earlier film versions appear to be lost; the rest are foreign-made or made for television) is a 1937 movie with Errol Flynn and Claude Rains. It takes liberties, making both young men a bit more immature and dumber than they are in the novel, and making the villains at court more villainous without making life in the ghetto more cruel or brutal. It's another film that cuts against the claim that Warner Brothers was especially radical in its approach. Like other studios, they were prone to softening source material, stripping away ambiguity and complexity, and shying away from opportunities to make poor communities genuinely complex.

Pygmalion (1938), too, might be thought of as a precursor to *Trading Places*. A wealthy man with time on his hands wagers that he can take a poor, uneducated flower girl and, with a bit of time and effort, make her, for all appearances, a woman of wealth and breeding. "Deliciously low," Higgins calls Eliza, and "horribly dirty," when measuring the challenge he faces. "I shall make a Duchess of this draggle-tail guttersnipe," he says later. Then, "when we've finished with her, we'll throw her back in the gutter." Liza becomes a lady, over time—professing modestly that "the difference between a lady and a flower girl isn't how she behaves. It's how she's treated"—while it's Higgins who demonstrates himself less capable of learning, character development, or growth. Even her father, by his own proud admission, "one of the undeserving poor," winds up being "delivered ... into the hands of middle class morality," thanks to an un-looked-for inheritance. Anyone can, it seems, ascend above their station, even if they would prefer not to.

Finally, there's *The Bride Wore Red* (1937), in which, as a drunken joke, a rich Count finds the "lowest, most decrepit" bar in all of Trieste, and sets out to see if he can make Annie, the nightclub's poor singer (Joan Crawford), into a lady. He gives her money, buys her elegant clothes, and sets her up in the fine lakeshore hotel where a young acquaintance (Robert Young) is staying. Anne ultimately is forced to leave the young man in favor of a local postman (Franchot Tone), and the lesson of the film is to find your station in the world and be contented with it—to know your place, in other words. "I work from morning 'till night," says a chambermaid who used to work at the club with Annie, "and I've never been happier."

So, with those preliminaries out of the way, to *Trading Places*: The Duke brothers bet themselves that they can turn a homeless beggar (Eddie Murphy) into a commodities broker and a credible representative of the elite, while simultaneously turning a spoiled American Bertie Wooster type (Dan Ackroyd) into a criminal and thief. It is couched as a debate between the relative power of nature versus nurture, but we can also think of it as engaging the age-old debate about the roots of poverty discussed in the Introduction: is need principally the consequence of bad behavior, or of the structural and economic forces beyond an individual's control? At least part of it is an Eliza Doolittle story, albeit one played for laughs, written by Timothy Harris and Herschel Weingrod instead of George Bernard Shaw, and, unlike Shaw, offering only the most superficial social commentary. Ultimately, even the beggar turned broker winds up articulating unsympathetic ideas about why people are poor and in need and the importance of not coddling them, even if he's hungry enough to steal food. "Oh but he has money to buy drugs, right?" says the once-homeless man, Billy Ray Valentine, once ensconced in the executive suite. "You can't be soft on people like that. Take it from me, I know." Empathy, they would have us believe, can be erased that simply. For what it's worth, the other storyline offers another instance in which the so-called homeless or poor person isn't in fact homeless but is a man of privilege putting on a costume, and by the end, everyone but the Duke brothers is rich. Doesn't the ease with which Eddie Murphy becomes a respectable businessman suggest the possibility that his homelessness—although it's not clear that just because he was begging for change he was homeless, since as many as one-third of contemporary panhandlers have homes (Lee and Farrell, 2003)—could have been ameliorated easily with a bit of ingenuity and a bit of hard work? And because

FIGURE 15.1, 15.2, 15.3, AND 15.4 The deceitful beggar made rich and honorable, and the pompous rich man made poor and humble. *Trading Places*, Paramount Pictures, 1983.

his begging routine was to impersonate a disabled war veteran, this seems also designed to make him less sympathetic. Maybe here, unlike in *Pursuit of Happyness*, pretty much anyone can become a successful stockbroker.

The rich Duke brothers are villains, willing to destroy other people's lives merely for their own entertainment. To make the quality of their characters clear, not only do they call Billy Ray a "nigger" when they think no one else is around, but the younger Duke has a framed photograph of Richard Nixon on his desk (it's Reagan for the other), and their henchman is later seen reading the autobiography of Watergate conspirator G. Gordon Liddy. Their former protégé (Dan Ackroyd, as Louis Winthorpe III) is humanized and redeemed by his encounters with ordinary people, including, yes, a hooker with a heart of gold (Jamie Lee Curtis). But we shouldn't mistake the kind of anti-rich sentiment evident in some movies with empathy or support for poor and homeless people. These are, it seems to be, very different things indeed, as much of the history of American populism shows. "You know, it occurs to me that the best way to hurt rich people is by turning them into poor people," says Murphy to Ackroyd when the plan is finally revealed to them and they plot their revenge.

In *Pursuit of Happyness* (2006), Will Smith plays a San Francisco man who sells expensive medical devices of dubious worth. He and his wife are barely getting by, as he scrambles to sell the machines he foolishly bought in bulk and she works double shifts in a dry cleaners. He's smart, good-humored, hardworking, and clearly cares for their young son. Eventually, she leaves him, and down to one irregular income, he and his son move from the apartment to a cheap motel two blocks away. Meanwhile, after much effort, Smith gets an unpaid internship at a brokerage firm (he chooses his profession, we are led to believe, because he sees a broker getting out of a very expensive red sports car), from which only one (of twenty) will get hired, and the rest will be blacklisted from all jobs in all San Francisco investment firms. This is irrational, and perhaps even irresponsible. But then again, it's Will Smith in the lead, so we know it will turn out okay, and instead of castigating him for taking a foolish risk, we are meant to admire his courage, his determination, his chutzpah.

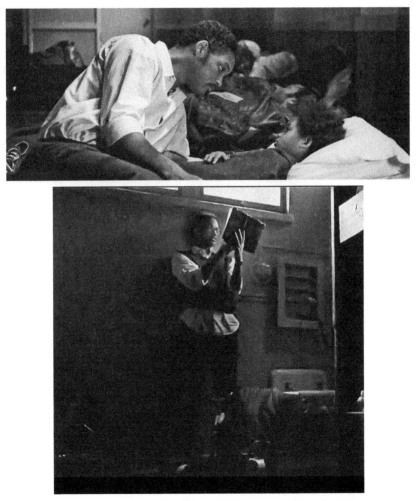

FIGURE 15.5 AND 15.6 In the shelter. *Pursuit of Happyness*, Columbia Pictures, 2006.

His bank account is suddenly seized for failure to pay back taxes; he loses a shoe crossing the street, adding to his public humiliation; he and his son are evicted from the motel; they sleep in a subway station bathroom; then finally, on those nights when they can get there early enough, in a large shelter; one night, to show us his determination, instead of sleeping, Smith stands up, with a book held just so to catch the light, so that he can read and prepare for the exam that will come at the end of his internship. Later, he sells blood.

We are supposed to be impressed by this labor and determination and general good-humoredness in the face of adversity. Unlike many of the movies of the 1930s, he is truly homeless; and unlike the horror films we've examined, he is the Hero. But should survival require such heroic acts? As with so many of these films, there is no politics, no analysis. We can feel sorry for Smith but are not prodded to believe that there's anything to be done. Indeed, the movie offers no insight at all. There is never any doubt that Smith will come out okay (it is Hollywood, after all), so there's no real dramatic tension. But, of course, none of all those other men at the mission will have stockbroker jobs at Dean Witter. We have not been asked to wonder how they will escape their plight, nor have the filmmakers given them or their condition much thought. They will be at the same place at the end of the film as they were at the beginning. The message, such as it is, is a common one—with determination, spunk, and hard work, anyone can survive and ultimately thrive. The causes of poverty and homeless are unexamined; the conditions merely exist, but the individual can rise above them. Or at least one individual can. How different, however, would this movie be and its predictable lesson, if at the end Smith didn't get the one job available? What then would the message be? How then would we judge his choices? That this film is "inspired by a true story" (see Gardner, 2006) isn't good enough, it seems to me.

Linda Chavez, writing for a very odd *National Review* article (Feb. 23, 2009) that lists the "Best Conservative Movies" (*Ghostbusters?!* *Brazil?!*), wrote of *Pursuit of Happyness*:

> This film provides the perfect antidote to Wall Street and other Hollywood diatribes depicting the world of finance as filled with nothing but greed.... Gardner never succumbs to self-pity, even when he and his young son take refuge in a homeless shelter. They're black, but there's no racial undertone or subtext. Gardner is just an incredibly hard-working, ambitious, and smart man who wants to do better for himself and his son.

Note that, for her, the failure to examine race is a virtue, and, presumably, those who are not perhaps quite as hard-working, ambitious, and smart should remain desperate and homeless. While few read the novels of Horatio Alger any more, they continue to serve as an example. With hard work, the moral is presumed to be, anyone can rise. But diligence is rarely, if ever, enough in Alger's tales, for luck, fortune, happy accident, happenstance—these, too, are central plot devices. Even in one of the core sources of American Dream mythology, hard work is never, by itself, enough. Contemporary American movies reinscribe these century-old notions of mobility and deservingness, and while there are individual cases of success, as Gardner attests, they are the exception rather than the rule, exceptions that dominate our storytelling and thus obscure the greater reality that rates of income and educational mobility are, in fact, lower in the United States than they are in many other rich democracies (Economic Policy Institute, 2013). Thus, the individual truth is wrapped in a greater lie.

Homeless to Harvard (2003) tells the story of Liz Murray (see Murray 2011), the child of a near-blind, schizophrenic, addict and alcoholic with AIDS (that's her mother) and an idiot-savant addict father. "I was always the smelly kid in class," she says in voice-over. "I itched from lice, and it burned between my legs . . . my teeth ached, and I was hungry." Despite being exceptionally bright and, thanks to the encyclopedia a neighbor rescues from the trash, well-read, Liz rarely goes to school. Child Services eventually takes her away. She's in a *Lord of the Flies*-like girls' group home for a while, then back, briefly, with her mother, until she leaves to help take care of a friend who escapes her own abusive home. They beg for change on the street and shoplift, sleep on the subway or on the streets, eat out of the trash, crash for a night here and there with friends. Upon the death of her mother, she hides her homelessness to enroll in school, where she thrives, "working as hard as I could so I didn't wind upon on food stamps, or hustling." And, as she says while looking up at the ivy-covered brick while on a school trip to Cambridge, "What if I worked even more?" (That she would have been better off on food stamps is not, apparently, considered.) This tale has much of the same false hope as the Alger stories do in the minds of people who cite them as examples without having read them; so, too, here, for while Liz works hard, to be sure, she is clearly blessed with a kind of innate intelligence that makes it possible for her to complete four years of high school in two, at the top of her class, despite not having regularly attended classes since grade school. She, like her father, is a savant.

The film is built upon the idea that for a homeless or formerly homeless child to find their way into Harvard is itself dramatic. Homeless to the City University of New York (CUNY) wouldn't make for as powerful a Lifetime movie, presumably, because CUNY does not occupy the same place in the public imagination—and yet homeless and formerly homeless students, in my experience teaching at CUNY, were no anomaly there. Implicit here is the idea that it's unusual for homeless children to be exceptionally bright and, perhaps worse, that only the exceptionally bright get into Harvard, suggesting that it's intellect, not wealth, that most dictates entrance. Of course, Harvard and other top-ranked elite colleges and universities are still overwhelmingly populated with the children of the wealthy and powerful. In 2004, merely three percent of students enrolled in the top 146 colleges came from the bottom fifth of the income distribution, while fully seventy-four percent came from the top (Carnevale and Rose in Century Foundation, 2004; see also Hoxby and Avery, 2012). Knowingly or not, the movie serves to buttress false claims that there is genuine equality of opportunity in America, reinforcing the myth that as long as young people demonstrate merit (and grit!) poverty and homelessness are no barriers to the very upper reaches of American society.

In their own way, that's the lesson of both *Upside Down* and *Elysium*, two science fiction tales of class-riven societies finally brought together by young men determined to, in one case, unite with the women he loves, and in the other, to secure medical care for those without it. *Homeless to Harvard* is the kind of story that we have told to ourselves and to the world for much of U.S. history—the streets are paved with gold, we are the land of opportunity, hard work makes everything possible—but even if such claims may have been true for a time in the late nineteenth century, they are not true today (see, e.g., Mishel, Bivens, Gould, and Shierholz, 2012, Chap. 3). *Upside Down* and *Elysium* tell us that even if the obstacles to equality (or, at the least, reduced misery) are monumentally large (gravity itself separates classes in *Upside Down*), there is still hope—but that hope is not rooted in the transformation of social or political instructions, a new economics, or a lengthy or bloody revolution, but simply in the power of earnest white people to seek to better themselves.

16 THE MODERN TRAMP

VICTIMS

Carrie, With Honors, Groundhog Day, The Saint of Fort Washington, Resurrecting the Champ, Sunday, Joe Gould's Secret, Homme Less, Angel of Abbey Street, Titanic, The Fisher King, Prince of Central Park, Treasure of the Sierra Madre, The Soloist, Brother to Brother, The Caveman's Valentine, Nothing Lasts Forever, Bulworth, Being Flynn, Time Out of Mind, Land of Plenty, Shelter, Eddie Presley, On the Bowery, On the Nickel, Gridlock'd, MacArthur Park, Factotum, Barfly, Mud

When not a danger or a lesson in the power of the individual to overcome all obstacles, the homeless man is a mere victim: a broken, helpless soul who, often thanks to mental illness or addiction, has fallen on hard times. These films, especially those about mental illness, are especially interested in origin stories. But also, harking back a bit to the Impostor Tramp, the homeless man is not necessarily the subject, even if he appears to be, but often merely the means by which another is redeemed. The Poor being used as a means of salvation is as old as the Church itself, of course, and while we have in some respects abandoned medieval ideas and practices of relief, this core principle remains suffused throughout modern charity, punishment, and public aid.

Carrie (1952) is an origin story, one about a homelessness caused by unrequited love rather than death or other trauma. It's an adaptation of Theodore Dreiser's *Sister Carrie* (1900), and, as in the novel, what's most relevant for our purposes is the descent of George Hurstwood (Laurence Olivier), Carrie's would-be suitor, from well-to-do restaurant manager ("the first grade below the luxuriously rich," Dreiser described him, "the picture of fastidious comfort") to hungry beggar. The stages of the decline are a bit off, as they are in *The Blot* (see Chapter 1): the New York tenement flat Hurstwood and Carrie live in, for example, has multiple rooms, ample furnishings, windows, light, appliances, and so on, while the "ghetto" streets are merely narrow and crowded, in contrast with the broad Chicago avenues his carriages rode along in better times. But a bit later, the flophouse he's in is unusually authentic, down to the chicken-wire ceilings, patched-together walls, and 7:00 AM mandatory check-out time. He's worn and sick, haggard, dirty, and dead-eyed by then, and carries his few possessions bundled together in old newspaper, stuffed into his thin coat. It's telling that the scene was not included in the movie's original release, "due to the political state of affairs in our nation during this era," according to a title card at the beginning of a 2005 DVD release. This presumably refers to the same anti-Communist hysteria that concluded that *Grapes of Wrath* was dangerous because of its unflinching portrayal of Depression-era desperation, and that *None But the Lonely Heart* was un-American because it was "gloomy." *Carrie* deviates from the novel in few respects (using Dreiser's last draft before others started to have their way with it), although the novel is filled with small scenes of subtle foreshadowing: an early glimpse of a beggar, who is ignored, for example. And Hurstwood's decline in the novel is not only slower (more like Lily Bart's in *House of Mirth*), but more clearly something for which he could be blamed, were one so inclined—he gives up, arguably, and his own

FIGURE 16.1 The Single Room Occupancy hotel/flophouse of *Carrie*, Paramount Pictures, 1952.

culpability for his poverty is more ambiguous and complicated than Olivier's is in the film.

More typical is *With Honors* (1994). Brandon Fraser plays Montgomery (Monty) Kessler, a Harvard senior writing a thesis that apparently asserts that elites must recognize that democracy has failed and step in to govern over the wastrels and the unemployables. Through a series of contrived events, Monty's thesis finds its way into the hands of Simon (Joe Pesci), who holds the pages for ransom. Monty has this "worthless, stinking, filthy human being" evicted from the library boiler room he's living in and arrested for trespassing and intoxication; later posts his bond in hopes of getting the thesis back; and then essentially adopts him, giving him an abandoned van as kennel. It's clear from the start that the irascible Simon will teach Monty Important Lessons About Life—and that the central character here is Monty, not Simon. And we know his thesis will be rewritten, informed by the democratic wisdom Simon provides. Sure enough, thanks in part to a confrontation with Monty's thesis advisor (Gore Vidal) and an (ultimately incoherent) debate about the democratic virtues of the U.S. Constitution, Monty revises it to make some ill-defined but presumably braver argument and, as he must, also gets the girl thanks to the Lessons About Love he also learns from Simon. It's a film that seems to want to be admired because it takes the brave, noble position that homeless people are human. It's not smart enough to know what that could really mean or what full citizenship for marginalized populations would look like. As with many such endeavors, it has no real politics to it, no analysis of power, no critical lens. And, of course, we find out, as we must, that Simon's homelessness is not his fault—he was fired after years of hard labor when asbestos rendered him unable to work.

Groundhog Day (1993) shows us how pervasive is this use of homeless people as tools for other characters' redemption. Bill Murray plays a television weatherman reporting on Punxsutawney Phil, the groundhog that people pretend predicts the onset of spring, but finds himself trapped in a time loop, with the same day repeating itself over and over and over. At first, when Murray sees a homeless old panhandler, he pats his pockets, pretending to be looking for change before passing him by, giving him nothing. By his hundredth or thousandth journey through the day, much of which is spent trying to make himself attractive to his producer (Andie MacDowell), he is trying to restore the homeless man to health and to prevent his death. The homeless man exists to aid the hero's education, humanization, and ultimate redemption. That's his only narrative function.

The Saint of Fort Washington (1993) opens with the demolition of the Jefferson Arms, an SRO hotel, a descendant of the Bowery flops of an earlier era. That event pushes Matthew (Matt Dillon) onto the streets, just as the end of SROs pushed many other people onto the streets. Meanwhile, Jerry (Danny Glover), who will come to be Matthew's protector, is a homeless vet, earning his living mostly as a "squeegee guy," one of the men who used to wash the windshields of cars stopped in traffic and then ask for payment. Before too long, we learn that Jerry was driven into bankruptcy by a business partner, while Matthew's story is one of multiple breakdowns and hospitalizations, and a schizophrenia diagnosis. "See that fella over there?" Jerry says while telling Matthew his tale. "He thinks everything honkey-donkey. A check don't come in, he only a coupla months short of homelessness." After hearing Matthew's tale, Jerry tells him that Joan of Arc and Moses heard voices, too. "Maybe you ain't schizophrenic, maybe you just a saint."

The film offers scenes of the processing and intake of the men and the transfer to the shelter where they will meet, and later offers glimpses of the routine of the shelter, with an authenticity—and general lack of prurient gaze—unusual to find on film, even accounting for Little Leroy (Ving Rhames), the one-dimensional villain who rules the shelter. Someone involved in the production of this movie had some experience with New York City shelters and some genuine affection for the men who live there, it seems to me. This carries through to the end of the film, when we visit another place we don't often find on film, Potter's Field, where Matthew joins the other paupers in their plain wooden coffins. *Saint of Fort Washington* is unusual for placing homeless men at the center of the story—this movie really is about them and not about the effects they have on others.

By contrast, there's *Resurrecting the Champ* (2007), which begins with a former boxer (Samuel Jackson) eating out of trash cans, then being beat up by teenagers. Erik, a struggling Denver sports reporter (Josh Hartnett) comes to his aid, and realizes that writing a story about this man, who claims to be a former champion, could be a way to resurrect his career. True to form, this is a story about the white sportswriter and his redemption, not a movie about the black homeless man, a movie about a journalist's efforts to piece together the Champ's life story, not a story about the Champ. (We can even see this in the title of the film: grammatically, the Champ is the object in the sentence, not the subject.)

Erik is not especially sympathetic—he's an ambitious but mediocre writer who tries to impress his son by lying to him about knowing famous athletes, deceives his editor to pitch the story, and then delays revealing that he's learned that Champ is just an old former boxer impersonating the real Champion, who's been dead for many years. The picture becomes a story about Erik forgiving the Champ, building a more honest relationship with

FIGURE 16.2 The Armory shelter. *Saint of Fort Washington*, Warner Brothers, 1993.

his son, and redeeming himself by writing a heartfelt, confessional article, one we hear in voiceover at the Champ's funeral, no less, making abundantly clear who it is who sits at the center of the story. There is one nice bit in the film: The reporter asks if he can go through Champ's shopping cart, saying people would be interested to know what he wheels around. Champ says sure, as long as he can go to Erik's house and rifle through *his* things.

This is not the only instance in which the homeless man turns out to be pretending to be something and someone he is not. *Sunday* (1997), a small film set in Astoria, New York (and a Grand Jury Prize–winner at Sundance), shows us some of the daily lives of a handful of shelter residents, but focuses most of its attention on Oliver, who is mistaken for, and then pretends to be, Matthew Delacorta, a film director. (Or is he actually Delacorta? The film seems to leave

FIGURE 16.3 The Champ with the real hero of the story. *Resurrecting the Champ*, 20th Century Fox, 2007.

FIGURE 16.4 From the ghetto to the supposed Promised Land; this time, the view of Manhattan is from Queens. *Sunday*, Goatworks Films, 1997.

open this possibility.) When asked what his new project is by a woman who seems to understand that he is not Delacorta, he tells what, we assume, is the story of his own life as an accountant who was laid off, only he tells it as if it were the plot of the movie he's researching. She responds: "That's good. It's a good idea for a story. A regular, middle-class guy just loses his job, and spirals downwards." She sighs. "God, you could fall in love or hate this country." As he says a bit later, "No work. No hope for work. Like every day's Sunday." There's some sympathy here for Oliver, or for the character Matthew's writing for the film, but the movie isn't much interested in the homelessness of the men in the shelter, even if it shows us what they do with their days, including those who work; it's the contrast that's meant to be important: the possibility of a film director living in such a grim place, or, nearly as dramatic, an accountant having fallen so low.

Joe Gould's Secret (2000) is the richer and more sophisticated version of this other kind of impostor story. Gould is a homeless man in early 1940s New York who has, in his own way, been adopted by group of artists, musicians, writers, and poets who slip him food and drink and contributions to the "Joe Gould Fund," so that he can finish his epic, sprawling oral history, a kind of "Song of Myself" for mid–twentieth century America, we are led to believe. He sleeps on benches, in doorways, in lodging houses and SROs, and now and then on the floors of his benefactors. Among the contributors to the Joe Gould Fund is Joseph Mitchell, who will come to write about Gould for *The New Yorker* and, in the process, learn that, while there are bits of writing here and there, there is in truth no grand oral history, just one lone chapter written over and again: "The Death of Clarke Storer Gould."

We know from Mitchell's *New Yorker* articles upon which the film is based (Mitchell, 1942; Mitchell, 1964) that Clarke is Gould's father, a man who had "given up on me," Gould told Mitchell. In those articles, we also learn that there are actually three or four chapters that seem to be written over and again, instead of just this one; the choice the film makes is more dramatic, even if it does make Gould seem that much more damaged and less pro-ductive. In those articles Mitchell also offers some insight and empathy that doesn't find its way directly into the film. Upon realizing that there is no book, Mitchell writes: "I suddenly felt a surge of genuine respect for Gould. He had declined to stay in [his home town] and live out his life as Pee Wee Gould, the town fool. If he had to play the fool, he would do it on a larger stage, before a friendlier audience. He had come to Greenwich Village and found a mask for himself, and he had put it on and kept it on. The Eccentric Author of a Great, Mysterious, Unpublished Book—that was his mask." In so doing, Mitchell writes, Gould wound up fashioning a character much or more interesting than those contained in most novels. The film does, however, periodically cap-ture Gould's self-awareness of his own state. Speaking of a noted artist, Gould observes: "Although our thoughts were the same, his meant something, because he was who he was; mine meant nothing, because I was who I am."

The movie has fine performances by Ian Holm as Gould and Stanley Tucci (who also directed) as Mitchell, along with Hope Davis and Susan Sarandon, among others, and it's smart and sharply observed and betrays a deft touch. We meet mostly three-dimensional characters living in a fully realized world. And more than most, the film manages to put Gould more or less at the center of the story, and the redemption of Mitchell isn't a part of the plot. Yet Gould's decline from Harvard student to a man who "looked like a bum and lived like a bum" is still explained, albeit obliquely, as the result of a single tragic event that, we presume, sent him into mental illness and the relentless recording of a single history. (And notice again how often Harvard serves narratively as the place to aspire to or to fall from.) In Mitchell's articles, Gould himself describes his turn to homelessness and dependence as a conscious decision, the only way he could have enough time to write the oral history. And he is not, to be sure, without some poetry to him. "Since that fateful morning," he intones to Mitchell in a passage that will find its way into the film, "the Oral History has been my rope and my scaffold, my bed and my board, my wife and my floozy, my wound and the salt on it, my whisky and my aspirin, and my rock and my salvation. It is the only thing that matters a damn to me. All else is dross."

Gould, though real, has something in common with the grand histrionics of Robin William's homeless character in *The Fisher King*: these are men both wiser and more otherworldly than they might seem, and their condition thus all the more tragic because of this (or is it their condition that makes them wise?). Gould is not entirely sympathetic, however—crude, selfish, demanding, disruptive, ungrateful, and worse; he even steals and sells the tools of a sculptor friend who gives him shelter for a night (containing a bit of Boudu in him, perhaps?). He's not someone most people would want hanging around regularly, especially once the novelty of him wears off. And he surely must reek, although no attention is paid to this either in Mitchell's writings or in the film; perhaps Gould manages a shower often enough to avoid this? (although Mitchell describes him as fairly consistently filthy).

Alice Neel (Susan Sarandon), offers this view of Gould: "I've always felt that the city's unconscious may be trying to speak to us through Joe Gould. The people who have gone underground in the city, the city's living dead. People who never belonged anyplace from the beginning. People sitting in dark barrooms. The ones who are always left out. The ones who were never asked." She worries that if Gould doesn't finish his oral history, "those anonymous voices might never speak to us." In Part II of Mitchell's 1964 follow-up on Gould, these lines are spoken by Sarah Berman, another of Gould's benefactors, but offer a more critical view, describing these "living dead" as "people who never belonged any place ... poor old men and women sitting on park benches, hurt and bitter and crazy—the ones who never got their share, the ones who were always left out, the ones who were never asked. Sitting there and dreaming of killing everybody that passes by, even the little children."

Homme Less (2014) doesn't give us an impostor, precisely, but a homeless man who effectively hides his status. This documentary first follows fifty-two-year-old photographer and former model and actor Mark Reay through his hectic schedule during New York's Fashion Week. There are some hints that all is not quite as it seems, but it is not until about seventeen minutes into this one-hour film, when he sneaks into an apartment building and beds down for the night on its roof under a tarp, that we realize that Mark is homeless. He works, has health insurance (through the Screen Actors Guild) and a bank account, and seems to eat reasonably well. He counts his "fixed" expenses, which include going out for drinks, as between $1,200 and $1,500 per month, and notes multiple times how much freer and simpler his life is without having to worry about paying rent. But he also calls himself an idiot, and says he's gotten what he deserves, having to sleep on a roof. Mark says that people should feel sympathy for people who are homeless, but he doesn't think people should feel sympathy for him, and that, therefore, he isn't homeless. "I just don't have a place, really. I just don't have a roof over my head." During the two years the film followed him, Mark is homeless by any conventional standard—but what do we make of his denial? Or of the fact that he does, in fact, have a stable abode, even if it is outside? Is its precariousness what makes him homeless? That he could be "evicted" (and perhaps arrested) at any time, should he be discovered?

There's yet another is this vein of films with homeless men pretending to be someone or something else, *An Angel on Abbey Street* (2003). In this TV movie, Briefcase (Christopher Michael Moore) is a middle-aged, homeless alcoholic, living in a cardboard box in an alley, whose begging rap is to say that he's the Tooth Fairy and that he needs change to put under children's pillows. It's clear within the first minutes of the film that his wife and daughter were killed in a car accident; that event, we are to presume, led to his decline and explains his current state. He's called Briefcase because when he first arrived on the street, he was carrying a briefcase; another signal we are meant to find him "worthy," being a respectable accountant brought low by tragedy beyond his control. He meets a young girl, Mary Elizabeth (Katelin Petersen), who informs him that her mother told her that people who beg for change are "winos and no-account drunks." He agrees. But then says that "sometimes, people can be two things at once," explaining that he is, in fact, a wino, but also the Tooth Fairy. When the girl loses a tooth—after having complained that Santa hasn't come for two years and the Tooth Fairy has never come—he doubles down on his panhandling, raises $11, and resists the persistent entreaties of the local liquor store owner so that he can give her the money. For no clearly discernible reason other than the fact that the plot requires it, Briefcase gets cleaned up, gets a job, and helps Mary Elizabeth's mother with a tax problem. He then contrives to steal money from a local drug dealer who is also the abusive boyfriend of the girl's mother, sacrificing himself to save them, reminding us again of how common it is for the homeless man to be dead at the end. We even see this in *Titanic* (1997): Jack (Leonardo DiCaprio), an orphaned, penniless, vagabond artist, slips into the frigid water to die so that Rose, set to be married into a fortune, may live.

I've mentioned *The Fisher King* (1998) briefly, but more needs to be said. I'm tempted simply to reprint Libby Gelman-Waxner's review and leave it at that (1994, pp. 171–173):

This is a film for people who thought that *Field of Dreams* and *Dances with Wolves* were too sarcastic. The homeless people in this movie are all winsome and sweet like a Children's Crusade; none of them ever spit at people or demand money. It's important to help the homeless, but maybe we shouldn't turn them into Cabbage Patch Kids.

She observes, correctly, that the homeless man played by Robin Williams:

> has developed the sort of lyrical mental illness that people only get in the movies.... *The Fisher King* is one of those movies that insist that insane people are really wiser and nicer than money-grubbing regular people and that only the homeless are truly sensitive and honest; in *The Fisher King*, all the street people are elves.

Jeff Bridges plays Jack, a shock-jock prone to tirades against many groups, including homeless people, whose rhetoric inspires a listener to go on a shooting rampage targeting "yuppies." Jack's life falls apart thereafter, and soon enough we find him dirty, drunk, and disheveled, appearing to be homeless himself. He's about to commit suicide when a group of teens beat him and pour gas on him, ready to set him on fire; he's rescued by Perry (Robin Williams) and a ragtag band of homeless people. The gunman Jack inspired killed Perry's wife, we discover, offering us a tidy explanation for his mental illness and for the homelessness that it creates, while simultaneously laying out the path for Jack's redemption: he will, in turn, save Perry, albeit by fostering the delusions that torment him.

FIGURE 16.5 Perry and Jack. *Fisher King*, Tri-Star Pictures, 1991.

Jack does rise to the top again, and is pitched a TV show:

> It's a weekly comedy about the homeless. But it's not depressing in any
> way. We want to find a funny, upbeat way of bringing the issue of home-
> lessness to television. So, we've got three wacky homeless characters.
> But they're wise. They're wacky and they're wise. And the hook is they
> love being homeless. They love the freedom, they love the adventure.
> It's all about the joy of living, not the bullshit we have to deal with—the
> money, the politics, and the best part is, it's called Home Free.

Jack leaves the room, to his credit, but that's a low threshold for what we're
meant to understand as heroic behavior. This is a film that clearly means well,
but it never escapes the saccharine naiveté that Gelman-Waxner complains of.
"You find some pretty wonderful things in the trash," the movie observes, but
it shouldn't seem brave and noble to assert that even homeless mentally ill
people are human and have redemptive qualities.

In addition to offering some of the same setting, *Prince of Central Park*
(1999), also taps into the notion of homelessness as freedom. J.J. (Frank
Nasso) lives in public housing on Staten Island with his foster mother (Cathy
Moriarty). We will learn that his mother died of cancer, and his foster mother
never told him of her request that J.J. visit her on her deathbed. Underfed and
abused, he runs away. It's made clear that his foster mother is only in it for
the money, but it's a sanitized movie-of-the-week kind of abuse he suffers, just
as it is a sanitized kind of homelessness—there's no real violence, no one's
too dirty, and the odd man he meets who lives under a bridge in Central Park
(Harvey Keitel) is meant to be endearing and harmless. Kathleen Turner plays
a well-to-do woman of the Upper West Side who brings food to Keitel (her
own son, we will learn, drowned), and the viewer knows from the outset that
Turner will adopt J.J., and he, in turn, will save her from despair. J.J., for his
part, finds homelessness an improvement over his previous state: "It's better
to be here in the Park living off scraps than trapped in that foster home with
that witch. I'm free here."

This "homelessness as freedom" trope is not new, and is part of the moral
landscape even of *The Treasure of the Sierra Madre* (1948). The film opens
with Dobbs (Humphrey Bogart), looking down-and-out, tearing up a losing
lottery ticket in Tampico, Mexico. He begs for money for food on the street,
and when he hits up a well-dressed American man (in a cameo by director
John Huston), he's met with this response: "Such impudence! ... You have
to make your way through life without my assistance." He sleeps on a bench,

where he meets Curtin (Tim Holt); then later in a flophouse, one that is not romanticized nor prettified, where he the meets Howard (Walter Huston) and hears a monologue about how gold can change a man's soul. The themes are laid out, and we soon see the contrast of the very poor, but amiable (if not happy) Dobbs and Curtis with their later selves, having found a vein of gold—paranoid, angry, fearful that the others will steal their share. This is a story about what money can do to a man, and the comparative virtues of poverty.

The Soloist (2009) is not, as I've previously noted, about Nathanial Ayers (Jamie Foxx), a Juilliard-trained musician who ends up homeless, as it might appear, but rather about Steve Lopez (Robert Downey, Jr.), a reporter who is writing a story about a Juilliard-trained musician who ends up homeless (the film is in fact based upon Lopez's book). Many reviews upon its release insisted that The Soloist was a significant cut above what one might expect, hearing the premise; but aside from a shared admiration for Downey's under-stated and typically intelligent performance, I don't see it. It's smarter than such films often are and perhaps more ambitious, but it's still a melodrama more concerned with Lopez (reasonably enough, given the source material) than Nathaniel. Indeed, the filmmakers have gone out of their way to make the movie even more about Lopez and his redemption by turning the real-world Lopez, who was married with a daughter, into a character who is separated from his wife and estranged from his son. Perhaps those who've admired the film have confused incoherence and sincerity for depth and insight, and noblesse oblige for activism and sharp political commentary. A movie that was actually about the travails of homelessness and schizophrenia would have made more of an effort to tell the story from Nathaniel's point of view, would have spent more time trying to represent on film what his mind was like (although there are non-trivial gestures in this direction), and would have shown more of his day-to-day struggle to survive.

That he's a former Juilliard student, although that's real, feels like narra-tive laziness in the way that Homeless to Harvard does—that someone who was homeless could end up at Harvard (so smart! so poised!), is meant to seem miraculous; so, too, are we meant to find it astonishing that someone with such talent (good enough for Juilliard, and "he seems so smart, and kind" we're told) could end up homeless (very much how people react to finding a "respected, published writer of the Harlem Renaissance" in a homeless shelter in Brother to Brother [2005]). Indeed, the reporter isn't even interested in this mentally ill man and his story until he makes reference to former classmates at the school. It does seem to get at something rather deep in our attitudes about poverty and homelessness and the assumption that to be so down and so out one must be deeply flawed—lazy, alcoholic, stupid, drug-addled, mentally unbalanced. "Normal" people don't find themselves in such straights, surely. But they do, hence the virtues of movies like *First, Last, and Deposit* or *God Bless the Child* (see Chapter 17).

Families in America become homeless all the time—over the course of their lives, some 14 percent of all Americans will be homeless at least once (Rank, 2007)—and it's often as much a slow, grueling slide as it is a dramatic event for which someone can be blamed. The instances in which extraordinary, and even "normal," people become homeless must be anomalies, for otherwise the prospect would be all too terrifying. So the animating question is, as always, what happened? How did you come to this? Almost never is the answer: low wages, a poor economy, high housing costs, lack of health care, weak social supports. It is never systemic or social failure, but individual failure or "natural" human frailty, and in the case of this film, it is a disease of the brain we can blame for human misery. The absurdly chaotic street scene near the mission reminds us that not only are homeless people crazy, but poor people are murderous, drug addicted, filthy, uncivilized, sexual libertines, even if, perhaps, it's not entirely their fault.

"A bum with a violin," is among Lopez's first thoughts suggesting that there was a story to be had here, we learn in Lopez's book (Lopez, 2008). Lopez notes that some of Nathaniel's ramblings remind him a bit of Joe Gould, as reported by Joseph Mitchell (see the discussion of *Joe Gould's Secret*). But it's an instructive comparison, given how fully human and intelligible, in his own way, Gould is. (It makes for a better film, too.) Still, there are some insights in Lopez's book and a depth that, perhaps inevitably, don't transfer to film. Notable was his recognition, after his research for his Ayers-related columns led him into conversations with a range of mental health experts, that to call Nathaniel "a bum with a violin," or even, more sympathetically, a mentally ill musician, was to make his economic status or illness his central identity. Better, he learns, to identify Ayers as a musician with schizophrenia. Lopez also relays another useful observation, even if it's a commonplace among mental health professionals: We treat mental illness as moral failure rather

FIGURES 16.6 AND 16.7 The chaotic scene at the Lamp mission, day (*left*), and night (*right*). *The Soloist*, Dreamworks Pictures, 2009.

than an illness, a reality succinctly embodied in the fact that we wouldn't tolerate encampments of homeless cancer patients, but we accept homelessness among the mentally ill as ordinary.

In a "making of" short film about *The Soloist*, the screenwriter, Susannah Grant, suggests that Lopez's stories were uniquely able to:

> humanize problems that the average American tends to overlook ... the problem of homelessness is so huge in our city ... and often those people feel foreign to us, feel frightening to us ... and I wanted to show in this movie that every one of those people on the street is somebody's daughter, somebody's mother, somebody's sister.... they were not born mentally ill, they weren't born homeless, and there's a story behind everyone that will break your heart of you take the time to learn it.

It's about as typical a Hollywood view of its own virtuous engagement as you're likely to find (Samuel Jackson said something similar about the character he played in *The Caveman's Valentine*, which is up for discussion next). It's less maudlin and self-congratulatory than is often the case, and it does feel more than a bit churlish to treat it so roughly, given such noble aspirations. But to steal a line from James Agee (2000, p. 141) from an unrelated 1945 review: "The picture is not as bad, I must admit, as I'm making it sound; but it is not good enough to make me feel particularly sorry about that."

Romulus (Samuel L. Jackson) in *The Caveman's Valentine* (2001) is also a homeless, black, former Juilliard student (and my observations about the function of Juilliard or Harvard in these kinds of narratives applies here, too), although this movie is based, not on a memoir, but on a mystery novel by George Dawes Green (1994). It opens with Romulus raving, social workers trying in vain to get him off the street; he says that Cornelius Gould Stuyvesant, an evil man who lives in the Chrysler building, controls the world. Romulus finds the frozen body of a young homeless boy near his "cave" in the park, a boy who turns out to be the one-time model of a famous photographer whom Romulus comes to believe committed the murder to cover up the young man's rape and torture. Romulus will, predictably enough, solve the mystery and prove himself a hero—with the inference that his mental illness connects him to some deeper truths hidden from the rest of us. This is another Prophetic Vagabond, another homeless-man version of the Magical Negro (see Hughey, 2009; Bogle, 1973/2007). He is wise beyond appearances, connected more deeply to the natural world, and possessed of a preternatural kind of insight. (There is no more striking example of this than in *Nothing Lasts Forever*

[1984], in which homeless men living on the street are revealed to be, in truth, "higher beings," and the "secret masters" of the City who determine who's worthy based upon how kind they are to their apparently downtrodden selves.) The rest of the film offers up other familiar storyline: Anthony Michael Hall plays a rich bankruptcy lawyer who invites Romulus home, gives him a suit, and cares for him a bit, acts which are meant to be both *brave* (for risking an encounter with this man) and *noble* (for caring at all). Ann Magnuson, playing the painter's sister, befriends and sleeps with Romulus—she too, is meant thus to be brave and bighearted.

There's another Prophetic Vagabond worth noting, although it's a character peripheral to the main story. *Bulworth* (1998) is in its own way a follow-up to *The Candidate*, depicting a tough-on-crime, anti-welfare, anti-affirmative action New Democrat (à la Bill Clinton) fighting to get back to his roots as a radical activist and idealist. Occasionally throughout the film, an old, black (presumably crazed) homeless man pops up to offer mysterious warnings or encouragements—among them a prophetic plea for Bulworth to "sing"—culminating in the final scene of the film in which he repeats his exhortation to the candidate, who may be dead, that he fight to be "a spirit, not a ghost." In a film with numerous references to slain black leaders, this is presumably meant to be a hope that Bulworth joins the ranks of the martyrs who motivate and inspire from beyond the grave. If we take this character seriously, one way of reading the film is that the homeless man was the catalyst that inspired Bulworth to finally sing out—in rap form—perhaps the modern equivalent of the ghost in the wind that set in motion the events of *Gabriel Over the White House* (see Chapter 12).

Being Flynn (2012) is based on Nick Flynn's fine memoir, *Another Bullshit Night in Suck City* (2004), but despite a screenwriting and producer credit for Flynn, it fails to capture the tone, communicate the substance, or approximate the power of the book. More important, it fails to include the ways in which Nick's own considerable addictions and run-ins with the law hover constantly and uncomfortably in the background of this narrative of his father's decline into homelessness, hinting of what may yet befall Nick. Part of what gives the book its fascination is that Nick's father, Jonathan, is something of an enigma, seen only through Nick's memories, stories from friends, and his eventual encounters with him once he's grown up. The movie, by contrast, is a story about Jonathan, and the camera sees the world through his eyes at least as much as through Nick's. Perhaps the inversion—making a book about the son into a movie about the father—was so that it could serve as a vehicle for Robert De Niro. Worse, in the film, Nick's drug use doesn't begin until after he discovers his father in the shelter—as if his addiction is produced by this

FIGURE 16.8 "What happened to me? What happened to my life? Why do I look like this?" *Being Flynn*, Focus Features, 2012.

traumatic event rather than being a part of him since his teen years. This alteration creates an opportunity for Nick's redemption through Jonathan that doesn't happen in the book, perhaps to comport with the deep, probably unconscious, notions of what Hollywood story structure demands when homeless men are concerned.

Many of the scenes in the shelter are good for Hollywood, but they look for dramatic events, for pathos, for conflict, missing the close observation and thick description of the day-to-day that characterize the book. A better adaptation would have taken the opportunity of the shower room to linger on the bodies of these old, battered, sick men (as the French film *Lovers on the Bridge* does, and as *Time Out of Mind* nearly does); it would have looked closely at their clothes; it would have taken more time to show the line outside, to let us see the sleeping areas in more detail. It would, in short, have taken some care to offer the audience a glimpse of places they don't see. It would have cared enough about those seeking refuge in the shelter to show us something about their lives. But whenever it's given the chance to offer depth or insight, the camera flinches, it pulls away: even when a group of men beats a homeless man with pipes and bats, it's obscured by a wall—it's unseen—and lasts only a few seconds. Brutality is hinted at, but not shown. Dirt and cold and fear and despair are gestured toward, but no more. And yet I suspect it, too, thinks it's being brave.

Time Out of Mind (2015) does better at conveying much of the day-to-day experience of living on the streets and struggling with the shelter system. It's an unusually quiet study of George Hammond, a homeless man in New York (Richard Gere), that subtly switches perspective. The camera is with him as he's thrown out of the abandoned apartment he's squatting in; when he's sleeping on a bench, trying unsuccessfully to stay warm; when he later sells his coat and uses the money to buy beer; and when he goes through the series of seemingly endless intake and evaluation processes at shelters and a range of public and nonprofit agencies. But other times we'll see him through glass, as if we were outsiders looking in at another bum asleep in the next subway car, or at a drunk lying on the floor of the ATM vestibule we want to enter. It's a lovely and largely successful effort to humanize this man, for whom things have, quite obviously, gone horribly wrong, and by (mostly) concerning itself with observing rather than explaining or moralizing, it ends up being among the few films about homeless people that seem made by people who have spent some time with them, and who have grown to like and care for them. It not only gives us the rarest of all things, a scene in which homeless people have sex, but it refuses to give us a pat ending. George is, at the end of the film, pretty much where he was when it started, except perhaps more keenly aware of his outsider, pariah status, and a shade closer to reestablishing a relationship with his estranged daughter.

A picture that also takes good advantage of the empathetic and radical opportunities of the shelter is *Land of Plenty* (2005). "There are more homeless and hungry in L.A. County than anywhere else in the States," says Henry (Wendell Pierce) as he is driving Lana (Michelle Williams) through makeshift homeless encampments in the city's downtown. "This is the hunger capital of America." And no one, he observes, is paying any attention, lamenting the lack of resources for the mission that he runs. The film spends a fair bit of time there, quietly observing its mundane day-to-day operations, some of which are seen through the eyes of Paul (John Diehl), Lana's racist uncle, who is probably suffering PTSD and perhaps neurological effects from Agent Orange exposure. Consumed with post-9/11 paranoia, Paul travels the city in a homemade surveillance van (where he seems also to sometimes sleep) looking for terrorists; when we meet him he's stalking a homeless turbaned man for no other reason, it would appear, than that he has a turban. What's unusual about this film is that what we see in the mission is not about the residents or about those who run it but, rather, an indictment of the city and the nation that create the need for it, one that is riddled with irrational fear of Muslims and Arabs and devotes extraordinary resources to their surveillance and control while allowing our fellow countrymen to go ill-fed, un-housed, unemployed, forgotten. When the homeless man is killed in a drug-fueled, drive-by, random shooting on skid row, the preacher reminds Lana that "nobody really cares about him" when she laments that he'll find himself in a pauper's grave. Nor do they care, by implication, about anyone like him. Lana enlists Paul's help in bringing the man, Hassan, to his family, 180 miles away. Here, in an area of desperate poverty with abandoned homes and burnt-out trailers, Paul can see only signs of criminals covering their tracks and ominous portents of conspiracy and sabotage. It's another angle on the ways in which people link poverty and criminality and deviance, here updated for the post-9/11 world, a world in which we pursue imagined threats while ignoring the real ones—homelessness, poverty, unemployment, stagnation, and despair.

There's another film, other than *Ironweed*, that shows us a relationship between a male-female homeless couple, as well as unusually authentic images of shelter life, and that's *Shelter* (2014). Tahir (Anthony Mackie) and Hannah (Jennifer Connelly) are homeless New Yorkers who are unusual film characters: They are both smart and thoughtful, neither shows any sign of mental illness, and while much of the film documents their struggles to find protection from the cold, food, and medical care, it is their relationship that sits at the center of the story. Their homelessness is hardly incidental, but it is not the most important thing about them. For a portion of the film they are not, in fact, even that: they happen upon an unlocked rooftop balcony door that leads to a wealthy family's home (it's vacant because they are on holiday), and take it over, so when they finally reveal to each other their own ugly personal histories, they do it as a well-dressed couple arguing in their New York townhouse. In those moments, they utterly cease to be homeless people on the screen, and are just a troubled couple, afraid, hurt, and in love.

We learn that both share similarly tragic pasts — Hannah's husband was killed while fighting in Iraq, and, in his native Nigeria, Tahir's wife was raped and murdered and then his young son was shot. Hannah became a heroin addict, while Tahir became a member of Boko Haram, an Al-Qaeda affiliate, for whom, in his words, "I became a murderer of women and children. I burned churches, I burned schools, police stations, military checkpoints. That's who I am. I watched people burn." So he is both villain and victim and, like so many of both categories, is dead in the end.

Eddie Presley (1992) is a more typical case in which trauma sits at the root of poverty and vagrancy. Eddie lives in a beat-up old van near the grimmer sections of Hollywood. We see him begin his day with Cheetos and a generic-brand cigarette, followed by checking his voicemail service on a payphone and then opening his post office box, in which he finds a "rent due" notice for the mailbox. He makes what may be his usual morning rounds, chatting with panhandlers getting ready for the day, sharing part of the paper with men sleeping on cardboard boxes, and stopping in the local diner for coffee where he tries to get the waitress, his girlfriend, to sneak him a couple of fried eggs. He nearly loses his job as a security guard when he leaves his post to take a shower, and not long after is suspended for falling asleep on the job, which coincides nicely with an opportunity to present—for one night only!—his

Elvis impersonator routine in a faded, desperate, dingy, little club. We know it's unlikely to end well, and his world is already closing in: the abandoned lot where he parks his van is being cleared for construction, he's unable to get an erection for his girlfriend, and flashbacks of happier times with his son and ex-wife, an onstage breakdown, and Eddie's subsequent institutionalization are increasingly intruding into his life. Predictably enough, he does melt down again onstage, in a long meandering monologue in which he tells the story of his life, and it's occasionally a bit poignant. It's the story of a man with dreams of grandeur cursed with realizing that "I'm not the best. . . . I'll never play the big rooms."

Finally, we should attend to the handful of films that place addiction at the center of their homeless narratives, starting with *On the Bowery* (1956). The Bowery was among the most famous of American skid rows (where we met George in *Carrie*), a long street in lower Manhattan filled with cheap rooming houses and the poor men, often alcoholic, who could afford nothing more, if they could even afford that. By day they scrounge for what little money they can, which they spend in the other institutions that dominated the Bowery, cheap bars (about the only place where we see the very occasional woman). At night they sleep (or pass out) on the sidewalks, in alleyways or on park benches. Some have dreams of the future that will never come to fruition, while most don't even have that, or don't talk of it. They share a bottle sometimes; sometimes steal from each other to pay for a flop for the night. When they don't have money for a beer or a bottle, they drink Sterno. Their work is sporadic—day jobs hauling trash or washing dishes, when they can get them and are sober enough and awake in time, or they beg for change on the street. They are all men, and most fairly old, though probably not as old as they look—haggard, unkempt, their face scarred and bruised, men deeply tired and beaten down. At the Bowery Mission, men are herded into the pews for a somber sermon of moral uplift, the usual price for a meal and a bed (or a space on the crowded floor for the new arrivals). Lodgers shave and shower while their clothes are being fumigated, none of which happens on camera. It's a grim, quiet film, no narration and an unobtrusive camera.

The Perfect Team: The Making of "On the Bowery" is a 2009 documentary by the director's son, Michael. As the elder Rogosin tells the story, he decided to become a filmmaker almost on a whim, concluding that "something was wrong with our society," and that he wanted to find out why, informed at least in part by a reaction to the horrors of the Holocaust. He wanted a subject that was dramatic and powerful for his first effort, and thought the Bowery men would fit the bill. He spent six months without a camera getting to know the scene and its inhabitants. He met James Agee in a bar and asked him to write

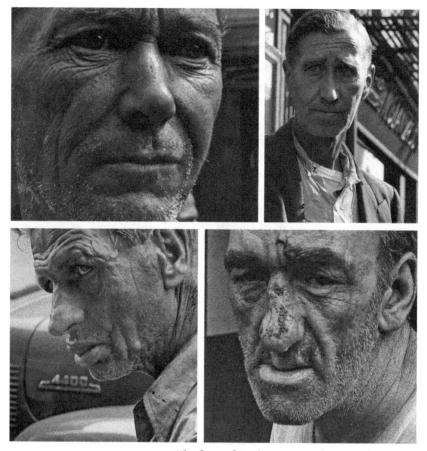

FIGURES 16.9, 16.10, 16.11, AND 16.12 The faces of *On the Bowery*, Milestone Films, 1956.

a screenplay, but Agee died shortly thereafter. So he improvised, "like *Bicycle Thief*," says Rogosin, based on just a bare outline based on Ray's own experiences and some prompting by the director. He says he had Rembrandt's portraits in mind when filming these men's cragged faces. When Rogosin was at the Venice Film Festival to receive the Grand Prize, Clare Booth Luce turned her back to him and refused to shake his hand for having made a film that offered such an ugly image of the United States, and Rogosin reports having heard rumors of some State Department efforts to limit the film's overseas exposure.

On the Nickel (1980) seems to owe a lot to *On the Bowery*, in subject matter if not in visual style. Set in Los Angeles rather than New York, it's a similar kind of glimpse into the alcohol-addicted men (and one woman) living on Skid Row, although here the flophouses are already gone from downtown, and they live instead on the streets, in alleys, and in one small park that hosts a lone, improbable tree. There much to admire here: the homeless men are treated sympathetically, almost lovingly, and they seem to care for each other, too; the uncleanliness of life on the streets is more convincing than is usual, and there's an acknowledgment of the fact that a committed drunk may find himself covered in his own urine, vomit, and feces after a bender. And there's a scene in which a doctor, doing rounds with his interns, coolly itemizes the physical deterioration of the body of a homeless, chronic alcoholic. But alcohol seems to be the sole cause of all the troubles here, and it feels as if the film presumes that if they could just get sober, most would find a way out. After all, the lead character, Sam (Donald Moffatt), got sober one day and thereby transformed his life. Perhaps this is a product of writer-director Ralph Waite's own experience in his younger days, before he, too, quit drinking. As he told one reporter: "I had a fairly clear picture I was going to end up on the Bowery. I was drinking heavily, living in a cheap hotel—I couldn't even wait on tables" (Jares, 1980). And yet this single-minded focus brings to the film, save for an awkward, too-earnest ending, a welcome lack of patronizing, evident in the eulogy Sam delivers to the friend he's spent the movie looking for:

> C.G., you died as you lived—wanting a drink. We don't know for sure where you are now, but we all hope somebody's keeping an eye on you. 'Cause you sure don't know how to look after yourself. There ain't nobody in the whole world gonna miss you, buddy, except us. And as soon as these guys have got some wine in them, they ain't hardly gonna miss you either. You got through, C.G. And now maybe there won't be no more arrests, no more time in jail, no more waking up sick as hell. No more of the world treating you like you didn't count. 'Cause you didn't. 'Cept to Rose, and a couple of us. Sleep well, C.G.

His life was lonely and rough, but a few people loved him. And now he will be forgotten, leaving no trace that he ever lived.

Gridlock'd (1997) offers one glimpse at what an effort to get sober might look like. It's a day-long struggle by two addicts to find a spot in rehab that turns into a day-long effort to secure a Medicaid card, as they escape both the police and various criminal types (we see Richard Gere go through a similar struggle trying to get a Social Security card in *Time Out of Mind*). Tupac Shakur and Tim Roth are terrific, and terrific together, playing, for all intents and purposes, a couple. It's not a bad take on bureaucracy, with some decent efforts to help them, some soulless and vindictive bureaucrats, and lots and lots of red tape. The best bit may be a diatribe of sorts from a caseworker responding to their anger and frustration at not being able to get a spot; he asks them if they think the whole system has simply been waiting around for them to decide that today, after five or ten years of using, they were going to try to get clean and that everything should stop and turn to assist them. But, of course, given what we know about the nature of addiction and the challenges of recovery, a system prepared for just such an occasion would be much more likely to succeed (National Institute on Drug Abuse, 2012).

MacArthur Park (2004) gives us homeless addicts in a Los Angeles park who smoke crack, hang out, hustle, and scheme and steal from each other, and engage in an increasingly far-fetched array of exploits. Addiction is the focus here, and the explanation for their state, their behavior, and their grim ends. They are even more isolated from the rest of the world than is often the case, but it's hard to see much more here than a "drugs are awful and hard to escape" message and a better-than-average effort to portray the daily grind of finding the next fix, all aided by some fine performances. It's a more human gaze than in the modern gangs-in-the-city pictures discussed earlier—a bit less voyeuristic, and it doesn't linger lovingly on the brutality as some of those other, courser, films do. It cares about the characters, and it's filled with empathy for their addictions and their state. And, to its credit, it offers no simple answers and no heroes, with the possible exception of an older woman who convinces a younger one to leave the Park and take a bus back home.

Factotum (2005), like its lesser cousin *Barfly* (1987), is a small, quiet, dour film based on the autobiographical works of Charles Bukowski. Matt Dillon plays Henry Chinaski, an alcoholic who works only when the unemployment checks run out and he has to—and then never for long—and appears content only when drinking, writing, or having sex. He suffers no delusions about his life or his place in the world, and he takes a certain kind of pride in his way of living: "If the poor aren't going to be decent with one another, no one else is going to be," he says, gently reprimanding a man at the racetrack. It's not a movie about poverty, but alcoholism, if anything, or one's man's effort to live a simple life. So, if poverty is defined as the inability to live the kind of life one values (to go back to the discussion in the Introduction), then Chinaski is not poor in any meaningful sense. He does eventually wind up homeless, sleeping on a bench, carrying all he owns in one small duffel bag. But it's still for him a kind of freedom. "If you're going to try," he says at the end,

FIGURES 16.13 AND 16.14 *Factotum,* IFC Films, 2005; and *Barfly,* American Zoetrope, 1987. Matt Dillon and Mickey Rourke as Charles Bukowski.

go all the way. Otherwise, don't even start. This could mean losing girl-friends, wives, relatives, jobs, and maybe your mind; it could mean not eating for three of four days, it could mean freezing on a park bench, it could mean jail, it could mean derision, it could mean mockery, isola-tion. Isolation is a gift. All the rest are a test of your endurance, of how much you really want to do it. . . . It's the only good fight there is.

It's the classic romantic vision of an artist's life, the self-imposed soli-tude and penury required to create. It has often been talked of as voluntary poverty—the kind that is often associated with mendicant orders, students, or "starving artists." But this is deeper than that: there's a suffering, a misery, a punishment that seems intrinsic to it. Or perhaps not. "Why do you live like a bum?" Chinaski is asked in *Barfly*. "Because I am a bum," he replies, and means it.

This is not the reaction we get from *Mud* (2012): When called a bum by one of the boys who find him living alone on a small island in Arkansas, Mud, played by Matthew McConaughey, replies: "I ain't no bum. I got money, boy. Now, you can call me a hobo, 'cause a hobo'll work for his living. And you can call me homeless, well, 'cause that's true for now. But you call me a bum again, I'm gonna' teach you something about respect your daddy never did." It's the same kind of defensiveness we saw from Stan in *Killer of Sheep*, and more evidence that we have been so effective in creating a hierarchy of deserv-ingness among the down and out that they, too, measure their worth against those even worse, and worse off, than they. It's an old American habit—to dream up and to blame down.

17 WOMEN AND CHILDREN LAST

Lady for a Day; Pocket Full of Miracles; Boxcar Bertha; Stone Pillow; God Bless the Child; First, Last and Deposit; House of Sand and Fog; Citizen Ruth; House of Mirth; Sidewalk Stories; Curly Sue; American Heart; Hidden in America; The Road; Where the Day Takes You; Streetwise; The Nickel Children; Smithereens; Slumdog Millionaire; Chop Shop; The Boxcar Children; Beasts of the Southern Wild

Even in film—perhaps *especially* in film?—women are treated differently, and often simply ignored. One set of studies that examined the 500 top-grossing movies from 2007–2012 found that men outnumbered women in speaking roles by as much as 2.5 to 1 (and that women were much more likely to be sexualized in their appearances). Women were even less well represented behind the scenes, accounting for between 2.7 and 8 percent of all feature film directors, between 11.1 and 13 percent of all writers, and between 18.3 and 20.5 percent of all producers. By 2013, women were still only 16 percent of the directors, producers, and writers of the top 250 movies. This matters: when there were women in senior positions behind the scenes, there were more likely to be women on screen (and they were less likely to be naked while they were there). The same general patterns held for television—when women were in control behind the scenes, there were more women on the screen, and those women were more likely to be featured characters who were permitted to be clothed (Women's Media Center, 2014; Smith, Choueiti, Scofield, and Pieper, 2013; Smith, Choueiti, Prescott, and Pieper, n.d.). When there were more women in decision-making positions, the films made were more likely to pass the "Bechdel Test," which requires, at minimum, that there be at least two female characters with names in a film, that they speak to each other at least once, and that that conversation not be about a man. To dispel claims that this is because that's what audiences demand—that the imbalance is only a product of the "free market" functioning—one analysis of more than 1,600 films released between 1990 and 2013 found that pictures that pass the Bechdel Test are just as profitable as those that do not (Hickey, 2014). While women are also under-represented on television, they were more likely to be writers and producers there: from 2012–2013, women were 34 percent of television writers (vs. 10 percent for film), 38 percent of TV producers (vs. 25 percent), and 12 percent of directors (vs. 6 percent) (Lauzen, 2013; Lauzen, 2014).

I had not initially intended to separate out portrayals of poor and homeless women into their own separate category, but as I started to identify the films that would be discussed in the book, a few things became obvious. First, women appear in the films under discussion here with less frequency than men do, just as they do in cinema more broadly. There is a total of 299 key films featured in this book, and if my count is correct, only forty-three of them—fourteen percent—have women clearly at the center of the narrative: *A Little Princess; A Tree Grows in Brooklyn; Angela's Ashes; Ann Vickers; Annie!; Beasts of the Southern Wild; Boxcar Bertha; Broken Blossoms; Citizen Ruth; Claudine; Coal Miner's Daughter; Country; Dangerous Minds; Don't Call Me a Saint; Entertaining Angels; First, Last and Deposit; Freedom Writers; Frozen River; God Bless the Child; Homeless to Harvard; It; Journey of Natty Gann; Just Another Girl on the IRT; Kit Kitridge: American Girl; Lady for a Day; Major Barbara; Mannequin; Music of the Heart; On the Outs; Places in the Heart; Pocketful of Miracles; Precious; Sister Act; Stone Pillow; The Blind Side; The Dollmaker; The House of Mirth; The Little Match Seller; The Little Princess; The Purple Rose of Cairo; Up the Down Staircase; Wendy and Lucy;* and *Winter's Bone.*

Yet, as I've noted, women in the United States are more likely than men to be poor (this has always been true), something you wouldn't know from what we've seen of high-profile films about poverty. Furthermore, while families with children constitute about one-third of those who are homeless on any given night, women are even harder to find when movies offers us portrayals of homeless people. But they can be found.

Lady for a Day (1933) is another Frank Capra picture. It introduces us to Apple Annie, a panhandler who sells, as you might guess, apples. She is also the good luck charm of Dave the Dude, a gangster who buys an apple from her before any important occasion. Annie, an alcoholic, writes letters to her daughter (who has been living overseas since she was small), pretending to be well-to-do, socially connected, and now married (though not to the girl's father). The bellman who has been sneaking out stationery from a fancy hotel and receiving Annie's letters for her is fired for "stealing" mail. Annie, more concerned about herself than her partner in crime, barrels her way into the hotel—to a cry of "Beggars are not allowed in here, madam!" and the horrified

FIGURE 17.1 AND 17.2 Apple Annie drinks and thinks of her daughter, in *Lady for a Day*, Columbia Pictures, 1933 (*left*); and *Pocket Full of Miracles*, United Artists, 1961 (*right*).

stares of hotel patrons—to retrieve the latest letter from her daughter. She learns, to her own horror, that the young woman is coming for a visit, bringing her fiancé and his father, a Count. Distraught at being finally found out, Annie pleads with the manager to tell her daughter that she is dead when she arrives looking for her; so great is her shame at her condition, she would rather have her daughter believe her dead than poor. All the other Broadway panhandlers go round to see Dave, worried that Annie might harm herself, and implore him to help. Fearing that he'll ruin his luck if he refuses, he agrees to put her up in the hotel for a week while her daughter's in town. (Note that rescuing Annie is a means toward his own end.) This effort spirals into an increasingly elaborate production, even enlisting the Mayor and the Governor, who join in on the ruse, not to help Annie, but as a means toward *their* own ends, in this case getting the Dude to release the reporters he has kidnapped in order to keep the charade under wraps. The film ends as Annie's daughter, future son-in-law, and his father return to Spain, the caper having been a success, and none of them the wiser. But what happens to Annie next? We get no hint.

Pocketful of Miracles (1961) is Capra's own remake of *Lady for a Day*, here with Glenn Ford and Bette Davis as Dave the Dude and Annie. The opening shot of this version is Annie on the street taking a swig from a bottle, Christmas music playing in the background. At first she seems more the leader of a protection racket, in charge of the Broadway panhandlers, extracting a few coins from each for working the street. Later we will learn that they allow her to do this because they know that the money they give her goes to her daughter (they have come to think of the girl as their goddaughter). These panhandlers are even more prominent than in the first film, though their behavior is consistent—here they come up with sixty-five dollars to try to get Annie into the hotel for a week, and their determination is what prods the Dude into action. But, as in *Lady for a Day*, they are all misfits: one is missing his legs and gets around on a board with wheels; one is blind; one deaf; one is a little person or a dwarf. We can read this in at least two ways: (1) they are beggars only because they can't work; they're among the "deserving poor" and not to blame, or (2) beggars are abnormal (perhaps even freaks) and the only (potentially) legitimate excuse for this is disability: they are not like us. It's a more richly textured film than the original, and while Annie is not the sad, lost, angry, and pitiable woman of *Lady for a Day*, she is possibly mentally ill here, talking to Dude of the "little people" you can't see. Or is she putting him on?

Annie's tale is essentially the same, but it's no longer the center of the movie: *Pocketful of Miracles* is a story about Dude and Queenie, and it's even revealed in passing that Dave escaped from an orphanage, rising to a position of wealth and power because "I'm good, and I'm lucky." As he'll tell Annie later, in her grungy, small, flat, "I was born in a place like this, and I don't want to come back to it." Annie notes of her daughter, and her fear of her finding out: "She thinks I'm . . . *somebody*." When Annie faints on the street upon learning that her daughter is coming for a visit, as she does in the first film, we hear a voice in the background say, "With Prohibition repealed, you see our streets full of nasty old drunks like that." (But strangers nonetheless help her up.) After Annie's "makeover," one of Dude's henchmen notes, "She's like a cock-a-roach what turned into a butterfly," while Annie, staring at her remade self in the mirror, simply notes: "I don't know who that is in there." There are echoes of Eliza Doolittle here (and the remaking of the "draggle-tailed guttersnipe"), except that for Annie, all that's required is a change of clothes—she is otherwise suitable to "pass" for wealthy. Annie is supposed to be heroic for her sacrifice, and Louise innocent, but it's hard not to feel some contempt for Louise. Whatever peace she may have had has been, at least in part, because of the penury her mother lives in; and Annie's shame is not really questioned, but assumed to be rational and justifiable. What's curious about both versions is that there is no husband at the end for Annie, no simple solution that gives her a permanent life free from begging. Even in *Lady for a Day*, when her story is more central to the film, she does very little, and says very little, once she is in disguise—her bravery is not in words or deeds, but in deceit, for her act of heroism is to lie to her daughter to conceal how bad her life is, how much she has sacrificed on her behalf, and, as a result, she loses an opportunity to demonstrate the depth of her love. Annie instead keeps her daughter free from the shame of having a poor mother, thus, we are to presume, making it possible for her to marry the rich, Spanish prince, who will ensure that Louise never has to beg.

Despite the title, *Boxcar Bertha* (1972) bears little relation to *Sister of the Road: The Autobiography of Boxcar Bertha* (1937), although the credits note that the film is "based on characters contained in" Ben Reitman's (fictionalized) biography of the Depression-era female tramp. There's not much of a plot here. Orphaned, Bertha travels around by rail, prostituting and grifting; she kills a man in card game. Her path periodically crosses with Big Bill Shelly's, a union organizer (and other various "Commies and coons") who's beaten periodically by police for making speeches to strikers, riding the rails, or befriending black men. Soon, they're escaping from chain gangs, robbing trains (and then they steal the train itself), and robbing banks (and giving the proceeds to workers and strike funds). There's no need for this to be set during the Depression—it's at best a peripheral context, and rarely even that, despite the fact that the opening credits present us with images of Roosevelt, dire newspaper headlines, and soup lines. Big Bill is literally crucified in the end—nailed to a boxcar, which then pulls away—as Bertha is made into Mary Magdalene, chasing after him until she can no longer follow. The shame here is not merely that it's such a bad movie (John Cassavetes said to Scorsese afterwards: "You just spent a year of your life making a piece of shit" [in Kirshner, 2012, p. 128]) but that Reitman's book could make such a good one.

Stone Pillow (1985) is the first of a series of television movies about homeless women we'll discuss, this one starring Lucille Ball. We first meet Florabelle sleeping on a New York subway grate covered with a trash bag. "Well, I'm still here," are her first words upon waking. Meanwhile, Carrie (Daphne Zuniga), a young, naïve, and not especially competent employee of a homeless shelter, befriends Flora at her boss's urging, to learn something about the actual lives of homeless people. It's a transparent device to get a character to stand in for the viewer, and one that telegraphs how urgently the film will seek to educate the audience. Flora is looked after by neighborhood residents: a patrolman brings her a sandwich, delivery men slip her other bits of food, a store owner—although he tries to get her to move to another corner—shoos away teenagers who are meant to be menacing, and passers-by give her money and buy her coffee, calling her "Grandma." Soon enough, Carrie is mugged and Flora is assaulted by the gang, and they form a friendship, Carrie allowing Flora to believe she's a runaway so that she will show her how to get by on the streets. When Flora scolds Carrie for not thinking of how worried the people she left behind must be, Flora sobs "Sonny! Sonny!" giving us the first hint of the Dramatic Tragic Event that, we know, must sit at the foundation of a film character's homelessness. "I wasn't always this," she says, before telling the story about being sick and hospitalized and coming home to find her husband and son gone, leaving no trace. She found herself on welfare, then in a shelter,

FIGURE 17.3 Lucille Ball as Florabelle, waking up from her bed on the street, wrapped in a trash bag. *Stone Pillow*, Gaylord Productions, 1985.

then on the streets. As I've complained, it's the triteness of the ultimate lesson that grates: The homeless are people, too! We should pity them (from a safe distance, of course), not hate them!

All that said, this is a film that has some virtues. It takes the time to offer us a sense of how clever Florabelle needs to be to survive on the streets: she shows Carrie where and how to find the trash that's not spoiled and is safe to eat; explains that she won't go into the shelters because she would have to surrender her possessions, be chemically deloused, and still be no safer; shares strategies to avoid being raped, since "all men think that women on the streets is tramps"; and offers pointers on how to stay warm at night and keep your feet dry. We see the endless, daily grind that is managing basic needs and the constant avoidance of the police.

But much of this effect is diminished when we are beaten about the head with Important Lessons. For example, while there are some awful shelters with cruel or indifferent administrators, and it's useful to point out how demeaning and controlling those places can be, those who run the Brooklyn shelter in *Stone Pillow* are cartoon villains, and not especially well developed even for a cartoon. For another example, when a shelter resident complains, "I'm sick of this charity. I want a job. I want what I had. I want a decent place of my own. Don't I deserve that?" it's clumsy and poorly executed, but it is trying to suggest that there's ambition and frustration among homeless women, whose efforts are blocked by other forces. Similarly, while searching for a place to sleep, Carrie whines, "Life is so hard! I had no idea," just before they walk past a series of women in fur coats coming in and out of doorman buildings. It's good that these points are being made, but it's hard not to wish they were being made with a bit more grace and skill.

God Bless the Child (1988), another television movie, offers something rare: an extended look at a homeless mother. Theresa (Mare Winningham) has been abandoned by her husband and is evicted from her apartment when the building was torn down; with no family or friends willing or able to take them in, and unable to come up with the first and last month's rent for new place, she and her young daughter are in dire straits. They wind up first in a church-run women's shelter, and the film shows us some of the challenges people there face: couples forced to separate, the expense of having to buy prepared foods, decent people doing their best to get by. When Theresa slips out of work early to find a space at a longer-term shelter, she's fired. Now, with no place to stay and no income, things go from bad to worse, and the difficulty of finding work while homeless and without childcare is pretty well realized. She applies for AFDC, is rousted by the police, bounces from shelter to shelter (each worse than the once before) and then to the street; her shoes are stolen, she skips out on diner meals without paying, goes to soup kitchens and later an empty-shelved food pantry, and struggles to keep her daughter fed and safe. It's nicely done, all in all, and even makes some effort to portray the other poor and homeless families as people with their own stories. There is one particularly stunning scene later in the film: when threatened with eviction by the landlord of a rat-infested apartment she finally finds (she reported him to the health department), her daughter asks if they will have to go back into the shelters; when Theresa answers yes, maybe, for a little while, the girl runs to the bathroom to throw up. Seldom has such a short scene so well captured the emotional and physical effects of homelessness on children. Ultimately, Theresa abandons her daughter, surrendering her to the foster care system, in hopes that she'll at least consistently have food, shelter, and clean clothes. It's a bit heavy-handed, but even so winds up being among the better portrayals of homelessness to be found on film.

First, Last and Deposit (2000) is a small independent movie made on digital video, but not without a sense of style, and there are some truly fine performances, showing the reality of the slide into homelessness. A mother, Christine (Sara Wilcox) and her middle-school-age daughter Tessa (Jessica White) move with the mother's boyfriend from Tempe to Santa Barbara so that he can take a new job, which he soon loses. Not long after, he leaves, and she falls even further behind on the rent and is evicted. When Christine is asked by her own mother why she won't apply for welfare, she responds simply: "Because

FIGURE 17.4 *God Bless the Child*, Alliance Entertainment, 1988. Theresa abandons her daughter rather than subject her to being homeless.

welfare is for other people." (There's a lovely scene in which the girl goes to the home of one of her well-off friends that captures the casual affluence from the perspective of a child with nothing, and doing her best to hide the fact from her friends.) They move in with one of Christine's fellow supermarket cashiers, but that doesn't last because it can't; so they have no place left but the car until they can add to the paltry $482 they have saved for a new apartment—the first and last month's rent plus security deposit (which she hopes to avoid by letting the landlord sleep with her). It is in capturing some of the mundane things that the film does especially well: driving around looking for a safe place to park or for a place to pee, setting up the bedding in the cars, looking for bathrooms. (*House of Sand and Fog* [2003] offers another instance of a woman living her car, in this case after being made briefly homeless when the county mistakenly seizes her home for failure to pay back taxes.) It makes it a double shame when Christine's car is stolen—it seems a contrived, cheap plot device when the film has otherwise been so sure-footed. Moreover, there are so many more likely scenarios whereby they would have lost the car. Likewise when Christine steals her landlord's car: she's too sensible and too cautious to have done such a dumb thing, for which she had to know she'd be arrested. That it resists a tidy ending (or any ending at all, really) is to its credit.

FIGURE 17.5 *First, Last, and Deposit*, Vanguard, 2000. "I'm gonna get our apartment today." Deciding to sleep with the landlord in exchange for a place for her and her daughter to stay.

A very different kind of homeless mother appears in *Citizen Ruth* (1996). Ruth is an addict who's already surrendered four children when she is found passed out in an alley, pregnant again. She's arrested for huffing inhalants and later charged with the felony endangerment of her fetus. Bailed out and taken in by anti-abortion activists, her homelessness recedes in importance, as Ruth becomes a pawn torn between abortion rights and anti-abortion activists.

The House of Mirth (2001) is another story about a woman's fall, written in the first Gilded Age/Progressive era and made into a film during the second Gilded Age. Like the 1905 Edith Wharton novel it's based on, it's a film about the insularity of the rich, their deep ignorance of what daily life is like for the majority, and how trivial their concerns are. Lily Bart slips out of her protected, insular class, thanks to gambling debts, bad financial management, and a scandal manufactured by a rival, into the worries of work, then unemployment, and poverty. "I can't think of anything worse," she says once she begins to see what it looks and feels like, "can you?" Her response is laudanum, and an overdose. Part of what makes *The House of Mirth* so tragic is that Lily is presented with opportunity after opportunity to rescue herself, and while, admittedly, some of those opportunities are less savory than others, she rebuffs every last one. She is brought so low, to the "rubbish heap," she sobs (unemployed and likely to be evicted soon from a working-class rooming

FIGURES 17.6 AND 17.7 *Sidewalk Stories,* Island Pictures, 1989; and *The Kid,* First National, 1921.

house, one that is positively luxurious by early-twentieth-century slum standards), thanks to her own foolishness and stubbornness. The film, like others in this section, draws attention to the fact movies usually want to show us escapes from poverty, not the descent into it.

Not all homeless families in film are headed by women: we have discussed *Pursuit of Happyness* as well as *Paper Moon,* and there is, of course, Chaplin's *The Kid,* which is updated in Charles Lane's *Sidewalk Stories* (1989).

In this more recent (also silent) film, a homeless street artist (played by Lane himself) takes in a small child when her father is killed in a fight. Like Chaplin, he initially considers abandoning the child, but can't bring himself to do it. He brings her to the building he squats in, feeds her, hangs hand-drawn cartoon-character pictures on the wall, steals clothes for her, brings her to the playground, and takes her to work, where he discovers that an adorable child is good for business. When they end up in separated in a homeless shelter, he contrives a kind of Rube Goldberg contraption, as Chaplin did in *The Kid,* to watch over her—here, it's an elaborate pulley system that wakes the man when the child stirs. Like Chaplin, he's charming and clever and loving and responsible—precisely the kind of homeless man Chaplin made a career out of and who hadn't been seen on screen much since.

In *Curly Sue* (1991), a ruthless, high-priced divorce attorney thinks she has hit a homeless man with her car; in fact, the man (James Belushi) and the young girl he's raising as his daughter (Alisan Porter) use this scam to get free meals and cash. They make a point, as does the director, of letting us know they never steal, and only lie and cheat for the necessities; they never beg,

FIGURES 17.8 *Sidewalk Stories,* Island Pictures, 1989.

either, finding that also beneath their dignity. The film sees this as a mark of their worthiness, even if it means they are occasionally hungrier. The woman makes them her project, starting with baths and fresh clothes, transforming them from homeless to respectable. But the young girl, Curly Sue, recognizes this game and is angry and ashamed: "It's no fun being someone's toys, and that's what we are." Confronted by this, the lawyer is even a bit chastened, and agrees to let them take her out for an evening as they would spend it. So, they hitch a ride on the back of a garbage truck, crash a wedding, and sneak into a movie theater. It's John Hughes (director of *Home Alone, Pretty in Pink, Mr. Mom*), so it's John Hughes, and it's a Cabbage Patch Kids kind of home-lessness, as Gelman-Waxner said of *Fisher King*. Being homeless here is a bit dirty and occasionally a bit too cold, but nothing truly dire, and nothing like the more authentic portrayals we see in *God Bless the Child* or *First, Last, and Deposit*. They all end up together, as we know they will, and thus we get one of the more unusual solutions to homelessness that is offered by an American film: get adopted by, or marry, a rich white lady.

In Seattle, Jack Kelson (Jeff Bridges), a just-released ex-convict, struggles to get by with his teenage son Nick (Edward Furlong) in *American Heart* (1993), made by the same director as *Streetwise* (see this chapter). They occupy a room in an SRO for seventy-five dollars a week while Jack works as a high-rise win-dow washer. Nick hangs out with a group of street kids, some of whom sell sex and few of whom seem to be actually homeless, but we don't get much in the way of information about them—it's a story about the father and son's *rapprochement*, and the setting is almost incidental. The son steals, gets in a few fights, drinks a bit, and smokes a few joints, while the father resists pleas to help plan the kind of heists that got him in jail in the first place. They fall behind on the rent, get robbed, get evicted, fight, and separate in anger; Jack gets fired and eats in a soup kitchen, while Nick sleeps in an abandoned building and starts stealing and robbing houses. They reconcile, and then Jack gets shot and dies, which continues to be the cinematic fate of so many homeless men.

Jeff Bridge's brother, Beau, also takes a turn as a lone father (Bill) trying to keep his children fed and housed after the death of his wife (Jeff also appears, as a doctor). A Showtime TV movie, *Hidden in America* (1996), charts their precarious existence. They are just barely hanging on, with Bill fighting for low-wage service jobs and begging for more hours at work after having been laid off from his seventeen-year stint on an assembly line. There's never quite enough for groceries, but he won't seek help, even though he finds himself pulling food from the trash at the fast food restaurant where he works, his daughter steals food from the house of a well-off friend of hers, and his son, who also picks through the trash for food, skips school to collect and redeem cans and bottles. "You'll never catch me taking a handout," boasts Bill. "That's what's wrong with this country. No one wants to work for a living." Even when things go from bad to worse—he's promised a job, it falls through, and he's already quit the other—he refuses the help offered by Dr. Millerton, the well-intentioned father of his daughter's friend. "I can't digest charity food," he says when invited over for a cookout.

It's slow, earnest, and well meaning, like the TV movies about homeless women and their children discussed above. If there's a signature difference, it's that Bill is willing to let his pride get in the way of providing for his family—they regularly lack food, he forgoes medicine for his sick daughter, and the electricity gets turned off. It gets so bad that his young son tries to kill himself. Bill finally applies for food stamps, battling an indifferent bureaucracy; at a food pantry, he's consumed with shame and makes constant excuses and apologies for his need, and the look on the staffer's face is long and pitying—as if, somehow, he *should* be ashamed. As is so often the case, the movie ultimately becomes as much about the transformation and redemption of Millerton, who, thanks to his encounters with Bill and family, reevaluates his work and his worth. Of course, in a braver world, he would reevaluate his politics, too, which are, instead, absent from this film, as they often are.

The Road (2009) gives us another father-son team struggling to survive, although one with a twist. Covered with filth, shoes bound together with scraps of cloth and tape, teeth dirty and crooked, unshaven, haggard, the

FIGURE 17.9 *The Road,* The Weinstein Company, 2009.

man (Viggo Mortensen) and his son (Kodi Smit-McPhee) roam the landscape in search of food, water, shelter, and, above all, safety. It is not alcoholism, drug abuse, disability, or unemployment that has brought them to this state; a nuclear holocaust (or its equivalent) has destroyed most of civilization, and the homelessness of these two tramps is no aberration, but the normal state of affairs for those few who remain alive. What distinguishes homeless men in other movies, and in the world itself, is that they exist while the "normal" world goes on around them; they are identified by what they do not have, by what they are not.

Other than the landscape, which is bleak even for those occasions when we see burned-out urban ghettos on film (think *Fort Apache, the Bronx,* or the ruined rural scene of *Winter's Bone*), the film does follow some of the conventions: it's a buddy picture (something like *Saint of Fort Washington*), with the elder man as protector, showing the younger how to survive in this merciless and dangerous environment. They sleep fitfully, worried about gangs attacking and killing them (though here, it's to take them as meat), and are constantly hungry. The Man is both comforted and tormented by memories of his former life. But there is no judgment, for they can't be blamed for their state; and there is no one better off to compare them to. And that may be the ultimate lesson: if everyone is homeless, then no one will be stigmatized for it.

Before homeless adults appear on film, we can find them in paintings and photographs, but in a limited way; in the late nineteenth and early twentieth centuries, just prior to the advent of movies as mass entertainment, it was more likely to be American children who were the subjects in paintings, not adults, and those children were typically represented in idealized, romanticized ways. Not until the social-realist works of Lewis Hine and Jacob Riis does a more authentic and more varied perspective enter the frame (Peters, 1987). The brief *Little Match Seller* (1902), based on the Hans Christian Andersen story, offers a view of this woeful street urchin type: it depicts a very young, poor, girl who hovers on the edge of an alley trying to sell matches to passers-by. She's taunted by a schoolboy, pelted with snowballs, and cries and shivers pitifully while dreaming of a warm fire and a table laden with food. She dies from the cold, then is taken away by an angel, her frozen body left to be discovered by a police officer in the morning.

We've seen, above, the relative abundance of poor children in films about crime and the city and in those about the Great Depression; gangs of home-less children can be found in more recent films, too. In *Where the Day Takes You* (1992), Dermot Mulroney is King, the leader of a varied group of home-less runaways in Los Angeles who live, for the most part, under a freeway bridge. It's not a film with much of a plot, a good thing in this instance. It mostly offers the viewer vignettes of the group's day-to-day activities: hanging out, riding trains, petty thievery, begging for change, eating, drinking, fight-ing, having sex, getting high, getting by. One turns to prostitution. One's an addict spiraling out of control, heading inexorably toward an overdose, who is ultimately thrown out with the trash. One shoots a man who's beating up on King. There's a mix of reasons they left home, and they comport with what we know about homeless teens: sexual abuse, physical abuse, drugs and alcohol, neglect. But the film's not too concerned with explanations or with the past, although that's a noise that hums in the background. It's not a morality tale and not even a tragedy (there's not really anywhere to fall from, after all). King is dead at the end, protecting the friend who was earlier protecting him, although in an act more stupid than noble. And the rest return to the street, to the bridge.

There's a documentary from 1984, *Streetwise*, from Martin Bell, the director of *American Heart* and *Hidden in America*, that seems to have had some influ-ence on *Where the Day Takes You*. It follows a handful of homeless preteens and teens in Seattle as they go through the day: they hang out, beg for change (while experimenting with new approaches and comparing techniques), pros-titute themselves, goof off, flirt, die, drink and do drugs, comb through the trash for food, and talk about the often abusive homes they've left behind and their fantasies for a better life. They're just kids, of course, which may be the film's power, since they are allowed to be just kids, and the contrast between their age and their circumstances is awful. That it doesn't purport to offer answers is welcome, too, since there are no simple ones.

Less closely observed is *The Nickel Children* (2005), which chronicles the day-to-day efforts at survival of two preteens who hook and steal for money and are homeless when they are not crashing at a cheap, dirty, run-down motel. The young boy, Nolan (Reiley McClendon), is an orphan. Cat (Tamara Hope) escaped sexual abuse at the hands of her father. How they wound up together is unclear, as is what we are meant to make of the story. Nolan dies, stabbed by a john. And Cat goes home to her mother, her future unclear. The end title card offers data about child prostitution in the United States (*Where the Day Takes You* and *Streetwise* ended with data about homelessness).

In *Smithereens* (1982), young Paul (Brad Rijn), a would-be portrait artist from Montana, lives in New York City in a van parked in an abandoned lot near the West Side Highway. Wren (Susan Berman), an aspiring punk musician, is evicted from her apartment after falling four months behind on her rent. She moves into Paul's van for a while, which she describes as a mobile home. The poverty here, such as it is, recalls the kinds of "voluntary" poverty associated with students or "starving artists," a sacrifice many are willing to make in pursuit of a better life. And if, indeed, it is short-term and merely a stage on a path toward something better or even fulfilling a dream, it does distinguish it from the kinds of poverty that do not offer anything in exchange for privation (the way that, say, riding the rails did for some; or pursuing an acting career does for others; there's an understanding that this may be necessary in order to build the kind of life one wants, although it is typically assumed to be temporary, a stage in life, not the condition of life itself). There's a similar kind of "voluntary" poverty evident in *Mouth to Mouth* (2005), which introduces us to a young American girl traveling through Europe who falls in with a group of misfits that calls themselves SPARK, or Street People Armed with Radical Knowledge. They are former prostitutes, addicts, and runaways heading off to the group's camp *cum* commune, where it becomes increasingly clear that it's more a cult than anything. Poverty and homelessness aren't the focus here, although they are poor by any typical standard—they live in the vans they travel in, and pick through dumpsters for food.

Slumdog Millionaire (2008) gives us a young boy from the Mumbai slums who finds himself on "Who Wants to be a Millionaire," and is accused of cheating as he advances further and further into the game. Since doctors and lawyers seldom get so far, the assumption goes, this "slumdog" clearly must be getting help: he's poor and must, therefore, be stupid. Perhaps the most important observation to make about the film is how popular it was in America, and to wonder why (with a budget of $15 million, it grossed over $141 million in just its first year here). It is, among other things, a story ostensibly about the ghetto in which the focus is on one very special individual who rises to the top and is celebrated by all those he left behind. It's the kind of Horatio Alger-ish approach that's so familiar, wrapped up in a love story. He wins the money and gets the girl, and it's all quite pat in a predictable kind of way—in which the opportunities to examine the reality of life in Mumbai for many millions is passed up for a feel-good story of one improbable success, so that we can leave the theater happy. It's propaganda of the worst kind, in this way, shifting our focus away from the millions who will not thrive, may not even survive. It's a tactic common in both film and political debate—I have an uncle who arrived with nothing but the clothes on his back and look what he made of himself! Why anyone can, if they just try hard enough! Although, to be fair, the victory here is, like in the Alger tales, an almost mystical one, in which he succeeds only because of extraordinary happenstance, because of sheer, improbable luck (or perhaps it's meant to be divine intervention?). Surprisingly, given the enduring power of his morality tales, there have been no film versions of any of Horatio Alger's rags-to-riches novels. There was a stage musical called *Shine!* (see http://www.shinethemusical.com/), from the same team that created the musical *Chaplin,* based in part on *Ragged Dick* and *Silas Snobden's Office Boy;* and the movie musical *Newsies* (1992) is arguably indebted to Alger in an oblique kind of way, with its newsboys' lodging house setting. But that's it, as far as I can tell.

Alejandro, in *Chop Shop* (2007), could be the face of a grim but ultimately inspiring story of child trying to make a go of it against great odds in a slum in India, and after a long rainstorm, the landscape does indeed look Third-Worldly. But Alee, as he's called, lives in Willet's Point, an industrial area of Queens, New York, near Shea Stadium, in a tidy room at the back of an auto-body repair shop. About ten or twelve years old, he scrounges for work by the highway with other brown-skinned day laborers, hunts for spare parts to resell to other nearby junkyard shops, works in the auto shop as an apprentice of sorts, sells candy bars on the subway, and aspires to set up his older teenage sister and himself with a food truck (she cooks in someone else's now). He is a hustler, in the best sense. It's not a terrible life—he and his sister are close and good to each other and happy when together, the adults in his life treat him reasonably well, he has a friend to work and play with, and he's diligently saving up for the truck. Upon realizing that his sister is turning tricks at night to make extra money, however, he steps up his efforts (after quietly urging her to be more forthright about soliciting tips at work), stealing hubcaps, sell-ing DVDs, and helping to strip down stolen cars. He eventually does buy a used food truck for $4,500, only to discover that it's essentially worthless; he recoups $1,000 by selling it for parts, and steals a purse and tries, and fails, to sell the cell phone from within it. And the movie ends—or stops, really—with Alee and his sister more or less where they started, although she now knows he's aware that she's been working as a prostitute. What's so unusual about this film is that there are no real dramatic climaxes, no plot twists, no events that intrude into the observation that is the heart of it. It's a simple study of a young man—bright, ambitious, good-natured, hard-working—who lives on the margins and may or may not make a better life for himself one day, or may

FIGURE 17.10 *Chop Shop*, Axiom Films, 2007. Alee confronts his sister, who's been prostituting herself.

get caught and end up in prison. There is no moralizing and no explanations. We don't know why he and his sister are alone, or how they came to be at the chop shop. The stadium is nearby, and we do get occasional glimpses of it or hear the crowds, and know that many with better lives are nearby, but there's no hammering home of some trivial point or a reach for some banal lesson. It's as respectful (without being reverent or sentimental) and closely observed a portrait of another America as you'll find, and reveals by contrast what a plot-driven exercise in sentimentality *Slumdog* is.

The film of *The Boxcar Children* (2014) makes them slightly more pitiable and increases the danger they are in, but otherwise it follows closely the 1926 book upon which it's based. It's not really homelessness they experience, and even if so, it's not for long, since they are finally rescued by their rich uncle; instead, it's like so many children's stories, about kids who are on their own and having exciting adventures. The youngest does, in the film, when hungry, complain: "I just want to go home," an utterance not, as far as I can tell, made in the book—indeed, their former home in the early volumes is an abstraction at best, not a real place so much as an idea, if even that. Their home is with each other, we are meant to believe, and wherever they are, thanks to their own individual talents and special penchant for resourcefulness, is home. It seems sloppy of the film to miss that, or foolish to trade that for the easier, cheap sentiment. The point is made in the books, when the boxcar that was their home in Book One becomes little more than a clubhouse or fort in subsequent adventures, moved by their grandfather into his spacious back yard.

FIGURE 17.11 *Beasts of the Southern Wild*, Fox Searchlight, 2012.

They then play at being alone without actually having to be alone. And, as is often the case, there's no problem that can't be solved by a rich man.

Beasts of the Southern Wild (2012) gives us a more recent vision of a homeless child. Hushpuppy (Quvenzhane Wallis) and her father, Wink (Dwight Henry), are survivors of Hurricane Katrina (or some other disaster), cut off from the city, living in squalid shacks, amidst their pets and their food animals; but that material poverty does not seem to be the point. Another storm comes and puts what little they have left underwater, displacing them, making them refugees and members of a small floating society of survivors, until they are carried off against their will to shelters as part of a mandatory evacuation. They escape as quickly as they can, desperate to get back to the land, to their homes, to what they know. The collapsing polar ice caps that have helped put them in such precarious terrain also released large, prehistoric animals that have been working their way toward Hushpuppy, who is destined to be King of the Bathtub (what they call where they live), her father says. The animals, though they have eaten their own to survive the trip, leave Hushpuppy be. This land is hers, somehow, and she may well rebuild civilization upon this swampy land: We all are doomed, but maybe we are not. And that may be as hopeful a message as there is to be found in films about homeless families.

CONCLUSION

THE PROPERTIED GAZE

American film has a blind spot when it comes to poor and home-less people. Some years ago, Laura Mulvey (1999) showed us that most films possess a *male gaze*. That is, the viewer was assumed to be a (straight, white) man, and most films were created by men to entertain and engage other men like them. I've reviewed some of the evidence showing how few women appear on screen and how overwhelmingly male the overall production of U.S. films is, and that's been true of the films discussed in this book, too. But I want to argue that American movies have also had a *propertied* gaze—the viewer is never assumed to be poor or homeless, and films are never meant for them, even when they are ostensibly about them.

Perhaps this should not be surprising. While a novel can be written by a poor person (although it will still be difficult to get it to market, even with innovations in self-publication and distribu-tion), and people of limited means can paint or sculpt, and even though someone with relatively inexpensive equipment can make a movie, film remains largely the province of large corporations. As a result, poor people don't typically make movies, and even movies ostensibly about poor people are not written, produced, or directed by them: these are, almost always, an outsider's perspective and, therefore, rooted in ideas that come from some place other than experience (this is true of movies about CIA agents, too, so this isn't the only way in which this plays out).

Furthermore, because film is a collaborative medium, a movie is rarely the product of a singular vision—it's a group decision-making process. Many of those decisions are made by businesspeo-ple. But they are businesspeople who think they know something about movies, and sometimes even think they know something about "art." Pauline Kael (1994, p. 818) wrote that, "they feel that they are creative people—how else could they have made so much money and be in a position to advise artists what to do?" Perhaps Stanley Kubrick was right when he observed (in MacDonald, 1962, p. 30): "The reason movies are often so bad out here isn't because the people who make them are cynical money hacks. Most of them are doing the very best they can; they really want to make good movies. The trouble is with their heads, not their hearts."

Throughout the history of the medium, there have been obvious efforts by filmmakers to have social or political impact, Samuel Goldwyn's famous advice notwithstanding (he supposedly once declared, "If you want to send a message, send a telegram"). As director John Frankenheimer said, "Hollywood has nothing against message films as long as they make money" (in Christensen and Haas, 2005, p. 22). Otis Ferguson (in Wilson, 1971, p. 47) agreed: "As the stuff of a great popular art it is inevitable that such material should mirror the ruling-class ideals of its time. But what is often confused is that in making use of it the movies are consciously trying to meet with, rather than mold, popular taste." But there's more to it than this. Steven J. Ross (in Stokes and Maltby, 1999) is right that there's something too simplistic in suggesting that Hollywood produces the films that sell, and, in that sense, is merely responding to market demand. Audiences can only go to see the movies that are produced and distributed, so they are hardly choosing from the full range of possible subjects and styles. But more importantly, and this is Ross's point, such claims leave out the varied pressures and interests that affect studio decision making. As Sarris notes (1998, p. 18), "the studios were never a monolithic bloc of crass commercialism, but rather many raging torrents of conflicting tastes and aspirations." For example: Why did the number of class-conscious, radical films decline in the 1920s? Because of local and state censors, to be sure, but also because when the big "movie palaces" took over, they lured patrons in from neighborhood cinemas, and the palaces were less likely to screen "radical" pictures because they needed to attract a broader audience (Ross in Stokes and Maltby, 1999; Ross, 1998). The space available to distribute pictures with a narrower appeal declined, so, over time, fewer of such pictures were produced. There's an ideology at work when decisions are made about which movies to make, but it's one mediated through a complex institutional relationship. Complaints about how the business of filmmaking constrains its politics (and, in another vein, sacrifices its art for commerce) are nearly as old as commercial filmmaking itself. In 1930, Potamkin grumbled that:

> The movie is concentrated in the hands of the financial powers along with the various other media of rapid intelligence—radio and television, and, as of old, the press.... During the more-or-less free-for-all

days it was still possible to get a film made of Upton Sinclair's "The Jungle." It was still possible to have Essanay produce a picture condemning the exploitation of the poor house-owner and farmer by the sellers of marshlands. Today the worker is either a clown, or a populist swashbuckler who gets the girl. . . . Social criticism has dwindled in the American film. All that remains is a gaiety uninformed by sincerity or intelligence. (in Jacobs 1977, p. 153)

As Sarris notes: "The exact date the cinema lost its soul to commerce is difficult to determine" (Sarris 1998, pp. 16–17).

The cinematic language used to describe poor and homeless people is constrained, as we have seen, and that is partly because the people making movies are trying to appeal to a broad audience, one with the time and money required to invest in a movie. But the limited frame is also because filmmakers have little knowledge of poverty and homelessness to draw upon. Even when they are trying to send a useful social message—even when they mean well—they often wind up reinforcing pernicious stereotypes and relying on the same clichés and narrative tropes. I won't recount all the patterns I've identified in these pages, but I want to briefly review a few of them before considering the implications of this for people who go to the movies, people who make them, and those who make policy that affects poor and homeless Americans.

First, as I've just discussed, there are relatively few films that take poverty or homelessness as their subject, and those that do are rarely made by people with substantive experience or deep knowledge of those conditions. That has consequences. But although depictions of poverty are more authentic when writers or directors have had some firsthand encounters with poverty or poor people, that is itself no guarantee (see the discussion in Chapter 2, for example). The power of American political culture is great, which is why even women on welfare have historically lambasted *other* welfare recipients as lazy and unworthy (Edin and Lein, 1997; Seccombe, 2010).

Second, while there are relatively few films that have presented themselves as interested in these most marginalized populations, even those movies turn out not to really care too much about them. We have, for example, seen Impostor Tramps in films that seem to be about homeless men when, in fact, the main character is a rich man in disguise. Or, think of a movie like *The Fisher King*, which appears to be about a mentally ill homeless man, but is most interested in the journey of the washed-up disc jockey played by Jeff Bridges. The homeless man is ignored by American popular culture just as he is by American politics—unless he is called upon, as he was in films like *Scanners*, *C.H.U.D.*, and *Prince of Darkness*, to represent a nameless dread that, sometimes quite literally, rises up from the sewers to threaten the well-being of the middling classes and the rich. That's as clear a metaphor as you're likely to find for the ways in which Americans' post-1970s anxiety about their economic well-being has manifested as contempt for the poor. Take *The Soloist* as an example of another way this plays out. This is not a story about the homeless former Juilliard student played by Jamie Foxx. It's a tale about what lengths the reporter played by Robert Downey, Jr., will go to to rescue the homeless man, and how the reporter is made better for having done so. In many religious traditions, service to "the poor" is a means by which one might enter heaven, and the American cinema likewise has a Protestant streak, treating poor and homeless people is a means toward someone else's ends. They are *redeemers*. In extreme cases of this we find a Prophetic Vagabond, who, like the Magical Negro, has mystical powers that will come to the aid of the protagonist. The function of the tramp on film is to transform others.

Third, when they are not tools to be used for other's enlightenment, poor and homeless Americans are *objects of fear*: dangerous villains who will destroy the social order. Alternately, they are *objects of pity*, passive, pathetic people with little agency or power. They are typically not allowed to be mad about their state, however, and the audience is not meant to be, either. We may feel sympathy, or even gratitude ("there but for the grace of God go I"), but seldom is the audience called upon to react with anger or indignation, nor are we called upon to take action. It's a way in which politics and questions about power get stripped out.

Fourth, when movies try to explain why people are homeless or poor, the causes are generally rooted in individual failure or a dramatic, tragic event. If poverty or homelessness come to an end in a movie, it is thus often the result of an individual transformation or a *deus ex machina*. There is almost never a sense of the social and economic forces that make poverty possible. It's another way we can see how films about poverty have no policy analysis and no real concern about power.

Finally, if a character is poor or homeless on film, then their poverty or their homelessness is the thing about them that most matters. There are a few exceptions: In *The Stranger in Us* (2010), a man in the midst of a break-up befriends a young homeless street hustler, but the most salient fact about this character is not his homelessness. Only recently have we begun to see gay men and lesbian characters on film whose reason to be in the film is not (or not merely) their sexual orientation, so perhaps there is hope for progress. Homeless people in the movies tend not to have love interests, for example, unless it's the failed love affair, divorce, or death that caused their homelessness, and almost never do poor or homeless people on screen have sex—although poor women can sometimes be saved by marrying. Representations of poor and homeless people in American film are one-dimensional. The challenge, of course, is to decide if that's more common when the subject is poverty than it is for other topics.

Lessons for Filmgoers

So what? If what I've argued about how American films represent poverty and homelessness is true, why should we care? And if we do care, what can we do about it? The short answer to why we should care is because, as political scientist Murray Edelman (1995, p. 128) put it: "We are socialized into the dominant ideology from infancy on . . . and works of art accomplish a great deal of the training." We learn lessons about other people, about politics, and about policy from the movies we see, and if those movies are consistently wrong, then we risk misunderstanding the world and our place in it. This is especially troubling given that the people we've been talking about are already marginalized. If you act upon this misinformation—as voters, say—you risk doing harm.

The caution I offer to the movie-goer is not to imagine that the depiction of poverty or homelessness you see on film—either its causes, its conditions, or its remedies—is offering you insight. If you have had experience with poverty or homelessness yourself, you already know this. I would urge you to be especially cautious if what you've seen on film reaffirms what you already thought—*Precious* remains a useful example in this regard, a movie that regurgitates the worst, racist stereotypes of welfare-reliant Americans and presents it as fact. But throughout these pages I've also identified films that comport pretty well with what we social scientists know about poor places and the people who live in them, and those are worth your time. If you're not sure where to begin, start with the following: *Chop Shop, God Bless the Child, Winter's Bone, Ballast, Grapes of Wrath, Heroes for Sale, Make Way for Tomorrow, City Lights, Claudine, King of the Hill, The Cool World, Killer of Sheep, The Pruitt-Igoe Myth, Major Barbara,* and *Angela's Ashes.*

If you would like to supplement your viewing with some reading, begin with Linda Tirado's *Hand to Mouth: Living in Bootstrap America* (2014) and *So You Think I Drive a Cadillac?* by Karen Seccombe (2010). You'll learn a lot about low-wage workers from Barbara Ehrenreich's *Nickel and Dimed* (2001), and for a full-scale history of homelessness in the United States, examine Kenneth Kusmer's *Down and Out, On the Road: The Homeless in American History* (2002). My previous publisher would be very annoyed with me if I didn't also point you to my own book that tells the history of poverty and homelessness from the perspective of poor and homeless people themselves, *A People History of Poverty in America* (Pimpare, 2008).

Having made yourself more knowledgeable and more attuned to some of the narrative tricks common to movies about poor and homeless people, if you do encounter them, now you can do something about it. What bell hooks wrote about film and race is also true of class: "Since movie culture is one of the primary sites for the reproduction and perpetuation of white supremacist aesthetics, demanding a change in what we see on the screen—demanding progressive images—is one way to transform the culture we live in" (hooks, 2012). And remember, as I discussed in the Introduction, over the course of their lives most Americans will have at least one spell of poverty or homelessness, so if you won't demand better representations of poor Americans for altruistic reasons, then do it for selfish ones.

Lessons for Filmmakers

I have complained about the inauthenticity of films about people in need, and, I hope, have convinced you that such complaints are justified. The solution to this problem is ostensibly simple: include more people with relevant expertise in the development and production of such films. It is common to hire consultants with military or law-enforcement background for films about war or policing. That's a product of wanting to get it right, and of recognizing your own ignorance in such matters. Some similar humility in the face of poverty, hunger, homelessness, and welfare receipt might help make your project not only more accurate, but *better*, too, offering viewers a more complicated, more provocative, and more human perspective.

Beyond the problem of the *quality* of films about poverty and homelessness—keeping in mind the many exceptions I've noted in this chapter and throughout the book—there is a problem of quantity. Hollywood tends not to pay too much attention to poor and homeless people, although it's perhaps not as bad as you might guess. To use one very crude measure, of the films on the American Film Institute's list of the 100 Best Movies of All Time (AFI 2007), seven are significantly concerned with the issues raised by this book: *City Lights, Grapes of Wrath, Treasure of the Sierra Madre, Midnight Cowboy, Intolerance, Sullivan's Travels,* and *Do the Right Thing* (it's nine if we wanted to include *The Gold Rush* and *Modern Times*). But critical success is not commercial success, and only two films even passably about poverty—*My Fair Lady* and *Lady and the Tramp*—can be counted among the 100 highest-grossing films in the U.S. (adjusted for inflation) (Dirks, n.d.). That offers one kind of explanation of why more movies about people in need are not made: perhaps it's because that's not what people want from their movies. Straight dramas of any kind are anomalies on that list, after all, which is dominated by epics, action-adventure, and big-budget science fiction spectacles.

Of the sixty-five directors represented on the AFI list, twelve of those men (there are no women there) have at least one film featured in these pages: Allen, Capra, Chaplin, Cukor, Curtiz, Ford, Griffith, Huston, Lee, Polanski, Schlesinger, Sturgis, and Wyler. But many famous and accomplished directors never made a film about poverty or homelessness, including Steven Spielberg, Robert Altman, Stanley Kubrick, and Francis Ford Coppola. Alfred Hitchcock was also uninterested in such issues, with one possible exception to be found among his early British films: In *Young and Innocent* (1937), a man is searching for a raincoat that will clear him of murder (or so we are meant to believe), which ends up in the hands of "an old tramp," called "Old Will the china mender." Later, as part of the plan to catch the murderer, Old Will will be dressed in a tuxedo, and we are meant to find funny this incongruity and his obvious discomfort in the costume.

I am not suggesting that Hitchcock is a lesser director for never having turned his attention to people in need—nor am I arguing that because they made movies about poverty, Woody Allen and Roman Polanski should be absolved of their crimes—but I am arguing that in a world in which the lived experience of poor and homeless Americans is so poorly understood, high-profile films by high-profile filmmakers is one way to help generate more empathy among the broader public, and maybe help open up some spaces for better policies. Return to the Introduction for a review of the research that shows that films can affect public attitudes and even political behavior.

As to the substance of those portrayals: Blaming poor people for their poverty serves a political function, obviating the need for action, for policymaking, for a reallocation of resources. Don't feed ignorance and make it worse. Don't legitimize or enable more bad policy. Similarly, one-dimensional portrayals of poor and homeless people on film serve a social and cultural function: they relieve the viewer of the need to do anything, to act, to press the political system to act more fairly. It reassures the viewer that the world is as it is for a reason, and even if things are grim for some people, it's ultimately their own fault. There is nothing to be done. A more thoughtful and more three-dimensional portrayal of poor and low-income people, families, and communities would have radical implications, showing how even the "worthy poor" can suffer, and that, often, hard work and determination do not lead to improved circumstances. Grit is not an anti-poverty program. More films should recognize that, and not valorize those who undertake heroic efforts just to survive. But they should do so with Pauline Kael's (1994, p. 4) admonition in mind: "Films made out of social conscience have generally given an even more distorted view of America than those made out of business sense, and are much less amusing." That is, don't make the goal the message, but, rather, the close observation, the story, the intersection of human behavior and social conditions, and recognize that most people don't triumph against the odds—they succumb to them.

This calls for a kind of deep empathy. Not a superficial kind of "I feel your pain," but a serious effort to understand behavior and attitudes from the perspective of another, and to consider the range of their actually existing choices and the forces that constrain them. It also, as a consequence, requires deep knowledge, and the implication is simple: Do not show us movies about poor and homeless people until you have spent time with them and learned about their worlds.

Lessons for Policymakers and Journalists

If what you know about people living on welfare is from *Precious* and your insight into homelessness comes from the *Pursuit of Happyness*, you're doing it wrong. Better to see some of the films I recommended to movie-goers. Or, even better, spend significant time with poor and homeless people in order to get a fuller perspective of what their lives truly look like. Visit homeless shelters—and more than just once—to see what it's like to live there and to have no place else to go. Spend a month living on a food stamp budget, and consider what it must be like to live with such scarcity not knowing it's just an experiment that will be over in thirty days. The readings suggestions for audience members are good ones for you, too, but that's not enough. Ask one of your staff members to put together a reading list of the best, current research on the topics. Or drop me an email and tell me what you'd like to read about, and I'll make some suggestions.

If these are issues you are already well versed in, then act upon that knowledge. When you see a one-dimensional, stereotypical, or inaccurate portrayal of poor and homeless people on screen, say something. Out loud. In front of a microphone or a camera. Or write something (or have one of your staff do it). If you have a public platform: use it. Not to censor, but to censure, to let people know that the myths and stereotypes that permeate our culture bear little relation to the people and programs and they actually exist in the real worlds. Undertaking a public critique requires care, however: Criticism of art and culture from people with power over the purse can look like censorship even when it's not intended to be, and that's potentially dangerous. Hollywood should make all the bad movies they want, but it's incumbent upon us to call them out when they are doing harm to our political culture, our policy making, and our fellow citizens. Maybe, as a result, in the future they will want to make better movies, with more three-dimensional portrayals. Finally, remember that poor and homeless people are your constituents, too, and there are probably more of them than you think. And if you don't know any of them personally, you can remedy that. And you should.

The advice I offered to filmgoers is also useful here: "Demanding a change in what we see on the screen—demanding progressive images—is one way to transform the culture we live in" (hooks, 2012). One of the ways in which norms of thought, behavior, politics, and policy are generated, reproduced, and calcified, is through the movies. Yes, and television, too, but that's another book.

KEY U.S. FILMS DISCUSSED, 1902–2015 (FILMS REFERENCED IN THE TEXT BUT NOT INCLUDED HERE CAN BE FOUND IN THE INDEX)

Year	Title	Director
1902	*The Little Match Seller*	James Williamson
1904	*The Ex-Convict*	Edwin S. Porter
1905	*The Kleptomaniac*	Edwin S. Porter
1909	*A Corner in Wheat*	D. W. Griffith
1912	*From the Submerged*	Theodore Wharton
1912	*One Is Business, the Other Crime*	D. W. Griffith
1912	*The Musketeers of Pig Alley*	D. W. Griffith
1912	*The Usurer's Grip*	Bannister Merwin
1913	*The Reformers*	D. W. Griffith
1914	*A Film Johnnie*	George Nichols
1914	*Between Showers*	Henry Lehrman
1914	*Face on the Bar Room Floor*	Charles Chaplin
1914	*Kid Auto Races at Venice*	Henry Lehrman
1914	*Mabel's Strange Predicament*	Henry Lehrman
1915	*A Night Out*	Charles Chaplin
1915	*In the Park*	Charles Chaplin
1915	*Regeneration*	Raoul Walsh
1915	*The Champion*	Charles Chaplin
1915	*The Tramp*	Charles Chaplin
1915	*Work*	Charles Chaplin

Year	Title	Director
1916	*Intolerance*	D. W. Griffith
1916	*Police*	Charles Chaplin
1916	*The Pawnshop*	Charles Chaplin
1918	*A Dog's Life*	Charles Chaplin
1919	*Broken Blossoms*	D. W. Griffith
1921	*Orphans of the Storm*	D. W. Griffith
1921	*The Blot*	Lois Weber
1921	*The Idle Class*	Charles Chaplin
1921	*The Kid*	Charles Chaplin
1922	*Oliver Twist*	Frank Lloyd
1922	*Pay Day*	Charles Chaplin
1922	*Robin Hood*	Allan Dwan
1925	*The Gold Rush*	Charles Chaplin
1927	*It*	Clarence G. Badger
1928	*Beggars of Life*	William Wellman
1928	*The Circus*	Charles Chaplin
1931	*City Lights*	Charles Chaplin
1931	*Sidewalks of New York*	Zion Myers, Jules White
1931	*Street Scene*	King Vidor
1932	*I Am a Fugitive from a Chain Gang*	Mervyn LeRoy
1932	*Washington Merry-Go-Round*	James Cruze
1933	*Gabriel Over the White House*	Gregory La Cava
1933	*Hallelujah, I'm a Bum*	Lewis Milestone
1933	*Heroes for Sale*	William Wellman
1933	*Lady for a Day*	Frank Capra
1933	*Man's Castle*	Frank Borzage
1933	*Wild Boys of the Road*	William Wellman
1933	*Gold Diggers of 1933*	Mervyn LeRoy
1933	*Ann Vickers*	John Cromwell
1934	*Beggars in Ermine*	Phil Rosen
1934	*Our Daily Bread*	King Vidor
1934	*Stand Up and Cheer*	Hamilton MacFadden
1934	*Tomorrow's Children*	Crane Wilbut
1936	*Modern Times*	Charles Chaplin
1936	*Mr. Deeds Goes to Town*	Frank Capra

Year	Title	Director
1936	*My Man Godfrey*	Gregory LaCava
1936	*The Plow That Broke the Plains*	Pare Lorentz
1937	*Boy of the Streets*	William Nigh
1937	*Dead End*	William Wyler
1937	*Make Way for Tomorrow*	Leo McCarey
1937	*Mannequin*	Frank Borzage
1937	*Prince and the Pauper*	William Keighley
1937	*Swing It, Professor*	Marshall Neilan
1937	*The Bride Wore Red*	Dorothy Azner
1937	*The River*	Pare Lorentz
1937	*Young and Innocent*	Alfred Hitchcock
1938	*Angels with Dirty Faces*	Michael Curtiz
1938	*Boys Town*	Norman Taurog
1938	*Crime School*	Lewis Seiler
1938	*Little Tough Guy*	Harold Young
1938	*Merrily We Live*	Norman Z. McLeod
1938	*Adventures of Robin Hood*	Michael Curtiz and William Keighley
1939	*Fifth Avenue Girl*	Gregory La Cava
1939	*Hell's Kitchen*	Ewald DuPont and Lewis Seiler
1939	*One Third of a Nation*	Dudley Murphy
1939	*The Angels Wash Their Faces*	Ray Enright
1939	*The Little Princess*	Walter Lang
1939	*They Made Me a Criminal*	Busby Berkeley
1940	*Boys of the City*	Joseph H. Lewis
1940	*Grapes of Wrath*	John Ford
1940	*Pride of the Bowery*	Joseph H. Lewis
1940	*The Fight for Life*	Pare Lorentz
1940	*The Great Dictator*	Charles Chaplin
1940	*The Great McGinty*	Preston Sturges
1941	*Bowery Blitzkrieg*	Wallace Fox
1941	*How Green Was My Valley*	John Ford
1941	*Major Barbara*	Gabriel Pascal
1941	*Meet John Doe*	Frank Capra
1941	*Men of Boys Town*	Norman Taurog
1941	*Sullivan's Travels*	Preston Sturges

Year	Title	Director
1941	*Tobacco Road*	John Ford
1942	*Mr. Wise Guy*	William Nigh
1944	*None But the Lonely Heart*	Clifford Odets
1944	*Sunday Dinner for a Soldier*	Lloyd Bacon
1945	*A Tree Grows in Brooklyn*	Elia Kazan
1945	*The Southerner*	Jean Renoir
1946	*From This Day Forward*	John Berry
1947	*Body and Soul*	Robert Rossen
1947	*It Happened on Fifth Avenue*	Roy Del Ruth
1947	*Monsieur Verdoux*	Charles Chaplin
1948	*Easter Parade*	Charles Walters
1948	*In the Street*	James Agee, Helen Levitt, and Janice Loeb
1948	*Treasure of the Sierra Madre*	John Huston
1952	*Carrie*	William Wyler
1952	*Limelight*	Charles Chaplin
1955	*Blackboard Jungle*	Richard Brooks
1955	*Lady and the Tramp*	Clyde Geronimi, Wilfred Jackson, and Hamilton Luske
1956	*On the Bowery*	Lionel Rogosin
1960	*Harvest of Shame*	Fred Friendly
1961	*A Raisin in the Sun*	Daniel Petrie
1961	*Pocketful of Miracles*	Frank Capra
1961	*The Hoodlum Priest*	Irvin Kirschner
1964	*My Fair Lady*	George Cukor
1964	*The Cool World*	Shirley Clarke
1964	*Robin and the Seven Hoods*	Gordon Douglas
1964	*The Pawnbroker*	Sidney Lumet
1967	*To Sir, with Love*	James Clavell
1967	*Up the Down Staircase*	Robert Mulligan
1969	*Midnight Cowboy*	John Schlesinger
1970	*Trash*	Paul Morrissey
1970	*The Landlord*	Hal Ashby
1972	*Boxcar Bertha*	Martin Scorsese

Year	Title	Director
1972	*Sounder*	Martin Ritt
1972	*The Candidate*	Michael Ritchie
1973	*Emperor of the North (Pole)*	Robert Aldrich
1973	*Paper Moon*	Peter Bogdanovich
1973	*Robin Hood*	Wolfgang Reitherman
1974	*Brother, Can You Spare a Dime?*	Philippe Mora
1974	*Claudine*	John Berry
1974	*Conrack*	Martin Ritt
1975	*Welfare*	Frederick Wiseman
1976	*Bound for Glory*	Hal Ashby
1977	*A Piece of the Action*	Sidney Poitier
1977	*Billion Dollar Hobo*	Stuart E. McGowan
1977	*Killer of Sheep*	Charles Burnett
1977	*Stroszek*	Werner Herzog
1979	*The Jerk*	Carl Reiner
1979	*Orphan Train*	William A. Graham
1980	*Coal Miner's Daughter*	Michael Apted
1980	*On the Nickel*	Ralph Waite
1981	*Annie!*	John Huston
1981	*Fort Apache the Bronx*	Daniel Petrie
1981	*Pennies from Heaven*	Herbert Ross
1981	*Scanners*	David Cronenberg
1981	*Wolfen*	Michael Wadleigh
1982	*Smithereens*	Susan Seidelman
1983	*Trading Places*	John Landis
1983	*My Brother's Wedding*	Charles Burnett
1984	*C.H.U.D.*	Douglas Cheek
1984	*Country*	Richard Pearce
1984	*Places in the Heart*	Robert Benton
1984	*Nothing Lasts Forever*	Tom Schiller
1984	*Streetwise*	Martin Bell
1984	*The Brother from Another Planet*	John Sayles
1984	*The Dollmaker*	Daniel Petrie
1984	*The River*	Mark Rydell
1985	*Journey of Natty Gann*	Jeremy Kagan
1985	*Stone Pillow*	George Schaefer
1985	*The Purple Rose of Cairo*	Woody Allen

Year	Title	Director
1986	*Down and Out in Beverly Hills*	Paul Mazursky
1986	*Little Shop of Horrors*	Frank Oz
1987	*Barfly*	Barbet Schroeder
1987	*Ironweed*	Hector Babenco
1987	*Prince of Darkness*	John Carpenter
1987	*Street Trash* and *Meltdown Memoirs*	Mike Lackey
1987	*Suspect*	Peter Yates
1987	*The Principal*	Christopher Cain
1988	*God Bless the Child*	David Shire
1988	*Stand and Deliver*	Ramon Menendez
1988	*The Women of Brewster Place*	Donna Deitch
1989	*Do the Right Thing*	Spike Lee
1989	*Lean on Me*	John G. Avildsen
1989	*Sidewalk Stories*	Charles Lane
1989	*Up Your Alley*	Bob Logan
1991	*Boyz N the Hood*	John Singleton
1991	*Chains of Gold*	Rod Holcomb
1991	*Curly Sue*	John Hughes
1991	*Life Stinks*	Mel Brooks
1991	*The Super*	Rod Daniel
1991	*My Own Private Idaho*	Gus Van Sant
1991	*New Jack City*	Mario Van Peebles
1991	*Robin Hood: Prince of Thieves*	Kevin Reynolds
1991	*Soap Dish*	Michael Hoffman
1991	*Straight Out of Brooklyn*	Matty Rich
1992	*Candyman*	Bernard Rose
1992	*Eddie Presley*	Jeff Burr
1992	*Just Another Girl on the IRT*	Leslie Harris
1992	*Newsies*	Kenny Ortega
1992	*Sister Act*	Emile Ardolino
1992	*The Vagrant*	Chris Walas
1992	*Where the Day Takes You*	Marc Rocco
1993	*American Heart*	Martin Bell
1993	*Groundhog Day*	Harold Ramis
1993	*King of the Hill*	Steven Soderbergh
1993	*Menace II Society*	Allen Hughes
1993	*Robin Hood: Men in Tights*	Mel Brooks
1993	*The Saint of Fort Washington*	Tim Hunter

Year	Title	Director
1994	*Crooklyn*	Spike Lee
1994	*Fresh*	Boaz Yakin
1994	*Hoop Dreams*	Steve James
1994	*Surviving the Game*	Ernest Dickerson
1994	*With Honors*	Alek Kashishian
1995	*A Little Princess*	Alfonso Cuaron
1995	*Clockers*	Spike Lee
1995	*Dangerous Minds*	John N. Smith
1995	*Down, Out and Dangerous*	Noel Nosseck
1995	*Two Bits*	James Foley
1996	*Citizen Ruth*	Alexander Payne
1996	*Entertaining Angels*	Michael Ray Rhodes
1996	*Extreme Measures*	Michael Apted
1996	*Hidden in America*	Martin Bell
1996	*High School High*	Hart Bochner
1997	*Gridlock'd*	Vondie Curtis-Hall
1997	*Gummo*	Harmony Korine
1997	*Public Housing*	Frederick Wiseman
1997	*Riding the Rails*	Michael Uys and Lexy Lovell
1997	*Sunday*	Jonathan Nossiter
1997	*Titanic*	James Cameron
1997	*187*	Kevin Reynolds
1998	*Acid Rain*	Albert Johnson
1998	*Night of the Bums*	Charles E. Cullen
1998	*The Fisher King*	Terry Gilliam
1998	*Bulworth*	Warren Beatty
1999	*Angela's Ashes*	Alan Parker
1999	*Music of the Heart*	Wes Craven
1999	*Prince of Central Park*	John Leekley
2000	*Dark Days*	Marc Singer
2000	*Finding Forrester*	Gus Van Sant
2000	*First, Last and Deposit*	Peter Hyoguchi
2000	*George Washington*	David Green
2000	*Joe Gould's Secret*	Stanley Tucci
2000	*The Corner*	Charles S. Dutton
2000	*The Stray*	Kevin Mock
2001	*Hardball*	Brian Robbins
2001	*The Caveman's Valentine*	Kasi Lemmons
2001	*The House of Mirth*	Terence Davies

Year	Title	Director
2001	*Zoolander*	Ben Stiller
2002	*Gangs of New York*	Martin Scorsese
2002	*In America*	Jim Sheridan
2003	*An Angel on Abbey Street*	Jed Nolan
2003	*Homeless to Harvard*	Peter Levin
2003	*House of Sand and Fog*	Vadim Perelman
2003	*The American Hobo*	Bobb Hopkins
2004	*MacArthur Park*	Billy Wirth
2004	*On the Outs*	Lori Silverbush and Michael Skolnik
2005	*Brother to Brother*	Rodney Evans
2005	*Cinderella Man*	Ron Howard
2005	*Factotum*	Bent Hamer
2005	*Land of Plenty*	Wim Wenders
2005	*Mouth to Mouth*	Alison Murray
2005	*Rail Kings*	Bobb Hopkins
2005	*The Nickel Children*	Glenn Klinker
2005	*Waging a Living*	Roger Weisberg
2005	*Complex: Life Inside a Sect 8 Apt.*	Oliver W. Tuthill, Jr.
2006	*Ask the Dust*	Robert Towne
2006	*Don't Call Me a Saint*	Claudia Larson
2006	*Half Nelson*	Ryan Fleck
2006	*Kill the Poor*	Alan Taylor
2006	*The Architect*	Matt Tauber
2006	*The Pursuit of Happyness*	Gabriele Muccino
2006	*The Second Chance*	Steve Taylor
2007	*Bum Man: Hero of the Homeless*	Floyd Jones
2007	*Chop Shop*	Rahmin Bahrani
2007	*Freedom Writers*	Richard Lagravenese
2007	*Resurrecting the Champ*	Rod Lurie
2007	*Skid Row*	Ross Clarke et al.
2008	*Ballast*	Lance Hammer
2008	*Frozen River*	Courtney Hunt
2008	*Hancock*	Peter Berg
2008	*Kit Kitridge: American Girl*	Patricia Rozema
2008	*Voices in the Tunnels*	Vic David
2008	*Wendy and Lucy*	Kelly Reichhardt
2009	*Brick City*	Mark Benjamin and Marc Levin

Year	Title	Director
2009	*Precious*	Lee Daniels
2009	*The Blind Side*	John Lee Hancock
2009	*The Road*	John Hillcoat
2009	*The Soloist*	Joe Wright
2010	*Robin Hood*	Ridley Scott
2010	*The Stranger in Us*	Scott Boswell
2010	*Winter's Bone*	Debra Granik
2011	*Hobo with a Shotgun*	Jason Eisener
2011	*The Pruitt-Igoe Myth*	Chad Freidrichs
2012	*Beasts of the Southern Wild*	Benh Zeitlin
2012	*Being Flynn*	Paul Weitz
2012	*Bindlestiffs*	Andrew Edison
2012	*Mud*	Jeff Nichols
2012	*Red Hook Summer*	Spike Lee
2012	*Upside Down*	Juan Solanas
2013	*Elysium*	Neill Blomkamp
2013	*The Purge*	James DeMonaco
2014	*The Boxcar Children*	Daniel Chuba et al.
2014	*The Purge: Anarchy*	James DeMonaco
2014	*Rich Hill*	Andrew Droz Palermo and Tracy Droz Tragos
2014	*Homme Less*	Thomas Wirthensohn
2014	*Shelter*	Paul Bettany
2015	*Chi-Raq*	Spike Lee
2015	*Time Out of Mind*	Oren Moverman

BOOKS AND ARTICLES CITED

Adkins, Todd, and Jeremiah J. Castle. 2013. "Evidence of Cinematic Influence on Political Attitudes." *Social Science Quarterly* 95, no. 5: 1230–1244.

Agee, James, and Walker Evans. 1941/2001. *Let Us Now Praise Famous Men.* New York: Mariner Books.

Agee, James. 2000. *Agee on Film: Criticism and Comment on the Movies.* New York: Modern Library.

Albertson, Bethany, and Adria Lawrence. 2009. "After the Credits Roll: The Long-Term Effects of Educational Television on Public Knowledge and Attitudes." *American Politics Research* 37, no. 2 (March): 275–300.

Alesina, Alberto, and Edward Glaeser. 2004. *Fighting Poverty in the U.S. and Europe: A World of Difference.* Oxford: Oxford University Press.

Almy, Frederic. 1900. "Public or Private Outdoor Relief." *Proceedings of the National Conference on Charities and Corrections*: 134–145.

American Enterprise Institute. 2003. "Attitudes about Welfare Reform." Washington, DC: AEI (March 6).

American Film Institute. 2007. "100 Years, 100 Movies. 10th Anniversary Edition" at http://www.afi.com/100years/movies10.aspx. Accessed on Nov. 26, 2016.

American Psychological Association. 2000. "Resolution on Poverty and Socioeconomic Status" at http://www.apa.org/about/policy/poverty-resolution.aspx; and "Fact Sheets on Socioeconomic Status" at http://www.apa.org/pi/ses/resources/publications/index.aspx. Accessed Nov. 26, 2016.

Anbinder, Tyler. 2001. *Five Points: The 19th Century New York City Neighborhood That Invented Tap Dance, Stole Elections, and Became the World's Most Notorious Slum.* New York: Free Press.

Anderson, Craig A., Douglas A. Gentile, and Katherine E. Buckley. 2007. *Violent Video Game Effects on Children and Adolescents: Theory, Research, and Public Policy.* New York: Oxford.

Austin, Michael J., ed. 2006. "Understanding Poverty from Multiple Social Science Perspectives: A Learning Resource for Staff Development in Social Service Agencies."

UC Berkeley School of Social Welfare for the Bay Area Social Services Consortium (August).

Bailey, Blake. 2003. "How Not to Be Poor." Brief No. 426, National Center for Policy Analysis (January 15).

Barabas, Jason, and Jennifer Jerit. 2009. "Estimating the Causal Effects of Media Coverage on Policy-Specific Knowledge." *American Journal of Political Science* 53, no. 1 (January): 73–89.

Barboza, Craigh, ed. 2009. *John Singleton: Interviews.* Jackson, MS: University Press of Mississippi.

Barker, Clive. 1987. *Books of Blood Vol. 5.* New York: Warner.

Barrington, Linda, and Gordon M. Fisher. 2006. "Poverty." In Susan B. Carter, Scott Sigmund Gartner, Michael R. Haines, Alan L. Olmstead, Richard Sutch, and Gavin Wright, eds., *Historical Statistics of the United States,* Millennial Edition On Line. Cambridge, England: Cambridge University Press at https://hsus.cambridge.org/HSUSWeb/HSUSEntryServlet. Accessed Nov. 26, 2016.

Bateman, Thomas S., Tomoaki Sakano, and Mokoto Sakanao. 1992. "Roger, Me, and My Attitude: Film Propaganda and Cynicism toward Corporate Leadership." *Journal of Applied Psychology* 77, no. 5: 768–771.

Bazin, Andre. 1971. "The Western: or the American Film *Par Excellence*." In Andre Bazin, *What Is Cinema? Vol. II.* Oakland, CA: University of California Press.

Bekkers, Rene, and Pamala Wiepking. 2010. "A Literature Review of Empirical Studies of Philanthropy: Eight Mechanisms that Drive Charitable Giving." *Nonprofit and Voluntary Sector Quarterly* 40, no. 5: 924–973.

Benson, Jackson J. 1984. *The True Adventures of John Steinbeck, Writer: A Biography.* New York: Viking.

Bergman, Andrew. 1971/1992. *We're in the Money: Depression America and Its Films.* Chicago: Ivan R. Dee.

Berman, Marshall. 2009. *On the Town: One Hundred Years of Spectacle in Times Square.* London and New York: Verso.

Bernstein, Arnie, ed. 2000. *"The Movies Are": Carl Sandburg's Film Reviews and Essays, 1920–1928.* Chicago: Lake Claremont Press.

Bernstein, Irving. 1985. "Images of the Worker." Chap. 7 in Bernstein, *A Caring Society: The New Deal, the Worker, and the Great Depression.* Boston, MA: Houghton Mifflin Company.

Blay, Zandile. 2009. "W Magazine Pulls a Zoolander Derelicte." *The Frisky* (August 26) at http://www.thefrisky.com/2009-08-26/w-magazine-pulls-a-zoolander-derelicte/. Accessed Nov. 26, 2016.

Bodnar, John. 2003/2006. *Blue-Collar Hollywood: Liberalism, Democracy, and Working People in American Film.* Baltimore, MD; London: Johns Hopkins University Press.

Bogle, Donald. 1973/2007. *Toms, Coons, Mulattoes, Mammies, and Bucks: An Interpretive History of Blacks in American Films.* New York: Continuum.

Bourne, Mark. 2003. "The Great Dictator: The Chaplin Collection." *DVD Journal* at http://www.dvdjournal.com/reviews/g/greatdictator.shtml. Accessed Nov. 26, 2016.

Brigham, William. 1996. "Down and Out in Tinseltown: Hollywood Presents the Dispossessed." In P. Loukides and Linda K. Fuller, eds., *Beyond the Stars: Themes and Ideologies in American Popular Film*. Bowling Green, KY: Bowling Green State University Popular Press.

Brownlow, Kevin. 1990. *Behind the Mask of Innocence: Sex, Violence, Prejudice, Crime: Films of Social Conscience in the Silent Era*. Berkeley: University of California.

Buck, Phillip O., Paul A. Toro, and Melanie A. Ramos. 2004. "Media and Professional Interest in Homelessness over 30 Years (1974–2003)." *Analysis of Social Issues and Public Policy* 4, no. 1: 151–171.

Buhle, Paul, and Dave Wagner. 2002. *Radical Hollywood: The Untold Story Behind America's Favorite Movies*. New York: New Press.

Bunis, William K., Angela Yancik, and David A. Snow. 1996. "The Cultural Patterning of Sympathy Toward the Homeless and Other Victims of Misfortune." *Social Problems* 43, no. 4 (November): 387–402.

Burke, Thomas. 1932. "A Comedian." Chap. 5 in Burke, *City of Encounters: A London Divertissement*. London: Constable & Co.

Burston, Betty Watson, Dionne Jones, and Pat Robertson-Saunders. 1995. "Drug Use and African Americans: Myth Versus Reality." *Journal of Alcohol and Drug Education* 40 (Winter): 19–39.

Butler, Lisa D., Cheryl Koopman, and Philip G. Zimbardo. 1995. "The Psychological Impact of Viewing the Film 'JFK': Emotions, Belief and Political Behavior Intentions." *Political Psychology* 16, no. 2 (June): 237–257.

Campbell, John L. 2002. "Ideas, Politics, and Public Policy." *Annual Review of Sociology* 28: 21–38.

Canby, Vincent. 1974. "New York's Woes Are Good Box Office." *New York Times* (November 10).

Caro, Robert. 1975. *The Power Broker: Robert Moses and the Fall of New York*. New York: Vintage.

Cary, Nathaniel. 2010. "Bauer: Needy 'Owe Something Back' for Aid." *The State* (January 23), at http://www.thestate.com/news/local/article14373875.html, as accessed on Nov. 19, 2016.

Center for Tobacco Control Research and Education. 2013. University of California San Francisco, at http://smokefreemovies.ucsf.edu/, as accessed on Dec. 13, 2013.

Centers for Disease Control and Prevention (CDC). 2012. "Smoking in the Movies." At http://www.cdc.gov//tobacco/data_statistics/fact_sheets/youth_data/movies/index.htm. Accessed Nov. 26, 2016.

Century Foundation. 2004. "Left Behind: Unequal Opportunity in Higher Education." New York; Washington, DC: Century Foundation.

Ceplair, Larry, and Steven Englund. 1983. *The Inquisition in Hollywood: Politics in the Film Community, 1930–1960.* Berkeley: University of California Press.

Chaplin, Charles. 1964/2003. *My Autobiography.* London: Penguin Classics

Chetty, Raj, Nathaniel Hendren, Patrick Kline, and Emmanuel Saez. 2013. "The Economic Impacts of Tax Expenditures: Evidence from Spatial Variation across the U.S." *Journalist's Resource* at http://journalistsresource.org/studies/economics/inequality/economic-impacts-of-tax-expenditures-evidence-from-spatial-variation-across-the-u-s (July 30). Accessed Nov. 26, 2016.

Christensen, Terry, and Peter J. Haas. 2005. *Projecting Politics: Political Messages in American Films.* Armonk, NY: M.E. Sharpe.

Clawson, Rosalee, and Rakuya Trice. 2000. "Poverty and We Know It: Media Portrayals of the Poor." *Public Opinion Quarterly* 64: 53–64.

Conroy, Pat. 1972. *The Water Is Wide.* New York: Open Road.

Cresswell, Tim. 2001. *The Tramp in America.* London: Reaktion Books.

Daniels, Alex. 2015. "As Wealthy Give Smaller Share of Income to Charity, Middle Class Digs Deeper." *Chronicle of Philanthropy* (updated January 13) at https://www.philanthropy.com/article/As-Wealthy-Give-Smaller-Share/152481. Accessed Nov. 26, 2016.

Davis, Darren W. and Christian Davenport. 1997. "The Political and Social Relevancy of *Malcolm X*: The Stability of African American Political Attitudes." *Journal of Politics* 59, no. 2 (May): 550–564.

Davis, Natalie Zemon. 2000. *Slaves on Screen: Film and Historical Vision.* Cambridge, MA: Harvard University Press.

Day, Dorothy. N.d. The Dorothy Day Collection, at http://dorothyday.catholicworker.org/index.html. Accessed Nov. 26, 2016.

Delli Carpini, Michael X., and Scott Keeter. 1996. *What Americans Know about Politics and Why It Matters.* New Haven, CT: Yale University Press.

deLong, Brad. 2010. "G.H.M. in the *Atlantic Monthly* in 1905." September 20, at http://delong.typepad.com/sdj/2010/09/todd-hendersons-century-ago-predecessor-ghm-in-the-atlantic-monthly-in-1905.html. Accessed Nov. 26, 2016.

DeMott, Robert, ed. 1989. *Working Days: The Journals of* The Grapes of Wrath, *1938–1941.* New York: Viking.

Denning, Michael. 1997. *The Cultural Front.* New York: Verso.

Dickens, Charles. 1838. *Oliver Twist.* London: Richard Bentley.

Dickstein, Morris. 2009. *Dancing in the Dark: A Cultural History of the Great Depression.* New York: Norton.

Dirks, Tim. N.d. "All-Time Box Office 100." American Movie Classics Filmsite. Last retrieved June 17, 2016, at http://www.filmsite.org/boxoffice.html. Accessed Nov. 26, 2016.

Dodson, Lisa. 2009. *The Moral Underground: How Ordinary American Subvert and Unfair Economy.* New York: New Press.

Doherty, Thomas. 2007. *Hollywood's Censor: Joseph I. Breen and the Production Code Administration.* New York: Columbia University Press.

Draut, Tamara. 2002. "New Opportunities? Public Opinion on Poverty, Income Inequality, and Public Policy: 1996–2002." New York: Demos (October 1).

Dreiser, Theodore. 1900. *Sister Carrie.* New York: Doubleday.

Dyck, Joshua J., and Laura S. Hussey. 2008. "The End of Welfare As We Know It? Durable Attitudes in a Changing Information Environment." *Public Opinion Quarterly* 72, no. 4 (Winter): 589–618.

Ebert, Roger, ed. 1997. *Roger Ebert's Book of Film: From Tolstoy to Tarantino, the Finest Writing from a Century of Film.* New York: W.W. Norton.

Ebert, Roger. 2008. *Awake in the Dark: The Best of Roger Ebert.* Chicago and London: University of Chicago Press.

Economic Policy Institute. 2013. *State of Working America*, International, Income and Mobility Charts, at http://stateofworkingamerica.org/subjects/international/. Accessed Nov. 27, 2016.

Edelman, Murray. 1995. *From Art to Politics: How Artistic Creations Shape Political Conceptions.* Chicago and London: University of Chicago Press.

Edin, Kathryn, and Laura Lein. 1997. *Making Ends Meet: How Single Mothers Survive Welfare and Low-Wage Work.* New York: Russell Sage Foundation.

Edwards, Ashley N. 2014. "Dynamics of Economic Well-Being: Poverty, 2009–2011." Washington, DC: U.S. Census Bureau.

Ehrenreich, Barbara. 2001. *Nickel and Dimed: On Not Getting By in America.* New York: Henry Holt.

Elliott, William R., and William J. Schenck-Hamlin. 1979. "Film, Politics, and the Press: The Influence of 'All the President's Men'." *Journalism Quarterly* 56, no. 3: 546–553.

Everett, Anna. 2001. *Returning the Gaze: A Genealogy of Black Film Criticism, 1909–1949.* Durham, NC; London: Duke University Press.

Experimental Cinema (unsigned). 1934. "R-E-L-I-E-F." *Experimental Cinema* 5.

Ezell, Mark. 1993. "The Political Activity of Social Workers: A Post-Reagan Update." *Journal of Sociology and Social Welfare* 20, no. 4: 81–97.

Faderman, Lillian. 1999. *To Believe in Women: What Lesbians Have Done for America.* Boston: Houghton Mifflin.

Farleigh Dickinson University. 2012. "What You Know Depends on What You Watch: Current Events Knowledge Across Popular News Sources." May 3, at http://publicmind.fdu.edu/2012/confirmed/final.pdf. Accessed Nov. 27, 2016.

Feagin, Joe R. 1975. *Subordinating the Poor: Welfare and American Beliefs.* Englewood, NJ: Prentice Hall.

Flynn, Nick. 2004. *Another Bullshit Night in Suck City.* New York: Norton.

Fox, Liana, Irwin Garfinkel, Keeraj Kaushal, Jane Waldfogel, and Christopher Wimer. 2014. "Waging War on Poverty: Historical Trends in Poverty Using the Supplemental Poverty Measure." National Bureau of Economic Research Working Paper 19789 (January).

Freeman, Miriam L., and Deborah P. Valentine. 2004. "Through the Eyes of Hollywood: Images of Social Workers in Film." *Social Work* 49, no. 2 (April): 151–161.

Fremstad, Shawn. 2012. "Married ... Without Means: Poverty and Economic Hardship Among Married Americans." Center for Economic and Policy Research (November).

Fuller, Linda K. 1999. "From Tramps to Truth-Seekers: Images of the Homeless in the Motion Pictures." Chap. 10 in Eungjun Min, ed., *Reading the Homeless: The Media's Image of Homeless Culture.* Westport, CT: Praeger.

Gallup and Fannie Mae. 2007. "Homelessness in America: Americans' Perceptions, Attitudes and Knowledge." *General Population Survey & City Surveys* (November) at http://shnny.org/uploads/2007_Gallup_Poll.pdf. Accessed Nov. 27, 2016.

Gans, Herbert J. 1964. "The Rise of the Problem-Film: An Analysis of Changes in Hollywood Films and the American Audience." *Social Problems* 11, no. 4 (Spring): 327–336.

Gans, Herbert. 1993. "Hollywood Entertainment: Commerce or Ideology?" *Social Science Quarterly* 74, no. 1 (March): 150–153.

Gardner, Chris, with Quincy Troupe. 2006. *The Pursuit of Happyness.* New York: Amistad.

Gelman-Waxner, Libby [Paul Rudnick]. 1994. *If You Ask Me: The Collected Columns of America's Most Beloved and Irresponsible Critic.* New York: Fawcett Columbine.

Gibelman, Margaret. 2004. "Television and the Public Image of Social Workers: Portrayal or Betrayal?" *Social Work* 49, no. 2 (April): 331–334.

Giglio, Ernest. 2002. *Here's Looking at You: Hollywood, Film, and Politics.* New York: Peter Lang.

Gilens, Martin. 1999. *Why Americans Hate Welfare.* Chicago: University of Chicago Press.

Gilliam, Franklin D., and Shanto Iyengar. 2000. "Prime Suspects: The Influence of Local Television News on the Viewing Public." *American Journal of Political Science* 44, no. 3: 560–573.

Gonzales, Evelyn. 2006. *The Bronx.* New York: Columbia University Press.

Gordon, Linda. 1988. *Heroes of Their Own Lives: The Politics and History of Family Violence.* New York: Viking.

Gordon, Linda. 1994. *Pitied But Not Entitled: Single Mothers and the History of Welfare.* Free Press: New York.

Gowan, Teresa. 2010. *Hobos, Hustlers, and Backsliders: Homeless in San Francisco.* Minneapolis: University of Minnesota.

Graber, Doris. 1988. *Processing the News: How People Tame the Information Tide* (Second Ed.). New York: Longman.

Green, George Dawes. 1994. *The Caveman's Valentine*. New York: Warner Books.

Greene, Doyle. 2010. *The American Worker on Film: A Critical History, 1909–1999*. Jefferson, NC; London: McFarland.

Greig, David. 1996. *The Architect*. London: Bloombury.

Guetzkow, Joshua. 2010. "Beyond Deservingness: Congressional Discourse on Poverty, 1964–1996." *Annals of the American Academy of Political and Social Science* 629, no. 1: 173–197.

Gustafson, Kaaryn. 2011. *Cheating Welfare: Public Assistance and the Criminalization of Poverty*. New York: New York University Press.

Guttmacher Institute. 2016. "Fact Sheet: Unintended Pregnancy in the United States." (July) at https://www.guttmacher.org/fact-sheet/unintended-pregnancy-united-states. Accessed Nov. 27, 2016.

Hacker, Jacob, Philipp Rehm, and Mark Schlesinger. 2010. "Standing on Shaky Ground: Americans' Experiences with Economic Insecurity." Rockefeller Foundation (December).

Hall, Mordaunt. 1933. "Gabriel Over the White House." *New York Times* (April 1).

Hamilton, David, and David Fauri. 2001. "Social Workers' Political Participation." *Journal of Social Work Education* 37, no. 2 (Spring/Summer): 321–332.

Harcourt, Bernard E., and Jens Ludwig. 2006. "Broken Windows: New Evidence from New York City and a Five-City Social Experiment." *University of Chicago Law Review* 73: 271–320.

Harrington, Michael. 1962/1997. *The Other America*. New York: Scribner.

Haskell, Molly. 1987. *From Reverence to Rape: The Treatment of Women in the Movies*. Chicago and London: University of Chicago Press.

Hays, Sharon. 2004. *Flat Broke with Children: Women in the Age of Welfare Reform*. New York: Oxford University Press.

Herring, Scott. 2007. *Queering the Underworld: Slumming, Literature, and the Undoing of Lesbian and Gay History*. Chicago: University of Chicago Press.

Hickey, Walt. 2014. "The Dollars-and-Cents Case Against Hollywood's Exclusion of Women." FiveThirtyEight.com (April 1) at http://fivethirtyeight.com/features/the-dollar-and-cents-case-against-hollywoods-exclusion-of-women/. Accessed Nov. 27, 2016.

Hiersteiner, Catherine. 1998. "Saints or Sinners? The Image of Social Workers from American Stage and Cinema before World War II." *Affilia* 13, no. 3 (Fall): 312–325.

Hilliard, Robert L. 2009. *Hollywood Speaks Out: Pictures That Dared to Protest Real World Issues*. West Sussex, UK: Wiley-Blackwell.

Hiltzik, Michael. 2011. *The New Deal: A Modern History*. New York: Free Press.

Hmielowski, Jay D., Lauren Feldman, Teresa A. Myers, Anthony Leiserowitz, and Edward Maibach. 2014. "An Attack on Science? Media Use, Trust in Scientists, and Perceptions of Global Warming." *Public Understanding of Science* 23, no. 7 (October): 866–883.

hooks, bell. 2012. *Reel to Real: Race, Sex and Class at the Movies*. New York: Routledge.

Hoxby, Caroline M., and Christopher Avery. 2012. "The Missing 'One-Offs': The Hidden Supply of High-Achieving, Low-Income Students." Working Paper #18586, National Bureau of Economic Research.

Hughey, Matthew W. 2009. "Cinethetic Racism: White Redemption and Black Stereotypes in 'Magical Negro' Films." *Social Problems* 56, no. 3 (August): 543–577.

Hunter, Robert. 1904. *Poverty*. New York: Grosset & Dunlap.

Iceland, John. 2013. *Poverty in America: A Handbook* (Third Ed.). Berkeley: University of California Press.

Irvine, Leslie. 2013. *My Dog Always Eats First: Homeless People and Their Animals*. Boulder, CO: Lynne Rienner.

Iyengar, Shanto. 1990. "Framing Responsibility for Political Issues: The Case of Poverty." *Political Behavior* 12, no. 1 (March): 19–40.

Jacobs, Lewis, ed. 1977. *The Compound Cinema: The Film Writings of Harry Alan Potamkin*. New York and London: Teachers College Press.

Jares, Sue Ellen. 1980. "Ralph Waite Risks a Wad on a Wino Flick." *People* 14, no. 4 (July 28) at http://people.com/archive/ralph-waite-risks-a-wad-on-a-wino-flick-and-is-eased-out-of-the-waltons-yet-comes-up-beaming-vol-14-no-4/. Accessed Nov. 27, 2016.

Jargowsky, Paul A. 1997. *Poverty and Place: Ghettos, Barrios, and the American City*. New York: Russell Sage Foundation.

Johnson, Angela. 2013. "Seventy-Six Percent of Americans Are Living Paycheck-to-Paycheck." *CNN Money*, at http://money.cnn.com/2013/06/24/pf/emergency-savings/index.html. Accessed Nov. 27, 2016.

Joint Center for Political and Economic Studies. 2012. "Place Matters for Health in Cook County." Washington, D.C. (July) at http://jointcenter.org/research/place-matters-health-cook-county-ensuring-opportunities-good-health-all. Accessed Nov. 27, 2016.

Jütte, R. 1994. *Poverty and Deviance in Early Modern Europe*. Cambridge, England: Cambridge.

Kael, Pauline. 1994. *For Keeps: 30 Years at the Movies*. New York: Penguin.

Kelley, Beverly Merrill, ed. 1998. *Reelpolitik: Political Ideologies in '30s and '40s Films*. Westport: Praeger.

Kennedy, William. 1979/1984. *Ironweed*. New York: Penguin.

Kidd, David Comer, and Emanuele Castano. 2013. "Reading Literary Fiction Improves Theory of Mind." *Science* 342, no. 6156 (October 18): 377–380.

Kilty, Keith M. and Eric Swank. 1997. "Institutional Racism and Media Representations: Depictions of Violent Criminals and Welfare Recipients." *Sociological Imagination* 34, nos. 2–3: 105–128.

Kirshner, Jonathan. 2012. *Hollywood's Last Golden Age: Politics, Society, and the Seventies Film in America*. Ithaca, NY: Cornell.

Klinger, Barbara. 2006. *Beyond the Multiplex: Cinema, New Technologies, and the Home*. Berkeley: University of California Press.

Kneebone, Elizabeth, and Alan Berube. 2013. *Confronting Suburban Poverty in America*. Washington, DC: Brookings Institution Press.

Kneebone, Elizabeth, Carey Nadeau, and Alan Berube. 2011. "The Re-Emergence of Concentrated Poverty: Metropolitan Trends in the 2000s." Washington, DC: Brookings Institution (November).

Kneebone, Elizabeth. 2014. "The Growth and Spread of Concentrated Poverty, 2000 to 2008–2012." Washington, DC: Brookings Institution (July 31).

Kohut, Andrew. 2007. "What Americans Know: 1989–2007: Public Knowledge of Current Affairs Little Changed by News and Information Revolutions." The Pew Research Center for the People and the Press at http://www.people-press.org/2007/04/15/public-knowledge-of-current-affairs-little-changed-by-news-and-information-revolutions/. Accessed Nov. 26, 2016

Kolata, G. 2013. "Decades Later, Condemnation for a Skid Row Cancer Study." *New York Times* (October 17) at http://www.nytimes.com/2013/10/18/health/medical-experiments-conducted-on-bowery-alcoholics-in-1950s.html. Accessed Nov. 27, 2016.

Kort-Butler, Lisa A., and Kelley J. Sittner Hartshorn. 2011. "Watching the Detectives: Crime Programming, Fear of Crime, and Attitudes About the Criminal Justice System." *Sociological Quarterly* 52: 36–55.

Kracauer, Siegfried. 1947/2004. *From Caligari to Hitler: A Psychological History of the German Film* (Revised and Expanded Edition). Princeton and Oxford: Princeton University Press.

Kull, Steven, Clay Ramsay, and Evan Lewis. 2003/2004. "Misperceptions, the Media, and the Iraq War." *Political Science Quarterly* 118, no. 4 (Winter): 569–598.

Lankenau, Stephen E. 1999. "Panhandling Repertoires and Routines for Overcoming the Nonperson Treatment." *Deviant Behavior: An Interdisciplinary Journal* 20: 183–206.

Lauzen, Martha M. 2013. "Boxed In: Employment of Behind-the-Scenes and On-Screen Women in 2012–2013 Prime-Time Television." San Diego, CA: Center for the Study of Women in Television and Film.

Lauzen, Martha M. 2014. "The Celluloid Ceiling: Behind-the-Scenes Employment of Women on the Top 250 Films of 2013." San Diego, CA: Center for the Study of Women in Television and Film.

Lee, Barrett A., and Chad R. Farrell. 2003. "Buddy, Can You Spare a Dime? Homelessness, Panhandling, and the Public." *Urban Affairs Review* 38, no. 2 (January): 299–324.

Lee, Barrett A., Kimberly A. Tyler, and James D. Wright. 2010. "The New Homelessness Revisited." *Annual Review of Sociology* 36: 501–521.

Leiserowitz, Anthony A. 2004. "Before and After *The Day After Tomorrow*: A U.S. Study of Climate Change Risk Perception." *Environment* 46, no. 9 (2004): 23–37.

Lepianka, Dorota, Wim Van Oorschot, and John Gelissen. 2009. "Popular Explanations of Poverty: A Critical Discussion of Empirical Research." *Journal of Social Policy* 38, no. 3: 421–438.

Leuchtenburg, William E. 1963/2009. *Franklin D. Roosevelt and the New Deal, 1932–1940.* New York: Harper Perennial.

Lewis, Sinclair. 1932/1944. *Ann Vickers.* Lincoln, NB; London: University of Nebraska.

Liebow, Elliot. 1967/2003. *Tally's Corner: A Study of Negro Streetcorner Men.* New York: Rowman and Littlefield.

Lippman, Walter. 1925. "The Phantom Public." In Robert Jackall, ed., *Propaganda* New York: NYU Press.

Lonnborg, Barbara A., ed. 1992. *Boys Town: A Photographic History.* Boys Town, Nebraska: Boys Town Press/Donning Company Publishers.

Lopate, Phillip, ed. 2008. *American Movie Critics: An Anthology From the Silents Until Now.* New York: Library of America.

Lopez, Steve. 2008. *The Soloist: A Lost Dream, an Unlikely Friendship, and the Redemptive Power of Music.* New York: Penguin.

Lorentz, Pare. 1975. *Pare Lorentz on Film: Movies 1927–1941.* New York: Hopkinson and Blake.

Lowell, Josephine Shaw. 1884. *Public Relief and Private Charity.* New York: G.P. Putnam.

Ludwig, Jens, Greg J. Duncan, Lisa A. Gennetian, et al. 2012. "Neighborhood Effects on the Long-Term Well-Being of Low-Income Adults." *Science* 337 (September 21): 1505–1510.

Ludwig, Jens, Greg J. Duncan, Lisa A. Gennetian, et al. 2013. "Long-Term Neighborhood Effects on Low-Income Families: Evidence from Moving to Opportunity." National Bureau of Economic Research, Working Paper 18772 (February).

MacDonald, Dwight. 1962. *Against the American Grain.* New York: Random House.

MacDonald, Dwight. 1969. *On Movies.* Englewood Cliffs, NJ: Prentice-Hall.

Manning, Jason. N.d. "The Mid-West Farm Crisis of the 1980s." *The Eighties Club: The Politics and Pop Culture of the 1980s.* Retrieved Feb. 2, 2016, from http://eighties-club.tripod.com/id395.htm.

Mary, Nancy L. 2001. "Political Activism of Social Work Educators." *Journal of Community Practice* 9, no. 4: 1–20.

Massood, Paula J. 2001. "Which Way to the Promised Land? Spike Lee's 'Clockers' and the Legacy of the African American City." *African American Review* (Summer): 263–279.

May, Larry. 2000. *The Big Tomorrow: Hollywood and the Politics of the American Way.* Chicago: University of Chicago Press.

McConnell, Robert L. 1976. "The Genesis and Ideology of *Gabriel over the White House.*" *Cinema Journal* 15, no. 2 (spring): 7–26.

Mencken, H. L. 1949. *A Mencken Chrestomathy*. New York: Knopf.

Merritt, Russell. (1990). "D. W. Griffith's *Intolerance*." *Film History* 4, no. 4: 337–375.

Mishel, Lawrence, Josh Bivens, Elise Gould, and Heidi Shierholz. 2012. *The State of Working America* (12th Ed.). Washington, DC: Economic Policy Institute.

Mitchell, Joseph. 1942 and 1964. "Professor Seagull" and "Joe Gould's Secret, Parts I and II." *New Yorker* (December 12; September 19, September 26).

Morgen, Sandra, Joan Acker, and Jill Weigt. 2010. *Stretched Thin: Poor Families, Welfare Work, and Welfare Reform*. Ithaca, NY; London: Cornell University Press.

Morone, James A. 2003. *Hellfire Nation: The Politics of Sin in American History*. New Haven, CT: Yale University Press.

Muhammad, Khalil. 20111. *The Condemnation of Blackness: Race, Crime, and the Making of Modern Urban America*. Cambridge, MA: Harvard University Press.

Mulligan, Kenneth, and Philip Habel. 2011. "An Experimental Test on the Effects of Fictional Framing on Attitudes." *Social Science Quarterly* 92, no. 1 (March): 79–99.

Mulligan, Kenneth, and Philip Habel. 2013. "The Implications of Fictional Media for Political Beliefs." *American Politics Research* 41, no. 1: 122–146.

Mulvey, Laura. 1999. "Visual Pleasure and Narrative Cinema" In Leo Braudy and Marshall Cohen, eds., *Film Theory and Criticism: Introductory Readings* (pp. 833–844). New York: Oxford University Press.

Murray, Charles. 1994. *Losing Ground: American Social Policy, 1950–1980* (10th Anniversary Edition). New York: Basic Books.

Murray, Liz. 2011. *Breaking Night: A Memoir of Forgiveness, Survival, and My Journey from Homeless to Harvard*. New York: Hyperion.

National Association of Social Workers. 2008. "Code of Ethics." NASW at https://www.socialworkers.org/pubs/code/code.asp. Accessed Nov. 27, 2016.

National Conference on Charities and Corrections, Proceedings. Various years. Available at https://catalog.hathitrust.org/Record/005709465 Accessed Nov. 27, 2016.

National Institute on Drug Abuse. 2012. *Principles of Drug Addiction Treatment: A Research Based Guide* (Third Ed.). Washington, DC: U.S. Department of Health and Human Services.

Nealand, Daniel. 2008. "Archival Vintages for *The Grapes of Wrath*." *Prologue* 40, no. 4 (Winter) at https://www.archives.gov/publications/prologue/2008/winter/grapes.html. Accessed Nov. 26, 2016.

Neve, Brian. 1992. *Film and Politics in America: A Social Tradition*. London and New York: Routledge.

New York Times. 1981. "'Apache Film's Debut Protested." (February 7) at http://www.nytimes.com/1981/02/07/movies/apache-film-s-debut-protested.html. Accessed Nov. 27, 2016.

Newport, Frank. 2012. "Americans Like Having a Rich Class, as They Did 22 Years Ago." Gallup.com (May 11).

Parchesky, Jennifer. 1999. "Lois Weber's *The Blot*: Rewriting Melodrama, Reproducing the Middle Class." *Cinema Journal* 39, no. 1: 23–53.

Parini, Jay. 1995. *John Steinbeck: A Biography*. New York: Henry Holt & Company.

Parkinson, David, ed. 1993. *The Graham Greene Film Reader: Reviews, Essays, Interviews and Film Stories*. New York: Applause Books.

Payne, Robert. 1952. *The Great God Pan: A Biography of the Tramp Played by Charles Chaplin*. New York: Hermitage House.

Peters, Lisa N. 1987. "Images of the Homeless in American Art, 1860–1910." In Rick Beard, ed., *On Being Homeless: Historical Perspectives*. New York: Museum of the City of New York.

Pew Research Center. 2012. "In Changing News Landscape, Even Television Is Vulnerable Trends in News Consumption: 1991–2012." September 27, at http://www.people-press.org/2012/09/27/section-4-demographics-and-political-views-of-news-audiences/. Accessed Nov. 26, 2016.

Pierce, David. 2013. "The Survival of American Silent Feature Films: 1912–1929." Council on Library & Information Resources and the Library of Congress (September).

Pimpare, Stephen. 2004. *The New Victorians: Poverty, Politics and Propaganda in Two Gilded Ages*. New York: New Press.

Pimpare, Stephen. 2008. *A People's History of Poverty in America*. New York: New Press.

Pittenger, Mark. 2012. *Class Unknown: Undercover Investigations of American Work and Poverty from the Progressive Era to the Present*. New York: NYU Press.

Piven, Frances Fox, and Richard A. Cloward. 1971/1993. *Regulating the Poor: The Functions of Public Welfare*. New York: Vintage

Platt, Dave. 1933. "Movie Snapshots." *Harlem Liberator* (December 23).

Platt, Dave. 1934. "Movie Snapshots." *Harlem Liberator* (December 30).

Polito, Robert, ed. 2009. *Farber on Film: The Complete Film Writings of Manny Farber*. New York: Penguin.

Pollan, Michael. 2006. *The Omnivore's Dilemma: A Natural History of Four Meals*. New York: Penguin.

Prior, Marcus. 2005. "News vs. Entertainment: How Increasing Media Choice Widens Gaps in Political Knowledge and Turnout." *American Journal of Political Science* 49, no. 3: 577–592.

Queenan, Joe. 2009. *Closing Time*. New York: Viking.

Rafter, Nicole. 2006. *Shots in the Mirror: Crime Films and Society*. New York: Oxford.

Rank, Mark Robert. 2007. "Rethinking the Scope and Impact of Poverty in the United States." *Connecticut Public Interest Law Journal* 6, no. 2 (Spring/Summer).

Rector, Robert, and Sheffield, Rachel. 2011. "Understanding Poverty in the United States: Surprising Facts about America's Poor." Backgrounder #2607. Washington, DC: Heritage Foundation (September 13).

Reilly, Hugh, and Kevin Warneke. 2008. *Father Flanagan of Boys Town*. Boys Town, Nebraska: Boys Town Press.

Reisch, Michael, and Janice Andrews. 2002. *The Road Not Taken: A History of Radical Social Work in the United States*. New York: Routledge.

Reitman, Ben. 1937/2002. *Sisters of the Road: The Autobiography of Boxcar Bertha*. Edinburgh: AK Press.

Riis, Jacob. 1890/1993. *How the Other Half Lives*. New York: Hill and Wang.

Roberts, Lisen. 2003. "Using Feature Films to Teach Poverty." *Journal of Teaching in Marriage and Family* 3, no. 1: 47–70.

Robinson, David. 1985/1994. *Chaplin: His Life and Art*. New York: Da Capo Press.

Rogin, Michael Paul. 1987. *Ronald Reagan The Movie, and Other Episodes in Political Demonology*. Berkeley: University of California Press.

Rose, Max, and Frank R. Baumgartner. 2013. "Framing the Poor: Media Coverage and U.S. Poverty Policy, 1960–2008." *Policy Studies Journal* 41, no. 1: 22–53.

Rosenbaum, Jonathan. 1997. *Movies as Politics*. Berkeley: University of California Press.

Ross, Steven J. 1998. *Working-Class Hollywood: Silent Film and the Shaping of Class in America*. Princeton, NJ: Princeton University Press.

Rowling, J. K. 2010. "The Single Mother's Manifesto." *Times of London* (April 14).

Russo, Vito. 1987. *The Celluloid Closet: Homosexuality in the Movies* (Revised Ed.). New York: Harper and Row.

Rynell, Amy. 2008. "Causes of Poverty: Finding from Recent Research." Heartland Alliance/Mid-America Institute on Poverty (October).

Saad, Lydia. 2011. "Most Americans Believe U.S. Crime Is Worsening." *Gallup* (October 31) at http://www.gallup.com/poll/150464/americans-believe-crime-worsening.aspx. Accessed Nov. 27, 2016.

Sampson, Robert J., and Stephen W. Raudenbush. 2001. "Disorder in Urban Neighborhoods—Does It Lead to Crime?" National Institute of Justice, Research in Brief (February).

Sanders, James. 2001. *Celluloid Skyline: New York and the Movies*. New York: Alfred A. Knopf.

Sandfort, Jodi R., Ariel Kalil, and Julie A. Gottschalk. 1999. "The Mirror Has Two Faces: Welfare Clients and Front-Line Workers View Policy Reforms." *Journal of Poverty* 3, no. 3: 71–91.

Sante, Luc. 2003. "My Lost City." *New York Review of Books* (November 6) at http://www.nybooks.com/articles/2003/11/06/my-lost-city/. Accessed Nov. 27, 2016.

Sapphire. 1996/1997. *Push*. New York: Vintage.

Sargent, James D., Michael L. Beach, Madeline A. Dalton, et al. (2001). "Effect of Seeing Tobacco Use in Films on Trying Smoking among Adolescents: Cross Sectional Study." *British Medical Journal* 323 (December 15): 1394.

Sarris, Andrew. 1996. *The American Cinema: Directors and Directions, 1929–1968*. Chicago: Da Capo.

Sarris, Andrew. 1998. *"You Ain't Heard Nothin' Yet": The American Talking Film, History and Memory, 1927–1949*. New York: Oxford.

Scarry, Elaine. 2012. "Poetry Changed the World: Poetry and the Ethics of Reading." *Boston Review* (July/August) at http://bostonreview.net/poetry-arts-culture/poetry-changed-world-elaine-scarry. Accessed Nov. 26, 2016.

Schickel, Richard. 1975. *The Men Who Made the Movies: Interviews with Alfred Hitchcock, Raoul Walsh, Frank Capra, Vincente Minnelli, George Cukor, Howard Hawks, William A. Wellman, King Vidor.* New York: Athenaeum.

Schiller, Bradley R. 2007. *The Economics of Poverty and Discrimination.* New York: Prentice-Hall.

Schneider, Saundra K., and William G. Jacoby. 2003. "A Culture of Dependence? The Relationship Between Public Assistance and Public Opinion." *British Journal of Political Science* 33: 213–231.

Schwartz, Joel. 2000. *Fighting Poverty with Virtue: Moral Reform and America's Urban Poor, 1825–2000.* Indianapolis: Indiana University Press.

Seccombe, Karen. 2010. *"So You Think I Drive a Cadillac?" Welfare Recipients' Perspectives on the System and its Reform* (Third Ed.). Boston: Pearson.

Seldes, Gilbert. 1924/2001. *The Seven Lively Arts.* Mineola, NY: Dover.

Seldes, Gilbert. 1937. *The Movies Come from America.* New York: Scribner's.

Sen, Amartya. 1999. *Development as Freedom.* New York: Anchor.

Shannon, Lyle W. 1963. "The Public's Perception of Social Welfare Agencies and Organizations in an Industrial Community." *Journal of Negro Education* 32, no. 3 (Summer): 276–285.

Shapiro, Robert Y. 2011. "Public Opinion and American Democracy." *Public Opinion Quarterly* 75, no. 5: 982–1017.

Shaw, George Bernard. 1906. "Preface to Major Barbara." In *Prefaces by Bernard Shaw*, 1934. London, Constable and Company.

Shelden, Randall G. 2004. "Assessing 'Broken Windows': A Brief Critique." *Center on Juvenile and Criminal Justice* (April 1) at http://www.cjcj.org/uploads/cjcj/documents/broken.pdf. Accessed Nov. 27, 2017.

Sherman, Arloc, Robert Greenstein, and Kathy Ruffing. 2012. "Contrary to 'Entitlement Society' Rhetoric, Over Nine-Tenths of Entitlement Benefits Go to Elderly, Disabled, or Working Households." Washington, DC: Center on Budget and Policy Priorities (February 10) at http://www.cbpp.org/research/contrary-to-entitlement-society-rhetoric-over-nine-tenths-of-entitlement-benefits-go-to. Accessed Nov. 27, 2016.

Shields, Todd G. 2001. "Network News Construction of Homelessness: 1980–1993." *Communication Review* 4, no. 2: 193–218.

Shindler, Colin. 1996. *Hollywood in Crisis: Cinema and American Society, 1929–1933.* London and New York: Routledge.

Short, Kathleen. 2015. "The Research Supplemental Poverty Measure: 2014." Washington, DC: U.S. Census Bureau (September).

Sklar, Robert. 1975/1994. *Movie-Made America: A Cultural History of American Movies* (Revised and Updated). New York: Vintage.

Skocpol, Theda. 1992. *Protecting Soldiers and Mothers: The Political Origins of Social Policy in the United States*. Cambridge, MA: Belknap/Harvard.

Sloan, Kay. 1988. *The Loud Silents: Origins of the Social Problem Film*. Urbana and Chicago: University of Illinois Press.

Smith, Adam. 1776/1904. *An Inquiry into the Nature and Causes of the Wealth of Nations*. London: Methuen.

Smith, Betty. 1943/2001. *A Tree Grows in Brooklyn*. New York: HarperCollins.

Smith, Stacy L., Marc Choueiti, Ashley Prescott, and Katherine Pieper. N.d. "Gender Roles and Occupations: A Look at Character Attributes and Job-Related Aspirations in Film and Television." Los Angeles: USC Annenberg School for Communication and Journalism, Geena Davis Center Institute on Gender and Media at http://seejane.org/wp-content/uploads/full-study-gender-roles-and-occupations-v2.pdf. Accessed Nov. 27, 2016.

Smith, Stacy L., Marc Choueiti, Elizabeth Scofield, and Katherine Pieper. 2013. "Gender Inequality in 500 Popular Films: Examining On-Screen Portrayals and Behind-the-Scenes Employment Patterns in Motion Pictures Released Between 2007–2012." Los Angeles: USC Annenberg School for Communication & Journalism, Geena Davis Center Institute on Gender and Media at http://annenberg.usc.edu/pages/~/media/MDSCI/Gender_Inequality_in_500_Popular_Films_-_Smith_2013.ashx. Accessed Nov. 27, 2016.

Sobel, Raoul, and David Francis. 1977. *Chaplin: Genesis of a Clown*. London: Quartet Books.

Sontag, Susan. 1965/2001. "The Imagination of Disaster." In *Against Interpretation and Other Essays*. New York: Picador.

Soss, Joe. 1999. "Lessons of Welfare: Policy Design, Political Learning, and Political Action." *American Political Science Review* 93, no 2: 363–380.

Stamp, Shelley. 2004. "Lois Weber, Progressive Cinema, and the Fate of 'The Work-a-Day Girl' in *Shoes*." *Camera Obscura* 19, no. 2: 140–169.

Starpulse.com. N.d. *Mario Van Peebles, Biography*. At http://www.starpulse.com/Actors/Van_Peebles,_Mario/Biography/. Accessed Nov. 26, 2016.

Steinbeck, John. 1939/2006. *The Grapes of Wrath*. New York: Penguin.

Stokes, Bruce. 2013. "Public Attitudes Toward the Next Social Contract." New America Foundation (January) at http://www.pewglobal.org/files/pdf/Stokes_Bruce_NAF_Public_Attitudes_1_2013.pdf. Accessed Nov. 27, 2016.

Stokes, Melvyn, and Richard Maltby, eds. 1999. *American Movie Audiences: From the Turn of the Century to the Early Sound Era*. London: BFI.

Stroud, Natalie Jomini. 2007. "Media Effects, Selective Exposure, and *Fahrenheit 9/11*." *Political Communication* 24, no. 4: 415–432.

Taylor, Paul, Rakesh Kochnar, D'Vera Kohn, et al. 2011. "Fighting Poverty in a Tough Economy, Americans Move in with Their Relatives." Pew Research Center (October 3).

Tillmon, Johnnie. 1972/2002. "Welfare Is a Women's Issue." *Ms. Magazine* (Spring).

Tirado, Linda. 2014. *Hand to Mouth: Living in Bootstrap America*. New York: Penguin.

Toth, Jennifer. 1993. *The Mole People: Life in the Tunnels Below New York City*. Chicago: Chicago Review Press.

Tryon, Chuck. 2009. *Reinventing Cinema: Movies in the Age of Media Convergence*. New Brunswick, NJ: Rutgers University Press.

Turner, Kristin, Rebecca Kissane, and Kathryn Edin. 2012. "After Moving to Opportunity: How Moving to a Low-Poverty Neighborhood Improves Mental Health Among African American Women." *Society and Mental Health* 3, no. 1: 1–21.

Twain, Mark. 1882. *The Prince and the Pauper*. Boston: James R. Osgood and Company.

Tweed, Thomas Frederic. 1933. *Gabriel Over the White House: A Novel of the Presidency*. New York: Farrar & Rinehart.

U.S. Department of Agriculture, Economic Research Service. 2013. "Geography of Poverty" (Updated March 26).

U.S. Department of Health and Human Services, Substance Abuse and Mental Health Services Administration, Center for Behavioral Health Statistics and Quality. 2012. "Results from the 2011 National Survey on Drug Use and Health: Summary of National Findings."

U.S. Department of Housing and Urban Development. 2011. "Understanding Neighborhood Effects of Concentrated Poverty." *Evidence Matters* (Winter).

Valentine, Deborah P., and Miriam Freeman. 2002. "Film Portrayals of Social Workers Doing Child Welfare Work." *Child and Adolescent Social Work Journal* 19, no. 6 (December): 455–471.

Vidor, King. 1953/1981. *A Tree Is a Tree: An Autobiography*. Hollywood: Samuel French.

Wachowski, Larry, and Andy Wachowski. N.d. *Carnivore*. Unpublished screenplay.

Wacquant, Loïc. 2008. *Urban Outcasts: A Comparative Sociology of Advanced Marginality*. Cambridge, England: Polity.

Warshow, Robert. 2002. *The Immediate Experience: Movies, Comics, Theatre and Other Aspects of Popular Culture*. Cambridge and London: Harvard University Press.

Watkins-Hayes. 2009. *The New Welfare Bureaucrats: Entanglements of Race, Class, and Policy Reform*. Chicago and London: University of Chicago Press.

Weimberg, Gary. 1981. "*The China Syndrome*: Film + Reality = Awareness." *Jump Cut: A Review of Contemporary Media* 24–25 (March): 57–58.

Weiss, I., J. Gal, R. Cnaan, and R. Majlaglic. (2002). "What Kind of Social Policy Do Social Work Students Prefer? A Comparison of Students in Three Countries." *International Social Work* 45, no. 1: 59–81.

Wenocur, Stanley, and Michael Reisch. 2001. *From Charity to Enterprise: The Development of American Social Work in a Market Economy*. University of Illinois Press.

Wertheimer, Richard, Melissa Long, and Sharon Vandivere. 2001. "Welfare Recipients' Attitudes Toward Welfare, Nonmarital Childbearing, and Work: Implications for Reform?" *New Federalism Series B*, no. B-37. Washington, DC: Urban Institute (June).

Wilson, James Q., and George Kelling. 1982. "Broken Windows: The Police and Neighborhood Safety." *The Atlantic* (March 1) at http://www.theatlantic.com/magazine/archive/1982/03/broken-windows/304465/. Accessed Nov. 27, 2016.

Wilson, Robert, ed. 1971. *The Film Criticism of Otis Ferguson*. Philadelphia, PA: Temple University Press.

Wimer, Christopher, Liana Fox, Irv Garfinkel, Keeraj Kaushal, and Jane Waldfogel. 2013. "Trends in Poverty with an Anchored Supplemental Poverty Measure." New York: Columbia Population Research Center (December 5).

Women's Media Center. 2014. *The Status of Women in the U.S. Media*. New York and Washington, DC:

Wood, Robin. 1979/2002. "The American Nightmare: Horror in the 70s." In Mark Jancovich, ed., *Horror: The Film Reader*. London and New York: Routledge.

Zaller, John R. 1992. *The Nature and Origins of Mass Opinion*. New York: Cambridge University Press.

Zaniello, Tom. 2003. *Working Stiffs, Union Maids, Reds and Riffraff: An Expanded Guide to Films About Labor*. Ithaca, NY; London: ILR/Cornell.

Zongker, Brett. 2010. "Long-Lost Chaplin Film to Debut at U.S. Festival." *Globe and Mail* (July 16).

Zugazaga, Carole B., Raymond B. Surette, Monica Mendez, and Charles W. Otto. 2006. "Social Worker Perceptions of the Portrayal of the Profession in the News and Entertainment Media: An Exploratory Study." *Journal of Social Work Education* 42, no. 3 (Fall): 621–636.

INDEX

Page references for figures are indicated by *f* and for tables by *t*.